The Cinema of

FEDERICO FELLINI

The Cinema of
FEDERICO FELLINI

PETER BONDANELLA

WITH A FOREWORD BY
Federico Fellini

PRINCETON UNIVERSITY PRESS

PRINCETON, NEW JERSEY

Library of Congress Cataloging-in-
Publication Data

Bondanella, Peter E., 1943-
The cinema of Frederico Fellini / by Peter
Bondanella.
p. cm.
Includes bibliographical references and
index.
ISBN 0-691-03196-7—ISBN 0-691-00875-
2 (pbk.)
1. Fellini, Frederico—Criticism and
interpretation. I. Title.
PN1998.3.F45B66   1992
791.43'0233'092—dc20   91-25873

This book has been composed in
Linotron Trump Medieval

Princeton University Press books are
printed on acid-free paper, and meet the
guidelines for permanence and durability
of the Committee on Production
Guidelines for Book longevity of the
Council on Library Resources

Printed in the United States of America

10 9 8 7 6 5 4 3

Frontispiece: Black-and-white drawing of
Fellini playing all his major characters by
Ettore Scola

For Gianfranco and Sergio

CONTENTS

ILLUSTRATIONS

FOREWORD

THE CINEMA, at least here in Italy, has been reduced to a mere pretext for filling two hours of entertainment on commercial television with an unrecognizable pap of cinematic images chopped up by commercial spots.

How could anyone imagine, therefore, that books could still be devoted to films butchered in such a fashion? It seems like a dream from another era, and yet, here it is: making his way with difficulty through detergents and diapers, somebody with good will, competence, and love still exists who succeeds in reconstructing the parts of a work of artistic expression by accomplishing a heroic enterprise not unlike that of someone who pieces together a book by picking up off the street pages that have been torn out and scattered about.

The most exciting aspect of Bondanella's work is, in fact, his inextinguishable faith in the power of reason and systematization which reminds us in a nostalgic way of methods and choices inspired by respect and harmony. Without a doubt, the fact that Bondanella is an American provides him with enormous support in his activity as historian and critic, to which he devotes himself with that sense of pragmatic mysticism which has carried the nation to which he belongs to the highest technological achievements, enabling America to claim a place for herself, and not only just of late, as the custodian and repository of Western culture.

Surely in America things are very different if the legendary Japanese director Kurosawa succeeds in realizing his dreams protected by the magic shield of Spielberg and Lucas, glorious samurai of that cinema which transforms films into millions and millions into films, following the simplest formula of all—that is, to love one's work and to enjoy doing it. A book like the one Bondanella has written can be planned, born, and brought into being only in contexts that possess an indestructible faith in their own health and have not been undermined by years of protests, negations, acts of arrogance, and "periods of crisis," as we say in a phrase that explains both everything and nothing and is, therefore, adopted by everyone without explanation or the acceptance of responsibility.

Bondanella's book treats the cinema of a European director, and this,

too, is an even more obvious sign of a vitality that ignores geographical
boundaries and helps to unite two realities that, however historically
or culturally different they may be, can nevertheless live together and
coexist, drawing nourishment from a single expressive utopia. And
then the fact that Bondanella treats primarily my own films suggests to
me once again the sense of uneasiness and embarrassment I always experience when I feel myself being analyzed, diagnosed, and synthesized
into fixed attitudes and expressions set in stone, rather reminiscent of
a funeral, which I immediately feel overwhelmed by the desire to con-
tradict and to deny in the attempt to extract myself from the paralysis
of such an act of intellectual sorcery.

But I am also invited to write a few prefatory pages. Another serious
embarrassment: to put myself in the position of the judge, the one who
confirms and grants approval and blessings? Here I am overcome by
that uncomfortable sensation experienced by the most undisciplined
schoolboy who has been brought before his headmaster, before authority, feeling an irresistible desire to run away and to make funny faces.

The only inclination I recognize in myself is perhaps that of being
able, on some occasions and in a rather confused manner, to bear witness solely to myself and to those few things I seem to understand,
while refusing as long as I possibly can to venture out into other terri-
tories, theoretical systems, generalizations. I do not possess such qualities, and in order to write about this book, I should be both a critic and
a historian, roles and tasks that really do not suit me. Bondanella's conclusions and proposals will serve to nourish, independently of what I
could write, an analytical discourse and a speculative dialectic that
will, if nothing else, help to place the cinema in its true light among
the arts.

A professor of Italian literature, translator of our literary classics, an
attentive commentator and observer of our history, Bondanella is a
scholar of our political and social behavior, but above all else, of our
artistic expression, knowing and loving as few others do the fresco
paintings he tirelessly seeks out in the most remote little churches of
our country. I also want to add that our author is a scientific philologist
and that everything he describes or to which he refers rests upon serious affirmations and reflects well-prepared arguments according to a
procedure that excludes every kind of digression, even that which
might be suggestive from a literary point of view. His long, tenacious
training has ultimately brought him to devote himself, with extraordinary preparation and enthusiasm, to Italian cinema and subsequently
to my films, and now in this book once again to my films, as he offers
an unrelenting examination of them. I know that in Italy he has spent
weeks and weeks in screening rooms seeing them over and over again,

and that he has also read everything written by others about my work. Not only that, but he has succeeded in meeting almost all those people who, for one reason or another, since they had belonged to my film crews, he felt could help him in writing his critical mosaic, seeking them out and collecting, with a faith that never failed him, testimonials, data, reports, and documents. Only from me did he receive very little, almost nothing.

And so now in front of this huge book that bears witness to his labor and love, I should feel a bit of remorse, but, instead, I believe that this situation has been beneficial to him, for while, and with every right, Bondanella hoped to obtain revelations and confidences, my evasions and my silences have forced him to search elsewhere and among other people, recovering old scripts and notebooks where a little drawing was sketched out with the outline of a dialogue, and where spots of color suggested the tones of a scene. And in this fashion, explorer, archeologist, bloodhound, and detective, he has gathered together notebooks, photographs, and scribblings, and he has carried this booty back to the archives of his university in a huge suitcase.

Generous America! Tenaciously optimistic and heedful, she has for some time been supplanting us, just like those provident children who show themselves wiser and more sensible than their reckless fathers.

There you have it: Bondanella is one of these children, and his book is a supreme example of all such protective qualities.

FEDERICO FELLINI
Rome
May 1990
[Translated by Julia Conaway Bondanella]

PREFACE

I'm a liar, but an honest one. People reproach me for not always telling the same story in the same way. But this happens because I've invented the whole tale from the start and it seems boring to me and unkind to other people to repeat myself.[1]

Many people say that I am a liar and repeat it continuously. But other people also tell lies; and I have always heard the greatest lies about me told by others. I could deny them, and I have even tried. Unfortunately, since I am a liar, nobody believes me.[2]

I'm not a man who approves of definitions. Labels belong on luggage as far as I'm concerned; they don't mean anything in art.[3]

What is extraordinary about film critics is that they apply critical methods which are a hundred years old to work which couldn't have existed a hundred years ago.[4]

FEDERICO FELLINI'S critical reputation was rapidly established with his early successes during the 1950s and 1960s. The release of his major works constituted important milestones in the rise of an *auteur*-oriented cinema in Europe that for a decade managed to challenge, if not displace, Hollywood's hegemony. Perhaps more than any other director of the postwar period, Fellini's public persona has projected the myth of the director as creative superstar, as imaginative magician. His name has become synonymous with fantasy and exuberant creativity and is recognized even by people who have never seen any of his films. With a number of works, such as *La strada, Le notti di Cabiria, La dolce vita, 8 1/2, Fellini Satyricon,* and *Amarcord,* Fellini managed the almost impossible task of reconciling original artistic genius with record profits at the box office.

---

[1] Federico Fellini, *Fellini on Fellini*, eds. Anna Keel and Christian Strich, trans. Isabel Quigly (London: Eyre Methuen, 1976), p. 49.

[2] Cited in Tullio Kezich, *Fellini* (Milan: Camunia, 1987), p. 5. All translations from the Italian are my own unless otherwise indicated.

[3] Cited in Suzanne Budgen, *Fellini* (London: British Film Institute, 1966), p. 92.

[4] Fellini, *Fellini on Fellini*, p. 113.

In preparing this book, which has been in germination for many years, I have tried to place Fellini's individual films in their appropriate aesthetic and intellectual contexts within Italian culture. Too often characterized by reviewers and critics as a madcap Latin genius with a charming and seductive public personality who lacks the critical mind typical of a European intellectual, Fellini in his work has consistently anticipated shifts in cinematic tastes or intellectual trends. Unlike many great artists who are understood fully only after their deaths, Fellini may well be *no longer* completely understood by public and critics today, as Milan Kundera has claimed.[5] Kundera argues that Fellini's particular brand of cinema suffers contemporary critical neglect because the director's private fantasy world finds no comfortable home in an era dominated by kitsch culture and mass media. Fellini's cinema aims at demystifying this very mass culture mesmerizing contemporary audiences, a critical operation in which "the voice of culture is always less audible, as little by little man loses his faculty to think, to doubt, to ask questions, to slowly examine the meaning of things, to be surprised, to be original."[6]

To comprehend the complexity of Fellini's long career, we must briefly examine Fellini's artistic origins and the sources of his imaginative creativity in Italian popular culture during the Fascist period. Moreover, a close look at the years Fellini spent as a scriptwriter before turning to direction clarifies many of the important aesthetic choices he was subsequently to make when he began his work behind the camera. Fellini's cinema develops in a relatively traditional manner through *La dolce vita* as he first explores and eventually exhausts the heritage of Italian neorealism, a moment in film history he did so much to create as a scriptwriter. I have treated his early career chronologically, but after *8 1/2* and Fellini's shift to an entirely different kind of cinema, I organize the treatment of the director's later career around key thematic concerns.

Such an approach proves more illuminating in treating Fellini's cinema than the conventional chronological perspective, since it serves to underscore what is most original in his latest films. This will be particularly clear in Chapter 4, dealing with Fellini's metacinematic films. Chapter 5 focuses on Fellini's original use of literary sources in *Fellini Satyricon* and *Toby Dammit*, films that cannot be called "adaptations" in the conventionally accepted sense of the term. The critical commonplace that Fellini is completely uninterested in social or political prob-

[5] Cited in Dario Zanelli, *Nel mondo di Federico* (Turin: Nuova ERI Edizioni Rai, 1987), p. 126.
[6] Ibid.

lems will be examined in Chapter 6, devoted to *Amarcord* and *Prova d'orchestra*. Chapter 7, analyzing *Giulietta degli spiriti, Casanova*, and *La città delle donne*, will tackle the complex problem of Fellini's representation of sexuality and women. Finally, Chapter 8 considers Fellini's latest film, *La voce della luna*, and underlines its links with ideas and images from his early "cinema of poetry." All of my observations are based on screenings of the original Italian prints, although I have also examined the prints distributed in either subtitled or dubbed versions outside of Italy.

Like the bemused but nonjudgmental observer of life that he is, Fellini never preaches or patronizes, never assumes the position, in Ezra Pound's words, of a poet on a perch. Above all else, Fellini considers himself an entertainer and a storyteller rather than an intellectual, and he gauges the results of his films by how well he has evoked an *emotional* response in his audience with a *visual* experience rather than how successfully he has raised the spectator's consciousness with a logical argument or a rational demonstration of an ideological position. Fellini's films allow us the luxury of regressing along with the director and of viewing the world he creates with the wonder and freshness of the child concealed in every one of us underneath the adult spectator. Yet, in spite of Fellini's desire to remain the eternal adolescent of the imagination, the corpus of his work has produced a complex of cinematic narrative that must be considered one of the most imposing *intellectual* achievements of contemporary Italian culture. This paradox will be explored at length in the following pages.

ACKNOWLEDGMENTS

WITHOUT THE friendship and counsel of Gianfranco Angelucci and Sergio Ercolessi during an extended stay in Rome while I was writing this book, I could never have completed my work. The following people have all assisted me in various ways on this project: Manuela Gieri, Ben Lawton, Millicent Marcus, Bernardino Zapponi, Brunello Rondi, Aureliano Luppi, Fiammetta Profili, Tullio Kezich, Dario Zanelli, Norma Giacchero, Mario Longardi, and Ettore Scola. At Princeton University Press, Joanna Hitchcock was the perfect editor.

I owe a profound debt to Federico Fellini. During the past decade, he has allowed me to visit his set on a number of occasions. In 1987, he and his scriptwriter Tullio Pinelli graciously agreed to the transfer of a large body of their original manuscripts to Indiana University's Lilly Library of Rare Books, establishing the first Fellini archive in a major research library. Large portions of this book would have been impossible to complete without this material, and I was privileged to be the first scholar to have had access to it. Needless to say, I was honored by Fellini's willingness to contribute a foreword to this work, for it quite accurately reflects Fellini's generosity and kindness as a man, qualities that nourish his artistic creations and endow them with such humanity and warmth.

A Lilly Foundation fellowship allowed me an entire year in Rome to study cinematography. During that period, the archival materials obtained from Fellini and Pinelli were assembled and brought back to Indiana University's Lilly Library. Without the vision of librarian William Cagle, who arranged for the reception of these materials, the Fellini archive would not have been acquired. The American Council of Learned Societies provided a fellowship for the basic research for this book. Indiana University's Office of Research and Graduate Development and its West European Studies program also provided funding for bringing the research to its final form. For all of this support, both moral and financial, I am very grateful.

The Cinema of
FEDERICO FELLINI

CHAPTER ONE _____

Origins

JOURNALISM AND THE

COMIC STRIPS

I learned the essence of comedy from _____
the first comic strips.[1]

T HE GENESIS of most of Federico
Fellini's artistic and intellectual concerns, as well as many of his thematic preoccupations in his films, must be traced to his early days as
an artist, gagman, journalist, and scriptwriter, vocations he practiced
for over a decade before turning to filmmaking. His long and successful
career reflects no unilinear development. On the one hand, Fellini returns again and again, but always in subtly different ways, to treat
many of the same basic themes. On the other hand, the cinematic style
in which these ideas find concrete artistic expression undergoes substantial alterations and even revolutionary shifts at crucial moments in
his career. Fellini may present a key idea in an early film—for example,
the notion of redemption in *La strada*—which in later works, such as
La dolce vita or *Fellini Satyricon*, returns to play an important role in
his narrative. However, the transformations that take place in Fellini's
cinematic style between 1954 and 1969 are so profound that these three
films could easily be taken to be creations of different directors.

Fellini's relationship to his producers and critics has often been curious. On the one hand, his producers are consistently reluctant to support the new projects the director proposes. On every occasion that Fellini sets out to explore new territory, his proposals are greeted with
suspicion and incomprehension, and the producers invariably prefer to
finance a sequel to his last successful film rather than a new project,
conveniently forgetting the fact that they had expressed similar doubts

[1] Cited in Oreste del Buono, "Da Fortunello a Giudizio, passando per Little
Nemo," in Federico Fellini, *I clown*, 2d ed., ed. Renzo Renzi (Bologna: Cappelli,
1988), p. 73. For other versions of this statement in English, in which the English
translation has somewhat confused Fellini's meaning, see Fellini, *Fellini on Fellini*,
p. 140; or Fellini's introduction to James Steranko, *The Steranko History of Comics*
(Reading, Pa.: Supergraphics, 1970), which renders Fellini's statement as "I began to
understand the essence of comics when I was a child" (p. 3). It is evident from the
original Italian ("l'essenza della comicità l'ho imparata nei primi fumetti") that Fellini intends a general statement on the nature of comedy.

about the project that eventually proved to be a success. Fellini invariably refuses to make a sequel, and his search for a producer always takes a great deal of his time and energy despite his track record at the box office. On the other hand, critical assessments of Fellini's films often complain that the director repeats his characteristic thematic concerns and frequently ignore the important departures in theme and content that producers fear but acknowledge.

In the evolution of his cinema, Fellini's past experiences are never discarded or rejected. Elements of his previous works and concerns reappear in successive works in new contexts and are viewed from ever different and more ironic perspectives. Over the past fifty years, from the first comic sketch he published until the present, Federico Fellini has gone through a number of important transformations in his cinematic style, moving almost effortlessly through over four decades of complicated technical changes that have taken place in the film industry. However, during this long period of time, he seems to have abandoned or rejected nothing from his rather humble artistic origins, no matter how lacking in seriousness or significance they may seem to his critics. In his artistic maturity, more and more of this legacy from Italian popular culture has surfaced, now that his international reputation and phenomenal critical successes no longer cause him irritated embarrassment when his obscure and unpromising artistic or intellectual beginnings are mentioned. Fellini is the first to underline the influence of his early experiences as a journalist upon his later films: " 'Not only do I not deny this experience, but it seems to me that in my films, situations linked to this type of experience continuously exist.' "[2]

A fine example of how such situations, themes, and images from Fellini's early pre-cinematic career eventually return to influence work completed much later by the mature director can be found in a particular collection of some forty articles under the general rubric of *Il raccontino pubblicitario* (*The Advertising Story*). Fellini published these brief pieces in 1939 in *Marc'Aurelio* to parody the sometimes ridiculous advertising claims for various products in tabloids and radio programs of the period. An article appearing in September 1939 treated a fictitious brand of macaroni, an enormous plate of which is spilled on an angry client whose outrage is calmed immediately when he learns that he has been "honored" by being covered with "Maccheroncini Pop" rather than any pedestrian brand. As the consummate gag-writer he had become, Fellini brings the story to a conclusion by having the now delighted customer order two additional plates of macaroni to be

---

[2] Cited in Angelo Olivieri, *L'imperatore in platea: i grandi del cinema italiano dal "Marc'Aurelio" allo schermo* (Bari: Edizioni Dedalo, 1986), p. 64.

poured over his head, so overwhelmed is he by the prestige of "Maccheroncini Pop"! In the same year, assisted by his growing reputation as a comic writer, Fellini began working on film scripts, usually providing one-liners for the actors—much the same job he had first done on the editorial staff of *Marc'Aurelio*. The comic tale of the plate of pasta dropped on the customer's head in *Il raccontino pubblicitario* was reused as a gag performed by the immensely popular actor Erminio Macario in *Lo vedi come sei?* (1939), directed by Mario Mattoli and scripted by two of the *Marc'Aurelio* staff, Vittorio Metz and Steno (the pen name of Stefano Vanzini).[3]

This brief story, really more of a gag than a narrative, is only the first of Fellini's frequent references to advertising during the course of his career. Extremely sensitive to all developments in contemporary mass culture, Fellini returns to advertising in a number of films, from *Le tentazioni del dottor Antonio* in the early 1960s to *E la nave va*, *Ginger e Fred*, and *Intervista* in the 1980s. Over the five decades since his contributions to *Marc'Aurelio*, however, Fellini's view of advertising changed drastically. What he first viewed as an amusing aspect of popular culture safely relegated to magazines, newspapers, or billboards developed into an uncontrollable monster in the consumer society of the 1980s that threatened the integrity of an artist's films when shown on television by destroying the particular rhythm and tone of the picture with commercial interruptions. As Fellini indignantly declared, "the insolence, aggression, and massacre of television publicity inserted within a film! It is like violence committed against an artistic creation."[4]

Fellini's decision to shoot two commercials in 1984 for Campari soda[5] and Barilla pasta[6] might seem to be contradictory, given his vehement opposition to their use during the broadcasting of his own feature films. Fellini's decision to shoot the commercials, however, was part of a project undertaken by the Italian advertising industry to convince the greatest talents of Italian cinema to produce commercials in their characteristic styles without sacrificing artistic integrity or crea-

[3] For the text of this particular narrative, including a photograph of the gag in the film, see ibid., p. 103; another example of these satirical parodies of popular advertising may be found reprinted in Adolfo Chiesa, ed., *Antologia del "Marc'Aurelio" 1931–1954* (Rome: Casa Editrice Roberto Napoleone, 1974; rpt. in 1988 as *Il meglio del "Marc'Aurelio"*), pp. 233–34.

[4] Federico Fellini, *Ginger e Fred*, ed. Mino Guerrini (Milan: Longanesi, 1986), p. 75.

[5] For the original script of the Campari commercial, modified in various particulars in the final commercial film, see "Filmetto pubblicitario per la soc. Campari: 'Oh, che bel paesaggio!'—sceneggiatura (Roma, 19 febbraio 1984)," Fellini MS. 7 (Box 2).

[6] No script of this commercial exists. My references are transcribed from a videotaped copy of the commercial as broadcast over Italian public television.

tivity. Not only Fellini but also Michelangelo Antonioni and Franco Zeffirelli responded with interesting spots reflecting their particular cinematic signatures. Only Fellini's commercials, however, aimed not only at selling a product but also at making a complex statement about the nature of advertising itself.

The spot Fellini created for Campari soda presents a bored young woman looking out the window of a moving train. In her compartment a fellow passenger picks up a remote-control device, like that for a television set, and begins to push the buttons, changing the landscapes outside from one exotic location to another. The woman remains uninterested in the various scenes, until the man asks her if she would prefer an Italian landscape. As she presses the remote-control device once again, a huge bottle of Campari appears alongside the Leaning Tower of Pisa, provoking an animated expression on the young woman's face. This brief spot contains an implicit critique of the commercial's intended audience, for Fellini believes that this very same public, remote-control device in hand, has been corrupted by the leveling of critical taste following the spread of commercial television in Italy. If the obvious and explicit message of Fellini's commercial tells the viewer to buy Campari soda, the more interesting theme of the brief film analyzes the public's inability or unwillingness to *look* carefully at a visual image. The contemporary audience's constant lack of attention or concentration, the most obvious symptom of which is its constant switching from channel to channel, has destroyed its capacity for interpreting serious cinematic works. The entire film reflects the parodic intent and the ambivalence typical of postmodern works of art. On the one hand, the director, whose previous masterpiece, *8 1/2*, may be quite rightly called the modernist film par excellence with its focus upon the self-reflexive nature of film, reaffirms his own prerogatives to control and manipulate the spectator's attention. On the other hand, the commercial embodies a subtle postmodernist perspective, since its creator visualizes, without approval, the way in which every spectator has become, with his remote-control device, his own editor. The postmodern audience produces a montage of televised images and therefore challenges the selection process formerly dominated by the director, who now loses control of the image he has created.

This duality of messages, where the director provides both an artistic creation and a critique of some of that same work's values, is even more pronounced in the more complex spot Fellini produced for Barilla, one of Italy's largest food companies. The spot was shot on a set similar to that of the luxurious dining room of the ocean liner Fellini used in *E la nave va*. The protagonists of the commercial are a couple engaged in an illicit love affair. This is revealed to the viewer by the suggestive, sensual glances the woman provocatively directs toward her companion. They are seated at a small table, toward which a number of stuffy and arrogant waiters are marching in a formal procession. The headwaiter begins to run off a long list of extremely pretentious-sounding dishes on the menu, pronouncing each entrée in French. At a certain point in this catalogue of foreign culinary delicacies, the sensuous woman turns to her friend and with a suggestive smile whispers a single word: "Rigatoni!" At the sound of this magic word, all of the waiters relax and breathe a sigh of relief. They are obviously Italians who have been ordered to pretend to be French to enhance the so-called atmosphere of the restaurant. In a chorus, they exclaim: "And we respond like an echo, Barilla, Barilla!" A voice-over then announces: "Barilla always makes you feel 'al dente.' "

The success of the Barilla commercial was unprecedented: it was solemnly announced as forthcoming in the major Italian newspapers, analyzed after its transmission by important media commentators, and reached a huge commercial audience. However, Fellini managed to turn the tables on the avowed commercial purpose of television advertising by producing a sixty-second spot containing not one but several messages. First, Fellini very neatly deflated the arrogant pretensions of French cooking by showing us how much more satisfying a simple dish of Italian pasta really is. He then fulfilled his contractual obligation by persuading his audience that Barilla pasta is superior to others with the excited reaction of the professional waiters. Such an exaggerated claim to superiority recalls the hilarious claims made in his comic article about the virtues of "Maccheroncini Pop."

More importantly, Fellini also linked the pleasure of eating Barilla rigatoni with sexual pleasure, the classic means of selling any product in advertising the world over, by showing us a couple engaged in a love affair who choose Barilla pasta over French cuisine for their sustenance. Fellini makes explicit the traditionally implicit linkage of a product with sexuality in his commercial by stressing a particular kind of pasta: "rigatoni," a word uttered by the sexy young woman, has a magical effect on the waiters and her companion. In a first viewing of the commercial, the effect of this rather common word seems inexplicable, and a great many Italians completely missed the point of Fellini's subtle innuendo. Some decades ago, and especially in Fellini's native Emilia-Romagna, "rigatoni" was a popular slang term for oral sex. Its precise English translation would be "blow job." Once we understand the subtext of the commercial's final voice-over, the brief film assumes an entirely different meaning. If "rigatoni" refers to an oral sex act as well as a kind of pasta, then "rigatoni" certainly makes one feel "al dente" (or "hard"), both literally and figuratively!

I have traced Fellini's interest in advertising from his simple gags for *Marc'Aurelio* to the far more interesting and sophisticated role advertising plays in his own commercials to emphasize how his characteristic themes constantly evolve from his earliest career as a writer and a cartoonist. Rarely has Fellini completely abandoned the intellectual or emotional baggage of his past in the many stylistic transformations that mark his career. The distance Fellini has traveled from simple gags parodying advertising claims in 1939 to postmodernist commercials revealing the artifices involved in advertising's psychological manipulation of an audience is emblematic of equally sophisticated transformations of ideas, images, and themes during his later career that reveal a constantly expanding visual imagination.

It is always surprising to be reminded of the fact that Federico Fellini, a director who has become practically synonymous with personal expression and artistic fantasy in the cinema, eventually arrived at his chosen profession without even the minimum of formal technical training. Born in Rimini in 1920, Fellini spent most of his childhood and adolescence in that city until he abandoned the provinces forever in 1938 and moved to Rome. Initially Fellini enrolled in the law school at the University of Rome, but he never completed his degree.[7] He never once considered attending Rome's Centro Sperimentale di Cinematografia, the important school founded by Mussolini in 1937, many of whose faculty and graduates later played a crucial role, with Fellini, in the rebirth of postwar Italian cinema. Moreover, unlike so many of the young Italians who grew up during the Fascist era, Fellini never frequented the film clubs ("Cinegufs") organized by the regime that screened not only the best work by native Italian directors, such as Mario Camerini or Alessandro Blasetti, but also important film classics from France, Germany, and, most importantly, Russia. When asked to recount the fifty films he loved the most, Fellini immediately replied: " 'Fifty films? Are you kidding? I never saw that many in my entire life!' "[8] From the group of forty-two works Fellini reluctantly agreed to list, such names as Dreyer, Griffith, and Eisenstein are conspicuously absent. Instead, Fellini prefers comic works (Chaplin, Buster Keaton, Laurel and Hardy, the Marx brothers, Pietro Germi, the black humor of Buñuel), as well as such popular films as *King Kong* and the James Bond series (*From Russia with Love* and *Goldfinger*).

---

[7] For a detailed discussion of Fellini's life, see Kezich, *Fellini*, to which my discussion of Fellini's early years is deeply indebted; see also Hollis Alpert, *Fellini: A Life* (New York: Atheneum, 1986), for the most current English biography of Fellini.

[8] Zanelli, *Nel mondo di Federico*, p. 130; Zanelli's discussion of what Fellini calls his "deficient" background in film culture is the best available treatment of Fellini's knowledge of film history.

Fellini's anti-intellectual attitude toward filmmaking and the history of his profession, one of the most refreshing aspects of his personality, has always puzzled film scholars, especially those unfamiliar with Italian popular culture during the Fascist era and the immediate postwar period. But when Fellini's intellectual origins are examined closely, the truly formative influences upon his early career emerge from popular Italian culture of the period and not primarily from the cinema: cartoons (or *fumetti*, as they are called in Italy), caricature sketches, variety shows, and even radio comedy. Fellini's intellectual odyssey through these fascinating but often neglected popular art forms toward his initial encounter with the cinema as a gagman and scriptwriter therefore deserves special attention.

The most intelligent evaluation of the impact of popular culture on the origins of Fellini's visual language has been provided by the late Italo Calvino, the brilliant novelist whose own prose style, like Fellini's cinema, moved from an interest in realism during the immediate neorealist era with a first novel, *Il sentiero dei nidi di ragno* (1947), toward metaliterary themes and techniques typical of postmodernist fiction in his mature literary works. In an important preface to an edition of four Fellini scripts published in 1974, "Autobiografia di una spettatore," Calvino notes that

> the force of the image in Fellini's films, so difficult to define because it cannot be contained in the codes of any figurative culture, has its roots in the superabundant and disharmonious aggressivity of journalistic graphic art, the aggressivity of which is capable of imposing upon the entire world cartoons and strips that seem as much characterized by individual stylization as they are capable of communication at the level of mass culture.[9]

Long before Italian film scholars had begun to pay much attention to the popular sources of Fellini's creativity, Calvino's precociously original essay on Fellini's style noted that the influence of Italian mass culture was not only crucial to Fellini's intellectual formation but had never been abandoned in his later and more sophisticated cinematic language: "what has been many times defined as Fellini's baroque [style] derives from his constant forcing of the photographic image in a direction that carries it from an image of caricature toward that of the visionary."[10] As such, Fellini's visual universe, according to Calvino, "corresponds to an infantile, disembodied, pre-cinematic visualization

[9] Italo Calvino, "Autobiografia di uno spettatore," in Federico Fellini, *Quattro film* (Turin: Einaudi, 1974), p. xxii.
[10] Ibid., pp. xxii–xxiii.

of an 'other' world (an 'other' world upon which the cinema confers an illusion of carnality that confuses its phantoms with the attractive-repulsive carnality of life itself)."[11]

By Fellini's own testimony, the comic strips and cartoons he eagerly read in the pulp magazines of his adolescence in Rimini constituted a crucial element in his early artistic formation:

> I began to understand the essence of what is comic when I was a child, in the comic-strips of Frederick Burr Opper and George McManus, *Happy Hooligan, Maud, Alphonse and Gaston* and *Bringing Up Father*. In those days they were published in Italy without balloons containing the dialogue, but with rhymes of a sort underneath the picture, rhymes that were never quite detailed enough—since, as we all know, rhymes may alter things a little. In other words, a fundamental part of the composition was missing: the text which is included in the image and forms part of the image itself. But, all the same, I did get an idea of this ingenious and already highly delicate art, and it even provided me with a way of looking at the world.[12]

Cartoons, both American and native Italian versions, have played an important role in popular culture in Italy, and their consumption is not limited to the less educated classes. It is not unusual in Italy to see an elegantly dressed businessman on a first-class train reading the equivalent of the American *New York Times* (the Roman daily, *La repubblica*), as well as "Topolino," the Italianized version of Walt Disney's Mickey Mouse cartoons. As early as 1908, a children's publication, *Il corriere dei piccoli*, presented the kinds of cartoons Fellini mentioned above—that is, without the traditional balloons.[13] The more familiar American form with balloons was introduced in 1932. The entire range of American cartoon characters was eventually introduced to the Italian reading public, although their names were often substantially al-

[11] Ibid., p. xxi.

[12] Fellini, *Fellini on Fellini*, p. 140.

[13] For a detailed history of cartoons and comic strips in Italy and their links to American artists, see Gaetano Strazzulla, *I fumetti*, 2 vols. (Florence: Sansoni Editore, 1980). For Fellini's own influence on contemporary cartoonists, see Vincenzo Mollica, ed., *Il fumetto e il cinema di Fellini* (Montepulciano: Editori del Grifo, 1984). In particular, Fellini's films have constituted a crucial source of visual inspiration for Milo Manara, one of Italy's best-known cartoon artists, who has based a series of cartoon adventures on Fellini's story entitled "Viaggio a Tulun" (first published in installments by Milan's *Corriere della sera* in 1986 and subsequently reprinted in Federico Fellini, *Block-notes di un regista* [Milan: Longanesi, 1988], pp. 9–39). Manara's cartoon, "Viaggio a Tulum" (the change in title reflects his modifications of Fellini's original story) began running in the Italian cartoon magazine *Corto maltese* beginning with vol. 7, no. 7, in 1989.

tered. Jiggs and Maggie became Archibaldo and Petronilla; Hans and Fritz Katzenjammer became Bibì and Bibò; Popeye was renamed Braccio di Ferro. Other characters that became household names in Italy include Barney Google (Barnabò Goggoloni), Sergeant King (Audax), Mickey Mouse (Topolino) and all of Walt Disney's creations, Buck Rogers (whose name was changed to Elio Fiamma in 1936 when the Fascist regime Italianized foreign strip heroes), Flash Gordon, Mandrake (Mandrache during the Fascist era), Buster Brown (Mimmo Mammolo), Felix the Cat (Mio Mao), Superman (the Nembo Kid), and the Phantom (L'uomo mascherato).

Fellini himself seems to have been blessed with a precocious talent for sketches and caricatures. His first publication as a young boy of sixteen occurred in a 1937 issue of a magazine published by Rimini's Opera Balilla (the Fascist youth organization designed to replace the more traditional and only slightly less militaristic Boy Scouts). It was a caricature of some of his Balilla friends from a camping trip in August 1936.[14] Subsequently, during the 1937 vacation season, Fellini joined the painter Demos Bonini to create a sketch and caricature shop called Febo that catered to the summer tourist trade in Rimini. Both Fellini and Bonini also provided caricatures of film stars to decorate the marquees of the Fulgor, a local movie theater in Rimini. The aspiring artist also began sending fictitious postcards to the *Domenica del corriere*, which paid twenty lire for any humorous sketches accompanied by one-liners that they found worthy of publication. Some twelve of Fellini's entries were accepted, all signed "Dis. di Fellini" (Sketch by Fellini). The first such card was published on 6 February 1938 and shows an animal trainer scolding his acrobat wife with the caption: " 'When you do the leap of death on the trapeze, you don't need to hold Giorgio's hands so tightly. Understand?' "[15] The same talent for inventing one-liner gags and illustrating them with clever sketches would later serve Fellini well as a journalist and scriptwriter after his move to Rome. While still in Rimini, Fellini encountered one of his adolescent idols, the artist Giuseppe Zanini, known as Nino Za. Za had made his fortune in Germany publishing caricatures of the world's great actresses and actors (Marlene Dietrich, Greta Garbo, Clark Gable) as well as important historical figures (Mussolini, d'Annunzio). For Fellini, Nino Za's art always remained linked to the dreamlike world of Rimini's Grand Hotel, later immortalized in *Amarcord*, with its wealthy Nordic tourists, exotic automobiles, expensive clothes, and beautiful but unapproachable women. The music played there was usually of the popular

[14] Kezich, *Fellini*, p. 26.
[15] Cited in ibid., p. 30.

American variety, and the hotel's heady atmosphere symbolized for Fellini all of the admittedly shallow aspirations he and his *vitelloni* friends experienced during their adolescent years in the provinces:

> The orchestra was playing "Following the Fleet," the sky had become velvet blue like the jacket of the famous sketch artist. It seemed like being in Los Angeles, who knows why. Nino Za. Grand hotels. Success. Golden cigarette cases. English shoes. I envied him with all my might. German movie actresses made appointments months ahead of time to have him do their picture; do you remember Zarah Leander with her quivering lips and her eyelids heavy with insatiable desires? And Brigitte Helm? . . . He certainly must have made love to them all. What aggravation! And during the winter at Cortina, the Hotel Cristallo gave him the most beautiful apartment, and he spent Christmas in Berlin. Then, who knows, February in London and afterwards perhaps Honolulu. I envied him with my every breath. I wanted to become just like him.[16]

When Fellini eventually moved to Rome, he met Za in the café society both men frequented, and Za did a fine caricature sketch of Fellini— then a rather serious, thin figure—the style of which is not too far removed from the artistic style Fellini himself developed during this period.

Before going to Rome, Fellini made more substantial contributions to the Florentine weekly humor magazine *420*, then directed by Mario Nerbini. Fellini presented himself at the editorial office late in 1937 and became, in his own words, "something between an office boy and an editorial secretary."[17] During a six-month period between 1937 and 1938, before his departure for Rome, Fellini became a close collaborator with its staff. Fellini's Florentine period has also given birth to an interesting and possibly apocryphal story concerning his work with cartoons. Mario Nerbini and his general editor, Gino Schiatti (a sketch artist who used the pseudonym Gischiat), were faced with mounting pressure from the Ministry of Popular Culture to substitute Italian cartoons for American ones. According to Fellini himself, "I boldly agreed, along with Gino Schiatti, to continue writing the texts while Giove

---

[16] Cited in Luigi Lambertini, *Nino Za: il caricaturista degli anni '30* (Bologna: Edizioni Bora, 1982), p. 17.

[17] Federico Fellini, *Comments on Film*, ed. Giovanni Grazzini, trans. Joseph Henry (Fresno: The Press of California State University at Fresno, 1988), p. 47; this is a translation of Federico Fellini, *Intervista sul cinema*, ed. Giovanni Grazzini (Rome: Laterza, 1983). As Kezich, *Fellini*, notes (p. 31), the disastrous 1966 flood in Florence destroyed many of the extant numbers of *420* and other magazines reflecting the popular culture of the period, making any analysis of Fellini's work in Florence today extremely difficult.

2. Federico Fellini (1942) by Nino Za

Toppi illustrated them, imitating their drawings perfectly. After accurate research, one commentator says that this story about homemade *Flash Gordon* cartoons is one of the many con jobs in my autobiography. Could be. . . ."[18] Tullio Kezich's recent biography casts some doubt on this episode, given that extant copies of the "Flash Gordon" strips during the period seem not to bear the mark of either Fellini or Giove Toppi. But there is little doubt that Fellini was profoundly influenced by "Flash Gordon" during this period. As he has noted, the character created by Alexander Raymond added an element of adventure to Fellini's understanding of comic strips after his notions of comedy had already been shaped by reading them. The exotic adventures unfolding on distant or fantastic worlds in the American comic strips were far more attractive to Fellini than the militaristic brand of Fascist heroism preferred by the Ministry of Popular Culture. Fellini has also admitted that in some of his mature works (*Fellini Satyricon*, for example, or *I clowns*), he attempted to recapture the peculiar colors typical of the comic strips of his youth.[19]

In addition to the impression made upon the young Fellini by Flash Gordon, a number of American cartoon figures have proved particularly stimulating to Fellini's visual imagination. Happy Hooligan, created between 1896 and 1899 by Frederick Burr Opper, was a melancholy clown anticipating not only the Little Tramp, the character immortalized by Charlie Chaplin in numerous comic films, but also a number of figures sketched by Fellini himself during various stages of his career. In Italy Happy Hooligan was renamed Fortunello and was extremely popular during Fellini's youth. The particular style of drawing in Opper's comic strip struck a responsive chord in Fellini's own cartoon style and can be seen in sketches done by Fellini throughout his entire career. On the manila folder containing the original manuscript of a film story entitled *La famiglia*, undated but certainly written between 1947 and 1950 when Fellini worked for the Lux Film Studio as a scriptwriter, there are a number of cartoons or caricatures in Fellini's hand. The inside front cover contains two caricature sketches of a man's head; on the inside back cover is the figure of a variety hall dancer in an Oriental costume, reminiscent of the clothes several characters wear in Fellini's first films, *Luci del varietà* and *Lo sceicco bianco*. Most interesting of all, and drawn in a style obviously indebted to Opper (as are all of the sketches on this manuscript), is the caricature of an entire family on the front cover. While engaged in creating a script containing a naturalistic portrait of Italian family life over three decades, Fellini's attention

[18] Fellini, *Comments on Film*, p. 48.
[19] Fellini, *Fellini on Fellini*, p. 140; del Buono, "Da Fortunello a Giudizio," p. 75.

3. Fellini's sketch on the cover of the manuscript of *La famiglia*

is instead focused upon the comic possibilities of distorting the realism of the story by representing the entire family as cartoon figures.[20]

Fellini continues the same graphic style in cartoons done at various stages of his career depicting characters interpreted by his wife, Giulietta Masina, famous for her moving performances as Gelsomina in *La strada*, Cabiria in *Le notti di Cabiria*, and Giulietta in *Giulietta degli*

[20] Federico Fellini and Tullio Pinelli, "La famiglia," Pinelli MS. 12 (Box 5, IIIA), front cover of manila folder.

spiriti.[21] It has long been a critical commonplace in the literature on Fellini to emphasize how for Fellini, Giulietta Masina embodies a particular combination of mannerisms, facial expressions, and gestures reminiscent of Charlie Chaplin. In fact, she has often been called "the female Chaplin." Fellini's particular sympathy for the figure of the clown, so important a character in many of his greatest films, thus owes a debt not only to the comic strip but also to the comic figure of Charlot and to Masina's comic talents as an actress. In fact, in 1957 Fellini wrote a script for a film eventually directed by Eduardo De Filippo entitled *Fortunella*. As the feminine form of the Italian name for Happy Hooligan implies, the film was both a vehicle for Giulietta Masina and a showcase for the comedic qualities the actress had already displayed in *La strada*. Fellini himself has declared that *La strada* arose primarily from a visual inspiration rather than a narrative one: "There are even ideas that are born all at once in the form of an image. 'Reading' it all comes later. This was particularly so with the character of Gelsomina."[22] When the visual inspiration for the comic type appropriate to Giulietta Masina's character came to Fellini, she was immediately associated with the persona of a clown:

> For some time, I had been thinking of a film for Giulietta. As an actress, she seems to me particularly capable of expressing spontaneously the amazements of a clown. There you have it—Giulietta is really an actress-clown, a true female clown. . . . I think I made the film because I fell in love with that *bambina-vecchina* who is both a little crazy and a little saintly; with that ruffled, funny, clumsy, and very tender clown whom I called Gelsomina, who even now manages to bend my mind with melancholy whenever I hear the music of her trumpet.[23]

Fellini has also remarked that both Gelsomina and Cabiria represent clowns of the *augusto* type—the anarchical, irrational, sympathetic clown usually set in contrast to the authoritarian disciplinarian known

[21] For examples of Fellini's various sketches of Giulietta Masina, see Pier Marco De Santi, *I disegni di Fellini* (Rome: Laterza, 1982), sketches 17, 21–22, 24, 25–28 (Gelsomina from *La strada*), 34 (Cabiria from *Le notti di Cabiria*), and 55 (Giulietta from *Giulietta degli spiriti*). Sketches 17 and 24 are reproduced in Federico Fellini, *"La Strada": Federico Fellini, Director*, ed. and trans. Peter Bondanella and Manuela Gieri (New Brunswick, N.J.: Rutgers University Press, 1987), title page and pp. 18, 182. For a consideration of Giulietta Masina's acting career, see Tullio Kezich, ed., *Giulietta Masina (La Chaplin mujer): Entrevista realizada por Tullio Kezich* (Valencia: Fernando Torres, 1985).

[22] Fellini, *Fellini on Fellini*, p. 100.

[23] Fellini, "The Genesis of *La Strada*," in *"La Strada": Federico Fellini, Director*, pp. 182, 184.

as the "white clown"—and that such figures are "not feminine; they are asexual. They are Fortunello."[24]

The visual link between Opper's Happy Hooligan and Fellini's graphic interpretation of Gelsomina remains constant throughout Fellini's career. One of the manuscripts from the Lilly Library archive reflecting various stages of the scripting of *La strada*, apparently the next-to-last draft of the film's script, contains cartoon sketches of Gelsomina in ballpoint pen on the front cover and inside the manila folder. In them, Gelsomina's clownish nature as well as her visual source in Opper's cartoons can be clearly discerned.[25] Years later in 1976, when Fellini completed his most comprehensive theoretical statement on the art of the cinema, *Fare un film*, he did another sketch of Gelsomina in felt-tip pen for the cover of the published book, the original drawing of which can be examined on the cover of the original manuscript.[26] Gelsomina's representation continues to repeat that established early on in Fellini's career and maintains the links to his sources—both the image of the clown in Opper's comic strips and that popularized by Chaplin's interpretation of the Little Tramp.

This particularly Fellinian comic type, derived both from contemporary cartoons and from various characters from film comedies created by such non-Italian actors as Chaplin, Buster Keaton, and Laurel and Hardy, obviously has deep-seated psychological roots in Fellini's visual imagination. Moreover, the appeal of this Fortunella figure continues throughout Fellini's career and is not confined merely to the early years of his career or his first films. As Oreste Del Buono, an expert on *fumetti* and a close personal friend of Fellini for many years, has astutely noted, the opening sequence of one of Fellini's most original films, *I clowns*, is actually a citation from the American comic strip called "Little Nemo," first created by Winsor McCay in 1905 for the *New York Herald*. The Italian edition of McCay's cartoons also served as Fellini's bedside reading during the shooting of this film. *I clowns* begins with a young boy awakening in his bedroom as he hears what are to him the mysterious sounds of the erection of a circus tent and then catches his first glimpse of a circus inhabited by clown types. The boy and his bedroom are clearly an homage to McCay's Little Nemo, underlining the director's debt both to the comic strip and to the circus clown as formative influences on his visual imagination.[27] Years after his first encounter with American comics and cartoons, at the retro-

---

[24] Fellini, in *I clown*, ed. Renzi, p. 44.

[25] Federico Fellini and Tullio Pinelli, "La strada: soggetto e sceneggiatura—Tullio Pinelli/Federico Fellini," Pinelli MS. 5 (Box 2, IE), front cover of folder.

[26] Federico Fellini, "Fare un film," Fellini MS. 1 (Box 1), title page.

[27] Del Buono, "Da Fortunello a Giudizio," p. 75.

4. Fellini's sketches for the front and back of the folder holding the original manuscript of *La strada*: Gelsomina as a clown figure

spective honoring his career at the Lincoln Center Film Festival in 1985, Fellini organized his acceptance speech around his recollections of the comic strip character Felix the Cat, bringing the house down with laughter. As he later explained,

> the American films and comic strips showed me that there was a place where you could grow up and become president without studying Latin and Greek. To me, American films have always been propaganda . . . not for the usual causes but for the idea of a freer life. The concept was gotten across through such figures as Charlie Chaplin, the eternal tramp, or such images as horses running wild in the fields. This world and the idea behind it had enormous appeal for me as a child and there was not one American film shown in Rimini when I was young that I didn't see, whether it was good or bad.[28]

Elsewhere, Fellini has declared that " 'America, democracy for me were Fred Astaire who danced on highly polished terraces or Greta Garbo who looked at us with that melancholy air, like a headmistress.' "[29]

[28] Federico Fellini, "America and I," *Amica—International Italian Fashion*, Autumn 1987—Winter 1988, p. 39.
[29] Cited in James Hay, *Popular Film Culture in Fascist Italy: The Passing of the*

5. Fellini's sketch of Gelsomina for the cover of the manuscript of *Fare un film*

As a mature director, Fellini seems to have retained a certain number of characteristics from his work as a cartoonist. In some of his films in color (*Fellini Satyricon, I clowns, Intervista*), the specific lighting and colors he employs are often informed by the peculiar kinds of vivid colors, or colors set against each other in sharp and violent contrast, usually found in comic strips. But if this kind of artistic contribution to Fellini's works is, of necessity, based upon an impressionistic judgment (since assessing the *quality* of a color must surely represent one of the most subjective of all problems in any critical evaluation of visual materials), there is no question that the brief and episodic nature of comic-strip narrative suited Fellini's artistic temperament perfectly. Comic strips usually either present a brief adventure or story within a single issue—a narrative composition not unlike a sequence in the structure of a fiction film—or are actually issued in weekly or monthly installments, an even more obvious division of narrative time with analogies to the cinematic sequence. Fellini's entire career may be viewed, at least from the perspective of the development of the narrative structure of his films, as a slow but deliberate move away from narrative closure toward episodic, open, and even plotless films. Surely the influence of the comic strip contributed in at least a small way to this pronounced narrative preference for episodic, sequential storytelling.

It is also possible that the comic strips Fellini read while a young man also influenced his view that the visual image of a film narrative must take precedence over any verbal dialogue. It must be remembered that until 1932 in Italy, Italian comic strips lacked the balloons containing the characters' dialogue; dialogue was physically absent from the section devoted to the visual image printed in color. During the postwar period and until only relatively recently, few Italian directors made films with synchronized sound. Instead, most have chosen to dub their sound tracks after work on the set is completed. In Fellini's case, however, this choice is deliberate and a matter of artistic choice, as it was with the late Pier Paolo Pasolini, since both directors equate synchronized sound with a search for cinematic naturalism, something they both seek to avoid at all costs. It is easy to see how the physical separation of visual narrative from verbal dialogue characteristic of comic-strip narration would appeal to a director such as Fellini who privileges images over ideas and pictures over words.

In Fellini's daily routine during the making of his films, his career as a cartoonist continues to play an important role, since the preparation

Rex (Bloomington: Indiana University Press, 1987), p. xii (Hay's translation); the original Italian statement is found in Corrado Augias, "Ho inventato tutto—anche me: conversazione con Federico Fellini," *Panorama*, 14 January 1980, p. 95.

and shooting of his works involve hundreds of sketches, usually caricatures, that he employs to capture the exact kind of lighting, makeup,
costume, and facial expression or physical type he desires for a particular character or scene. It is sufficient here to note not only that Fellini
conceives of his film characters as comic *types*, but that he usually (as
in the examples of Gelsomina or Zampanò in *La strada*, to mention
only the most celebrated characters) *visualizes* his characters first and
sketches them out as cartoon figures long before a narrative story line
emerges to match their physical features. In some of the original manuscripts of his scenarios or scripts (in those of *Roma* in particular), such
drawings actually constitute the nucleus of the projected film, while
the dialogue plays a secondary role.

Yet, in spite of the comic strip's constant fascination for Fellini, the
director recognizes its limitations as an artistic source for the cinema.
In a recent preface to a collection of cartoon work inspired by his films,
Fellini has reconsidered his debt to the comics. Defining the essence of
the comic strip as "that of fixity, the immobility of butterflies pierced
by a pin" or "those situations which are fixed forever, immobile like
puppets without wires," Fellini believes that such artistic stasis is "impossible to propose in the cinema, which has its seduction in movement, rhythm, and dynamism"; the comic strips may contribute their
scenographies, their characters, and their stories to the cinema but lack
the cinema's essential quality, which is dynamic motion.[30]

After his brief but fruitful association with Nerbini's *420* in Florence,
Fellini moved to Rome in 1938, where he first supported himself as a
wandering caricature artist providing sketches for clients of the restaurants and cafés, as well as painting shop windows. The artistic style
Fellini learned from his early readings of the comic strips, or his imitation of the caricatures of Nino Za, and which he has consistently employed to render his clown figures, may be discerned in most of the
cartoons and sketches he produced for Fascist Italy's most important
humor magazine, *Marc'Aurelio*.[31] Like almost everything else in Felli-

[30] Fellini, Introduction to *Il fumetto e il cinema di Fellini*, ed. Mollica, p. 7.

[31] For examples of both cartoons and articles written by Fellini and others for
Marc'Aurelio, see Chiesa, *Antologia del "Marc'Aurelio" 1931–1954*, or the reprint
entitled *Il meglio del "Marc'Aurelio."* See also Kezich, *Fellini*, pp. 39ff.; Olivieri,
L'imperatore in platea; and Françoise Pieri, "Federico Fellini écrivain du *Marc'-
Aurelio*," *Positif* 244–45 (1981): 20–32, and "Aux sources d'*Amarcord*: les récits felliniens du *Marc'Aurelio*," *Études cinématographiques* 127–30 (1981): 19–36. For a
completely negative and surprisingly insensitive view of Fellini's debts to the graphic
popular culture of the *fumetti* and the humor magazines of the prewar period, see
Paolo Bertetto's *Il più brutto del mondo: il cinema italiano oggi* (Milan: Bompiani,
1982), which juxtaposes Buñuel's background in French surrealism with Fellini's interest in cartoons. Bertetto remarks sarcastically, "but while Buñuel read *The Sur-*

ni's early career, his association with *Marc'Aurelio* was serendipitous. *Marc'Aurelio* was a twice-weekly periodical appearing on Wednesday and Saturday that eventually enjoyed a circulation of some 350,000. It was then published by Angelo Rizzoli, later to become the producer of *La dolce vita*, whose offices were in the same building as those of the editorial staff. Its golden age of popularity in Italy coincided with the last decade of the Fascist era until the chaos accompanying the fall of the Fascist government forced it to cease publication in September 1943. It resumed publication in 1946 and ran until 1954, but with less success, since by that time the cinema had replaced the general appeal of the weekly humor magazines in Italian popular culture.

In 1939, at the editorial offices of *Marc'Aurelio* in Via Regina Elena 68 (now Via Barberini), Fellini encountered Stefano Vanzini (known as Steno), the editorial secretary of the magazine, who immediately recognized Fellini's genius and eventually hired him to invent gags for the vignettes and comic drawings the journal published. Fellini's arrival at the editorial office made quite an impression on Steno. After the doorman announced the arrival of the callow provincial carrying a stack of vignettes under his arm, "as soon as he turned them over on the table, I saw that they were promising; they looked as if they had been sketched by Grosz. I therefore kept him there waiting for the director."[32] Fellini thus entered the fascinating world of Roman popular journalism. But Steno's perceptive judgment of Fellini's talent as an artist was far more important to Fellini's future career in the cinema than anyone could have imagined at the time, for in the editorial offices of *Marc'Aurelio* Fellini joined a group of journalists and artists who were also closely connected to the Italian film industry. As Steno has noted, *Marc'Aurelio* served as a kind of unofficial training ground for scriptwriters and directors. The gags Fellini and others wrote requiring visualization in comic sketches constituted a form of pre-cinematic humor that would later find its fullest expression not only in Fellini's cinema but also in many of the most important Italian film comedies of the 1950s and 1960s, the so-called *commedia all'italiana*. In fact, the writers associated with *Marc'Aurelio* during the 1940s and 1950s were to become Italy's greatest scriptwriters during the last years of the Fascist era and the immediate postwar period. Besides Steno, these included Vittorio Metz, Cesare Zavattini, Age (Agenore Incrocci), Ruggero Mac-

---

realist Revolution, Fellini did not miss a number of *Marc'Aurelio*" (p. 34). Bertetto apparently ignores the fact that the surrealists also found inspiration in film comedy and cartoons and that film cartoons embody many of the characteristics of surrealism in other genres.

[32] Cited in Franca Faldini and Goffredo Fofi, eds., *L'avventurosa storia del cinema italiano raccontata dai suoi protagonisti 1935–1959* (Milan: Feltrinelli, 1979), p. 39.

cari, Ettore Scola, Furio Scarpelli, and Bernardino Zapponi (later Fellini's scriptwriter on *Toby Dammit, Fellini Satyricon, Roma,* and *Casanova*). By Tullio Kezich's count, Fellini made some seven hundred
different contributions of various kinds to *Marc'Aurelio* between 1939
and 25 November 1942 (the date of his last contribution) totaling more
than two thousand pages of text, including cartoons, gags, and comic
columns of some duration.[33] The humor of the magazine was typically
Roman, vulgar and rather sophisticated at the same time. Its tone was
very far from that typical of the English *Punch*, a literary magazine
Marc'Aurelio frequently attacked during the war years, even while implicitly acknowledging it as a model.

Fellini's job with *Marc'Aurelio* introduced him to the kind of group
activity typical of film production. The editorial staff met at regular
intervals and worked as a team to produce the magazine's material, just
as scriptwriters collaborate to construct a script for a film. At first, the
inexperienced Fellini was obliged to prove his talent by completing relatively simple chores—writing captions for cartoons as well as gags or
"battute." After successfully passing this trial period, he was permitted
to write brief and anonymous articles from time to time. Finally, as
a seasoned veteran, Fellini was given his own byline and allowed to
produce a series of articles based upon similar themes, the comic rubrics that constituted the most authentic proof of his journalistic maturity.[34] At this point, Fellini's name had already become familiar to the
thousands of readers of the magazine, and his popular reputation as a
comic writer was well established.

Many of the recognizably Fellinian themes in the future director's
cinema can be identified in a formative stage in the rubrics Fellini
wrote for *Marc'Aurelio* and often reused in scripts he contributed to
various radio programs between 1941 and 1943. Fellini's treatment of
popular advertising has already been mentioned. A number of the stories Fellini wrote are bittersweet portraits of provincial life and love
that recall his early cinema. This connection is most striking in a trilogy of narratives entitled, respectively, *Primo amore* (*First Love*, eighteen texts between 9 November 1940 and 11 January 1942), *Piccoli fidanzati* (*Little Fiancés*, six texts contributed between 29 March 1941
and 1 July 1942), and *Oggi sposi* (*Today's Married Couples*, twelve texts
completed between 28 February and 22 April 1942). In the first group of
stories, Fellini recounts a rather infantile and naive love affair, what
used to be called "puppy love," between an innocent and pure girl

[33] Kezich, *Fellini*, pp. 50, 57.

[34] Bernardino Zapponi's description of the working methods of the editorial staff is
cited in Pieri, "Federico Fellini écrivain du *Marc'Aurelio*," p. 21.

24

6. A typical Fellini cartoon for *Marc'Aurelio* (1942) that prefigures the ending of *Toby Dammit*. The cartoon's caption reads: "*Plausible Mistakes*: Damn! Instead of taking the balloon from the little man, I took the little man with the balloon!"

named Bianchina and a narrator named Federico. In contrast to his first films, which mercilessly satirize provincial attitudes toward love and marriage, these early stories are less cruelly ironic, since they lack the presence of an omniscient narrator recounting the tale from the perspective of acquired adult experience that characterizes many of Fellini's later treatments of provincial Italy. But the genesis of Fellini's demythologizing irony, so integral a feature of his early films, is already present. In "Pronto Bianchina" ("Hello, Bianchina"), of 30 November 1940, for example, he mixes tenderness, humor, and satire in describing a long-distance telephone call made by Federico, his alter ego, to Bianchina. The comic force of the narrative arises from the juxtaposition of the young man's meticulous preparations to make the call and the unexpected results the conversation produces. Federico's dreams of a romantic link to his young girlfriend over the long distance separating the two are dashed by the sordid condition of the telephone booth, an interruption by a vulgar fat man, the interference of the static covering Bianchina's "sweet" voice, and the banality of the commonplaces that emerge during his long-awaited conversation. The story concludes as the narrator, having spent all of his money on the useless call, stands heartbroken in the pouring rain. The clash of romantic illusions with bittersweet reality, and the slow movement from dream to disenchantment, cannot but remind us of the films from Fellini's early period— *Luci del varietà, Lo sceicco bianco,* and *I vitelloni.*

In the *Piccoli fidanzati* cycle, the two protagonists Federico and Bianchina are replaced by a young man named Roberto and a number of female characters (Nadia, Adrianella, Mirella) in some of the stories, while other texts are presented as love letters from Bianchina to Federico, who is off to war. As Fellini's fictional characters draw closer to engagement and marriage, they begin to lose their original innocence and are treated with increasing pessimism. For example, in a story with Roberto and Adrianella as protagonists (6 June 1942), Roberto one day discovers that he is no longer in love. Previously, as both are illiterate, they had exchanged blank love letters, only imagining their unwritten contents. But Roberto learns to read and write, eventually marrying another woman and fathering two children, all the while continuing to send his former girlfriend, who remains illiterate, blank pages falsely testifying to his continued affections. One of the few critical articles devoted to these early narratives quite rightly underlines the affinities between this vignette treating the eclipse of adolescent love and an early short story eventually made into a brief play by Luigi Pirandello entitled *Lumíe di Sicilia* (*Limes of Sicily*) which first appeared in 1920.[35] This first connection between Fellini and Pirandello, Fascist Ita-

---

[35] Ibid., p. 27.

ly's most influential writer, is worthy of note, since years later, Pirandello's revolt against realism in the theater provided Fellini with a
model for his move away from neorealism and its socially derived concept of film character. The example of Pirandello's metadramatic revolution would be even more important as inspiration for Fellini's own
metacinematic examination of the cinema as an art form. In spite of
Fellini's often expressed antipathy for comparisons between his films
and Pirandello's plays,[36] a possible influence of the playwright upon the
filmmaker at such an early stage in his career should not be ruled out.
Given the importance of Pirandello to Italian theater at this time, and
Giulietta Masina's early dramatic training in the theater, it is likely
that Fellini knew Pirandello's works quite well, even if today he objects
to searching for the sources of his visual imagination because he feels
that such a search reduces his creative inspiration to a mechanical operation of assimilation and imitation.[37]

   In the third collection of stories, Oggi sposi, Fellini returns to Federico and Bianchina to recount the imaginary history of their marriage:
their honeymoon, their first night together, their return to their new
home, their friends, a description of their kitchen, and their first anniversary. Now the mood of Fellini's narrative becomes more somber. Fellini interprets the passage from young love to marriage and responsibility as a fall from grace and innocence and a betrayal of greater potential.
The young couple has been inevitably trapped within the strict conventions and social conformity of bourgeois family life. Once again, the
juxtaposition of the young couple's illusions and the more sordid reality they face points toward themes in Fellini's early films: the long-
awaited honeymoon lacks the luxury hotels and expensive wagon-lits
train they had imagined, while the Venetian location is dirty and teeming with stray cats; a very unromantic gondola ride through the dark
canals of the city ends in seasickness. The diminutives Cico and Pallina
for Federico and Bianchina appear in these stories for the first time and
would be reused only a few years later in radio sketches inspired by the

[36] In Comments on Film, p. 151, Fellini includes Pirandello among his other dislikes, which include film festivals, interviews, music in restaurants, ketchup, and
"hearing people talk about Brecht over and over."
[37] Kezich's biography (pp. 74–75) notes that in 1925, Masina was taken by her relatives at the early age of four during an intermission in the theater to see Pirandello
in person. During a rehearsal for one of the dramas produced by the Teatro Guf (the
theatrical group sponsored by the Gruppi universitari fascisti), her admission to
drama school included the reading of a scene from Pirandello's Vestire gli ignudi.
One of her first performances was as a prostitute in a program including Pirandello's
All'uscita. As we shall see in the next two chapters, Fellini practically typecast his
wife as a prostitute in films he scripted during the 1940s and early 1950s and in a
number of his own works during his early career.

same characters. But the dark vision of the institution of marriage that these stories contain reappears in the equally unhappy portrayals of such early Fellinian characters as Ivan and Wanda in *Lo sceicco bianco* or Fausto and Sandra in *I vitelloni*. Federico now feels "nothing" for Bianchina, where once he could dream only of being alone with her (4 March 1942); he experiences a feeling of terror (18 March 1942) when he recognizes that she will be his wife forever.[38] Completely successful and mutually satisfying marriages are conspicuously absent in all the films Fellini has made during the course of his lengthy career, and his views on the subject today seem not to have changed substantially from these early narratives.

Another popular rubric Fellini created for *Marc'Aurelio*, with some forty articles between 7 December 1940 and 4 October 1941, was entitled *Seconda liceo* (*Second Liceo*). This is a seemingly autobiographical portrait of a provincial high school that seeks to reflect experiences from Fellini's youth, on the one hand, and may well constitute, on the other, an artistic precursor to the justly famous satire of school life under fascism in *Amarcord*. One of the recurrent elements of Fellinian narrative—the sexual encounter of an inexperienced young male with an older, sexually mature woman in the darkness of a provincial cinema—appears in a humorous description of an article from this series dated 12 February 1941. The same kind of sexual encounter will appear again and again in a number of Fellini's films. Fausto meets an attractive woman in a cinema in *I vitelloni* and attempts, without success, to set up an amorous rendezvous with her outside in the street. In *Roma*, the narrator notes that the pharmacist's wife would allow men to touch her while the lights were turned down in the local cinema; the film then transforms this woman into Messalina, wanton wife of the cuckolded emperor Claudius. Perhaps the most memorable of these Fellinian sexual encounters in the cinema may be found in a famous scene from *Amarcord* in which the young Titta attempts to seduce the beautiful Gradisca in the smoke-filled local movie theater but meets with ignominious failure. In the *Seconda liceo* narratives, the protagonist of these schoolboy adventures is Fellini himself (called Federico or Fellini in the text), but the stories are never recounted in a subjective style as in *Roma* or *Amarcord*. Moreover, Fellini insists that such humorous vignettes set in a time and place that would seem to be his native Rimini are completely fictitious: "You know how one produces an artistic creation. . . . A creation is never invented and is never true. It is, first and foremost, itself. What an idea to want to know if my tales were invented! From what point of view? Of course they are true. For the

---

[38] Pieri, "Federico Fellini écrivain du *Marc'Aurelio*," pp. 31–32.

simple reason that they are invented, they become truer than any other kind of reality."[39]

Another interesting rubric, comprising some eighty different articles between 26 October 1940 and the end of 1942, bears the title *Come si comporta . . . l'uomo* (*How the Man Behaves . . .*), where "the man" is almost always the author himself. In November 1940, for example, in *Come si comporta . . . l'uomo al cinematografo* (*How the Man Behaves . . . at the Movies*), we have an interesting subjective view of the thoughts of a man who edges closer and closer to a woman seated in the darkened movie theater, the magic location, in Fellini's view, where sexual fantasies are permitted free expression.[40] Besides providing proof, if any were needed, that Fellini has always regarded the dreamlike atmosphere of a darkened movie theater as a place where normal sexual inhibitions are overcome, this particular rubric also contains another suggestive "meta-article" entitled *Come si comporta . . . l'uomo quando deve scrivere questa rubrica* (*How the Man Behaves . . . When He Has to Write This Rubric*, 15 March 1941), which cannot but remind us of the self-reflexive, metacinematic works of Fellini's mature career, such as *8 1/2, Block-notes di un regista, Roma*, or *Intervista*.

Of all the various rubrics Fellini created and wrote for *Marc'Aurelio*, none was as popular as that which began on 26 July 1939 and continued during the entire year of 1941, including an edition in German for the Axis troops allied with Mussolini's Italy. Its title was *Ma tu mi stai a sentire!* (*But Are You Listening to Me?*), and the various articles were structured around the author's plaintive and often romantic address to some one hundred different and vividly rendered comic characters—the vaudeville star, the waiter with the white shirt, the lady friend of the family, the chaplain with the false smile, the ex–school friend, and so forth. Inevitably, these articles dealt with the bittersweet effects of adolescent or unrequited love and evoke, as many of Fellini's early articles do, the same detailed portrait of seemingly insignificant events from Italian provincial life so typical of his early cinema.[41]

Given Fellini's increasingly recognized talent as a gag-writer and his association with the editorial board of *Marc'Aurelio*, it was perhaps inevitable that the young man would eventually try his hand at writing for the other two popular sources of mass entertainment in Fascist Italy that were nourished by the Roman humor magazine's genius: the cin-

[39] Cited by Pieri, "Aux sources d'*Amarcord*," pp. 20–21.

[40] For the text, see Olivieri, *L'imperatore in platea*, p. 104.

[41] For several examples of this rubric, see either ibid., pp. 101–2, 104–5; or Chiesa, *Antologia del "Marc'Aurelio" 1931–1954*, pp. 247–48, 256, 258–59, 272–73.

ema and popular radio programs.[42] By and large, the scripts Fellini provided for various radio programs, beginning in 1940 and continuing until the fall of the Fascist regime in 1943, do not depart significantly from the style and themes of the articles he had already written for *Marc'Aurelio*. It is interesting, however, that these radio scripts contain a number of the crucial ideas that would guide the work of the mature film director in later years. For example, the script for a broadcast of 24 April 1941 contains the statement that "dreams are the cinema of the indigent," whereas in a script dated 22 May 1941 the theme of Fellini's future comic masterpiece, *Lo sceicco bianco*, is neatly summarized: "But when dreams become reality, they make no one happy."[43] Immediately after the war, from 17 November 1946 until the first months of 1947, Fellini returned to the material he had developed in his early narratives for *Marc'Aurelio* (*Primo amore, Piccoli fidanzati, Oggi sposi*) to re-create a popular radio program entitled "Le avventure di Cico e Pallina" ("The Adventures of Cico and Pallina") that ran for twenty minutes every Sunday evening. Giulietta Masina, Fellini's wife since 1943, read the part of Pallina. By this time, however, Fellini had already begun to write regularly for the film industry, abandoning his early dreams of becoming a famous journalist.

[42] For Fellini's career in radio, see Kezich, *Fellini*, pp. 60–72, to which my discussion is indebted.

[43] For these two citations from the mass of radio scripts Kezich examined for his biography, see ibid., p. 62.

CHAPTER TWO

Neorealist Apprenticeship

FELLINI AS SCRIPTWRITER

The script is like the suitcase you carry with you, but you buy a lot of things on the way.[1]

IN THEIR understandable desire to do justice to Fellini's contributions as a director, most studies of Fellini have neglected his almost equally significant career as a scriptwriter. Apart from the hundreds of awards Fellini has received during his lifetime from a variety of Italian and international organizations, his films have garnered a total of twenty-three nominations for Oscars in America, seven of which were successful.[2] Of these twenty-three nominations, eight were for Fellini's work as a scriptwriter on neorealist films directed by Roberto Rossellini, *Roma città aperta* (1945) and *Paisà* (1946), as well as scripts for his own films. Before turning to the actual direction of feature films in the 1950s, Fellini had already established himself as one of the Italian industry's most versatile writers. This crucial apprenticeship over a decade enabled him to master all of the traditional skills of professional scriptwriting within several different settings. Fellini's experiences introduced him to a variety of cinematic styles, and without a consideration of their importance to his

---

[1] Federico Fellini, *E la nave va*, ed. Federico Fellini and Tonino Guerra (Milan: Longanesi, 1983), p. 166; also cited in Kezich, *Fellini*, p. 104.

[2] His Oscars are as follows: four for Best Foreign Film (*La strada*, 1956; *Le notti di Cabiria*, 1957; *8 1/2*, 1963; *Amarcord*, 1974); and three for Best Costume Design (*La dolce vita*, 1961; *8 1/2*, 1963; *Casanova*, 1976—the first two films being designed by Piero Gherardi and the last by Danilo Donati). His sixteen unsuccessful nominations are as follows: Best Original Screenplay (*Roma città aperta*, 1946; *La strada*, 1956; *Amarcord*, 1975); Best Story and Screenplay (*Paisà*, 1946; *I vitelloni*, 1957; *La dolce vita*, 1961; *8 1/2*, 1963); Best Screenplay from Another Medium (*Casanova*, 1976); Best Director (*La dolce vita*, 1961; *8 1/2*, 1963; *Fellini Satyricon*, 1970; *Amarcord*, 1975); Best Art and Set Direction (*La dolce vita*, 1961; *8 1/2*, 1963); Best Costume Design (*Giulietta degli spiriti*, 1966); and Best Color (*Giulietta degli spiriti*, 1966). These data are taken from Richard Shale, ed., *Academy Awards*, 2d ed. (New York: Frederick Ungar, 1982); the dates above do not always correspond to the Italian release dates but refer, rather, to the time when each film was submitted to the Academy for consideration.

intellectual development we can make little sense of his subsequent artistic choices when he began his own work behind the camera.

Italian screenplays differ, in some respects, from those created within the traditional Hollywood studio system. Contrary to Hollywood practice, adaptations from literary works are relatively few in the Italian cinema. In the postwar period, some 80 percent of Italian production has been based upon original scripts.[3] Fellini's own directing career has continued this pattern. Only four of his films (*Toby Dammit*, *Fellini Satyricon*, *Casanova*, and *La voce della luna*) are even loosely based on or suggested by literary sources, and they are idiosyncratic interpretations rather than true adaptations faithful to the spirit of the original text.

The Italian cinema has also always depended on extended periods of intimate collaboration between the same directors and scriptwriters. As a result, the scriptwriter functions more as a dependent of the director than of a producer or his studio. The entire history of postwar Italian cinema could be written from the perspective of such teams: Vittorio De Sica and Cesare Zavattini; Luchino Visconti and Suso Cecchi d'Amico; Rossellini and Sergio Amidei, as well as Fellini; and Fellini's own associations with Ennio Flaiano, Tullio Pinelli, and Brunello Rondi. When artistic disagreements and the inevitable passage of time broke up Fellini's lengthy teamwork with these three men, he would subsequently work on equally intimate terms over a number of years with Bernardino Zapponi, Tonino Guerra, and, most recently, Gianfranco Angelucci. Close personal friendships and similar intellectual backgrounds usually characterize these collaborations. In addition, an Italian director almost always works with his scriptwriters throughout the creation of both stories and screenplays. Most of them would consider the standard Hollywood studio practice of circulating scripts until they encounter willing producers and appropriate directors unacceptable. Italian stories and screenplays are tailor-made vehicles for an individual director working in a symbiotic relationship with scriptwriters familiar with his vision of the world and comfortable with his cinematic style or sense of humor. On the infrequent occasions when one Italian director has taken over a project originally written by or intended for another director, the resulting films have rarely proved satisfactory. When Fellini sold a script he wrote in 1957, *Viaggio con*

---

[3] Marie-Christine Questerbert, *Les Scénaristes italiens: 50 ans d'écriture cinématographique* (Renans: 5 Continents/Hatier, 1988), p. 9. This interesting book contains chapters devoted to Fellini's major collaborators on scripts: Sergio Amidei, Ennio Flaiano, Tonino Guerra, and Tullio Pinelli.

Anita, to Mario Monicelli, the film Monicelli produced was a disappointment.[4]

An Italian film usually begins its long odyssey from ideation to final editing and release with the producer's acceptance of an original *soggetto* (subject or story) or *trattamento* (treatment), a prose narrative lacking dialogue but written much like a short story. The soggetto sketches out the atmosphere of the intended film, its major characters, and predominant themes. Little or no attention is given to the specifically cinematic problems of transforming the story into a film (camera angles, number and kinds of shots, style of editing, and so on). The passage from soggetto to *sceneggiatura* (script or screenplay) involves a major transformation. The greatest part of the labor consists of adding dialogue to the story and rendering more precisely how each sequence advances the plot, but again, in the Italian system little direction is provided as to how the film will actually be shot. Scriptwriters generally leave such technical questions to the director, who decides from day to day on the set how the larger sequences should be broken down into individual shots and what specific kinds of shots should be employed. Transitions between shots and sequences, of course, are selected by the director alone, who directs the work of the editor during the editing phase of production after work on the set has been completed. The Italian director's contribution to the editing is far greater than that of his American counterpart, and some Italian directors, such as Ermanno Olmi, even edit their own films. How much the scriptwriter influences the specific manner in which a film is created from a technical perspective will thus vary from director to director, as we shall see from a consideration of some of Fellini's original scripts. Rossellini's films, for example, were shot with a good deal of improvisation on the set by the director, and the scripts Rossellini required of Fellini contained few technical details, although the scriptwriters were allowed a great deal of freedom to fill the script with their own ideas. In the case of directors working within a commercial studio organized on the Hollywood model, Fellini might well provide some specific technical directions, but he would usually follow the director's own original story line closely without the freedom to make the kinds of major changes in the film's content that he enjoyed under Rossellini.

The actual physical structure of what is essentially a *literary* narra-

[4] For the English translation of the script, see Federico Fellini, *"Moraldo in the City" and "A Journey with Anita,"* ed. and trans. John C. Stubbs (Urbana: University of Illinois Press, 1983). The original script was written with Tullio Pinelli; in 1978, Fellini sold the screen rights to producer Alberto Grimaldi, who hired Monicelli to shoot it. *Viaggio con Anita* appeared in 1979 starring Giancarlo Giannini and Goldie Hawn and was released in the United States in 1981 under the title *Lovers and Liars*.

tive in the soggetto becomes, in the Italian sceneggiatura, a double-columned text oriented toward the film to be shot. On the left side of the manuscript, writers describe all information necessary to understand the development of the story (location, time, atmosphere, attitudes of the protagonists, and so on), while on the right side of the page, the actual text of the dialogue and the various elements of the sound track that are to be dubbed appear parallel with such descriptions. Ennio Flaiano once remarked that the passage from the soggetto to the sceneggiatura always disappoints its reader, particularly producers, for

> the story is a narrative, enjoyable for good or ill immediately, while the script is the structure of a work not yet completed, the film. Everything has to be transformed: and the writer imagines locations, characters, situations, tones, silences, lights, approaches, allusions that the reader later substitutes with others taken from his own experience, even if the action and the dialogue can seem to be following an unequivocal track.[5]

Much the same opinion was expressed by Pier Paolo Pasolini in a theoretical definition of the screenplay as a genre, "The Screenplay as a 'Structure That Wants to Be Another Structure.' " Pasolini, who provided Fellini with some dialogue for Le notti di Cabiria and La dolce vita,[6] believed that a screenplay's essential nature consisted in its con-

---

[5] Cited in Omaggio a Flaiano, ed. Gian Carlo Bertelli and Pier Marco De Santi (Pisa: Giardini, 1987), p. 6.

[6] The original manuscripts for both of these films, as well as the story for Le notti di Cabiria, are now preserved in Indiana University's Lilly Library of Rare Books and are catalogued, respectively, as follows: Federico Fellini, Tullio Pinelli, and Ennio Flaiano, "Le notti di Cabiria: sceneggiatura di Federico Fellini, Ennio Flaiano, Tullio Pinelli," Pinelli MS. 8 (Box 3, IIB); Federico Fellini, Tullio Pinelli, and Ennio Flaiano, "Le notti di Cabiria: soggetto di Fellini, Flaiano, Pinelli," Pinelli MS. 9 (Box 4, IIB-1); Federico Fellini, Tullio Pinelli, and Ennio Flaiano, with the collaboration of Brunello Rondi, "La dolce vita: soggetto e sceneggiatura di: Federico Fellini, Ennio Flaiano, Tullio Pinelli: collaboratore alla sceneggiatura: Brunello Rondi," Pinelli MS. 10 (Box 4, IIC-1); and Federico Fellini, Tullio Pinelli, and Ennio Flaiano, with the collaboration of Brunello Rondi, "La dolce vita (secondo tempo)," Pinelli MS. 11 (Box 4, IIC-2). The scripts for both Le notti di Cabiria and La dolce vita have also been published, although the story of the first film survives only in Pinelli MS. 9 (see note 8 below for details). A recent article in Rome's most important newspaper announced the acquisition of Pasolini's papers by the Gabinetto Vieusseux in Florence, which are conserved in Palazzo Corsini Suarez in Via Maggio. The article claims that the scripts for both Le notti di Cabiria and La dolce vita are included in this material. ("Nasce l'archivio dedicato a Pasolini," La Repubblica, 19 August 1989, p. 19). However, Pasolini's papers are as yet uncatalogued and cannot be examined by scholars without the permission of the donor, Signora Graziella Chiarcossi, Pasolini's heir. It is unlikely that Pasolini would have the final version of any of Fellini's scripts, although it is possible that his papers do contain carbon copies of the originals at the Lilly Library or, more probably, Pasolini's carbon copies of the dialogue he submitted

tinuous allusion to another, as yet uncompleted, work, and its consequent "desire for form."[7]

Both the collective authorship of a screenplay and its existence in limbo, suspended between the traditional prose fiction of the soggetto and the collection of images constituting the completed film, make specific attribution of authorship in various parts of an individual script a vexing critical problem. As Cesare Zavattini is reported to have remarked, the relationship of director and scriptwriter resembles the *caffélatte* Italians drink for breakfast: it is a mixture that can be separated into its constituent parts only with great difficulty. It is, however, an issue not without parallel in the discipline of art history. A film historian must approach a script written by several hands in much the same way that an art historian analyzes a fresco cycle or a panel painting from the traditional Renaissance *bottega* or workshop. The director's decisions, like those of the shop master, are final, but the scriptwriters' contributions, usually discernible through a connoisseurship not unlike that practiced by art historians, may be compared to work on a shop project executed by apprentice painters.

Another serious obstacle to any clear understanding of a scriptwriter's contribution either to a story or script with multiple authors or to the completed film is the status of the manuscripts involved in the film's production. In all too many cases, these documents have been lost or destroyed by directors, writers, producers, or production companies. When such original manuscripts are no longer extant, anyone attempting to define the scriptwriter's contribution to a story, screenplay, or completed film must rely heavily on secondhand testimony provided by interviews and memoirs. In Fellini's case, there is fortunately a particularly rich secondary literature treating the films on which he collaborated. Moreover, thanks to the recent acquisition of a large number of original manuscripts of *soggetti* and *sceneggiature* by Indiana University's Lilly Library of Rare Books, materials obtained directly from Tullio Pinelli and Fellini himself, scholars now have available for the first time archival documents with direct bearing on Fellini's work as a scriptwriter.[8]

---

to Fellini, and which was subsequently revised by Fellini, assisted by Pinelli and Flaiano.

[7] Cited in *Heretical Empiricism*, ed. Louise K. Barnett, trans. Ben Lawton and Louise K. Barnett (Bloomington: Indiana University Press, 1988), p. 188.

[8] See the bibliography for a complete listing of the Lilly Library materials. As a writer and the person who actually typed most of these manuscripts, Pinelli not only recognized their historical value but had carefully bound and preserved them over the course of many years. Thus, what few documents remain from the many scripts and stories Fellini wrote with Pinelli for other directors in the 1940s and 1950s were preserved only by Pinelli. Fellini, on the other hand, detests saving materials from

Fellini's move to scriptwriting from journalism came about as a direct result of his position on the editorial staff of *Marc'Aurelio*. A number of the magazine's writers made regular contributions of gags, dialogues, and entire scripts to various comic films shot at Cinecittà. As he had been forced to do when he initiated his journalistic career, Fellini began this new activity by providing gags without a byline before gradually moving toward his own credits and complete artistic collaboration with other writers and directors. The gag-writer played a key role not only in film and radio comedy but also in the very popular *avanspettacolo* shows. This peculiarly Italian variety theater, similar in many respects to the American vaudeville shows, was staged before the screening of feature films in major urban theaters (hence the name "before the show"). Fellini's first efforts, uncredited by printed titles, were gags in three comic films directed by Mario Mattoli as vehicles for the comic talents of Erminio Macario: *Lo vedi come sei!* (1939), *Il pirata sono io* (1940), and *Non me lo dire!* (1940). It is significant that three writers from *Marc'Aurelio*—Steno, Metz, and Marcello Marchesi—were the principal credited scriptwriters on the three projects.

---

past projects, his or those of other directors, and the materials acquired from Fellini were in an entirely different state, often incomplete or fragmentary and obviously overlooked in previous attempts to throw away such materials. They are less interesting from a literary point of view than as precious evidence of how Fellini's process of artistic creation works, and such materials contain a number of very important sketches and drawings that will help to explain the genesis of certain major films. Something of Fellini's lack of concern for the ultimate disposition of these written materials can be seen by the fact that as late as 1989 (a full year after I had personally provided Fellini with a detailed listing of the materials Pinelli was adding to the materials Fellini had turned up in his own office for the Lilly Library) Fellini continued to claim in print that the original soggetto for *La strada* had been lost (Fellini, *"I vitelloni" e "La strada"* [Milan: Longanesi, 1989], p. 175). Yet, Pinelli had carefully guarded several versions of the soggetto of *La strada*: they are catalogued in the Lilly Library as Federico Fellini and Tullio Pinelli, "La strada," Pinelli MS. 7 (Box 3, IIA); and Federico Fellini and Tullio Pinelli, "La strada: soggetto e sceneggiatura—Tullio Pinelli/Federico Fellini," Pinelli MS. 5 (Box 2, IE). The materials acquired from Pinelli also contained several drafts of the original script for *La strada*, which are contained, respectively, in the manuscript listed above as Pinelli MS. 5 (Box 2, IE) and in *another* manuscript, Federico Fellini and Tullio Pinelli, "La strada," which is listed as Pinelli MS. 7 (Box 3, IIA) but is separate from the manuscript with the same listing mentioned above. In the preface to the published script for *Le notti di Cabiria*, which contains a printed version of the original manuscript material conserved in the Lilly collection as Pinelli MS. 8 (Box 3, IIB), Fellini declares: "I have not saved or cannot find any longer the original treatment of *Le notti di Cabiria*. To be sincere, I can't even remember if we wrote one" (Federico Fellini, *Le notti di Cabiria* [Milan: Garzanti, 1981], p. 5). In fact, among materials Pinelli provided to the Lilly Library, original manuscripts of both the story and the screenplay are to be found, previously referred to in note 6 above as Pinelli MS. 8 (Box 3, IIB) and Pinelli MS. 9 (Box 4, IIB-1).

Although Fellini was primarily identified with comic screenplays, he was also brought into the scripting of an action film by Alfredo Guarini entitled *Documento Z3* (1942), a tale of Italian wartime espionage in Yugoslavia, again without receiving credit for his contribution.[9] Fellini's close contacts with people employed by the Roman avanspettacolo and comic theater led to an important friendship with Aldo Fabrizi, one of the most popular comedians of the moment. Fabrizi was undoubtedly responsible for Fellini's jump from uncredited gagman to credited scriptwriter for three of his own comedies. In Mario Bonnard's, *Avanti c'é posto* (1942), Fellini shared the scripting credits with Fabrizi, Piero Tellini, and Zavattini. In Bonard's *Campo de' fiori* (1943), Anna Magnani and Fabrizi were paired together before their brilliant performances in *Roma città aperta*; the cast also included Peppino De Filippo, a member of the famous Neapolitan acting family who later starred in two of Fellini's films, *Luci del varietà* and *Le tentazioni del dottor Antonio*. The third, *L'ultima carrozzella* (1943), directed by Mario Mattoli, included Magnani in the cast with Leo Catozzo as assistant director. Catozzo, later to become famous as Fellini's editor for *8 1/2*, invented the celebrated "Catozzo suture," the simple yet revolutionary tool permitting editors to replace cumbersome acetone connections with ordinary Scotch tape. Catozzo's patent, rarely acknowledged by film historians, provided the technical foundation for many of the revolutionary shifts in film editing that emerged in the 1960s. While Fellini's participation in Fabrizi's three very successful comedies marked his debut as a professional scriptwriter, the vehement critical attacks on these lighthearted films by leftist critics associated with the review *Cinema*, who were paradoxically working under the patronage and protection of Vittorio Mussolini, the dictator's son, already anticipate postwar polemics over the role realism ought to play in Italian cinema. This controversy would culminate in the battle over Fellini's *La strada* and Luchino Visconti's *Senso* at the Venice Film Festival of 1954.[10]

With the increasing ferocity of the war, Fellini divided his time between scripting films and staying one jump ahead of the draft. Between 1942 and 1943, he apparently worked at the office of the Alleanza Cinematografica Italiana, a company directed by Vittorio Mussolini,

---

[9] The most reliable list of Fellini's contributions to the works of various directors may be found in the following books: Kezich, *Fellini*; Stefano Masi and Enrico Lancia, *I film di Roberto Rossellini* (Rome: Gremese Editore, 1987); Callisto Cosulich, *I film di Alberto Lattuada* (Rome: Gremese Editore, 1985); Alberto Farassino and Tatti Sanguineti, *Lux Film: Esthétique et système d'un studio italien* (Locarno: Éditions du Festival international du film de Locarno, 1984); and Ugo Pirro, *Celluoide* (Milan: Rizzoli, 1983).

[10] See Kezich, *Fellini*, pp. 94–95.

where he met Rossellini for the first time. Fellini was dispatched to Tripoli to work on a film derived from the adventure novels of Emilio Salgari provisionally entitled *Gli ultimi Tuareg* and directed by Gino Talamo. According to Guido Celano, who played a major role in the ill-fated production, Fellini scripted the film. The on-location production of this desert drama was abruptly cut short with the American invasion of North Africa, and just before Tripoli fell to the English in January 1943, Fellini managed to find a seat on a German military plane that skimmed the waves to escape Allied fighters during a hair-raising return to Sicily and relative safety. Celano also claims that Fellini directed several scenes while Talamo was ill.[11] If the actor's account is true, this incomplete film marks Fellini's debut behind the camera.[12] Fellini's adolescent admiration for adventure stories in the comic strips probably explains why in at least two instances (*Documento Z3* and *Gli ultimi Tuareg*) he abandoned his normal work in the comic genre to try his hand at spy and adventure stories.

Fellini's chance encounters and subsequent friendships with both Aldo Fabrizi and Roberto Rossellini were soon to catapult him into the intellectual ferment of Italian cinematic culture that began with the downfall of the Fascist regime and the appearance of Rossellini's *Roma città aperta*. Rome was liberated on 4 June 1944 by General Mark Clark's Fifth Army, but when Italian geography and fierce German resistance slowed the Allied push up the boot of Italy, the war naturally constituted the major topic of conversation for all Italians, including those who worked in the cinema. Almost everyone had a war story worth recounting. In Fellini's case, his famous sense of humor saved his life on 29 October 1943 when he was suddenly arrested by a German patrol detaining Italian men out of uniform. Just before boarding

[11] For Celano's account of this incident, see Francesco Savio, *Cinecittà anni trenta: parlano 116 protagonisti del secondo cinema italiano (1930–1943)* (Rome: Bulzoni Editore, 1979), 1:304.

[12] Other accounts of Fellini's first shots behind the camera differ from Celano's. In *Celluloide* (p. 161), Pirro claims that Fellini's debut took place when he replaced Gianni Puccini (oddly enough, one of the *Cinema* intellectuals who generally opposed films Fellini scripted or directed in his early career) on the set of *Persiane chiuse*, a work completed by Luigi Comencini and released in 1951. The soggetto of this film, 108 pages written by Fellini, Pinelli, and Puccini, is now in the Lilly Library and catalogued as Federico Fellini, Tullio Pinelli, and Gianni Puccini, "Persiane chiuse," Pinelli MS. 15 (Box 5, IIID). Comencini's film credits Leo Benvenuti and Piero De Bernardi for the story and Massimo Mida, Gianni Puccini, Franco Solinas, and Sergio Sollima for the screenplay without mentioning either Fellini or Pinelli (see Jean A. Gili, *Luigi Comencini* [Paris: Edilig, 1981], pp. 19–21, 121). Tullio Kezich is probably correct, however, when he claims that Fellini's first work with a camera took place when he substituted for Rossellini on the Florentine episode of *Paisà* (*Fellini*, p. 126).

the truck that would probably have taken him to either execution as a deserter or enforced military service on the Axis side, Fellini pretended to recognize a Wehrmacht officer, embracing him with a hearty "Fritz, Fritz!" as the Germans in the truck drove off and left him behind, fooled into thinking he was the officer's friend. Fellini then apologized to the officer for having mistaken him for someone else and raced off to safety in nearby Via Margutta, where, perhaps not by accident given his superstitious nature, he currently lives.[13] With the cinema not yet even beginning its slow recovery from wartime devastation and the resulting chaos, the regime's radio programs canceled, and the avanspettacolo theater in disarray, Fellini was forced to employ his talents as a caricature artist in order to survive. He established an extremely profitable shop on Via Nazionale called "The Funny Face Shop," where he sold Allied soldiers humorous drawings, superimposing original heads for each new client upon a large supply of previously sketched body caricatures. Rossellini came to the shop one day to ask Fellini if he would convince Fabrizi to play the leading role in a new film he was planning.[14] In return, Fellini was offered the job of writing Fabrizi's part. The film was tentatively entitled *Storie di ieri* and was to treat the events leading to the execution on 4 April 1944 of Don Giuseppe Morosini, a Catholic priest. Previously, Sergio Amidei, an extremely talented scriptwriter of Communist sympathies, had already begun a script on the black market. After discussing his work with Rossellini, the two men decided to include Amidei's material in a new episodic film on the Nazi occupation of Rome. Subsequently, a Neapolitan journalist named Alberto Consiglio suggested the addition of a story about a partisan priest named Don Pappagallo, and after a producer was found, Consiglio (never credited in the eventual film produced) combined this character with the figure of Don Morosini to produce the figure that eventually, after subsequent revisions, would become the film's Don Pietro. Before the Liberation, Amidei had read about another striking incident in *L'unità*, the clandestinely published Communist newspaper, that recounted the savage machine-gunning of a pregnant woman in Viale Giulio Cesare as she ran after her husband, arrested during one

[13] The anecdote is recounted in Kezich, *Fellini*, p. 114.

[14] For the story of the relationship between Rossellini and Fellini, see ibid., pp. 119–36; Masi and Lancia, *I film di Roberto Rossellini*, pp. 21–37; Pirro, *Celluloide*, an entire book devoted to a detailed account of the creation of *Roma città aperta*; and Faldini and Fofi, *L'avventurosa storia del cinema italiano . . . 1935–1959*, pp. 90–97. I follow the accounts of Masi, Lancia, and Pirro when they differ from Kezich's narrative, since they contain more details. Fellini's own account of this fateful encounter may be found in his *Fare un film*, pp. 70–74, or *Comments on Film*, pp. 58–69.

7. Federico Fellini and Enrico De Seta outside The Funny Face Shop on Via
Nazionale in Rome

of the dragnets Fellini narrowly escaped. This woman evolved into Pina, whose dramatic death in *Roma città aperta* launched Anna Magnani to international stardom, culminating in an American Oscar for Best Actress in *The Rose Tatoo* (1955). Finally, Amidei insisted on the addition of a fictitious Marxist, Giorgio Manfredi, to the plot in order to ensure, at least to his own satisfaction, that one model hero in the film reflected his own ideological views.

While *Roma città aperta* announced the rebirth of a new and revolutionary cinema in post-Fascist Italy, it is most certainly not a film that follows recognizably realist canons. In fact, its appeal derives primarily from its unconventional juxtaposition of traditional styles and moods, ranging from the use of documentary-like footage, creating a texture of journalistic immediacy, to the most blatant melodrama and spellbinding suspense, moving the audience's hearts more than raising its ideological consciousness.[15] The critical evaluation of Italian neorealism has long suffered from a series of myths and misunderstandings—that it was even a movement at all, with consistent aesthetic principles and programs; that it required amateur actors and a rejection of Hollywood cinematic codes and theatrical conventions; that it avoided traditional film genres and substituted the "realism" of on-location shooting for the "artificiality" of the studio. Of course, *some* of these characteristics fit *some* neorealist films, but the very fact that Federico Fellini played such a major role in scripting a number of the most interesting neorealist works by Rossellini, Alberto Lattuada, and Pietro Germi should have caused critics decades ago to temper their too often ideologically slanted judgments of this moment in cinematic history. By any traditional definition of the term, realism has always been antithetical to Fellini's temperament. What emerged with *Roma città aperta* was a hybrid style, a mixture of historical facts and pseudo-documentary aimed at a moving evocation of the German occupation of Rome through the employment of tear-jerking melodrama and slapstick comedy.

Even with the scanty means at Rossellini's disposal, the production was a highly professional one, and its cast, as well as its writers, all had extensive experience in the entertainment business. Fabrizi and Magnani came from the music hall, avanspettacolo world of Roman theater,

---

[15] For a more complete reevaluation of Italian neorealism than is possible here, see my *Italian Cinema: From Neorealism to the Present*, 2d ed. rev. (New York: Continuum, 1990), chaps. 2–4; and Millicent Marcus, *Italian Film in the Light of Neorealism* (Princeton: Princeton University Press, 1986). The most comprehensive discussion of Rossellini is now Gianni Rondolino's *Rossellini* (Turin: UTET, 1989). For a discussion of Rossellini's films in English, see Peter Brunette, *Roberto Rossellini* (New York: Oxford University Press, 1987).

even though they were better known for comic than tragic roles. Marcello Pagliero, who played the role of Manfredi, was a friend of Rossellini's who had already directed a film of his own in 1943 and would later work with Rossellini and Fellini on the script of *Paisà*. Maria Michi, who plays Marina, the friend of Pina's corrupt sister Lauretta and the betrayer of both Manfredi and Don Pietro, was a friend of Amidei's and a dancer, as was Harry Feist, who portrayed the homosexual Nazi, Major Bergmann. Nando Bruno (the sacristan) and Edoardo Passarelli (the policeman), two actors used in the film to provide moments of comic relief, came from similar experiences in the variety hall theater. The massive sets of Cinecittà were admittedly occupied by refugees at the time, as traditional definers of neorealism point out in their attempts to raise on-location shooting to a formulaic rule. But Rossellini's crew merely constructed four perfectly conventional sets for the locations where most of the film's action unfolds (the priest's sacristy, Gestapo headquarters, the torture room, and the living room where the German officers relax) in a vacant basement of a building in Rome's Via degli Avignonesi. As Fellini has recounted the story, the location of these sets had surprising consequences for Fellini, Rossellini, and the reception of postwar Italian cinema abroad. It was on the same street (number 36) that a celebrated Roman institution, the brothel operated by Signora Tina Trabucchi, was located. One night, while Rossellini was shooting, an American soldier named Rod Geiger, presumably exiting Signora Trabucchi's establishment, staggered drunkenly across the street and tripped over the crew's electric cables. Geiger was steadied by a solicitous Fellini, and as the American watched the shooting, he became fascinated with the film in progress. Eventually, Geiger convinced Rossellini to sell him the American rights for the completed film for only $20,000. Once again, another coincidental encounter, this one more hilarious than most, produced a fateful turn in Fellini's career. The incredible popular and critical appeal of the film abroad brought Rossellini, Fellini, and the Italian cinema in general to the attention of the entire world.[16]

[16] Fellini's account of his meeting with Geiger is to be found in Fellini, *Fare un film*, pp. 73–74; or in Fellini, *Fellini on Fellini*, pp. 42–43. It is only fair to record that in a personal telephone conversation with me (31 March 1990), Rod Geiger denied the most colorful details of Fellini's account: his inebriated state and his visit to Signora Trabucchi's establishment. Geiger was also involved with the financing of Rossellini's second neorealist work, *Paisà*, conceived with the provisional title *Sette americani*. After the acclaim for *Roma città aperta*, Geiger wanted to exploit Rossellini's newly won fame. Rossellini was also at this time considered for a number of Hollywood projects, including an adaptation of Pietro Di Donato's *Christ in Concrete*, eventually shot by Edward Dmytryk and produced by Geiger. For the link between Italian neorealism, Geiger, and Dmytryk, see my "*Christ in Concrete* di Ed-

All accounts of the production of *Roma città aperta* unanimously agree that Federico Fellini's assignment on the original script (which no longer exists) focused on the character of the priest, Don Pietro. Aldo Fabrizi's performance, requiring an almost impossible combination of perfect comic timing and serious tragic dignity, owes a great deal to Fellini. For example, it was certainly Fellini's brilliant inspiration to insert the frying-pan gag into the action, a slapstick routine typical of earlier comic films that he worked on. In order to silence an old man lying on a bed near some contraband weapons, Don Pietro hits him over the head with the only implement he can find, an old skillet, just as Fascist soldiers enter the apartment. When Rossellini accepted Fellini's comic interpretation of Don Pietro and, in the final editing, juxtaposed this sequence of hilarious slapstick comedy from the avanspettacolo with the moment of darkest pathos in the film—the sequence in which Pina is machine-gunned to death outside the apartment immediately follows Fellini's gag—the two men had succeeded in producing one of the most moving moments in the history of the cinema. It was a mark of Rossellini's genius as a director that he was able to temper Amidei's ideological fervor with Fellini's comic wit and surer awareness of how to manipulate the audience's emotions.

If *Roma città aperta* established Fellini as a serious scriptwriter, and as one of Rossellini's closest collaborators, it was *Paisà*, by Fellini's own testimony, that convinced him of his future vocation as a director. Before working on *Paisà*, Fellini considered himself a writer rather than a filmmaker and had never seriously considered changing his profession. An episode film in six parts, *Paisà* follows the Allied invasion of Italy from Sicily through Naples, Rome, Florence, and a monastery in the Apennines to conclude in the Po River valley. Rossellini does indeed employ stylistic elements that leftist critics would later attempt to codify into fixed rules for acceptable neorealist style—the conventions of newsreel documentary (authoritative voice-overs, pincer movements on a map, the combination of fiction with actual documentary footage); amateur actors; grainy photography and stark, realistic lighting; avoidance of "artificial" commercial studios in favor of "authentic" on-location work; an immediacy of subject matter the public would instantly associate with the morning news. But the true subject of the film can be comprehended only through a Christian rather than a Marxist perspective; it represents an empathetic portrayal of the encounter between two alien cultures (Italian and American) and the growth of mutual understanding and brotherhood between them. While

ward Dmytryk e il neorealismo italiano," *Cinema e Cinema* 11, no. 38 (1984): 9–16. For more detailed information about *Paisà*, see Adriano Aprà, ed., *Rosselliniana: bibliografia internazionale—dossier "Paisà"* (Rome: Di Giacomo, 1987).

amateur actors do provide a sense of authenticity in the film, and the vast complex at Cinecittà was still occupied by refugees at the time, traditional sets were nevertheless built in many cases rather than employing "actual" locations. For example, the Florentine sequence was substantially completed in Rome on Via Lutezia near the home of Giulietta Masina's aunt. Many of the other locations were not actual ones but were found near Maiori on the Amalfi coast where Rossellini and Fellini would later shoot *Il miracolo* (1948).[17] The fact that numerous critics praised the veracity of the film's locations without recognizing the artifice of their traditional, cinematic character reveals more about their prejudices than their critical insight.

It was on the Amalfi coast just before the monastery episode was shot that Fellini made his most important contribution to the script, creating an entirely different episode from the one originally written down by Amidei:

> I discovered a little convent of Franciscan friars and, since as a young boy I had often been sent to a boarding-school kept by friars, I entered it full of curiosity and actually discovered a charming place, very much resembling a picture. There were five or six friars, very poor, extremely simple. I don't exactly recollect, now, whether the idea of that episode was already written in the story or if it was suggested by this little convent. I remember anyway that, one evening, I took Rossellini to dine with me in the convent, so that I started to suggest to him the possibility of filming an episode. At first, the idea was to achieve a meeting between two quite different ways of conceiving religion, through a meeting between American chaplains and Italian friars; between an active belief, as that of military priests should be, and this kind of faith, so meditative, a life of prayers only, as it was lived in some little medieval convents that are to be found here and there in Italy. The idea was there, but not yet the episode. I wrote the episode in that convent.[18]

While the original manuscript of the script does not survive, Italian biographers of both Rossellini and Fellini agree that Amidei's original script included a monastery episode that was entirely different from the final version Fellini provided.[19] In Amidei's story, the American chaplain kills two Germans at Anzio and reaches the monastery during a

[17] See Kezich, *Fellini*, pp. 124–26.

[18] Federico Fellini, "My Experiences as a Director," in *Federico Fellini: Essays in Criticism*, ed. Peter Bondanella (New York: Oxford University Press, 1978), p. 4. The translator of this passage rendered the word Fellini used, *convento*, as "convent," but English practice generally requires that a convent be inhabited by nuns while a monastery houses only monks. The Italian word *convento* can cover both possibilities.

[19] See Kezich, *Fellini*, p. 126; and Masi and Lancia, *I film di Roberto Rossellini*, p. 27.

crisis of conscience. There his resolve hardens, he decides against desertion, and he returns to face the action at the front. Such a figure would suit Amidei's ideological requirements for an active, politicized protagonist: even a Catholic chaplain could be transformed into an Italian version of an idealized hero who, in good social realist fashion, struggles for a better world. Fellini's revisions of Amidei's script may have been suggested by a reading of the celebrated story of Melchisedech and the three rings in Giovanni Boccaccio's *Decameron*, a novella treating religious tolerance and the difficulty of reaching absolute truth. Fellini considered adapting the Italian classic into a film for a number of years.[20] When the simple monks of the monastery discover that the Catholic chaplain, Captain Martin, has never attempted to convert his two friends and colleagues (a Protestant and a Jew) to the "true" faith, they begin to fast in order that God may provide the grace to lead these "two lost souls" toward salvation. Thus, when the three chaplains are brought into the refectory, they find themselves eating alone and surrounded by a group of silent, fasting friars. When Captain Martin realizes why the monks are behaving in such a strange fashion, he addresses them in an extraordinary manner that the film's viewers have always found puzzling: "I want to tell you that what you've given me is such a great gift that I feel I'll always be in your debt. I've found here that peace of mind I'd lost in the horrors and the trials of the war, a beautiful, moving lesson of humility, simplicity, and pure faith. Pax hominibus bonae voluntatis."[21]

Such a statement delivered in this emotionally charged context, where the Catholic monks could easily be suspected of bigotry and intolerance of their Protestant and Jewish brothers, underlines the vast emotional distance separating the active chaplains from such simple (and even simpleminded) friars. And yet Captain Martin accepts their fasting as an act of genuine, pure faith. The key to the entire sequence must be found in Fellini's own conception of Catholicism, one which suited Rossellini's sensibilities as well. While rejecting the institutional trappings of the Church, particularly its doctrinaire stands on social issues, Fellini, like many Italians, has always responded to the

[20] For Boccaccio's story, placed near the beginning of his *Decameron* (Day 1, Story 3) to underline his own attitude of complete religious tolerance, see Giovanni Boccaccio, *The Decameron*, ed. and trans. Mark Musa and Peter Bondanella (New York: New American Library, 1982), pp. 36–38. If Fellini was influenced by Boccaccio's original, as I believe he was, he transformed Boccaccio's three rings representing the three great monotheistic religions (Christianity, Judaism, and Islam) into three military chaplains of three different faiths—a Catholic, a Protestant, and a Jew.

[21] Cited in Stefano Roncoroni, ed., *Roberto Rossellini: The War Trilogy* (New York: Grossman, 1973), pp. 315–16. The Italian original may be found in Stefano Roncoroni, ed., *La trilogia della guerra* (Bologna: Cappelli, 1972).

Church's evangelical message of love and human brotherhood and has consistently shown an unabashed admiration for the simple acts of faith on the part of its humblest believers, especially when such acts fly in the face of contemporary religious indifference.

It would not be an exaggeration to state that the fateful and hotly contested movement away from social realism in the postwar Italian cinema toward what Rossellini once called "the cinema of Reconstruction" begins here in the enigmatic monastery episode scripted by Fellini with Rossellini's full approval of the drastic alterations Fellini made to Amidei's original screenplay.[22] The direction Fellini's script takes was even better described by Michelangelo Antonioni as a cinema that no longer was so concerned with a man whose bicycle is stolen (in reference to De Sica's masterpiece, *Ladri di biciclette*) but would, instead, eliminate the metaphoric bicycle and "see what there is in the mind and in the heart of this man who has had his bicycle stolen, how he has adapted himself, what remains in him of his past experiences, of the war, of the period after the war, of everything that has happened to him in our country."[23] The "road beyond neorealism" was thus traveled by Fellini even as he worked within the neorealist style Rossellini was practically inventing before his very eyes on the set of *Paisà*. Fellini's peculiar notion of a deinstitutionalized Christianity enlightened by the central values of innocence, grace, and human brotherhood would provide the ideological underpinning not only for a number of Rossellini's subsequent films but also for Fellini's own cinema in the 1950s.

For an entire generation of Italian filmmakers (not to mention the French New Wave), Rossellini's *Paisà* and films he made in the early 1950s provided not only a stylistic model to follow but also personal inspiration and encouragement. Gillo Pontecorvo, Ermanno Olmi, and the Taviani brothers have all declared that a screening of this particular work inspired them to become directors.[24] Fellini's even more intimate experience on the set of *Paisà* had much the same effect. The artistic direction that his own career would subsequently take differed radically from an ideologically committed cinema of "realism" typical of early films by these men or by younger directors, such as Bernardo Bertolucci and Pier Paolo Pasolini, all of whom used Rossellini's *Paisà* as a springboard for their own hybrid brand of cinematic realism. While

[22] Maurice Sherer and François Truffaut, "Interview with Roberto Rossellini," *Film Culture* 1 (1955): 12. The original French interview appeared in *Cahiers du Cinéma* 37 (1955).

[23] Cited in Pierre Leprohon, *Michelangelo Antonioni: An Introduction* (New York: Simon and Schuster, 1963), p. 90.

[24] For their testimony, see Faldini and Fofi, *L'avventurosa storia del cinema italiano . . . 1935–1959*, p. 110.

8. Roberto Rossellini, Federico Fellini, and Giulietta Masina try a new dance step during a pause on the set of *Paisà*

familiar Fellini themes can be seen germinating in *Paisà*, what he learned specifically about the technical nature of the cinema from his work with Rossellini is less obvious. Fellini's remarks on *Paisà* have always presented a deceptively simple but consistent version of Rossellini's lesson:

> I think I may honestly say that what I mostly owe to Roberto Rossellini's teaching is his example of humility, or better, a way of facing reality in a totally simplified way; an effort of not interfering with one's own ideas, culture, feelings. . . . When I came in touch with Rossellini, I saw at first a completely new world, the loving eyes through which Rossellini observed everything to make things alive through his framings. It was actually through his attitude that I thought that, after all, films may be created without deceits, without presumptions, without thinking of sending around quite definite messages.[25]

What Fellini most certainly did not inherit from Rossellini was a desire to pursue cinematic realism in any programmatic fashion. In fact, Fellini reached quite opposite conclusions. He came to understand that the cinema offered a personal and individual means of self-expression capable of communicating *any* kind of artistic message, provided that it was honestly felt. And far from being awed by the technical difficulties of this industrialized art form, Fellini declared that *Paisà* convinced him of the utter simplicity of this medium: "I had the chance of realizing that I myself might screen my stories, that filming would not be so difficult. I definitely realized that the camera, the film apparatus on the whole are not so very mysterious, so terribly technical. It was just a matter of relating quite simply what one was looking at."[26]

Fellini enjoyed one opportunity to direct on the set of *Paisà* during a day when Rossellini fell ill. The scene to be shot was from the Florentine segment treating the internecine struggle between partisans on one side of the city and Fascist sharpshooters on the other. Fellini was supposed to complete a relatively simple shot of a demijohn of water being pulled by a rope under sniper fire across a street. While lacking even the minimum of authority that would have come from experience, Fellini immediately contested the manner in which Otello Martelli, one of Italy's greatest cameramen, conceived the scene. Martelli, who would go on to create some of Fellini's most brilliant photography (particularly in *La dolce vita*), insisted on shooting the demijohn from a high position, taking an objective view. Fellini, on the other hand, wanted the camera as low as technically possible and threatened to dig a hole in

---

[25] Fellini, "My Experiences as a Director," p. 3.
[26] Ibid., p. 4.

the ground if Martelli did not accept his "rat's eye view" of the scene.[27] The shot eventually used in the final film represents something of a compromise. This anecdote reveals, however, how clearly Fellini had instinctively grasped the fact that a subjective shot from the ground would reflect the emotional state of mind of men dodging sniper fire more effectively than a more conventional shot of higher elevation. Moreover, Fellini had bravely followed the example of his mentor in refusing to be cowed by the technical aspects of the cinema—for him, as for Rossellini, the camera was merely a means of reproducing his own perspective, and the so-called rules applied only if they furthered the narrative. Fellini's desire to add a moment of subjectivity to the film that critics have always interpreted as the epitome of objective realism would, of course, reach fullest expression when he took complete control of his own camera, script, and film crew.[28]

As his desire to work toward a "cinema of Reconstruction" demonstrates, Rossellini, like Fellini and Antonioni, was also interested in moving beyond what he considered a stultifying emphasis on cinematic realism. His own ideology of Catholic humanism corresponded to many of Fellini's admittedly vague and even unsophisticated ideas about the need for love and humanity in the world. In three other films on which Fellini collaborated with him as a scriptwriter—the episode entitled *Il miracolo* of the two-part film *L'amore* (1948), *Francesco, giullare di Dio* (1950), and *Europa '51* (1952)—Rossellini continues and broadens, again employing crucial contributions from Fellini's scripts,

[27] This anecdote is recounted in Kezich, *Fellini*, p. 126; while Kezich believes this is Fellini's first actual work behind a camera, see notes 8 and 9 above for the possibility that his first shots were made much earlier during his trip to North Africa, or even later in 1950.

[28] Two other important moments of extreme subjectivity occur in *Paisà*, and given Fellini's work on the script, he may well have encouraged Rossellini to shoot them. The first is the flashback in the Roman episode, in which an American GI named Fred picks up a prostitute and fails to recognize that she is the same innocent girl he met outside his tank during the liberation of Rome. The second is the celebrated sequence in the final Po Valley episode in which the camera captures the partisans' perspective, never peering over the thin row of reeds in the marshy river basin. As André Bazin notes in a beautiful description of the sequence, the film thus provides "the exact equivalent, under conditions imposed by the screen, of the inner feeling men experience who are living between the sky and the water and whose lives are at the mercy of an infinitesimal shift of angle in relation to the horizon" (*What Is Cinema? Vol. II*, trans. Hugh Gray [Berkeley and Los Angeles: University of California Press, 1971], p. 37). The purpose of the sequence justly praised by Bazin is to create the same kind of subjective emotion in the viewer that Fellini was aiming to achieve with Martelli. It is even possible that Rossellini may have been inspired by Fellini's earlier experiment in the Florence episode and that in this case, the master learned from his precocious pupil.

the new thematic direction opened by Fellini's monastery episode. When Fellini joined the production of *L'amore*, Rossellini had already shot the first part of the film, *La voce umana*, an adaptation of a play by Jean Cocteau. He now needed another brief film to construct a feature-length work, since *La voce umana* lasted only forty minutes. By this time, Fellini had begun to write film scripts for the Lux Film Studio with Tullio Pinelli. The two men had met in 1947 while they were both reading opposite sides of a newspaper displayed by a street kiosk. This serendipitous encounter, one of many in Fellini's life, soon led to a close friendship and an artistic collaboration that has endured, with a long hiatus between 1965 and 1985 based on artistic rather than personal disagreements, until his most recent film, *La voce della luna*.[29]

When Rossellini asked Fellini for something suitable for Anna Magnani's personality, Fellini offered a strange story about a poor prostitute who is picked up by a famous movie star, later to become a key episode in *Le notti di Cabiria*, but Magnani rejected it.[30] Fellini then satisfied both Magnani and Rossellini with yet another original story, that of a simpleminded peasant girl named Nannina who meets a man she believes to be Saint Joseph. When she discovers that she has become pregnant after her encounter with this mysterious stranger (who never says a single word in the film), she proclaims her pregnancy to be divinely conceived and withdraws from her scoffing and disbelieving neighbors to a deserted sanctuary, where her baby is delivered. At the last minute, Rossellini convinced Fellini to play the part of Saint Joseph, forcing him to wear a beard and dye his hair blond.

Il miracolo's plot obviously owes a debt to the story of the Immaculate Conception, a central tenet in the Christian faith, and the peasant woman is but the first of a number of simpleminded Fellinian protagonists (such as Gelsomina of *La strada*) who compensate for their lack of intellectual depth with their special capacity for innocence and the reception of grace. Fellini and Rossellini offered the film as a parable treating the role of sainthood and grace in a skeptical contemporary world, and it provoked the first of the many polemical debates that would rage around the films of both men produced during the late 1940s and the 1950s. In America, Cardinal Spellman attacked the film as blasphemous. As a result, the work was censored, forcing its Ameri-

[29] Pinelli recounts the story of their meeting in Faldini and Fofi, *L'avventurosa storia del cinema italiano . . . 1935–1959*, pp. 127–28; their association together with the Lux Film Studio is discussed by Farassino and Sanguineti in *Lux Film*.

[30] Fellini's account of the first script offered is to be found in *Fare un film*, pp. 61–62. For the recollections of Rossellini, Pinelli, and Aldo Tonti (the cameraman), see Faldini and Fofi, *L'avventurosa storia del cinema italiano . . . 1935–1959*, pp. 199–200.

can distributor, Joseph Burstyn, to take the case all the way to the United States Supreme Court, where it was the occasion for an important decision declaring religious censorship of films illegal.[31]

Rossellini, however, viewed *Il miracolo* as "an absolutely Catholic work," and declared that a theme that obsessed him, not only in this film but in others he made during the period, was the "absolute lack of faith . . . typical of the postwar period."[32] Furthermore, he found arguments to counter the charge of blasphemy leveled against his paradoxical fable by his critics in one of the sermons delivered by San Bernardino of Siena. The sermon recounted the story of a man who killed his dog Bonino by mistake. Repenting of his tragic error, the man buried his animal in a tomb bearing the inscription "Here Lies Bonino: Killed by the Ferocity of Man." Years later, after everyone had forgotten that the tomb contained a dog, a cult of Christian devotion grew up around it, miracles began to occur, and a church was built on the site. The discovery that Saint Bonino was actually a dog occurred only after its bones were transferred to the church.[33] San Bernardino argued that the discovery did not undermine the purity of the faith inspired by the dog, nor were the miracles performed through such fervent belief any less authentic. In like manner, Fellini and Rossellini admired the faith of the simpleminded Nannina regardless of the true identity of her mysterious visitor. For both director and scriptwriter, the film underlined the essential ambiguity of true religious sentiment and set into relief its inevitable conflict with conventional wisdom in the everyday working world. In this sense, *Il miracolo* continues the discourse begun by the enigmatic speech Fellini wrote for Captain Martin in *Paisà*.

At first glance, *Francesco, giullare di Dio*, the subsequent film on which Fellini collaborated with Rossellini, may seem aimed at placating the attacks upon *Il miracolo* by the Catholic hierarchy. However,

[31] In a 1952 decision in the case of Burstyn v. Wilson, the United States Supreme Court reversed a 1915 ruling, declaring that films such as *Il miracolo* were protected by constitutional guarantees of free speech. For a discussion of this decision, see Ellen Draper, " 'Controversy Has Probably Destroyed Forever the Context': *The Miracle* and Movie Censorship in America in the Fifties," *The Velvet Light Trap* 25 (1990): 69–79.

[32] Roberto Rossellini, "Ten Years of Cinema," in *Springtime in Italy: A Reader on Neo-realism*, ed. David Overbey (Hamden, Conn.: Archon Books, 1979), p. 102.

[33] Ibid., pp. 101–2; while Rossellini cites San Bernardino's sermon as close in spirit to the theme of his film, it is hardly likely that Fellini used such an erudite document as his inspiration for the story. Given his comic bent, Fellini was much more likely to have found inspiration in a far more famous story, that of Ser Ciappelletto (Day 1, Story 1) in Boccaccio's *Decameron*, which deals precisely with the difference between the ambiguous nature of human personality and the paradoxically genuine quality of the miracles such questionable individuals inspire. Given Fellini's likely use of *The Decameron* to structure the monastery episode of *Paisà*, this source is certainly a possibility. For the text, see Boccaccio, *The Decameron*, pp. 21–32.

the kind of Catholic ideology the two men had pictured in *Il miracolo* was not without its admirers among progressive circles and Catholic film critics, who preferred Rossellini's message of Christian humanism to ideologically motivated neorealist works such as those directed by Luchino Visconti or Giuseppe De Santis, which were championed by the intellectual adversaries of Rossellini and Fellini—Marxist critics and their leftist intellectual fellow travelers. Defending Rossellini, however, became increasingly difficult, given the scandalously un-Catholic private life Rossellini was leading at the time. While still married, he moved from a public affair with Magnani to another and even more notorious liaison with Ingrid Bergman in 1949. Besides Fellini's important contribution to the script of *Francesco* and the fact that his monastery episode from *Paisà* was the immediate inspiration for this adaptation of the collection of popular legends surrounding Saint Francis (the medieval book entitled *I fioretti di San Francesco*), Rossellini preferred to hedge his bets with the Church and gained the collaboration on the screenplay of two Catholic priests (Felix A. Morlion, s.j., and Antonio Lisandrini, o.f.m.), who lent an air of theological acceptability to his film even if they actually contributed very little to the script.[34]

Francesco courageously avoids the kind of pious hagiography one might expect of a portrayal of a saint's life and shows us Franciscan monks who are simple to the point of simplemindedness. They are truly "fools for Christ" in the New Testament sense, and a great deal of Fellini's contribution to this script consists of various gags that underline their humility and innocence. Irritated by the din of their singing, Francesco asks the famous birds to whom he is usually shown preaching if they would lower their voices so that he can complete his prayers. The comic figure of Brother Ginepro seems inspired by such literary characters as the hapless Calandrino of Boccaccio's *Decameron*. He constantly follows Francesco's instructions to the letter, which results in numerous comic gags. Told that he should give his belongings to the poor, Ginepro returns to the monastery again and again stark

---

[34] Morlion was a strong defender of the Catholic foundations of Italian neorealism, which he naturally found better expressed in Rossellini's cinema than in films made by leftist directors. His essay "The Philosophical Basis of Neo-Realism," first published in *Bianco e nero* in 1948, makes the following observation that neither Fellini nor Rossellini would probably have opposed, although neither was much interested in theology or approved of the Church's frequent interventions into Italian politics as an *institution*: "In Italy, intelligence, imagination, and sensitivity are immensely creative because they are linked to a simple and rich human tradition, the fruit of twenty centuries of heroism and sacrifice: the Christian tradition. There is only one danger for the neo-realist school: a loss of contact with the deep source of human reality, which in Italy is either Christianity or non-existent" (cited in *Springtime in Italy*, ed. Overbey, p. 122).

naked, in a parody of San Francesco's original rejection of his father's possessions. When one of the monks falls ill and asks for a *zampone di maiale* (a sausage shaped in the form of a pig's foot popular in Emilia-Romagna), Ginepro takes the request literally and cuts off the foot of a pig that is very much alive. But the grace of God touches the injured pig's angry owner, who eventually donates the rest of the poor animal to the monks for supper. And finally, Ginepro's simplicity moves an evil tyrant named Nicolaio (played by Aldo Fabrizi in a comic manner reminiscent of his music hall roles) to raise the siege of a town. At the film's conclusion, when Francesco orders his disciples to go forth into the world and preach the Gospel, choosing their directions by twirling around and around until they fall, it is Giovanni, the humblest of the group, who remains balanced on his feet. For Rossellini and Fellini, it is clear that the simple and pure of heart are, paradoxically, the least confused about their direction in life.

With *Europa '51*, a film scripted in important sections by Fellini and Pinelli even if they never received credit for their work, Rossellini turns from the simple peasant girl of *Il miracolo* and the medieval monks of *Francesco* to examine the status of sainthood and religious faith in his own middle-class society. *Europa '51* was one of a series of films Rossellini made to showcase Ingrid Bergman's acting talents. As Rossellini recalls, the inspiration for the film came from Aldo Fabrizi's cynical remark on the set of *Francesco* that San Francesco was "a madman"; the example of Simone Weil, who starved herself to death during the Second World War in sympathy with her occupied compatriots, also played a role in the evolution of the story.[35] Ingrid Bergman has stated that Rossellini was even more explicit about the purpose of the film, telling her just after making *Francesco*, "I am going to make a story about St. Francis and she's going to be a woman and it's going to be you."[36] With the character named Irene (played by Bergman), Rossellini demonstrates that today, the simple religious faith of the early Franciscans is totally incomprehensible to a wide range of ideologies and traditional institutions and can be understood in our times only as a form of mental illness. After Irene's son unsuccessfully attempts to commit suicide, he subsequently dies mysteriously, not from a tangible disease but as if he had merely lost his will to live. This event shocks Irene into examining her comfortable, middle-class life. In time, she begins to help the sick and the needy, even filling in at a dreary factory job for a poor unmarried woman with too many children nicknamed Passerrotto ("Little Sparrow"), played by Giulietta Masina, while Passerrotto

---

[35] See Faldini and Fofi, *L'avventurosa storia del cinema italiano . . . 1935–1959*, p. 250.
[36] "Ingrid Bergman on Rossellini," *Film Comment* 10, no. 4 (1974): 13.

has a rendezvous with her boyfriend. Eventually her efforts to practice simple Christian charity cause her to be declared insane by everyone from the society with which she once identified. Not only do her relatives consider her mad, but both her Communist cousin and representatives of the Church concur with the court's shallow and insensitive judgment. The film concludes with Irene's commitment to a mental institution, while a crowd of the poor people who have benefited from her charity gathers under her hospital window, crying and proclaiming her sainthood. While completely unconcerned with Rossellini's polemical intentions in using this film to attack both his leftist critics and those in the Church, Fellini worked with Pinelli on one of the major episodes of the film, that of the young boy's enigmatic death by suicide.

In spite of their long friendship and similar ideas about Christian charity, Fellini would never again work with Rossellini, although he did complete several simple shots on *Dov'è la libertà?* (1952–1954) for Rossellini while the director was ill. This gave Fellini his only opportunity to direct, even briefly, the great comic actor Totò.[37] By the time *Europa '51* was screened at the thirteenth Venice Film Festival, Fellini was already engaged in presenting a film of his own at the festival, *Lo sceicco bianco,* and had scripted another film directed by Pietro Germi (*Il brigante di Tacca del Lupo*), which had been entered in Venice in competition with both his own film and that of Rossellini. Both in private and in public, with the exception of *Il bidone,* Rossellini would consistently criticize Fellini's subsequent films, from the beginning of his career as an independent director down to *Casanova,* which Rossellini saw shortly before his death.[38] Not always generous in evaluating the work of others, Rossellini may well have become jealous of his young understudy's meteoric rise to fame, and their extremely fruitful artistic collaboration eventually soured into rancor on Rossellini's part. Fellini, however, consistently acknowledged the important lessons he had learned from the man he always regarded as his teacher and master.

Fellini's experiences with Rossellini took place in an atmosphere that was as far removed from the industrial system of Hollywood filmmaking as could be imagined, with scripts written and rewritten the night before shooting was to begin, constant lack of funding, and questions

[37] Fellini describes this event in "Totò: per pochi minuti fui il suo regista," *La Repubblica: Il venerdì* 2, no. 29 (4 June 1988): 96–105.

[38] For example, Rossellini denigrated *La dolce vita* as the "work of a provincial" (see Fellini, *Fellini on Fellini,* p. 154). When Brunello Rondi argued with Rossellini that *La dolce vita* marked a new direction in film narration, Rossellini retorted that Fellini's film reached the lowest depths the Italian cinema had experienced since the advent of neorealism and went on to remark testily: "I think I knew very well after making *Paisà* what one means by modern narrative techniques" (cited in Franca Faldini and Goffredo Fofi, eds., *L'avventurosa storia del cinema italiano raccontata dai suoi protagonisti 1960–1969* [Milan: Feltrinelli, 1981], p. 16).

about who was actually financing the pictures or providing the troupe's salaries, all of which reflected Rossellini's extravagant personality and the fact that he was directing his films in the midst of critical controversy and extreme personal tension caused by his flamboyant love affairs with Magnani and Bergman. The precarious nature of such an operation was precisely what Fellini enjoyed about working with Rossellini, however, and Fellini would subsequently try to create such a chaotic mood on his own sets during the rest of his career. His collaboration with Pietro Germi and Alberto Lattuada, in contrast, took place within a traditional studio environment, that of the Lux Film Studio. Lux had been organized in 1934 and played a major role in the Italian industry until 1964. Tullio Pinelli joined the company in 1940 at what was at the time a handsome salary and was contracted to provide three scenarios per year, in addition to reading countless novels in search of useful story ideas. Given Fellini's friendship with Pinelli, it was inevitable that the two men should eventually work together for Lux. Fellini met a number of extraordinary men in the company, including Dino De Laurentiis, Carlo Ponti, and Luigi Rovere, all of whom would eventually produce some of his most interesting films, including *Lo sceicco bianco*, *La strada*, *Le notti di Cabiria*, and *Le tentazioni del dottor Antonio*. His contacts with Riccardo Gualino, the Pietmontese industrialist who founded the studio, and with Guido Gatti, the artistic director of the studio—remembered by Fellini as a man who hated the cinema and preferred music instead—taught the young scriptwriter a great deal about the practical side of his profession. Gatti's brilliant intuition in hiring Nino Rota as a studio musician would lay the groundwork for a lifetime of affectionate collaboration with Fellini that lasted until Rota's death just after completing the music for *Prova d'orchestra*.

Much has been written about the anticommercial, almost artisanlike quality of neorealist cinema, but as even a summary analysis of the history of the Lux Film Studio demonstrates, many of the most interesting works filmed between the end of the war and the advent of a second, postneorealist generation of young directors in the 1960s were produced precisely within a complex commercial company organized along the same industrial lines as its Hollywood competitors.[39] Thus, historical discussions of the films made during the neorealist period that assume that neorealist films rejected the traditional capitalist stu-

---

[39] For an exhaustive study of Lux, see the previously cited study by Farassino and Sanguineti, *Lux Film*. Further evidence of the studio system's contributions to the Italian cinema in the postwar period may be found in two studies of another major studio: see Guido Barlozzetti, Stefania Parigi, Angela Prudenzi, and Claver Salizzato, eds., *Modi di produzione del cinema italiano: La Titanus* (Rome: Di Giacomo, 1985); and Aldo Bernardini and Vittorio Martinelli, eds., *Titanus: la storia e tutti i film di una grande casa di produzione* (Milan: Coliseum Editore, 1986).

dio system of film production, along with their equally questionable assertions that neorealist films demanded amateur actors, "actual" locations, and an avoidance of traditional Hollywood cinematic codes and generic conventions, must be discarded or, at least, questioned seriously. In fact, Fellini remembers that Ponti and De Laurentiis tried to imitate the brash style commonly associated with Hollywood moguls, displaying three or four telephones on their desks and working in their shirtsleeves (a habit, like propping up one's feet on a desk, Italians associated at the time with Americans). Their offices were on opposite sides of a narrow corridor, an arrangement that enabled them to exchange obscenities in scenes worthy, as Fellini has remarked, of a "Neapolitan avanspettacolo show."[40]

After producing what may arguably be called the greatest film made during the Fascist era, Alessandro Blasetti's *La corona di ferro* (1940), Lux was responsible for a surprising number of first-rate films in the postwar era, many of which must be taken into account in defining neorealist style: *Il bandito* (1946), *Il delitto di Giovanni Episcopo* (1947), *Senza pietà* (1948), and *Il mulino del Po* (1949), all by Alberto Lattuada; Luigi Zampa's *Vivere in pace* (1947); Giuseppe De Santis's *Riso amaro* (1948); Luchino Visconti's *Senso* (1954); *In nome della legge* (1949), *Il cammino della speranza* (1950), and *Il brigante di Tacca del Lupo* (1952), all by Pietro Germi; *Persiane chiuse* (1951), by Luigi Comencini; and *Il passatore* (1947), by Duilio Coletti, the first film on which Fellini and Pinelli worked together for the studio.

The importance of the Fellini-Pinelli scriptwriting team to Lux is evident from the fact that of the films listed above, the two men worked on three of the films by Lattuada (the exception being *Il bandito*), all three of Germi's productions, and the two works by Comencini and Coletti. In addition, they completed a number of scripts for the Lux group that never reached final production. And unlike the case of Fellini's collaboration with Rossellini, a number of these precious original manuscripts of stories or scripts survive. These documents include the following materials: the script for Lattuada's *Senza pietà*; a lengthy treatment of Germi's *Il brigante di Tacca del Lupo*; the story of *La famiglia*, a film intended for Germi but never made; a long treatment of *Persiane chiuse* written for Gianni Puccini but eventually shot by Luigi Comencini; the first half of a script for Giorgio Pastina entitled *Il diavolo in convento*, which was never shot; and a script for a Lux production entitled *Happy Country (Paese felice)*, designed for Mario Camerini but never realized.[41]

[40] Farassino and Sanguineti, *Lux Film*, pp. 284–85.
[41] Kezich, in *Fellini* (p. 140) refers to the film's provisional titles as *Nice Country* and *Oil in Tuscany*; he apparently did not examine the original manuscript, Federico Fellini and Tullio Pinelli, "Happy Country (Paese felice)," Pinelli MS. 13 (Box 5, IIIB),

Fellini's work with Lattuada involved two adaptations of preexisting
literary texts whose titles were retained in the filmed versions: *Il delitto di Giovanni Episcopo* was adapted from a novel of the same title
by Gabriele d'Annunzio, while *Il mulino del Po* was an adaptation of
the second part of a trilogy by Riccardo Bacchelli. The first film, of particular interest since it employs the kind of first-person, subjective
voice-over that Fellini would often use in his later films and that was
infrequently employed by neorealist directors, recounts the tale of a
mild-mannered man, convincingly played by Aldo Fabrizi, who murders his wife's ex-lover to keep her from abandoning his family. The
production was intended to embody the themes of the classic nineteenth-century Russian novels and is shot in a style reflecting Lattuada's admiration for the American film noir. The rapid conversion of
Episcopo's wife from a wayward woman to a penitent supporter of her
husband as he goes to the police station to turn himself in to the au-
thorities for his crime cannot but recall the equally sudden and sometimes inexplicable changes of character in the figures of Nannina and
Irene that Fellini scripted for Rossellini. Besides gaining experience in
writing a script following American generic conventions, Fellini also
met Alberto Sordi during the production, who acquired his first important part here and would later be brilliantly cast by Fellini, over the
objections of his producers, in both *Lo sceicco bianco* and *I vitelloni*.

Senza pietà is without question the most important of the films Fellini scripted for Lattuada, and its subject, the encounter of Italy and
America after the Liberation, continues the theme Rossellini had developed in *Paisà* and writers such as Cesare Pavese and Italo Calvino
popularized in literature immediately after the war.[42] The original idea
of the film came from Ettore M. Margadonna, who had called his story
Good-bye Otello before Fellini and Pinelli, working with Lattuada,
completely rewrote the story into the screenplay that survives. Its daring plot treats an interracial love affair between Jerry (John Kitzmiller),
a black GI, and Angela (Carla Del Poggio, Lattuada's wife, later cast by
Fellini and Lattuada in *Luci del varietà*), an Italian girl who is forced to
become a prostitute to survive. The film is set in Tombolo near the port
of Livorno, where deserters, bandits, and corrupt Allied soldiers con-

now in the Lilly Library. Pinelli also refers to the film on occasion as *Petrolio in
Toscana* (Faldini and Fofi, *L'avventurosa storia del cinema italiano . . . 1935–1959*,
p. 128). Since the script was never shot, I use the title appearing on the manuscript.

[42] For a survey of this theme in the Italian cinema, see my "America in the Postwar
Italian Cinema," *Rivista di studi italiani* 2, no. 1 (1984): 106–25. For the debt of
postwar Italian literature to American culture, see Donald Heiney, *America in Modern Italian Literature* (Ann Arbor, Mich.: University of Michigan Press, 1964); and
Angela Jeannet and Louise Barnett, eds. and trans., *New World Journeys: Contemporary Italian Writers and the Experience of America* (Westport, Conn.: Greenwood
Press, 1977).

spire to plunder army supplies for sale on the black market. The criminal activities there are controlled by a sinister character named Pier Luigi, whose effeminate mannerisms, white linen suits, and even his initials associate him with similar roles played by Peter Lorre in the American film noir Lattuada admired so much. Giulietta Masina appears in a supporting role as a plucky young prostitute named Marcella, a character invented by Fellini. Marcella, also in love with another black soldier, dreams of leaving "the life" and making a fresh start in America. Masina's performance earned her a Nastro d'Argento (the Italian equivalent of an Oscar) for a supporting role and launched her on a career of such characterizations of fallen women with golden hearts in films either scripted or directed by Fellini.[43] Fellini would employ the figure of the prostitute in his own subsequent work as the prototype of a human being hungering for a new life and consequently open to the reception of a secularized form of Christian grace.

Senza pietà does not paint a particularly favorable picture of America: the white guards at the prison camp are violent racists, while most of the prisoners they guard are black. Jerry falls into Pier Luigi's clutches because the criminal mastermind exploits his love for Angela to draw him into his organization. A number of the film's most important sequences owe much to the American gangster film, a genre Lattuada also imitated and one not usually associated with Italian neorealism: there are several gun battles and car chases with automobiles careening around corners, pistols blazing; there is a melodramatic prison break by Jerry and a black friend, who is wounded and must be left behind; and we see an American-style jazz nightclub that serves as the headquarters of Pier Luigi's activities. In a desperate effort to escape Pier Luigi's clutches, Jerry and Angela rob him and attempt to flee; Angela steps in front of Jerry and receives a bullet meant for him. As she dies, Jerry vows never to abandon her, leaps into his truck filled with contraband goods to the tune of a crescendo of black spirituals, brilliantly set to a score written by Nino Rota, and drives his truck into the ocean. The film's final shots portray a spinning truck wheel, Angela's head, and her arm clutching Jerry, as the two lovers are finally united in death.

A glance at a single but typical sequence from the original manuscript of *Senza pietà* reveals that the script Fellini and Pinelli provided for Lattuada departs in important respects from traditional Italian prac-

---

[43] Besides *Senza pietà*, Fellini creates practically the same role in *Lo sceicco bianco* for Masina. In addition, Masina plays wayward women hoping to change their lives in *Persiane chiuse*, *Europa '51*, and, of course, *Le notti di Cabiria*; *Giulietta degli spiriti* also proposes Masina as a woman in mid-life crisis who must choose between continuing to be a faithful wife or becoming a sexual libertine like Susy, her next-door neighbor.

tice. It seems closer to a screenplay intended for the American studio system:

A COMPLEX OF SHACKS IN AN AMUSEMENT PARK. OUTSIDE (NIGHT)
156.157.158.159.160.161.162.163.164.
165.166.167.168.169.170.171.172.173.
174.175.176.177.178.179.180.

CRANE AVAILABLE FOR THE SEQUENCE. MUSIC

> A very loud Italian song transmitted by the loud-speaker.

A detail of the model train of the test of strength which completes three, four, five turns around the circular tracks in the midst of multicolored little lights.

Following the train going backwards, we discover Jerry, Angela, two white sailors, and a number of curious bystanders—predominantly young boys—all gathered around the departure track. Jerry has launched the train.

> FIRST SAILOR:
> "Seven."
> JERRY:
> "Seven."

The sailor takes several dollars out of his pocket and places them by his side as he says:

> SAILOR:
> "What do say wanna bet five bucks?"

Jerry is rather excited; there is also a bit of excitement among the spectators, as in all contests. Angela, who is eating an ice-cream cone, still unhappy and silent, and with a certain apprehension, looks on, first at the sailor and then at Jerry, who takes the bills out of his pocket he has received from Pier Luigi and begins to count them.[44]

---

[44] The broken English, reproduced exactly as it was typed on the original manu-

Written for a studio production that employed the rational industrial procedures typical of an American studio—a standardized method of production that would never have tolerated the haphazard and provisional atmosphere characteristic of Rossellini's early neorealist films—the manuscript prepared by Fellini and Pinelli for *Senza pietà* contains numerous technical details. The precise number of shots allowed for the sequence above (25) is specified. The sound to be added after location work was completed is indicated for postproduction dubbing. Somewhere in the sequence, it is suggested that the director employ a crane shot, and while the script specifies this choice, it does not indicate in which shot or shots the crane will actually be used. Elsewhere in the script, there are more concrete directions about the camera: "the camera drops down upon the girls to reach a medium close-up shot" (p. 21), or "the scene ends with a close-up of Angela" (p. 26); a crane shot is called for (p. 10) as Angela descends from a carriage of a train. All transitions between sequences are marked in the script with editing suggestions (dissolve, fade to black, and so on), thus separating the film's sequences into their constituent shots, which the script lists as a total of 480, well below the average number of shots in a typical American studio production of the period. There are also very few modifications from the written script during its transformation into the completed film. A studio script based on a recognizable American film genre, the film noir, thus seemed to require a tightly written and minutely organized screenplay, which, unlike Rossellini's normal practice, was designed to support a commercial operation attempting to avoid costly improvisation.

The films Fellini scripted with Pinelli for Pietro Germi also follow American generic conventions. *In nome della legge, Il cammino della speranza*, and *Il brigante di Tacca del Lupo* all transpose the formula of the American western, especially various masterpieces by John Ford, into specifically Italian settings. The first work uses the time-honored plot of the new marshal who cleans up a lawless town: a young *pretore* is sent to a Mafia-infested village in Sicily and eventually has a showdown with criminals there. The script contrasts an old and honorable Mafia of the past with a new breed of common criminal lacking *onore* in a conclusion presenting the Mafia in a surprisingly romanticized light. In the second film, a group of impoverished Sicilian sulphur miners and their families replace the more familiar Western wagon train in a migration to France in search of a better life. Finally, in the third

script—Federico Fellini, Tullio Pinelli, and Alberto Lattuada, "Senza pietà," Pinelli MS. 1 (Box 1, IA), p. 82—represents the scriptwriters' attempt to render English slang at a time when neither writer knew the language very well. The rest of the passage is translated by the author.

work, the climactic and inevitable scene of the cavalry arriving at the last possible moment to save a threatened fortress or wagon train is transformed into an equally dramatic rescue in the Mezzogiorno during the nineteenth century, where troops of the fledgling Italian republic battle merciless rebels still faithful to the deposed king of Naples. The manuscripts in the Lilly collection unfortunately include only two samples from Fellini's collaboration with Germi: a lengthy and detailed treatment (103 pages) of *Il brigante di Tacca del Lupo*; and the story of the unfilmed *La famiglia*.[45] According to Pinelli, Germi not only helped Fellini and Pinelli write his scripts but also edited his own films as well. Apparently, he rarely allowed any rewriting or changes in his final ideas.[46] Thus, it is not surprising that Fellini and Pinelli enjoyed less liberty working for Germi than for either Lattuada or Rossellini. It is much more difficult to detect their presence in either of the two extant manuscripts for Germi and in the films Germi completed.

The story of *La famiglia* is even further removed from the familiar plots and characters Fellini preferred. It offers an extremely naturalistic portrayal of twenty-five years in the life of an Italian family with strong affinities to the early novels of Italo Svevo or the Italian school of *verismo*. Only in its emphasis on the cycle of events recurring again and again in the life of an Italian household do we catch a glimpse of the provincial milieu Fellini was to represent so vividly in his early films. The humorous sketches and caricatures of a family and a dance-hall girl Fellini scrawled on the folder holding *La famiglia*'s manuscript, already mentioned in the discussion of Fellini's interest in cartoons, may actually reveal something of Fellini's attitude toward the story. It is possible that Fellini was simply bored by such unappealing material and imagined changing Germi's minute and naturalistic dissection of an average Italian family into something much more humorous and closer to Fellini's comic vision. The figure of the dancer anticipates his subsequent film *Luci del varietà*, which Fellini may well have been privately planning as he worked on Germi's project with Pinelli.

Three other projects—*Il diavolo in convento* and *Happy Country (Paese felice)*, two scripts never filmed, as well as *Persiane chiuse*, eventually completed by Comencini—return to more specifically Fellinian territory. The manuscript of *Il diavolo in convento*, the existence of which Fellini scholarship has never suspected,[47] has comic possibil-

[45] In the Lilly collection, these manuscripts are labeled respectively as Federico Fellini, Tullio Pinelli, and Pietro Germi, "Il brigante di Tacca del Lupo," Pinelli MS. 14 (Box 5, IIIC); and the previously cited "La famiglia," Pinelli MS. 12 (Box 5, IIIA).

[46] Farassino and Sanguineti, *Lux Film*, p. 298.

[47] The manuscript is catalogued as Federico Fellini, Tullio Pinelli, and Giorgio Pastina, "Il diavolo in convento," Pinelli MS. 16 (Box 5, IIIE). Kezich, certainly well

ities that must have intrigued Fellini. The manuscript unfortunately lacks an ending and, indeed, the entire second half of the script. The *primo tempo*[48] is relatively long (119 pages of narrative), and the text contains fewer technical directions than the manuscript of *Senza pietà*. The plot focuses on Angelo, a lay brother who attempts to foil the planned conversion of his monastery, situated on the Ligurian coast and of which he is the only surviving occupant, into a luxury hotel for tourists. The film traces Angelo's attempts to save the traditions of the monastery, while the townspeople, in contrast, are all delighted over the projected changes, since the construction will mean jobs and money for them all. At the end of the manuscript, Brother Angelo makes the tantalizing announcement that he has a "solution" to the problem, but as the second part of the manuscript is missing, we can only imagine what this solution might be. The title's reference to a devil in the monastery suggests that the wily friar may be planning to provide the old building with a poltergeist in order to thwart its transformation into a tourist attraction. Alternatively, he may be planning to use the presence of such an otherworldly tenant as a lure to attract visitors, thereby saving the integrity of the monastery.

Happy Country (Paese felice), scripted from an idea by Luigi Barzini, the author of the best-selling book *The Italians* and a well-known journalist with connections in America, was written to be directed by Mario Camerini for the Lux Film Studio. It may also have been aimed at the American market, since Tullio Kezich notes that Cary Grant was discussed for the leading role with David Selznick, a possible American coproducer with Carlo Ponti.[49] The script is an extremely long one (285 pages), containing a number of specific technical directions for transforming it into a film, following the pattern that we have observed in other Lux film scripts. The literary style of the work is so high that it

---

informed about the minute details of Fellini's life, apparently did not examine this script in his research for his biography, an inconsequential oversight given the quantity of previously unexamined archival material he cited in the book. But he does mention another unrealized project scripted by Fellini and Pinelli, an adaptation of Mario Soldati's novel *La ragazza di Trieste*, which Lux Film hoped to convince David Selznick to shoot starring Alida Valli and Gregory Peck (*Fellini*, p. 140). Another Italian film with the same title as the unrealized script, *Il diavolo in convento*, was made for the Taurus Film Studio in 1951 by Nunzio Malasomma, but it has nothing whatsoever to do with the project scripted by Fellini, Pinelli, and Pastina.

[48] In Italy, feature films are generally divided in half, the two parts of which are called *primo tempo* and *secondo tempo*. This produces an intermission in the screening similar to that between acts of a play.

[49] Kezich, *Fellini*, p. 140. While the first page of this document, Pinelli MS. 13 (Box 5, IIIB), suggests that the material contained in it includes both the trattamento and the sceneggiatura, in fact the story is missing and only the script is extant.

could well be published as a polished and entertaining short novel. Like the plot of Rossellini's *Paisà* or Lattuada's *Senza pietà*, the story line of *Happy Country* focuses on the different cultural values of Americans and Italians. An American oil company holds an option on territory owned by Count Della Robbia near the Tuscan town of San Quirico in the Sienese countryside. The idea that Americans might actually believe that oil existed there provides us with some notion of the kind of comedy of errors the script proposes to develop. An American engineer named Robert (presumably the role proposed for Cary Grant) is sent to tie up the deal by Mr. Harrison, the president of the petroleum company, whose daughter Mary is also Robert's fiancée. Robert is accompanied by some stereotypical American oil-rig rowdies named Jhonny (*sic*) and Blakey, and his initial meeting with the count concludes with a successful agreement to drill for oil. However, Robert is warned to beware of the reaction of the count's daughter Fernanda, whose objections to turning the Tuscan countryside into a Texas-style oil field eventually convince even Robert.

Although written in a comic vein, *Happy Country* seems closer to the somewhat negative portrait of American culture in *Senza pietà* than the more positive one in *Paisà*. The script mercilessly satirizes the American obsession with progress and calls into question the idea that economic improvement brings an increase in level of civilization or culture. The confrontation of a new industrial culture from America and a more ancient form of civilization in Tuscany with deep roots in the soil and peasant folklore becomes the focal point of the script, as in a particularly important passage in which Robert argues with Professor Nicola Della Robbia, the count's brother:

> ROBERT: You're a town without a penny, and you permit yourself the luxury of making fun of someone who is bringing wealth to your door! . . . Civilization . . . !
>
> PROFESSOR DELLA ROBBIA: Excuse me . . . what do you mean by civilization . . . ? I have the impression that you are confusing it with mechanical progress; now look, they are, instead, two contrary things. . . .
>
> ROBERT: What does that remark mean . . . ? That we should go back to candles and hand carts?
>
> PROFESSOR (with a smile): Really . . . ! The fact remains that in the days of candles, the world slept more peacefully, and a masterpiece was born every day. . . .[50]

[50] Fellini and Pinelli, "Happy Country (Paese felice)," Pinelli MS. 13 (Box 5, IIIB), p. 211.

If the film thus begins by emphasizing the lack of comprehension between the two cultures, a situation similar to the one that opens the Sicilian episode of Rossellini's *Paisà*, the script of *Happy Country* completely reverses the direction of emotional development. Here, the Italians possess a culture that the scriptwriters obviously consider superior to the one the Americans seem to be trying to impose from abroad, and Robert is eventually convinced that living in the Tuscan countryside offers advantages the American way of life lacks. As he admits to Fernanda, with whom he has immediately fallen in love, "perhaps you are right . . . life shouldn't be wasted in worries and frenetic activity . . . it shouldn't be wasted that way . . . you still know how to enjoy it. . . . For us, the greatest crime is to waste time; and instead, perhaps wisdom lies precisely in knowing how to waste time. . . . You're right, Fernanda, perhaps it would have been best not to have found the oil. . . ."[51] This theme builds up to a dramatic conclusion as Robert tells Mr. Harrison that grain and olive oil, not oil rigs, should be sprouting up on the Tuscan hills: "We think we are coming here to colonize, to bring civilization. . . . But from the very beginning we are butting into things we don't succeed in understanding . . . another conception of life . . . another kind of civilization . . . much more ancient."[52] When Mary complains that Italy is backward and has the lowest percentage of indoor toilets in Europe, Robert, now a staunch defender of life in Italy, retorts that the Germans and the Japanese enjoyed the world's greatest number of such facilities but were not so civilized in the last war![53] The conclusion of the script is inevitable: Mary leaves Robert, who, a year later, is shown in a parting shot dressed as a Tuscan farmer and holding Fernanda's hand as he and the local peasants celebrate the annual August harvest festival that has been celebrated for the past four hundred years.

The most important technical device the script proposes for comic effects is the juxtaposition of an ironic narrative voice with contradictions in the dialogue or the visuals immediately following the narrator's supposedly objective and reliable remarks. The pattern is set during the first few pages of the script. After the narrative voice-over declares that Robert is arriving in the "land of the sun," the script calls for a dissolve to San Quirico being drenched with driving rain.[54] Before Robert leaves America, he informs his company that he cannot speak Italian, but he is assured that the town is populated by ex-emigrants to America who all speak English "PERfectly" (the emphasis is in the

---

[51] Ibid., p. 265.
[52] Ibid., p. 275.
[53] Ibid.
[54] Ibid., pp. 8–9.

script).[55] Naturally, when he reaches San Quirico, not only do very few people speak English, but their Tuscan dialect is sprinkled with colorful expletives found only in that region of Italy. Robert's lack of understanding of Italian art is underlined by one of the most interesting of the script's shots, also one of the few shots described in great detail by the scriptwriters:

> Atrium of the Villa, Interior during the Evening
> The Leaning Tower of Pisa . . . .
> which, during a track backwards, reveals itself
> to be one of those countless and horrible reproductions
> in alabaster of the famous bell tower.[56]

Robert had purchased the kitsch object because he knows Fernanda loves art and he wants to give her something suitable! Here, the object serves as a cue to Robert's lack of sophistication, set in contrast to the more cultured girl with whom he has fallen in love. Years later, as was noted previously, Fellini employed an equally artificial reproduction of the Leaning Tower of Pisa in his commercial for Campari soda. In both cases, the image serves as a symbol of Italy. However, the commercial employs the image in a self-conscious and ironic fashion, contrasting the object's obvious artificiality to the genuine goodness of the product standing beside it, while its appearance in the script of *Happy Country* merely emphasizes the fact that, like the alabaster statue, Robert comes from a world organized around the principle of mass production and replication, lacking a genuine core of humanist values.

If *Happy Country* and its ironic narrative voice point toward narrative techniques Fellini will employ in his early films set in a similar provincial setting, the script of *Persiane chiuse* returns to a familiar Fellini theme, that of prostitution. The story is set in Turin, not only because Pinelli was born there but also because the script calls for a modern urban environment to be photographed in the grim, gritty black-and-white style typical of American film noir. The analysis of what used to be euphemistically called "white slavery" emerging from the script employs American-style bars filled with black GIs drinking with white Italian prostitutes to underline the changes in social values brought about by the American occupation. The description of one particular night spot, the "Joe Louis Bar," recalls Pier Luigi's establishment from *Senza pietà*. The script's plot recounts the attempts by Sandra, a factory worker's daughter, to rescue her sister Luisa from a life of prostitution and, eventually, to reconcile her with her father, who has

---

[55] Ibid., p. 6.
[56] Ibid., p. 241.

driven Luisa out of the family home. One of the secondary characters in the film, a likable young prostitute named Pippo, is played by Fellini's wife, Giulietta Masina, in a role obviously inspired by that which Fellini created for *Senza pietà*. In order to introduce the reader to the kind of environment prostitutes must endure, the script portrays Sandra mistakenly arrested as a prostitute while searching for Luisa, a scene repeating the opening of *Senza pietà*, where Angela is first mistaken for a prostitute before she eventually becomes one herself.

One recent critic of Comencini's films believes that the only weak element in the film he eventually made from this script is the cliché of the father who drives his daughter as a fallen woman from his home but eventually and tearfully receives her back.[57] And yet, this is precisely the kind of scene we shall come to expect from Fellini's own films in the 1950s, such as *La strada*, *Le notti di Cabiria*, or *Il bidone*, all of which employ a personal interpretation of notions of Christian redemption and grace to treat radical transformations in various protagonists. For Fellini and Pinelli, the message of *Persiane chiuse* is probably summarized in a remark made by Sandra: "It's not fair . . . a woman who has made a mistake must have the possibility of saving herself . . . of leaving that hell. . . ."[58] In fact, at the end of the film, Sandra and Lucia return to Genoa for a reconciliation with their father. Just before they arrive, they encounter the same kind of itinerant musicians Fellini will later depict in *Luci del varietà*, *Lo sceicco bianco*, *La strada*, and, most importantly, *Le notti di Cabiria*. As the script notes, this sudden and quite unexplained presence of music represents "an unexpected light of humanity."[59] As so often is the case in Fellini's early films, the script calls here for music to underline the possibility of change and renewal. The music's effects on Sandra are profound and signal her final forgiveness of her sister's fall from grace: "It is as if an unexpected revelation touched her soul and kindled in her heart a deep and emotional hope."[60] After calling for a dissolve to end this penultimate sequence, the script's final sequence describes the tearful reconciliation of Luisa with her father, the classic return of the prodigal child to receive the paternal benediction.

As mentioned previously, Luigi Comencini took over the direction of *Persiane chiuse* after the producer, Luigi Rovere, had viewed some of the daily rushes shot by the original director, Gianni Puccini, and rejected his work out of hand. For a brief period, probably only a day or

[57] Gili, *Luigi Comencini*, p. 20.
[58] Fellini, Pinelli, and Puccini, "Persiane chiuse," Pinelli MS. 15 (Box 5, IIID), p. 72.
[59] Ibid., p. 104.
[60] Ibid.

two, Fellini was called in to keep the crew working while Rovere brought Comencini in to complete the rest of the film. Fellini was thus in charge of shooting the opening scene, the discovery of the body of a dead prostitute by policemen in the Po River.[61] This brief moment behind the camera working with Arturo Gallea, the director of photography for *Persiane chiuse*, proved to be an important break for the young scriptwriter, for Luigi Rovere was so impressed by the professional caliber of the rushes Fellini produced that he resolved to use him as the director of a future project. When Fellini made his first independent film, *Lo sceicco bianco*, only two years later, Rovere produced the work and Gallea was his photographer.

Because we know that nothing shot by Puccini was used in the final film, and that only the opening shots were completed by Fellini, there is no doubt that Comencini was responsible for the entire work. Yet, a number of intriguing annotations in Fellini's hand can be found on the verso of one of the last pages of the script. It outlines how the final sequence of the reconciliation between father and daughter might have been broken down into eight separate shots had Fellini directed the scene himself:

1) A shot of them from behind in the garden. They stop because the door opens.

2) The door opens, the father comes out—he turns and sees [the two daughters].

3) The two [daughters] stand immobile.

4) Close-up of the father.

5) The two [daughters] ~~move forward   they reach "home"~~ standing   "L[ucia] has returned home."

6) Close-up of the father (a match) ~~they enter the scene~~.

7) Reverse angle shot fixes them from the father's shoulders.

8) ~~Close-up~~   the door opens   they enter.[62]

Up to this point in his career, Fellini had been content to provide such scenes for other directors in a strictly *literary* form. The content

---

[61] Kezich, in *Fellini* (p. 158), identifies the specific scene Fellini shot and also notes that it was Fellini who suggested to Rovere that Comencini be hired to complete the film.

[62] Fellini, Pinelli, and Puccini, "Persiane chiuse," Pinelli MS. 15 (Box 5, IIID), p. 105, verso. The canceled words are marked through but still legible in the original document; I have added the material in brackets for clarity.

of this last sequence certainly reflects ideas about the need for redemption in a fallen world that will mark his best works in the 1950s. Now, however, for perhaps the first time in his life, and certainly the first time in any extant document, Fellini reinterprets his written material from a completely visual perspective, employing the eye of a director rather than the mind's eye of a scriptwriter. The transition is a fateful one, however, for Fellini's handwritten notes are the first tangible proof we have of the genesis of his new vocation as a film director, a storyteller who employs pictures as well as words. These few precious notes scribbled on the back of a script represent Fellini's final arrival at a destination toward which all his previous work as cartoonist, gagman, journalist, and scriptwriter seemed to be inexorably drawing him. The next developments in Fellini's career, nourished to this point as much by popular Italian culture as by the cinema, would change the direction of Italian film history itself.

CHAPTER THREE

Beyond Neorealism

CHARACTER AND

NARRATIVE FORM IN EARLY

FELLINI FROM *LUCI DEL*

VARIETÀ TO *LA DOLCE VITA*

*I don't want to demonstrate any-
thing; I want to show it.*[1]

I don't have any universal ideas and I think I feel better not having them.[2]

La Strada *is really the complete catalogue of my entire mythical world, a
dangerous representation of my identity, undertaken without precau-
tions.*[3]

When Rossellini said that **La dolce vita** *was the film of a provincial, he
didn't realize what he was saying, since my own feeling is that to call an
artist provincial is the best way of defining him. For an artist's position in
the face of reality must be exactly that of a provincial, he must be attracted by what he sees and at the same time have the detachment of a
provincial. What is an artist, in fact? He is merely a provincial who finds
himself standing between a physical and a metaphysical reality. Faced
with a metaphysical reality, we are all provincials.*[4]

WHEN FELLINI began to make
his first film as codirector of *Luci del varietà* with Alberto Lattuada in
1950, he brought to the project over a decade of experience in the film
industry. Fellini began his new career as a filmmaker during a time
(1945–1955) when critics on all sides of the ideological spectrum were
engaged in a heated debate over the direction Italian cinema ought to
take in the Reconstruction period.[5] Defining the specific artistic contri-

[1] Fellini, *Fellini on Fellini*, p. 52.

[2] Fellini, *Comments on Film*, p. 6.

[3] Federico Fellini, "The Long Interview: Tullio Kezich & Federico Fellini," in *Federico Fellini's "Juliet of the Spirits,"* ed. Tullio Kezich (New York: Orion Press,
1965), p. 26.

[4] Fellini, *Fellini on Fellini*, p. 154.

[5] For a sampling of the critical essays and reviews arising from this debate in Italy
and France, see Overbey, *Springtime in Italy*; Bazin, *What Is Cinema?* *Vol. II*; and
Fellini, *"La Strada": Federico Fellini, Director.*

butions made by such films as Rossellini's *Roma città aperta* and
Paisà, Luchino Visconti's *La terra trema* (1948), and Vittorio De Sica's
Ladri di biciclette (1948)—not to mention a great number of excellent,
if less influential, works by Germi, Lattuada, De Santis, and others—
became less important to many critics than dictating the direction Italian cinema should take in the future. After interpreting neorealist aesthetics along strict realist lines, the *description* of neorealism quickly
became a *prescription* for acceptable style. A film's critical importance
was directly proportional to how "realistically" it reflected Italy's social problems in the present and how "correctly" its ideology indicated
radical Marxist solutions for the future. Directors who wished to follow
their own artistic imperatives were considered either conservative or
reactionary. In the case of individuals such as Fellini whose careers had
begun during the neorealist era, the accusation was broadened to imply
an act of artistic as well as ideological betrayal. This simplistic interpretation of Italian neorealism as a cinema of pure, unmediated realism
never represented a satisfactory description of its great variety or originality.[6] In fact, Italian filmmakers were trying to develop a cinematic
language comparable to the new literary language contemporary writers
aimed to create, a nonrhetorical, elemental means of expression permitting an essentially poetic treatment of important social and political issues. In the fiction of the period, brilliant novels such as Elio Vit-
torini's *Conversazione in Sicilia* (1941), Cesare Pavese's *Paesi tuoi*
(1941) and *La luna e i falò* (1951), Carlo Levi's *Cristo si è fermato ad
Eboli* (1945), and Italo Calvino's *Il sentiero dei nidi di ragno* (1947) reflected as great a debt to American literature as Italian neorealism often
owed to the styles and generic conventions of Hollywood film. Moreover, these highly original works all dealt with social reality in a symbolic or mythical fashion, employed a subjective and usually unreliable
narrative voice, and embraced a clearly antinaturalistic narrative stance
quite far removed from the canons of literary realism established by the
European or American novel of the nineteenth century. Italo Calvino
best defined the poetics of both directors and novelists when he declared that neorealists "knew all too well that what counted was the
music and not the libretto . . . there were never more dogged formalists
than we; and never were lyric poets as effusive as those objective reporters we were supposed to be." Calvino also suggested that, rather
than neorealism, "perhaps the right name for that Italian season . . .

---

[6] For recent studies of neorealism that avoid ideological polemics and concentrate
on neorealist style, see Marcus, *Italian Film in the Light of Neorealism*; my own
Italian Cinema: From Neorealism to the Present, which contains an extensive bibliography on neorealism; and Roy Armes, *Patterns of Realism: A Study of Italian
Neo-Realism* (Cranbury, N.J.: A. S. Barnes, 1971).

should be 'neo-expressionism'."[7] Unfortunately, few of the period's film critics heeded his intelligent comments. Cesare Pavese's description of the innovative qualities his generation discovered in American fiction could just as well be applied to neorealist Italian filmmakers. For Pavese, American novelists sought to "readjust language to the new reality of the world, in order to create, in effect, a *new* language, down-to-earth and symbolic, that would justify itself solely in terms of itself and not in terms of any traditional complacency."[8]

There was, to be sure, a major shift in Italian cinema during the early 1950s, but the polemical debate between Italian and French critics on the right and those on the left often obscured precisely *how* Italian cinema changed during this period. The untenable dichotomy in the reviews and critical literature of the time between films analyzing Italian society and others that supposedly avoided the presentation of social problems derived primarily from ideological prejudice rather than a careful consideration of the various cinematic styles reflected in the major classics of Italian neorealism. Fellini's slow progress toward an individual cinematic signature of his own in his early films, a development whose outlines are already discernible in his contributions to screenplays for Rossellini and others, begins with a few simple but deeply held beliefs that represent both moral principles and aesthetic choices. Most importantly, Fellini felt no obligation to limit his subject matter to themes with immediate and obvious ideological significance. On the contrary, after the experience on the set of *Paisà*, Fellini redefined neorealism to mean the liberation of artistic expression, "looking at reality with an honest eye—but any kind of reality; not just social reality, but also spiritual reality, metaphysical reality, anything man has inside him."[9] Refusing to restrict his attention solely to those themes acceptable to "progressive" or Marxist ideology, Fellini would later declare that "it sometimes seemed as if the neorealists thought they could make a film only if they put a shabby man in front of the camera. They were wrong."[10] In a polemical exchange with a Marxist critic, Fellini further explained his aversion to a limited set of "acceptable" topics and rejected any pretense to objectivity as well:

> I feel that the historical process which art must discover, support, and illumine, can be seen in far less limited, and, particularly, far less tech-

[7] Italo Calvino, Preface to *The Path to the Nest of Spiders*, trans. Archibald Colquhoun (New York: Ecco Press, 1976), pp. vii, xi.

[8] Cesare Pavese, *American Literature: Essays and Opinions*, trans. Edwin Fussel (Berkeley and Los Angeles: University of California Press, 1970), p. 197.

[9] Fellini, "The Road Beyond Neo-Realism," in Fellini, *"La Strada": Federico Fellini, Director*, p. 217.

[10] Fellini, *Fellini on Fellini*, p. 152.

nical and political terms than those in which you see it. Sometimes a film, while avoiding any precise representation of historical or political reality, can incarnate in mythic figures, speaking in a quite elementary language, the opposition between contemporary feelings, and can become very much more realistic than another film in which social and political matters are referred to much more precisely. This is why I do not believe in "objectivity," at least in the way you people believe in it, and cannot accept your ideas of neorealism which I feel do not fully capture, or even really impinge upon, the essence of the movement to which I have had the honor, since *Open City*, to belong.[11]

Besides having absolutely no interest in an objective vision of Italian society (since "objectivity" and "realism" during the period had actually become code words for a specifically Marxist brand of cinematic realism), Fellini agreed with Rossellini that neorealist cinema should represent an act of humility toward life. But he defended the artist's absolute freedom to manipulate, interpret, and control his artistic creation:

> Yes, an act of humility towards life, but *not* towards the camera, there I *don't* agree . . . once you're in front of the camera, you ought to abandon this humility completely; on the contrary, you ought to be arrogant, tyrannical, you ought to become a sort of god, in total command not only of the actors, but also the objects and the lights. This is why, in my view, the confusion created by neorealism was a very serious matter, because if you have an attitude of humility not only towards life but towards the camera as well, carrying the idea to its logical conclusion, you wouldn't need a director at all. The camera can work by itself; all you need to do is set it up and make things happen in front of it.[12]

The films Fellini produced during the 1950s before the critical turning point of *La dolce vita*—*Luci del varietà, Lo sceicco bianco, I vitelloni, Un'agenzia matrimoniale, La strada, Il bidone,* and *Le notti di Cabiria*—reflect his increasingly mature control over the cinema's technical resources. But Fellini's development toward a personal cinematic style, that of an internationally recognized auteur, does not begin as a revolution of cinematic style. In this respect, Fellini's cinema was initially more conservative and traditional than that produced during the same period by either Rossellini or Antonioni, who both effected important technical changes in editing or photography that placed them squarely in the avant-garde of the 1950s. In many respects, the

[11] Fellini, "Letter to a Marxist Critic," in ibid., p. 63; also in Fellini, *"La Strada": Federico Fellini, Director*, p. 214.
[12] Cited in Budgen, *Fellini*, pp. 91–92.

technical components of Fellini's early cinema reflect the standard practice of the Italian studio system, itself based on the dominant Hollywood model.

The first significant innovations leading to what may be termed Fellini's "cinema of poetry" lie in his conception of film character, which drastically altered the neorealist view of character and had important implications for a subsequent development both in his typical themes and, to a lesser extent, in the structures of his plots.[13] Regardless of how critics approach the thorny problem of "realism" in Italian neorealism, there is general agreement that the neorealist film character was defined, as well as limited, by his or her social environment. Visconti's exploited fishermen in *La terra trema*, De Santis's rice workers in *Riso amaro*, De Sica's impoverished man in search of his bicycle in *Ladri di biciclette* or his retired pensioner in *Umberto D.*, all have at least one thing in common in spite of the diverse cinematic styles employed in representing them on the screen. These figures reflect specific historical conditions in postwar Italy and can be understood primarily in terms of their social surroundings. The unemployed worker in De Sica's *Ladri di biciclette*, a classic neorealist protagonist, derives almost all of his dramatic force from the fact that without a bicycle he will lose his hard-won job hanging posters on city walls; and without his job, his family will be doomed to a life of deprivation. His material circumstances determine his essential nature insofar as the spectator is concerned. And since he may be regarded as typical of many Italian workers in the immediate postwar period before the economic boom launched Italy into the vanguard of newly emerging industrial nations, this character serves to represent an entire class or generation of Italians. While such figures are not "types" in the same sense that figures from traditional comedy or Italy's *commedia dell'arte* embody recognizable stock characters, they are nevertheless "typical" in their reflection of the consequences of specific social conditions—widespread unemployment, poverty, and the chaos in Italian society immediately following the war.

Rather than concentrating on how a protagonist's environment shapes his character and destiny, thereby providing the audience with a story emphasizing social or economic problems, Fellini's first three films offer characters that are atypical and willfully eccentric. They exist in a particular Fellinian fictional world, an environment that privi-

[13] In some of my earlier work on Fellini, particularly "Early Fellini: *Variety Lights, The White Sheik, The Vitelloni*," in *Federico Fellini: Essays in Criticism*, pp. 220–39, I argued that Fellini's thematic concerns remained close to those of the neorealists. I now believe that a shift in his view of film character necessitated parallel modifications in content and narrative form.

leges the interplay of illusion or fantasy with reality rather than the representation of economic and social realities. In what I have elsewhere termed a "trilogy of character,"[14] *Luci del varietà, Lo sceicco bianco*, and *I vitelloni* dramatize the clash between a character's social "role" or "mask"—how a character tends to act in society—and the character's more authentic "face"—represented by the protagonist's aspirations, ideals, instincts, and fantasies. Fellini's protagonists may well embody certain values typical of a particular historical period or a specific social class, but they are closer in conception to the stock characters of the commedia dell'arte as well as the caricatures Fellini drew during his days with *Marc'Aurelio*, sketches capturing with a few strokes of the pen universal human qualities transcending a particular moment in time. Fellini's particular conception of character marks a shift in direction that is essentially *psychological* or *dramatic* rather than cinematic, for it initially did not require drastic changes in the cinematic style he had encountered at the Lux Film Studio. Such an essentially dramatic conception of film character, however, should come as no surprise. Fellini's transition to film direction began after a decade as a scriptwriter with a studio company that encouraged well-made plots. His chief collaborator, Tullio Pinelli, turned to scriptwriting immediately after beginning a promising career as a playwright.

The development of a specifically Fellinian concept of film character in the trilogy of character repeats a similar reaction against the conventions of theatrical realism in the early dramatic production of Luigi Pirandello. In Pirandello's early plays—works such as *Il piacere dell'onestà* (1918), *Così è (se vi parve)* (1918), and *Il giuoco delle parti* (1919)—a rejection of dramatic characters defined by their social or economic conditions led to a new psychological concept of character in Pirandello and marked a necessary first step toward an even more revolutionary shift in perspective in his later, metatheatrical masterpieces, such as *Sei personaggi in cerca d'autore* (1921), *Ciascuno a suo modo* (1924), and *Questa sera si recita a soggetto* (1930). A transition from realism through an intermediary stage of development calling into question realism's conventions toward a modernist concern with self-reflexive artistic statements is an extremely common pattern in twentieth-century culture. A similar trajectory may be seen in the career of Italo Calvino, Fellini's contemporary and one of twentieth-century Italy's most original novelists. Calvino's career begins with a neorealist novel, *Il sentiero dei nidi di ragno*; it moves toward an examination of character with the trilogy *I nostri antenati* (1952–1959); and it con-

---

[14] See Fellini, *"La Strada": Federico Fellini, Director*, p. 9; or my *Italian Cinema: From Neorealism to the Present*, p. 130.

cludes with the internationally celebrated postmodernist fiction of such works as *Cosmicomiche* (1965), *Le città invisibili* (1972), and *Se una notte d'inverno un viaggiatore* (1979).[15]

In the early drama of Pirandello and in Fellini's trilogy of character, a realist definition of character as socially determined, as a reflection of environmental influence and social pressures, is deepened by a fundamental philosophical inquiry into the nature of personality itself. The title of Pirandello's collected dramatic works, *Maschere nude* (*Naked Masks*) might well serve as an identifying tag for Fellini's trilogy of character. In Fellini's films, as in Pirandello's early theater, the notion of character as a function of social forces shifts to a basically subjective position. Character is now defined by an uneasy equilibrium between a character's outward social "mask" and his more authentic and often unconscious "face"—composed primarily of irrational dreams, instincts, drives, and emotions. With protagonists defined by such an unstable combination of seemingly rational social roles and irrational psychological forces, dramatic conflict may be produced, with either tragic, comic, or, more typically, tragicomic consequences when a character's mask is stripped off to reveal something of the intimate personality underneath. In Pirandello's case, the unmasking operation involves a polemical attack on the middle-class values of his contemporaries that force his characters to assume constricting social masks, and an impassioned defense of the authenticity of their private and usually irrational emotions or feelings hidden underneath. Fellini's trilogy of character employs equally dramatic moments of unmasking, but his intentions are less polemical, and his tone is less that of the moral reformer than that of the bemused onlooker who admits his own complicity in the comic flaws he portrays in his characters.

For Pirandello, a character could never reach a unified, static state or even be completely comprehensible to others. Influenced by Henri Bergson's philosophy, Pirandello conceived of human personality (and the fictional characters embodying his dramatic roles) as existing in a state of constant flux, an ever-changing entity beyond the grasp of conventional reason precisely because the foundation of both human personality and dramatic character—the face under the mask—derived from an irrational source whose outward expression in dramatic action remained incomprehensible to others. Pirandello's *L'umorismo* (1909), an essay constituting the philosophical basis of his collected literary works (both drama and fiction), is essentially a discussion of the tragi-

---

[15] For a superb examination of Calvino's works, see Gregory L. Lucente, *Beautiful Fables: Self-consciousness in Italian Narrative from Manzoni to Calvino* (Baltimore: Johns Hopkins University Press, 1986), pp. 266–300.

comic genre extended to encompass not only the playwright's generic preferences but his philosophy of life as well. Explaining the difference between writers who are "humorists," such as himself, and others who have a comic vision of the world, Pirandello provides the example of an old woman whose pathetically provocative dress and excessive makeup immediately strikes a spectator as foolish and comical. This merely intellectual perception of a disparity between the woman's inner personality and her consciously adopted social role produces an initial reaction, what Pirandello calls the "perception of the opposite."[16] However, deeper reflection on the compelling motives that might cause an elderly and otherwise respectable woman to assume such a ridiculous outward appearance—for example, the possibility that she is trying to save her marriage—moves the "humorist" beyond a superficially comic reaction to what Pirandello terms the "feeling of the opposite." This second and crucial phase in the development of such a moment of "unmasking" begins with a rational perception but concludes only when reason is joined to and then superseded by sentiment or empathy. Such a tragicomic view of character in an artist's fictional world finds a clear parallel in Fellini's trilogy of character. Fellini, like Pirandello, strips his figures bare of their posturing social masks to reveal their underlying faces. But, in contrast to Pirandello, Fellini does so without presuming to present moral judgments of either his characters or the society in which they live. Fellini's wrenching unmasking operations reveal the director's attitude as that of an accomplice, a witness for the defense, rather than a prosecutor or judge.[17] It is a special characteristic of Fellini's cinematic universe that its creator extends to every part of the fantasy world he has created what Pier Paolo Pasolini quite accurately described as an "undifferentiated and indifferent love."[18]

Fellini's directing debut in *Luci del varietà* plunges the spectator directly into a world far removed from that of Italian neorealism—the variety theater. It is a world of intriguing illusion and fantasy beneath which a tawdry and mundane reality will emerge during the course of the film. While there has been much speculation about the degree of Fellini's participation in this film, given the joint direction of Fellini

[16] For a complete translation of Pirandello's *L'umorismo*, see *On Humor*, ed. and trans. Antonio Illiano and Daniel P. Testa (Chapel Hill: University of North Carolina Press, 1974).

[17] See Budgen, *Fellini*, p. 99; or Gilbert Salachas, "Fellini's Imagery from *Variety Lights* to *Juliet of the Spirits*," in *Federico Fellini: Essays in Criticism*, ed. Bondanella, p. 214.

[18] Pasolini, "The Catholic Irrationalism of Fellini," *Film Criticism* 9, no. 1 (1984): 71. Pasolini's remarks refer to the characters of *La dolce vita*, but his perceptive evaluation fits all of Fellini's characters.

and Lattuada, there is general critical agreement that Lattuada controlled most of the technical aspects of the production, while the definition of the film's protagonists, as well as the general content and atmosphere of the film, reflects Fellini's fantasy.[19] In spite of the film's undeniable merits, its dismal performance at the box office during the 1950–1951 season, ranking sixty-fifth in gross ticket sales, came close to ending Fellini's career at its debut. *Luci del varietà* also failed to obtain the usual government subsidy bestowed on works of "artistic merit" and suffered from the competition of another, more popular film also treating the variety theater, *Vita da cani*, which was released during the same year and placed thirty-fourth in box office receipts for the season. *Vita da cani* was produced by Carlo Ponti and directed by Steno and Mario Monicelli. It was scripted by three of Fellini's friends: Steno and Maccari, two writers from *Marc'Aurelio*, and Sergio Amidei, Fellini's cowriter with Rossellini. It was edited by the same man who edited *Luci del varietà* (Mario Bonotti); the music was written by Nino Rota; and a young Marcello Mastroianni was part of the cast.[20] One might imagine that a group of Fellini's past and future collaborators had conspired with *Vita da cani* to sabotage *Luci del varietà*, even if the crucial contributions of Rota and Mastroianni to Fellini's future career would compensate for their limited responsibility in the early critical and commercial failure of his first film.[21]

[19] A number of such statements may be found in Faldini and Fofi, *L'avventurosa storia del cinema italiano . . . 1935–1959*. Lattuada claims that the direction was his while Fellini's spirit was reflected in the characters and the themes (p. 228); Lattuada's wife, Carla del Poggio, argues that the idea for the film was hers rather than Fellini's (pp. 227–28), a claim that can surely be discounted; one of the actors in the cast denies any real contribution to the film by Fellini (p. 228), while another actor maintains that the two men divided the work, with Lattuada handling the technical problems (p. 228). The original manuscript of the script may be examined in the Lilly Library: Federico Fellini, Tullio Pinelli, Alberto Lattuada, and Ennio Flaiano, "Luci del varietà," Pinelli MS. 2 (Box 1, IB). No published Italian screenplay of the film exists, although an English translation may be consulted in Federico Fellini, *Early Screenplays: "Variety Lights" and "The White Sheik"* (New York: Grossman, 1971). The original manuscript specifies the film's sequences, marking transitions with dissolves, and calls for a total of 769 shots. It is similar in structure and style to scripts produced by Fellini and Pinelli for the Lux Film Studio.

[20] Kezich, *Fellini*, pp. 167–68.

[21] The critical literature on *Luci del varietà* is sparse. The most sympathetic discussion of the film is by Brunello Rondi in *Il cinema di Fellini* (Rome: Edizioni di Bianco e Nero, 1965), pp. 43–67. In English, see my essay "Early Fellini: *Variety Lights, The White Sheik, The Vitelloni*," pp. 220–39, incorporated into my *Italian Cinema: From Neorealism to the Present*, pp. 116–18. Frank Burke's "Fellini's *Luci del varietà*: The Limitations of the Stage and the 'Morality of Movies,' " *Italica* 55, no. 2 (1978): 225–35, interprets the film as an implicit critique of theater and an affirmation of the moral supremacy of the cinema. Fellini's concentration on the

The variety theater and the glittering world of show business in general are employed by Fellini in his trilogy of character to dramatize his treatment of illusion and reality and the subsequent unmasking operation his major characters experience. *Luci del varietà* portrays the vagabond life of a second-rate troupe of players who wander through the small towns of provincial Italy. Its leader, Checco Dalmonte (Peppino De Filippo), suffers from an exaggerated sense of self-importance as an actor and is an essentially shallow, unreliable man. In contrast, his fiancée Melina Amour (Giulietta Masina) displays both a sensitive affection for Checco and a tough, resilient personality underneath an out-

9. *Luci del varietà*: the eccentric members of the theatrical troupe take a bow

nature of one artistic medium does point toward his eventual examination of the cinema in future works. Moreover, there are hints of a self-reflexive bent in the film that Burke overlooks—Lattuada appears in a nonspeaking role; glimpses of posters for two films Fellini scripted, Lattuada's *Il delitto di Giovanni Episcopo* and Germi's *Nel nome della legge*, are briefly shown. But there is really very little in *Luci del varietà* to support Burke's claim that the film's central theme argues for the superiority of the cinema over the theater. In fact, the aesthetics of Fellini's mature cinema are not far removed from those of the variety theater. Burke repeats his argument in *Federico Fellini: "Variety Lights" to "La Dolce Vita"* (Boston: Twayne, 1984), pp. 7–10.

ward sentimentalism that will inform all of the actress's future roles
for Fellini. The conflict in this comic film arises from the sudden appearance of Liliana Antonelli (Carla del Poggio), a star-struck amateur
with a beautiful body but little dancing talent, whose ambition to reach
the bright lights of big-city dance halls causes Checco to betray Melina.
Some indication of Liliana's talent is offered by the fact that her "discovery" comes about when her costume rips open, revealing a sensuous
body clad only in her underwear to a deliriously applauding audience!

In spite of the fact that *Luci del varietà* is Fellini's first work, a number of the recurrent visuals in the film that critics have traditionally
identified with Fellini's signature are already discernible—deserted piazzas reflecting the inauthentic existence, loneliness, and solitude of
the characters; frenzied nocturnal celebrations followed by the inevitable moment of truth at dawn; processions of numerous comic characters with grotesque or highly amusing physical traits captured by
traveling shots or surveyed by slow pans.[22] Since the variety theater
is an art form that privileges illusion over reality, fiction over fact,
and, like Melina Amour's quick-change routine, the effortless shift of
the characters from one dramatic role to another, it becomes the perfect background against which Fellini's comic unmasking of Checco's
weaknesses and flaws unfolds.

Checco's character is revealed most memorably by the confrontation
between Checco and Liliana after she has abandoned him for a more
promising night on the town with a rich theatrical producer, revealing
her mercenary nature in sharp contrast to the faithfulness of Melina
Amour. Checco waits dejectedly for her return, and when he reminds
Liliana of what he has done for her in the past and suggests that she
should share his bed as a demonstration of her gratitude, she demurely
agrees without a moment's hesitation. Checco thus catches a brief
glimpse of Liliana's true face behind the mask of innocence that usually
obscures her shallow character. In this moment of truth, Checco can no
longer maintain his own social mask as a worldly sophisticate. His con-
sternation at Liliana's immediate acceptance of his proposal is so complete that he, too, becomes a more sympathetic figure for an instant,
revealing his own genuine emotions and affection. Checco slaps Liliana
for agreeing to the very thing he most desires and rejects her lack of
morals and commitment.

As Checco walks away, climbing the stairs toward his hotel, we hear
what sounds like applause on the sound track. The poetic necessity of
this intrusive commentary by the directors is unassailable, even if to-

---

[22] For an excellent survey of Fellini's recurrent imagery, see Salachas, "Fellini's
Imagery from *Variety Lights* to *Juliet of the Spirits*," pp. 205–19.

tally out of place in a purely realistic version of the scene. In Fellini's opinion, we have indeed witnessed Checco's finest performance, an action that seems both based on genuine feeling and far removed from the ridiculous roles of the variety theater he usually performs. For a moment (and only a moment, as he subsequently reverts to character behind his pretentious mask), Checco becomes human, vulnerable, and sympathetic. Yet, only a few moments later he is persuading Melina to invest her life's savings in a new company he wants to form around Liliana. This project, too, proves to be an illusion, for without any warning Liliana abandons Checco for a sugar-daddy producer. The film concludes with a double journey in the train station: Checco, Melina, and the troupe head toward the south of Italy and its miserable provincial villages, while Liliana goes first class to Milan and, presumably, a life of stardom and wealth. As if to underline the static nature of Checco's character and his entrapment within his mask, the last shot of the film shows Checco making overtures to another pretty young girl on the train while Melina sleeps peacefully beside him. Checco has apparently learned nothing in his adventure with Liliana and will no doubt continue to betray Melina.

Luci del varietà presents Fellini's essentially dramatic conception of film character within the generic framework of comedy: the potential harm Checco's adventures could have caused Melina never materializes, and our distaste for his actions is mitigated by the sympathetic way in which he is presented to the spectator. "Hate the sin but love the sinner" might well be taken as Fellini's formula for the disclosure of Checco's flaws. The structural pattern inherent in the film's simple plot—the inevitable clash of dreams or illusions with a much harsher reality—will be repeated in the next two parts of the trilogy of character with far more interesting results. Fellini's subsequent ventures into the dynamics of mask and face create more complicated plot structures and join new elements to his narration: in *Lo sceicco bianco*, more sophisticated editing, and in *I vitelloni*, a more complex group of protagonists examined through the ironic perspective of a narrative voice-over.

Lo sceicco bianco marks Fellini's debut as an independent director, but the screenplay derived from a brief outline written by Michelangelo Antonioni.[23] Producer Carlo Ponti gave the Antonioni manuscript to Fellini and Pinelli for the preparation of a script; Ennio Flaiano eventually joined the two scriptwriters, marking the beginning of a collab-

[23] For a discussion of the evolution from Antonioni's story to Fellini's screenplay, quite different from Antonioni's original idea, see Faldini and Fofi, *L'avventurosa storia del cinema italiano . . . 1935–1959*, pp. 252–53; Oreste del Buono, "Un esordio difficile," in Federico Fellini, *Lo sceicco bianco* (Milan: Garzanti, 1980), pp. 7–8; and Fellini, *Fare un film*, pp. 48–50.

oration that lasted through the scripting of *8 1/2*. Eventually Antonioni rejected the script they provided, and it landed on the desk of Luigi Rovere, who occupied the office next to Ponti at Lux. Remembering how competently Fellini had filled in for Gianni Puccini on the set of *Persiane chiuse* until Luigi Comencini took control of the production, Rovere proposed that Fellini shoot the script, arguing that Fellini's past experience with *Marc'Aurelio* was similar to the film's setting in the world of the *fotoromanzo* or "photo-novel." These sentimental magazines were introduced into Italian popular culture in 1947 and soon sold millions of copies. Before the advent of mass-audience television in Italy, such pulp publications occupied the same position in popular culture that television soap opera fills today. There was a close connection between the world of the cinema and that of the fotoromanzo, a fact clearly underlined by the titles of the most popular ones: *Bolero Film, Sogno, Grand Hôtel*. Published in weekly or monthly installments, *fotoromanzi* had a mostly adult, female clientele. Their narratives were romantic tales of fatal passion employing black-and-white photographs of actors, rather than colored cartoon sketches; the balloon containing dialogue maintained the link of the photo-novel to the fumetti.

The passage from *Luci del varietà* to *Lo sceicco bianco* represents a qualitative leap rarely shown in the second film of a young director, underlining how quickly Fellini had mastered the essentials of his new trade by observing the practice of other, more experienced directors. Fellini remembers his first day on the set as a total disaster. His task was to complete a scene involving a small boat with two passengers in the middle of the sea. Having absolutely no idea how to approach such a difficult task, Fellini was understandably terrified. A flat tire delayed his arrival on the set but gave the young man the opportunity to pray for guidance at a roadside church. Unfortunately, in the church Fellini saw a catafalque he understandably interpreted as a bad omen. He spent the entire first day on his set walking around on the beach in the sun, pretending to his crew and producer that he was deep in thought, while actually trying to imagine how the directors for whom he had written scripts would have resolved the scene's technical complexities: "Rossellini, the inimitable, the unpredictable, came to mind almost exclusively. How would Roberto have done it?"[24]

That night, a worried producer called a meeting with Fellini that could have meant his dismissal, since Rovere had shown no hesitation in firing Puccini from the set of *Persiane chiuse* when Puccini's self-confidence failed on his first day of shooting. Rovere pointedly complimented Fellini on his magnificent suntan (the only positive thing to

---

[24] Fellini, *Fare un film*, p. 52.

emerge from the day's work) and asked what he intended to do on the following morning. Fellini's meditation on Rossellini's example must have served him well, for he calmly announced: "I'll do what we didn't do today . . . we'll shoot the ocean scenes on the beach."[25] By shooting the scene on the beach, Fellini meant exactly that—he wanted to set the boat on the sand without taking it (and the bobbing camera) out on the water; the boat's location on the ocean would be simulated by clever camera angles and, if necessary, subsequent process shots during editing. The director of the production immediately objected, but Fellini insisted on attempting his solution. His cameraman thought Fellini's ingenious solution was feasible, and on the next day Fellini completed the scene without difficulty. Shortly thereafter, Fellini ordered the production director off his set and asserted an absolute control over it that he has never since relinquished to anyone: "In short, I reappropriated my film and from that moment on, without knowing anything about lenses, technique, without knowing anything about anything, I became a despotic director, one who knows what he wants, demanding, picky, capricious, with all the defects and all the qualities that I have always despised or envied in true directors."[26] Fellini's biographer suggests that this amusing account may be apocryphal, one of the many legends to have sprung up around Fellini's personality that the director himself either invented or encouraged in order to provide provocative copy for his many interviewers. Indeed, other accounts of Fellini's first days on the set report that Fellini was well in command of the crew.[27] Regardless of the authenticity of his own recollections, Fellini's sudden burst of self-confidence and the clever solution he discovered to resolve a difficult technical problem cannot help but recall his earlier experience with Rossellini and his equally original interpretation of the demijohn shot on the set of *Paisà*.

Lo sceicco bianco expands Fellini's vision of film character beyond the rather simple comic caricature Checco represents within the static plot of *Luci del varietà*.[28] Now Fellini increases the complexity of his

[25] Ibid.
[26] Ibid., p. 53.
[27] Kezich, *Fellini*, p. 171.
[28] The original manuscript of the screenplay of *Lo sceicco bianco* is in the Lilly Library: Federico Fellini, Tullio Pinelli, and Ennio Flaiano, "Lo sceicco bianco," Pinelli MS. 3 (Box 1, IC). It is similar to that of *Luci del varietà* in that it specifies the total number of shots (718) and divides the major sequences with dissolves, numbering the shots within each sequence. It is substantially the same text as that published first in Federico Fellini, *Il primo Fellini: "Lo sceicco bianco," "I vitelloni," "La strada," "Il bidone,"* ed. Renzo Renzi (Bologna: Cappelli, 1969), and more recently in Fellini, *Lo sceicco bianco*. An English version may be found in Fellini, *Early Screenplays*. For critical analyses of *Lo sceicco bianco*, see Rondi, *Il cinema di Fel-*

cast, juxtaposing the personalities of two newlyweds, fresh from the provinces on a Roman honeymoon, and developing their stories within an extremely sophisticated plot structure requiring a very different and more aggressive, intrusive editing style.[29] Ivan Cavalli (Leopoldo Trieste), the husband, is a typical petit-bourgeois product of the Italian provinces, characterized by his mechanical obsession with time and order, physical fastidiousness, and a complete subservience to conventional morality. He is the antithesis of spontaneity and emotion, planning every moment of his visit to the Eternal City: first, the patriotic homage to the Tomb of the Unknown Soldier at Piazza Venezia; then, the obligatory deference to the Church during a papal visit at the Vatican with his relatives. Only after the demands of Church and State have been met does Ivan schedule the consummation of his marriage in the late evening. Given Ivan's priorities, it is no wonder that his wife Wanda seeks an emotional outlet in her photo-novels. In public, Ivan's social mask requires constant fretting over his outward physical appearance, and a burning desire to be perceived by others as a pious, patriotic *paterfamilias*. In the privacy of his new wife's company, Ivan's mask imposes a stern authoritarianism and an overbearing obsession with *her* respectability and purity. His worst fear is that his life will spin out of control, particularly as a result of some minor infraction of his strict moral code by his new wife, causing him a loss of face. Wanda (Brunella Bovo), a naive and romantic but likable daydreamer, has only a single thought during her honeymoon in Rome—to break away momentarily from the rigid conventions Ivan imposes to visit her idol, a ham actor named Fernando Rivoli, interpreted brilliantly by Alberto Sordi. Rivoli plays an exotic character named the White Sheik in one of the fotoromanzi, called *Incanto Blu* (*Blue Romance*), that Wanda avidly

---

lini, pp. 68–99; Claudio G. Fava and Aldo Viganò, *I film di Federico Fellini*, 2d ed. (Rome: Gremese Editore, 1987), pp. 54–59; my own interpretation in the previously cited works listed in note 21; and Jacqueline Risset, *Fellini: "Le Cheik Blanc"— l'annonce faite à Federico* (Paris: Adam Birro, 1990).

   [29] While contemporary critics praise *Lo sceicco bianco* as a comic masterpiece, the film was anything but a box-office and critical success when it first appeared. Initially selected for presentation at the Cannes Film Festival, it was eliminated from this forum at the last minute. After it was subsequently selected for showing at the Venice Film Festival, it was unfortunately screened in the afternoon rather than in the evening. Curtly dismissed by almost all of the critics, it received no prizes and was almost immediately withdrawn from circulation after its release. Its distributor went bankrupt, the film was impounded by the legal process, and the master print was almost destroyed until the rights to it were acquired in 1960 by Cineriz after the incredible critical and commercial success of *La dolce vita*. Re-released in 1961, the film now received favorable reviews, but the public continued to ignore it, and the ticket receipts barely covered the expenses of producing the prints. For details, see Oreste del Buono, "Un esordio difficile," pp. 13–15.

reads each week in the provinces. It chronicles the adventures of a hero recalling Rudolph Valentino and the romantic desert dramas that made the Italian immigrant an international star. Wanda has written fan letters to Rivoli, and after receiving an invitation to visit the editorial office of the magazine to meet him, she manages to sneak away from her hotel room and to elude Ivan's possessive grasp for what she believes will be only a few moments. Her momentary truancy turns out to last an entire day and to be filled with misadventures for both of the newlyweds.

The stage is thus set for a comic confrontation between the conventional values of a husband obsessed with his social mask, and the childishly romantic fantasies of a young woman equally obsessed with living, even for a moment, the illusions concealed beneath the role of respectable and faithful wife that Ivan expects her to perform throughout the rest of her married life. The complicated plot of the film reflects Fellini's ingenious decision to separate the newlyweds as soon as they reach their hotel. He narrates their misadventures in parallel fashion, employing abrupt and ironic cuts between sequences, avoiding more traditional dissolves or fade-outs. Separating the story line in this manner also underlines Fellini's theme of mask and face: one narrative concentrates on a figure dominated by his social mask, while the other traces a character attempting to reject the demands imposed upon her by her social mask and seeking to live out the compelling but secret desires concealed underneath. Ivan's sequences stress his slavish attempts to follow social conventions, while Wanda's sequences display her equally pathetic attempts to bring to life the romantic fantasies she devours in her photo-novels.

Wanda's escape from Ivan to the *Incanto Blu* office to meet her White Sheik, leaving the bath water running over in her excitement, sets the complicated cross-cutting under way. Great attention is paid to the links between the juxtaposed sequences: details in one sequence are subtly transformed or evoked in the next. As Wanda walks to the magazine office, the camera following her path catches glimpses of numerous movie posters, all pointing to the ultimate source of the romantic ideas defining her character in the cinema, the art form that provides the photo-novels with their romantic philosophy. Bells can be heard on the sound track, suggesting that an additional source of deception and illusion in Fellini's universe may also be the Church, a theory confirmed at the film's conclusion when the two separated story lines are finally united in front of Saint Peter's. Wanda enters the magazine's office as if she were entering another world, and Fellini never misses the opportunity to show his audience how silly Wanda's perceptions really are. She encounters an obviously Roman extra, whose accent pre-

10. *Lo sceicco bianco*: Wanda stares dreamily at her photo-novel hero, the White Sheik

cludes any possible doubt of his national origin, but Wanda only sees his bedouin costume and immediately connects him to the world of her White Sheik. She has a "serious" conversation with Marilena Alba Velardi, the magazine's editor, and agrees with her that "dreams are our true lives."[30] The editor suggests that she meet her idol, Fernando Rivoli, during shooting on the set of the photo-novel's production at the beach.

An abrupt cut transfers the action back to Ivan, who learns of Wanda's mysterious departure when her bath water overflows into the hallway and his room. A black African priest, speaking a completely nonsensical language—the comic counterpart of Wanda's Roman bedouin with an all too obviously artificial dark skin—tries to tell Ivan about the spill. Unlike Wanda's assimilation of the bedouin into her fantasy world, Ivan pushes the African away and races off in pursuit of his wife, carrying with him Rivoli's letter, which Wanda had dropped on the

[30] Fellini, *Early Screenplays*, p. 102.

bathroom floor. Another quick cut returns us to Wanda's starry-eyed
departure from the photo-novel office as she witnesses a strange procession of the characters from her hero's narrative, all decked out in Arab
costumes. In her imagination, Wanda's fantasy world merges here with
the world of everyday experience, for she imagines that she sees real
Arabs, not actors about to perform a role in a photo-novel. Nino Rota's
sound track underlines her confusion, for the music is extradiagetic,
not issuing from any rational source in the scene (such as a radio). It is
dubbed by Fellini as a commentary on the illusory nature of this procession of unusual characters. In addition, the strangely clothed characters move down a staircase without any apparent order or structure,
reminiscent of figures in a dream. A rapid cut returns to Ivan on the
street just after Wanda passes by. There, Ivan encounters an entirely
different kind of procession. It is a highly regimented group of *bersaglieri* (shock troops who characteristically march in double time rather
than at a normal pace) playing a patriotic march. Ivan is trapped in their
midst, as if to underline the stultifying effects of his shallow patrio-
tism. Now, the music on the sound track comes from the soldiers
themselves, emphasizing Ivan's domain, the world of everyday reality,
in contrast to the dreamy mood music that marks Wanda's fantasy
world of photo-novels and bedouin adventurers.

By now, Fellini's extremely clever cross-cutting between parallel sequences, each devoted to a single protagonist but containing ironic
commentary on the subsequent sequence treating the other protagonist, has defined the narrative structure of *Lo sceicco bianco*. Reaching
the sea, Wanda finally sees her idol, the White Sheik. His fantastic stage
entrance imitates the mechanism of a dream: we first view the Sheik
in a subjective shot from Wanda's point of view, high above her head
on a giant swing between two huge pine trees. No daydreamer himself,
Fernando Rivoli immediately realizes that Wanda's fascination with
the world of photo-novels might make her an easy target for his advances, and he quickly persuades her to dress as a harem girl and to
perform a role in the episode of the magazine to be shot that very day.
Once again, reality and illusion become fused in Wanda's imagination
as she takes part in the production, living a role the other actors only
feign. Earlier, Wanda had been asked by Marilena at the magazine's editorial office what kind of line might be appropriate for such a scene,
and she had replied: "I'd say . . . 'Oh . . . I feel so uneasy. . . .' "[31] Marilena immediately wrote Wanda's suggestion into the script, declaring
that it embodied "the simplicity of life itself."[32] During the next se-

[31] Ibid., p. 106.
[32] Ibid.

quence, Fellini uses a series of rapid still shots to capture the production of a photo-novel by a still camera. In the process, of course, Fellini reveals to the careful viewer the process of film montage that lies at the heart of his entire film. This sequence represents Fellini's implicit refusal to follow a principle advocated by some neorealist directors, especially Rossellini, who believed that the manipulative qualities of such dramatic editing failed to respect the "reality" they were filming.[33] Even without assuming any possible polemical intent on Fellini's part in fashioning this sequence around the act of montage, the sequence nevertheless demonstrates Fellini's rejection of "humility" toward the camera.

While Wanda performs her role as a harem girl with genuine involvement, Fellini returns to Ivan, who is entertaining his Roman relatives at a restaurant, all the while pretending Wanda is sick in her hotel room. Like Wanda, he too is forced to play a role, but one making him extremely uncomfortable, for Ivan must make imaginary telephone calls to his room to convince his relatives that Wanda even exists. Wanda's role-playing gives life to her fantasies, while Ivan's merely protects his social mask. Just as Fellini made the transition from beach to restaurant by showing the actors eating in both sequences, the shift from Ivan's restaurant back to Wanda's seashore is signaled by the sound track: diagetic music typical of Ivan's sequences, here played on a mandolin by a strolling musician near his table, points the spectator toward the narrative's next jump with its lyrics: "O sky, o sun, o sea."[34] The Sheik convinces the gullible Wanda to sail out into the ocean with him (the sequence that so terrified Fellini when he began the film), and Rivoli tells Wanda a fantastic lie about how he was tricked into marriage by his wife's deceitful use of a magic potion. Just as he tries to force a kiss on her, Rivoli loses control of the boat's sail and is struck several times on the head by the boom. An immediate cut to the opera house where Ivan and his relatives are witnessing a performance of Mozart's *Don Giovanni* follows. The fact that the opera treats one of our culture's most celebrated seducers completely undercuts Rivoli's bungling attempts to seduce Wanda.

By this time, both Wanda and Ivan are trapped in their respective roles. Wanda has tried to create a momentary realization of her empty romantic illusions, hoping to evade her social role as the faithful wife, but her attempts prove more and more unsatisfying. Ivan, on the other

---

[33] Rossellini thought such montage was absolutely essential for the silent cinema but was no longer required with the advent of a mobile camera: "Montage is no longer essential. Things are there, why manipulate them?" Cited in Gianni Rondolino, *Roberto Rossellini* (Florence: La Nuova Italia, 1974), p. 12.

[34] Fellini, *Early Screenplays*, p. 142.

hand, works desperately to protect the respectability his social mask
provides him, but he is equally hard pressed to maintain his performance. Neither of the two characters is really aware of the comedy of
errors Fellini's narrative presents to the spectator, since their role-playing lacks even the slightest bit of self-consciousness. While we laugh at
their mishaps, the other characters in the film begin to consider both
of them mad. When Ivan reports his wife's disappearance with a white
sheik to the police, the officials are ready to have him committed. De-
spairing of ever finding Wanda again, Ivan wanders aimlessly through
the dark streets of Rome and encounters two prostitutes. One, named
Cabiria (Giulietta Masina), will eventually become the protagonist of
Le notti di Cabiria. Ivan goes off with the other prostitute, who is older
and more maternal, thereby breaking his conventional code of ethics
and destroying whatever claim he might earlier have had to bourgeois
respectability. During Ivan's tryst, Wanda returns from the seashore in
the car of a man whose advances she, in contrast to her husband, firmly
rejects. But she realizes that her dream of actualizing her romantic illusions has been destroyed. Deciding to end her life, and bidding good-
bye to her husband, she exclaims: "Dreams are our true life . . . but
sometimes dreams plunge us into a fatal abyss. . . ."[35] Her absurd statement could have been lifted directly from the dialogue of the very
photo-novels that distort Wanda's perceptions of love and life. Her suicide attempt even culminates in a comic gag: Wanda jumps into the
Tiber at a location where the water is only high enough to dampen her
spirits. Rescued, she is taken to a mental hospital, where she seems to
belong.

Alerted by the police that Wanda has finally been located, Ivan rushes
to the hospital just after he has returned from his tryst with the prostitute and with only minutes to spare before the couple must meet his
relatives in front of Saint Peter's for the papal audience. The two
threads of the narrative, so carefully divided and interrelated throughout the film by Fellini's skillful montage, are now rejoined, and Ivan
and Wanda are forced to confront each other in a madhouse—for Fellini,
the ultimate destination of characters dominated by rigid social conventions or superficial romantic illusions. Ivan reverts to his authoritarian role as defender of the family honor, issuing orders to his frightened wife: "You have five minutes to get dressed . . . I don't want to
hear anything . . . now. First comes the honor of the family. . . ."[36]

Just before the couple enter Saint Peter's, Wanda attempts to maintain her innocence before her angry husband:

[35] Ibid., p. 183.
[36] Ibid., p. 194.

WANDA: It's the truth . . . It was ill-starred destiny. But I'm pure . . . pure and innocent . . .

A wave of relief breaks over Ivan, as if liberating him from a horrible, nightmarish dread. For a moment his legs seem to buckle beneath him. He is heart-stricken; a brief sob of release shakes him and he presses Wanda's arm strongly and tenderly against his side.

IVAN (in a whisper, almost to himself): Me too . . .

WANDA (still through her sobs): Now . . . you're my White Sheik . . .[37]

After making this declaration to Ivan, Wanda closes her eyes dreamily, almost swooning at the thought of finally reconciling her desire for a passionate love affair with her White Sheik and the social demands of her role as a faithful wife. But Ivan's worried look underlines his inability to accept Wanda's solution to their dilemma. Since he has been unfaithful to Wanda, he will never be quite certain that she will not pay him back in kind in the future. While Wanda fails in her attempt to substitute a life based on romantic illusions for a respectable, provincial marriage, she now transfers her illusions to Ivan as he becomes the unlikely substitute for her ill-fated White Sheik. Wanda embraces the social form of marriage as her new illusion, and in a sense, her solution merges the world of illusion and reality in an inauthentic and uneasy combination, the existence of which is clearly threatened by its shallow foundation. Ivan remains trapped in the social role that has dominated his actions throughout the entire film. But now his social mask has been cracked by a violation of his rigid moral code and his subsequent insincere declaration of his faithfulness to Wanda. As the couple head into the cathedral with Ivan's relatives, their brisk manner and orderly procession cannot help but recall the earlier regimented pace of the bersaglieri. Comic balance, disturbed by Wanda's escape from the hotel, has now been reestablished following a comic odyssey through Rome. Fellini then dissolves to a long shot of the group entering the cathedral, emphasizing the narrative distance between their inauthen-

[37] Ibid., p. 197. The published scripts in both English and Italian (Fellini, *Lo sceicco bianco*, p. 150; Fellini, *Early Screenplays*, p. 197) present the same misleading description of this crucial scene as follows: "Ivan turns to look at Wanda, but his face darkens again as he sees her gazing blissfully at something. He follows her eyes and finds that the object of her gaze is . . . the statue of an angel atop the colonnade" (*Early Screenplays*, p. 197). The statue in the film is not an angel but a saint giving his benediction. Far from gazing at anything, Wanda closes her eyes in a daydream, and Ivan could obviously never discover the object of a nonexistent gaze. This is only a single example of how unreliable most published scripts of Fellini's are. For obvious commercial reasons, they are usually published to coincide with the release of the film they treat and are usually based on the original screenplay or the shooting script.

tic reconciliation and his own humorous perception of it. The camera (probably placed on a building opposite the colonnade) then pans right to conclude the film with a medium close-up of one of the many statues on the colonnade of Saint Peter's. The statue bestows an ironic benediction on the uneasy compromise between Wanda's romantic illusions and Ivan's conformist morality.

Ivan and Wanda, like Checco before them, remain unchanged. No dramatic epiphany reflecting a modification of their basic nature takes place. Like the traditional comic types they are, they remain essentially mechanical figures, and the repetitive quality of their actions explains much of their humorous appeal. They remain trapped in their comic forms, while Fellini presents such figures without any truly passionate critique of the society to which they belong. The clash of mask and face in *Lo sceicco bianco*, and the subsequent unmasking of Wanda's romantic illusions and Ivan's hypocrisy, serve primarily as a structural device employed by the director in his humorous and sympathetic, and not harshly critical, representation of each character's predicament. From a thematic perspective, Fellini's first two films have much in common. But the greater complexity of *Lo sceicco bianco*'s plot and the more sophisticated technical means Fellini employs in its narration represent a major step toward his mature style. None of his films until *8 1/2* will depend as heavily and so successfully on a dramatic and intrusive type of montage as a means of advancing the story.

After two commercial failures, the astonishing critical and commercial success of *I vitelloni* established Fellini as a director worth a financial risk. Not only was the film the first of Fellini's works to go abroad, where it was warmly received, but it was awarded a Silver Lion at the Venice Film Festival by a jury headed by Nobel laureate poet Eugenio Montale. And yet, the film found a producer only after Luigi Pegoraro's adamant refusal to accept Fellini's proposal of *La strada*, a project on which Fellini and Pinelli had been working for some time. *I vitelloni* also gave birth to a new slang expression in Italian taken from its title. Scriptwriter Ennio Flaiano later explained the term as a corruption of the word *vudellone* ("large gut"), signifying a nonproductive person prone to stuffing himself—a gut suitable only for filling.[38] Fellini recalls hearing the word only once in his native province of Romagna, when an angry peasant applied it to him in a derogatory fashion. Later, when Fellini asked a philologist about the word's origin, he was told that it represented a cross between the Italian words for beef and veal, mean-

[38] Ennio Flaiano, "Il termine 'vitellone,' " in *Omaggio a Flaiano*, ed. Gian Carlo Bertelli and Pier Marco De Santi (Pisa: Giardini, 1987), p. 81. I have also heard another explanation of the term *vitellone* that interprets the word as a corruption of the name of a notoriously wasteful medieval family in the Romagna district.

ing an immature, lazy person without a clear identity or any notion of
what to do with his life.[39] The term was the perfect description for five
listless young males from the sleepy Italian provinces.

The techniques Fellini develops in *I vitelloni* reflect his increasingly
sophisticated narrative style. At the same time, the film's slow, episodic plot is somewhat more conventional than the rapid cross-cutting
between two parallel story lines in *Lo sceicco bianco*. While the editing
of *I vitelloni* is less daring, Fellini's subtle profiles of his more numerous protagonists represent an advance in the direction of increased psychological profundity that leaves behind the admittedly hilarious but
essentially unbelievable and stereotypical characters of *Lo sceicco
bianco*. Rather than a clear narrative separation of two parallel story
lines, in *I vitelloni* Fellini explores the interrelationships of a group of
protagonists whose actions (or, rather, inactions) constitute a form of
social ritual.

Fellini first outlines the pretentious social roles masking the personalities of his protagonists. Then, in moments of intense emotional crisis, these masks are torn away, as Fellini forces the vitelloni to confront
the reality of their faces and the emptiness of their respective illusions.
Three of the vitelloni—Fausto (Franco Fabrizi), Alberto (Alberto Sordi),
and Leopoldo (Leopoldo Trieste)—are examined in great detail. Fausto
is described by the narrative voice-over as the "leader and spiritual
guide" of the group,[40] and of the three central figures, he receives the
most attention. We are informed of his affair with Sandra Rubini, Moraldo's sister (Eleonora Ruffo), and of his attempt to avoid marrying her
when he discovers she is pregnant. We see him during both successful
and unsuccessful approaches to various women—a mysterious vamp in
a dark movie theater; his boss's wife, resulting in the loss of his job in
the shop selling religious objects; and a dancer. Finally, we learn of his
theft of a religious object from his former employer with Moraldo
(Franco Interlenghi) as his accomplice. Alberto, the most pathetic of the
vitelloni, is a weak and slightly effeminate wastrel who lives with his
mother off the wages of his sister Olga, while nevertheless pretending
to know how to protect the family honor from any slip in *her* behavior.

[39] Irene Bignardi, "Prefazione" to Fellini, *"I vitelloni" e "La strada,"* p. 11. This
Italian edition contains not only the screenplay of *I vitelloni* but also a version of the
original story, which differs in some important ways from the original manuscript of
the story conserved in the Lilly Library along with the original manuscript of the
screenplay: Federico Fellini, Tullio Pinelli, and Ennio Flaiano, " 'I vitelloni' (titolo
provvisorio): soggetto e trattamento di Federico Fellini, Tullio Pinelli, Ennio
Flaiano," Pinelli MS. 4 (Box 2, ID). For the English translation of the screenplay, see
Federico Fellini, *Three Screenplays: "I Vitelloni," "Il Bidone," "The Temptations of
Dr. Antonio"* (New York: Grossman, 1970).
[40] Fellini, *Three Screenplays*, p. 6.

Leopoldo is a would-be poet who dreams of staging his dreary plays and hunting in Africa in the style of Hemingway. Moraldo, the most sensitive of the group, is the only vitellone who has a conscience or self-consciousness, even though Fausto's influence often leads him astray. Fausto's friendship also prevents Moraldo from reporting his brother-in-law's escapades to his sister Sandra. Riccardo (Riccardo Fellini, the director's brother) receives practically no detailed attention at all, perhaps in order to avoid the kind of reductive autobiographical interpretation of his work that Fellini has always detested.

The moments of crisis that reveal the flawed personalities behind the roles the three major characters play all have some link to the world of make-believe—a beauty pageant, a movie theater, a carnival ball, and a variety theater performance. Thus, the various settings underline the clash of reality and illusion quite naturally, without the need for Fellini to insert philosophical arguments into his script to advance his discourse on character. We first meet Fausto at a beauty pageant while his future wife Sandra is elected "Miss Siren of 1953." Fausto flirts with another girl as Sandra receives the award and then promptly faints because of her ill-concealed pregnancy. Fausto's evasion of responsibility here will be repeated throughout the film. He immediately tries to leave town, only to be stopped and forced into a shotgun marriage by his respectable father. Just as Fellini had employed the backstage realities of the variety theater or the photo-novel in his first two films as a screen against which his protagonists were to be judged, each successive action set against an environment connected with make-believe reveals the vitelloni's shallow, superficial characters hidden behind their masks. Fausto tries to seduce a beautiful woman in a movie theater with his wife sitting right beside him; at the carnival ball, he begins his scheme to seduce his employer's wife; and during the variety theater performance, he is attracted to one of the lead dancers, with whom he later betrays Sandra. All these activities finally move Sandra to leave him, taking the young Moraldino with her. Her resolution reduces Fausto to tears and desperation, the reaction of a spoiled brat, which, rather than the provincial Casanova he pretends to be, is his true identity. Fausto is finally whipped by his father like the child he is and will always remain before a reconciliation takes place with Sandra that will most likely not last very long.

Alberto's moment of truth occurs during a masked carnival ball, an even more obvious arena for Fellini's presentation of the interplay of illusion and reality, mask and face. Fellini has Alberto dance about the ballroom in a drunken stupor, hugging a giant papier-mâché head while wearing an outlandish woman's costume, as if to set him apart from his stronger and self-reliant sister Olga. Perhaps no other image in all of

Fellini's early trilogy of character more clearly portrays his dominant theme of mask and face than this surrealistic dance between a man in drag and an empty carnival head.

Only while intoxicated does Alberto enjoy a moment of introspection or ask serious questions about the purpose of his life, as he does when he turns to Moraldo and says: "Who are you? . . . You're nobody. You're all nobody! . . . All of you. All."[41] Of course, Alberto really addresses this rhetorical question to himself, and he could never form the query or live with the brutal answer if he were sober. Alberto's illusions about himself are finally destroyed when he returns home from the ball and discovers that Olga has decided to leave with her lover, a married man. As usually occurs in Fellini's films, such a traumatic revelation

11. *I vitelloni*: Alberto dances drunkenly with a carnival head

41 Ibid., p. 68.

takes place in the early hours of dawn. When Olga abandons Alberto, his pompous declarations to his vitelloni companions that he knows how to protect his family's honor from scandal are revealed as the empty posturings they have always been.

The confrontation between Leopoldo's illusions and the sordid realities of his life takes place against the background of a variety hall performance, which features an aging homosexual actor named Sergio Natali. Leopoldo foolishly believes that Natali is interested in his miserable plays, while the old man actually hopes to seduce the naive poet on the beach later that evening. Racing away from Natali's overtures and the menacing shadows with which Fellini's expressionistic lighting envelops this mysterious homosexual, Leopoldo returns to his home, the maiden aunts who cater to his every need, and his comfortable literary dreams—sadder, but certainly no wiser.

Each of the three vitelloni experiences a crisis as his illusions collide with reality. The shock of this revelation causes their social masks to slip for a moment, revealing their more authentic personalities underneath. Their reaction represents a development beyond the completely unself-conscious reactions of Checco, Ivan, and Wanda in similar circumstances, but even the momentary glimpse of truth that occurs in these traumatic moments becomes unbearable in such essentially shallow figures. Their lives move on the surface of reality, and when superficial responses to serious problems no longer suffice, the vitelloni return to the soothing comfort of their womblike family shelters, outwardly pretending to their friends that nothing has changed, yet now privately conscious of the inadequacy of their damaged illusions.

Moraldo is treated differently, precisely because he is not forced to participate in the emotional trials his friends undergo. Instead, Moraldo bears witness to their failures and seems to profit from their mistakes. During the course of the film, he is frequently photographed by himself in lonely, desolate piazzas, often conversing with a young boy named Guido who works the night shift at the train station. Guido reminds Moraldo of his childhood, when personal problems seemed simpler and capable of resolution through facile illusions. As *I vitelloni* concludes, Moraldo bids farewell to Guido and leaves his provincial birthplace for an unspecified future in the capital city.

The story line of *I vitelloni* marks a giant step forward in Fellini's trilogy of character, and the film's undeniable quality has inspired a number of provocative studies.[42] Not surprisingly, these studies dis-

---

[42] For example, see Rondi, *Il cinema di Fellini*, pp. 100–27; Fava and Viganò, *I film di Federico Fellini*, pp. 60–66; Stubbs, *"Moraldo in the City" and "A Journey with Anita,"* pp. 1–16, which discusses Moraldo in terms of the development of an autobiographical hero in Fellini's works; Zygmunt G. Baranski, "Antithesis in Fellini's *I*

agree on the meaning of Moraldo's departure. The original manuscript of the film's story in the Lilly Library contains what most probably is the final version of this scene. Its conclusion differs substantially from that published in a recent volume containing a different, and what I believe to be an earlier, version of the story. Most significantly, the manuscript reports an important conversation between Moraldo and Leopoldo that explains Moraldo's motivations for leaving, material omitted both in the published version of the story and in the final film itself. It presents a strongly negative judgment of Moraldo's departure by the story's narrators:

> "At a certain point you get disgusted . . . ," Moraldo continues with his voice even more disturbed, as if to reinforce the idea that 'I can't take it anymore.'

> "You're right . . . disgusted . . . you've seen us in our true light . . . Yes! Yes! Escape . . ." [Leopoldo says].

> This time a true bitterness that is more accentuated can be heard in Leopoldo's ringing words.

> Escape. They have talked about it on many occasions, especially these two; this is escape. Neither of the two suspects at least for now that this "escape" is nothing but ultimately an act of cowardice: a flight. Neither of the two understands that each of them could attempt a truly courageous escape, and successfully, without needing to take the train to Rome.[43]

This unequivocally moralistic condemnation of Moraldo's departure, which the narrators define as a flight from responsibility rather than a courageous decision to make a new life for himself, at an early stage of

---

vitelloni," *The Italianist* 1 (1981): 24–42; or my own discussions in several works previously cited in note 21.

[43] Fellini, Pinelli, and Flaiano, " 'I vitelloni,' " Pinelli MS. 4 (Box 2, ID), pp. 83–84. This entire conversation is missing from the published story in Fellini, *"I vitelloni" e "La strada."* Since stories are rarely changed after their submission to producers, and most changes after that time are made directly in the screenplay, it is my opinion (based on a telephone conversation I had with Pinelli on 3 September 1989) that the Lilly manuscript is actually the *final* version of the story, since it was preserved by Pinelli himself, who always personally typed the final drafts of the projects on which he worked with Fellini and Flaiano. Given Fellini's complete lack of concern for the philological accuracy of his published scripts, it would not be at all surprising if he submitted an early version of the story to his publisher. See note 8 of Chapter 2 for a lengthy discussion of this question as it relates to two other films, *La strada* and *Le notti di Cabiria.* The published and earliest version of the story, however, represents a less judgmental view of Moraldo, and this interpretation eventually prevailed in both the screenplay and the actual filming of the sequence.

the film's conception underlines the fact that Fellini at first believed that growth toward maturity as responsible adults was the only true "escape" from the vitelloni's predicament. All the film's dissection of irresponsibility, set against the solid, comfortable, and respectable lives enjoyed by the adults of the provincial town, would thus *seem* to lead toward a similar view in the film's conclusion. And in fact, Moraldo's departure has been interpreted by various critics in such negative terms: it is described as "rooted in precisely the kind of mentality that has created all the problems in the film," failing to solve anything,[44] by one critic; as "aimless," and only slightly better than living in a dream-world, but not yet indicative of adult maturity, by another.[45]

While the manuscript of Fellini's original story contains a strong moralistic tone and a clear condemnation of Moraldo's cowardice, this judgmental tone is softened considerably in subsequent stages of the film's production. The screenplay omits the conversation between Moraldo and Leopoldo entirely. In the scene actually shot, one of the most original in the film, Fellini visualizes Moraldo's departure in an ambiguous but sympathetic manner. Moraldo first waves farewell from the train to the young Guido on the tracks. The camera then cuts to a brilliant subjective tracking shot past the four sleeping vitelloni Moraldo abandons. This perspective is clearly impossible from a logical point of view, but it is absolutely appropriate to indicate the character's subjective state of mind. The camera follows Moraldo's thoughts, moving through each of the bedrooms and passing over each of his friends with a nostalgic caress.

Fellini has always tried to avoid completely logical conclusions and moral judgments in his films, and the evolution in the ending of *I vitelloni* from story to screenplay to final film reflects such a refusal to pass final judgment on his characters:

My films don't have what is called a final scene. The story never reaches its conclusion. Why? I think it depends on what I make of my characters. It's hard to put it—but they're a kind of electrical wire, they're like lights that don't change at all but show an unchanging feeling in the director from start to finish. They cannot evolve in any way; and that's for another reason. I have no intention of moralizing, yet I feel that a film is the more moral if it doesn't offer the audience the solution found by the character whose story is told. . . . If films like *I vitelloni*, *La strada*, and *Il bidone* leave the audience with this feeling, mixed with a slight uneasiness, I think they have achieved their object. . . . If I were a political animal, in order to explain this I should hold meetings or join a political

[44] Burke, *Federico Fellini*, p. 24.
[45] Baranski, "Antithesis in Fellini's *I vitelloni*," p. 32.

party; or go out barefoot and dance in the streets. If I had found a solution, and if I were able to explain it convincingly and in good faith, then of course I should not be a storyteller or a filmmaker.[46]

At the end of *I vitelloni*, Moraldo seems to stand on the brink of experiencing an epiphany, the kind of conversion suggested by the protagonists and the moving conclusions of Fellini's subsequent works.[47] True to his preference for avoiding a clear message or moral, however, Fellini simply leaves the question of any resolution open for his audience. It is clear that Moraldo has learned something from his experiences, but we are offered no real means of confirming that his escape to Rome will have a maturing effect. We feel he hopes to accept the responsibilities of adult life and to abandon the puerile illusions dominating the lives of his vitelloni friends, but Fellini precludes the possibility of our ever knowing with any confidence whether he will succeed or not. And Fellini is quite correct in believing that this refusal to provide a "resolution" causes an audience to examine Moraldo's dilemma in a more honest manner than if he had provided an edifying finale.

A number of stylistic features set *I vitelloni* apart from Fellini's first two films. In the first place, Fellini seems to have found the perfect camera style to match the listless, purposeless lives of his characters, preferring slow tracks over any other kind of shot. His typical editing pattern combines dissolves between long sequences with more abrupt cuts within the individual sequences, producing a rhythm that strings together a series of what are essentially brief episodes governed by their own internal logic. There are a few notable and highly dramatic zoom shots—first of Sandra when she becomes ill at the beauty pageant; later upon Sandra again after Moraldino's birth; and finally of Fausto when his father beats him. There is also an unusual freeze-frame, something Fellini rarely employs in any of his films, which immobilizes the young Guido as he is walking the rails toward town after Moraldo's departure. In the Italian print, however, this shot is virtually covered up by the end titles, and its rather unobtrusive presence is perhaps not so significant, as a recent interpretation of the film argues.[48] But the few freeze-

---

[46] Fellini, *Fellini on Fellini*, pp. 150–51.

[47] In previous discussions of this film (see citations in note 21 of this chapter), I overemphasized the extent of Moraldo's change at the finale. Taking the original manuscript of the story and the film's evolution into account, it now seems clear to me that Fellini has moved from a condemnation of Moraldo's escape to a conclusion that leaves the meaning of his departure open to various interpretations.

[48] Burke, in *Federico Fellini* (p. 26) maintains that the freeze-frame "finalizes the victory of static convention over vital individuality and the reduction of love to paternal authority." But besides the extremely brief length of time the shot appears on the screen, the shot is subsequently obscured by the end titles, and Guido is far into

frames and zoom shots that exist fail to counter the predominance of slow tracks in *I vitelloni*.

While the camera usually respects the point of view of the narrator and is therefore objective, omniscient, and ironic, there are a number of extremely subjective shots that stand out in the film—the one reflecting Moraldo's emotions as he departs; several shots communicating Sandra's shame and guilt after she faints; and, perhaps most memorable, Alberto's drunken dance in drag around the ballroom floor. The most remarkable stylistic development in the film is produced by the presence of a narrative voice-over, which intervenes in the film some fourteen times. In traditional fashion, this narrator naturally serves to tie together the loose ends of the episodic stories, announcing the passage of time, new events that will influence the protagonists' lives, and so forth. But the point of view of Fellini's voice-over is purposefully ambiguous. At the beginning of the film, the voice-over introduces the five vitelloni and includes the narrator as one of their group: "Everybody's here, and of course we're here too—the Vitelloni."[49] Fellini never reveals the true identity of the voice-over. He may well represent Moraldo in the future, since the voice has an omniscient character and knows how the story will end. He may also represent Fellini's own point of view, since his public image is that of an ex-vitellone. Its last intrusion reports Fausto's shaky reconciliation with Sandra and announces Moraldo's departure: "The story of Fausto and Sandra ends here, for now. As for that of Leopoldo, of Alberto, of Riccardo, of all of us, you can imagine for yourselves. We were always talking about leaving, but one of us, one morning, without a word to anybody, did leave."[50] The foreboding words "for now" cast doubt on the future of Fausto's marriage and remind us that only Moraldo has any hope of escaping this provincial prison and changing his personality.[51] Elsewhere the narrator's ironic perspective provides the viewer with a cue as to how various events are to be interpreted. When Fausto's marriage takes place, the narrator's description ("it was a lovely wedding, even if it was prepared a little hastily")[52] confirms our earlier suspicions that Sandra was pregnant when she went to the altar. Later, before the crucial carnival scene, the narrator reports that the "most important

---

the background when the frame freezes. Since the most unusual shot of the entire film, that of Moraldo's departure, has just occurred, Burke may have forced a point here.

[49] Fellini, *Three Screenplays*, p. 5.

[50] Ibid., p. 130.

[51] Baranski, in "Antithesis in Fellini's *I vitelloni*" (p. 33) emphasizes the importance of this remark.

[52] Fellini, *Three Screenplays*, p. 23.

things that happened" in the vitelloni's lives were Riccardo's new moustache, Alberto's new sideburns, and Fausto's decision to shave his moustache,[53] thereby ironically emphasizing their static immobility. The narrative voice-over forces the viewer to share the narrator's sympathetic perspective on the vitelloni and undercuts any strongly negative moral judgment of the characters' lives. We are convinced that the vitelloni lack a sense of responsibility, yet we are also subtly persuaded by the narrator that the world of the vitelloni also contains a potential for joyful living that is not entirely to be disparaged. The narrative voice thus reinforces Fellini's ambivalent conclusion, in which any clear-cut denunciation of his protagonists becomes impossible.

Fellini's trilogy of character moves away from any programmatic notion of cinematic realism and points toward the evocative, poetic representations of a private fantasy world that characterize his next three feature films. His protagonists, engaged in comic defenses of social masks that are eventually uncovered to reveal more authentic emotions and fantasies, are obviously out of place in a neorealist cinema that explains characters by their socioeconomic status or ideological beliefs. Moreover, Fellini's settings—dance halls, movie theaters, beauty contests, carnivals, and photo-novels—underline his growing interest in the world of spectacle, illusion, and make-believe, which achieve artistic significance only in the private and personal mythology that Fellini is in the process of developing with these early works. The protagonists of these three films are measured, yet not judged, against the conventional morality of Fellini's middle-class background, and while they are always found wanting, they also reveal an intriguing capacity for dreams and fantasies that Fellini obviously admires. Various narrative techniques (aggressive editing, subjective shots at crucial moments in the narrative, an omniscient but ironic voice-over) all contribute in moving Fellini's cinema away from the mere representation of Italian society toward an independent and highly original vision of the world.

Immediately after *I vitelloni*, however, Fellini shot a single brief episode, *Un'agenzia matrimoniale*, as his contribution to *Amore in città*, a film composed of six different stories by six different directors.[54] The

[53] Ibid., p. 55.

[54] No published script of this film exists, nor does the Lilly collection contain any of the project's original manuscripts. Consequently, my comments are based on an analysis of both the Italian and the American prints. In addition to Fellini's episode, the other brief films are: *Paradiso per tre ore* by Dino Risi; *Tentato suicidio* by Antonioni; *Gli italiani si voltano* by Lattuada; *La storia di Caterina* by Francesco Maselli; and Carlo Lizzani's *L'amore che si paga*, which was cut from the original American version by the Italian government because it revealed that the world's oldest

project originated with Cesare Zavattini, the scriptwriter for Vittorio De Sica's neorealist classics, whose important theoretical statements on neorealism advocated the rejection of fictitious stories and a documentary style that avoided traditional Hollywood codes. Zavattini felt that even the most important neorealist classics, including the ones he scripted, were still tied too closely to fictional plots:

> This powerful desire of the cinema to see and to analyze, this hunger for reality, for truth, is a kind of concrete homage to other people, that is, to all who exist. This, among other things, is what distinguishes neorealism from the American cinema. In effect, the American position is diametrically opposed to our own: whereas we are attracted by the truth, by the reality which touches us and which we want to know and understand directly and thoroughly, the Americans continue to satisfy themselves with a sweetened version of truth produced through transpositions.[55]

With *Amore in città*, Zavattini proposed to avoid such "transpositions" by the creation of a new style of cinema, comparable to journalism and cinema verité—the *film inchiesta* or film inquiry. It would employ nonprofessional actors, the very people who had lived the events represented within the various episodes, and these film inquiries would appear on a regular basis like a magazine. Each film would treat the same topic but would be filmed by a number of different directors. Zavattini believed the project, if successful, would advance his desire to turn Italian neorealism away from presenting reality through metaphor toward the simple representation of daily life itself.

Almost everything about Fellini's episode undercuts Zavattini's intentions. Indeed, it is difficult to understand why Zavattini even asked Fellini to contribute to a project so far removed from Fellini's own style. A possible explanation may be found in the fact that some Italian critics viewed *I vitelloni* as a neorealist exposé of Italian provincial life and a denunciation of its shallow, bourgeois values. The frame surrounding the six different episodes opens with the somewhat pompous announcement that the film to follow will present a new kind of magazine journalism—cinema news—as a hand turning the pages of a mag-

---

profession was practiced in Italy! For discussions of Fellini's episode treating the film as a minor and somewhat insignificant work, see Rondi, *Il cinema di Fellini*, pp. 122–27; Fava and Viganò, *I film di Federico Fellini*, pp. 67–68; and Kezich, *Fellini*, pp. 207–11. Interpretations that stress, on the other hand, the crucial role the film plays in the evolution of Fellini's style beyond neorealism toward a cinema of poetry include my own *Italian Cinema: From Neorealism to the Present*, pp. 100–102; and Burke's *Federico Fellini*, pp. 31–35.

[55] Cesare Zavattini, "A Thesis on Neo-Realism," in *Springtime in Italy*, ed. Overbey, p. 69.

azine displays the credits; a narrative voice-over assures the viewer of the film's "objectivity" and notes that only the most unusual and poignant stories have been selected, portrayed by the very people who lived them.

Fellini's contribution is a fantastic invention that he apparently convinced the gullible Zavattini had actually occurred. In it, a reporter poses as a prospective client and goes to a marriage agency to find a woman willing to marry a friend who is a werewolf! Fellini employs a voice-over narrator, the technique of *I vitelloni*, but unlike the unidentified and ambiguous narrator of *I vitelloni*, the narrator here is clearly labeled as the reporter himself, who recounts the story from the perspective of the future after his investigation is completed. The narrator attempts to combine his objective account of the story and his own subjective involvement in it as a major character. The reporter (Antonio Cifariello) is introduced by the agency to Rosanna (Livia Venturini), who declares her willingness to marry the werewolf as long as he is "good." She comes from a poor family and obviously has no prospects of a better marriage.

By the time the reporter has convinced Rosanna that she would make a good match for his friend, he has become involved in the story itself. Far from being an objective observer of reality, his own fictitious cover story has begun to set in motion a chain of events that will profoundly alter Rosanna's life, causing her disappointment when she learns of his ruse after raising her hopes for a new life. Realizing the impact his desire for a "true story" has had upon the girl, the reporter abruptly tells Rosanna to forget the idea, drives her back to town without saying a word, and dismisses her with a curt "good luck" as he abandons her on the curb. The vaunted "objectivity" of Zavattini's investigative reporting has suddenly been revealed to be, instead, an insensitive exploitation of the intimate feelings of another human being. It promises no privileged path to the discovery of any important "truths" about the nature of love in the city. While evolving beyond his trilogy of character in his own films, Fellini turns the unmasking operation of his first three films against Zavattini's theories of cinematic realism and objectivity. Stripping away the presumptuous mask of "objectivity" worn by an investigative reporter reveals a far more arrogant and unlikable personality than any of those Fellini had created in his first three films. With *Un'agenzia matrimoniale*, Fellini boldly announces his determination to leave the dispassionate representation of social reality to others. His subsequent films embody an entirely different approach to the aesthetics of the cinema.

Following the trilogy of character, Fellini's subsequent trilogy of salvation or grace—*La strada, Il bidone, Le notti di Cabiria*—marks an

12. *Un'agenzia matrimoniale*: after raising a young girl's hopes of a good marriage, the journalist abandons her on the sidewalk

even sharper break with his neorealist heritage. *La strada*, a film Fellini has described as "really the complete catalogue of my entire mythical world,"[56] represents the director's first mature exposition of a personal mythology of his own creation within a self-consciously poetic cinema. Yet, the surroundings of the film's characters seem lifted directly from a textbook definition of neorealist style—stark landscapes, poverty-stricken peasant families, real locations in the small towns of provincial Italy, nonprofessional actors portraying a number of minor characters.[57]

[56] Cited in Federico Fellini, *Federico Fellini's "Juliet of the Spirits,"* ed. Kezich, p. 30.

[57] The Italian shooting script can be examined in Fellini, *"I vitelloni" e "La strada,"* although this edition ignores a number of major revisions of the script that took place during the shooting and editing. The most accurate guide to the film, containing minute descriptions of all shots and editing techniques, is Fellini, *"La Strada": Federico Fellini, Director,* which contains not only the continuity script but

In spite of his ambivalent views on the Church as a social institution, Fellini has never concealed his admiration for the ethical teachings of Christianity; in fact, he makes them the center of his trilogy of salvation or grace. He considers Jesus Christ "the greatest person in the history of the human race," and maintains that "he continues to live on in anyone who sacrifices himself for his neighbor."[58] If there is a "message" in the films Fellini produced before *La dolce vita*, it is a familiar one, Christ's admonition to love one's neighbor: "It seems to me that . . . yes, all my films turn upon this idea. There is an effort to show a world without love, characters full of selfishness, people exploiting one another, and, in the midst of it all, there is always—and especially in the films with Giulietta—a little creature who wants to give love and who lives for love."[59] In 1957, writing to a Jesuit priest, Fellini defined his views in this manner: "Perhaps my spiritual world is, in fact, this

---

a number of variants from the shooting script, as well as the most complete anthology of critical statements on the film. In spite of Fellini's declaration that the story for *La strada* has been lost (Fellini, *"I vitelloni" e "La strada,"* p. 175), the Lilly collection contains both an early and a final draft of the story, as well as an early and final draft of the screenplay. When Tullio Pinelli had these materials bound years ago, either he or the binder apparently switched their logical order. The earlier version of the story and the final version of the screenplay were bound in one volume: Fellini and Pinelli, "La strada: soggetto e sceneggiatura," Pinelli MS. 5 (Box 2, IE). The final copy of the story and an earlier version of the script were grouped together in another folder: Fellini and Pinelli, "La strada," Pinelli MS. 7 (Box 3, IIA). Unlike Fellini's first four films, the critical literature on *La strada* is voluminous and includes important statements by such critics as André Bazin and Guido Aristarco, to mention only those involved in the debate that erupted at the Venice Film Festival of 1954. The most accessible sampling of these materials may be found in either my *Federico Fellini: Essays in Criticism*; or Fellini, *"La Strada": Federico Fellini, Director*. The first volume reprints the major documents in the debate over neorealism and a number of major critical studies of the film. The critical edition of the continuity script includes the documents relevant to the Venice debate, a number of freshly translated articles on the film's creation, contemporary reviews of the film, and two critical essays by Peter Harcourt and Frank Burke. Additional material on the film's creation may be found in Faldini and Fofi, *L'avventurosa storia del cinema italiano . . . 1935–1959*, pp. 329–31, 374–75; in Kezich, *Fellini*, pp. 212–31; and in Bignardi, "Prefazione" to Fellini, *"I vitelloni" e "La strada."* See also the following detailed analyses of the film: Marcus, *Italian Film in the Light of Neorealism*, pp. 144–63, the best of recent discussions; Rondi, *Il cinema di Fellini*, pp. 128–41; Fava and Viganò, *I film di Federico Fellini*, pp. 69–74; and Donald Costello, *Fellini's Road* (Notre Dame, Ind.: University of Notre Dame Press, 1983), pp. 5–31. Almost every publication on Fellini mentions *La strada* in some detail, but see especially Stuart Rosenthal, *The Cinema of Federico Fellini* (South Brunswick, N.J.: A. S. Barnes, 1976). In addition, Fellini's own comments may be examined in *Fare un film*, pp. 57–60, or *"La Strada": Federico Fellini, Director*; and in Fellini, *Fellini on Fellini*.

[58] Fellini, *Fellini on Fellini*, p. 57.

[59] Ibid., pp. 56–57.

instinctive wish to do good to those who know only evil, to make them catch a glimpse of hope, of the chance of a better life, and to find in everyone, even the worst intentioned, a core of goodness. . . . My films are born not from logic but from love."[60]

Such a traditional Christian perspective could not fail to irritate "progressive" or Marxist critics. *La strada* was awarded a Silver Lion at the Venice Film Festival with a jury presided over by Ignazio Silone, the ex-Communist whose novels blend socialist ideals and Christian imagery. The same jury ignored Luchino Visconti's *Senso*, angering leftists who considered the film a major step beyond neorealism's accounts of Italian daily life toward a "critical" realism comparable to the grand tradition of the nineteenth-century European novel. As a result of the slight to Visconti, the critical debate boiled over into actual fisticuffs at the festival. Moraldo Rossi, Fellini's assistant director, attempted to take away a whistle that Visconti's assistant director, Franco Zeffirelli, was using to disrupt the ceremonies, and the police intervened to stop the ensuing brawl. It was not uncommon to hear such remarks as "Where was Zampanò when the partisan war was being fought?"[61] Guido Aristarco, the Marxist director of the influential journal *Cinema nuovo*, never stooped quite so low, but even Aristarco rejected *La strada* and its poetic cinema on purely ideological grounds, accusing Fellini of gathering up and jealously preserving "the subtlest poisons" of prewar literature, and carrying on "the tradition of the poetry of the solitary man, a poetry in which each story, instead of being reflected, lived within the reality of the narrative, is, through a process of individualization, reabsorbed into itself and nullified as an historical entity only to be converted into a symbolic diagram, a legend, a myth."[62] Praising both the earlier *I vitelloni* and the subsequent *Le notti di Cabiria* for their presumably realistic critiques of Italian social conditions, Aristarco liquidated *La strada* in a few words: "We don't say, nor have we ever said, that *La Strada* is a badly directed and acted film. We have declared, and do declare, that it is *wrong*; its perspective is wrong."[63] Astonished to this day by the ferocity of the debate swirling around him and his film, and entirely without having invited such an ideological battle, Fellini was surprised to find himself identified as the leader of a spiritualist reaction against cinematic realism even though extremely conservative church circles looked with equal suspicion on his

[60] Ibid., pp. 65–66.

[61] Cited in Bignardi, "Prefazione" to Fellini, *"I vitelloni" e "La strada,"* p. 17.

[62] Guido Aristarco, "Italian Cinema," in Fellini, *"La Strada": Federico Fellini, Director,* p. 204.

[63] Guido Aristarco, "Guido Aristarco Answers Fellini," in Fellini, *"La Strada": Federico Fellini, Director,* p. 209.

work and would eventually, in the case of *Le notti di Cabiria* or *La dolce vita*, even attempt to have his films censored. As Fellini remarked, "the trouble with *La Strada* is that the Church seized on it, used it as a flag. The return to spirituality. So *Cinema Nuovo* turned against it. I assure you, if *Cinema Nuovo* had praised it first, the Church might very well have turned against it. It is very hard to see a work for what it is, without prejudice."[64] The most original critic of the period, André Bazin, saw Aristarco's constrictive definition of Italian neorealism for what it really was, a "substitution for socialist realism, whose theoretical and practical barrenness unfortunately does not need to be demonstrated."[65]

Fellini's preference for a poetic or lyrical cinematic style over any realistic approach to his stories becomes immediately evident in his choice of protagonists for *La strada*. Fellini's characters reflect a multilayered array of symbolic possibilities not exhausted by their socioeconomic conditions. Gelsomina (Giulietta Masina), the young woman who is bought from her impoverished mother by Zampanò (Anthony Quinn), a performer and strongman in a traveling circus, is described by her mother as "a bit strange" and "not like the other girls" (shot 9).[66] A more uncharitable view of Gelsomina might even consider her retarded or dim-witted. Yet, this sympathetic waif who knows almost nothing about the everyday world possesses a special ability to communicate with children, animals, and even inanimate objects. She knows, for example, when it is about to rain (shot 60). She has a strange affinity with nature and seems most at home by the seashore, where Zampanò encounters her. Once, in a moving shot (133), Gelsomina walks by a solitary tree and imitates with her arms the angle of its only branch. Immediately afterward, she listens enraptured to the almost musical sound of the telegraph wires that only she seems capable of hearing. When she confronts Osvaldo, a freakish child whose embarrassed parents keep the little boy hidden in a farmhouse attic (shots 163–75), only Gelsomina understands the nature of his silent suffering, loneliness, and inner pain.

Characterized by her costume, makeup, and antics as a clown figure (with clear links to Fellini's past as a cartoonist-imitator of Happy Hooligan and Charlie Chaplin), Gelsomina possesses a special Franciscan

[64] Federico Fellini, "An Interview with Federico Fellini," in Fellini, *"La Strada": Federico Fellini, Director*, p. 206.

[65] André Bazin, *"La Strada,"* in Fellini, *"La Strada": Federico Fellini, Director*, p. 200.

[66] In my discussion of *La strada*, all citations are from the critical edition of the continuity script—Fellini, *"La Strada": Federico Fellini, Director*—and refer to shot numbers rather than page numbers.

simplicity and a purity of spirit that recall some of the characters scripted by Fellini for Rossellini. These unique qualities of hers more than compensate for her diminished intellectual capacity. Moreover, her emotional potential makes Gelsomina the perfect vehicle for Fellini's poetic mythology developed in this first part of his trilogy of salvation or grace. In an important scene (shot 236), Gelsomina is photographed during a religious procession against a wall upon which is affixed a poster reading "Immaculate Madonna." Gelsomina's function in life is to become the means through which her companion Zampanò begins to feel—learns, in effect, what it means to be a human being rather than an insensitive animal. Gelsomina's vocation is revealed to her in a conversation with another clown figure called the Fool (Richard Basehart), who relates to Gelsomina the celebrated "parable of the pebble" (shots 462–69). Discussing the ultimate mystery and meaning of life, the Fool takes up a common stone and declares: "I don't know what purpose this pebble serves, but it must serve some purpose. Because if it is useless, then everything is useless" (shot 466). The Fool convinces Gelsomina that she is somehow destined to remain with Zampanò, who, in spite of his brutish insensitivity, seems to care for her. This realization confirms Gelsomina's sense of purpose until her grief over Zampanò's accidental killing of the Fool leads to her madness, her subsequent abandonment by Zampanò, and finally her death.

Fellini's complex characterization of Gelsomina is paralleled by an equally ambiguous portrayal of the two male figures in her life, the Fool and Zampanò. When we first see the Fool, he is skillfully performing his tightwire act high above a crowd in a provincial square, wearing a pair of angel's wings (shot 244). The religious associations that began with the portrayal of Gelsomina as a Madonna or Virgin figure are taken up by the Fool's initial characterization as an angel, the heavenly figure traditionally linked to the delivery of special messages from the other world, as in the case of Gabriel and the Virgin Mary. At first, the Fool seems to serve precisely such a function in Fellini's poetic mythology. But the Fool also possesses a darker side to his character, a touch of Lucifer as well as Gabriel. Although he is the vehicle for confirming Gelsomina in her spiritual vocation, delivering the message that all human beings need others and serve some positive function, the Fool does not practice what he preaches and once declares: "I don't need anybody!" (shot 473). In claiming that he can survive perfectly well without love, the Fool resembles Zampanò in spite of his seemingly wiser, even religious nature.

The same kind of ambiguity can be found in Zampanò. He is constantly compared to animals in his speech, his behavior, his coarse treatment of Gelsomina, and his promiscuous sexuality. Even his

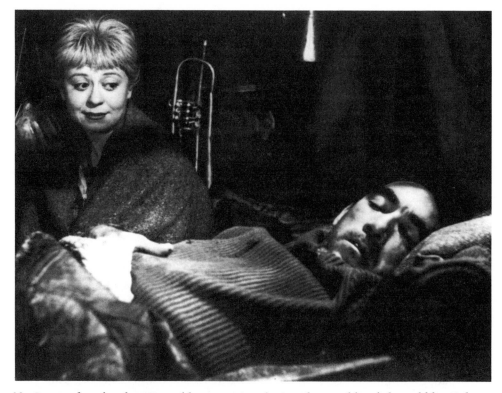

13. *La strada*: after learning of her vocation during the parable of the pebble, Gelso-mina sees Zampanò in a new light

strongman routine, which consists of breaking a chain with his chest muscles, seems devoid of any intelligence or style and depends only on brute force. Unlike Gelsomina, who has a special affinity for children and nature, or the Fool, who is most at home in the air high above the admiring crowds as he performs his amazing feats on the high wire, Zampanò's element is the solid earth. It is there on his knees that he shatters the chains around his chest, and it is there that he often lies in a drunken stupor. Yet, the Fool and Zampanò have qualities in common, particularly a form of selfishness. Each of them believes he can live without the love of his neighbor. When Zampanò staggers drunk-enly out of a bar after learning of Gelsomina's death, his pathetic cry echoes that of the Fool earlier: "Cowards . . . ! I don't need . . . I don't need anybody! . . . I . . . I want to be alone . . . alone" (shot 740). But unlike the Fool, Zampanò no longer really believes what he says. As he staggers toward the beach, that special place fraught with symbolic links to Gelsomina, Zampanò slowly looks up toward the stars, overcome by emotion. And it is in that moment that we discover how Gelsomina has profoundly changed Zampanò's character. It is a mark of Fellini's genius that he never specifies exactly what kind of experience Zampanò undergoes at the close of the film. It may well be a private revelation of an important truth. It may be the feeling of an emotion never before experienced, such as his recognition of Gelsomina's love and gratitude for her sacrifice. While this scene can most easily be compared to the religious experience of conversion, Fellini quite clearly stops short of providing the audience with a simple, unequivocal meaning for his closing shot. There is no "message" to draw the film to a comforting resolution. Instead, the film concludes on a moving, poetic image—Zampanò, prostrate on the beach, grasps the sand in desperation and finally sheds a tear (shot 745).

If Fellini's purpose in ending his films without a clear message was to provoke discussion, he was singularly successful with *La strada*. Almost all of the film's interpretations focus on the ending. Some critics argue that, in contrast to Gelsomina's gradual awareness of her spiritual vocation with the circus strongman, Zampanò remains a beast to the end.[67] Other more charitable critics believe that the last scene announces an apotheosis, a radical transformation caused by Gelsomina's benevolent influence.[68] Fellini provides a poetic and therefore ambiguous conclusion, because he is more concerned with the audience's open-ended discussion of the *possible* meanings of the film than with providing a single, ready-made explanation that limits the film's suggestive quality.

The transformation of Zampanò's character from the original story by Fellini and Pinelli through the shooting script to the final version of the film reveals a consistent move toward *rejecting* a definite, conclusive interpretation of the final sequence. Moreover, the transition from the literary phase of the film's production (story and shooting script) to the film itself shows a consistent desire on Fellini's part to replace either theological, philosophical, or literary clues explaining Zampanò's behavior with concrete, figurative, cinematic language, objective correlatives of emotional states. In the original manuscript of the story,

[67] See, for example, Burke, *Federico Fellini*, p. 262.
[68] See Marcus, *Italian Film in the Light of Neorealism*. Marcus believes that Zampanò never changes and is characterized by "stasis" while Gelsomina grows in understanding and love (p. 154); she later adds (p. 159), however, that Zampanò experiences a belated "breakthrough." Costello, in *Fellini's Road*, construes the ending in traditional Christian terms of "apotheosis, of beginning, of sacramental birth" (p. 30). Rondi, in *Il cinema di Fellini*, believes that "without a doubt at the end of the film Zampanò frees himself, with the most believable of cadences, from his mute, confused state of depersonalization and inauthenticity: he opens up to a sense of self and arrives at an understanding of his own situation in the world" (p. 141).

Zampanò is presented within a highly abstract narrative containing literary citations and philosophical concepts. A number of specific details in the story are also completely transformed in the final version of the film. For example, Gelsomina's famous trumpet, with which she plays her heartrending song composed by Nino Rota on a variant of a tune by Arcangelo Corelli, was originally a flute in the story.[69] Gelsomina's discovery of sexuality with Zampanò, very discreetly represented by Fellini, who leaves almost everything to the imagination (shot 64), is described in the story in great physical detail as a terrifying rape.[70]

The most interesting change in perspective revealed by the manuscript of Fellini's original story occurs in what would eventually become the key sequence of the final film, the parable of the pebble. Given the importance of this parable to understanding Gelsomina's influence on Zampanò, the modification of the sequence from story to screenplay and then to the final film provides us with precious insight into Fellini's artistic intentions and the evolution of his thinking during the making of *La strada*. In the story, before the Fool outlines his parable, he somewhat pedantically cites a passage from Dante's *Divina commedia*:

> The devil Charon, with eyes of glowing coals,
>   summons them all together with a signal,
>   and with an oar he strikes the laggard sinner.
>
> As in autumn when the leaves begin to fall,
>   one after the other (until the branch
>   is witness to the spoils spread on the ground).[71]
>
> (*Inferno* 3.109–14)

This celebrated description of Charon in Hell, who gathers the damned souls together for their journey into the depths of the underworld, has been depicted by a number of famous artists, most notably in Michelangelo's *Last Judgment* in the Sistine Chapel. In the original story, the Fool cites only the first part of the epic simile comparing the falling of autumn leaves to Charon's herding of the damned with the oar of his infernal boat, but every Italian schoolboy would recognize the context

[69] Fellini and Pinelli, "La strada," Pinelli MS. 7 (Box 3, IIA), p. 21.

[70] "She feels herself falling with the man pressing against her; this time she cries out from an obscure ancestral instinct, caught up more savagely in a terror she has never experienced. She bites and scratches. But it is a struggle against an implacable and brutal force that immobilizes and annihilates her. Her increasingly hoarse screams are lost in the nocturnal solitude of the fields" (ibid., p. 17).

[71] In the manuscript of the story, this section is in ibid., p. 49. The English translation of Dante is from the standard English version by Mark Musa in Dante, *The Divine Comedy—Volume I: Inferno* (New York: Penguin, 1971), pp. 92–93.

of the passage and the following line, which the Fool omits, that defines fallen humanity as "the evil seed of Adam's fall." Dante's verses imply that Zampanò represents a symbolic *figura* of fallen humanity without hope of redemption. Their presence in Fellini's original story calls for an essentially Catholic or theological interpretation of Zampanò which stands in marked contrast to the essentially poetic interpretation concluding the completed film. Moreover, the story's emphasis on the concept of "nothingness" suggests that Fellini was attempting to give visual expression to a key concept popularized by European existential philosophy, a Catholic variant of which was popular in France and Italy at the time the film was made and of which Fellini was well aware:

> Zampanò stops and listens. He listens to what he has never heard before: the silence. A sudden shiver shakes him from head to foot. It is a shiver of terror. And after the terror follows the dismay for something he has never experienced before, the fear of nothingness. Not the fear of hunger or of prison or of another man: the fear of nothingness. . . . As if struck by a terrifying disease of the senses, an illness he has never before experienced, Zampanò struggles within himself against something that is being born with great difficulty in his animal soul: anguish. In the shadow the noise of the waves repeats itself to infinity, and Zampanò, for the first time in his life, cries. A woman was born and has died for this. The dawn on the seaside is like the beginning of the world. Luminous, new, and innocent like the beginning of the world. Zampanò sleeps soundly on the sand, not like he always does, all curled up and contorted as if in an instinctive, animal-like defensiveness: his arms and legs lie open and abandoned, with the serene trustfulness of an infantile sleep. His face is at rest and human. The end.[72]

The ending proposed by *La strada*'s original story thus applies to Zampanò an orthodox Christian view of humanity (the "evil seed of Adam's fall"), presenting him as destined for damnation if divine grace fails to intervene. The story makes the parallel between Gelsomina's life and death and that of Christ almost too explicit, threatening to reduce the poetic potential in the final scene to a lesson in theology or philosophy. Gelsomina's sacrifice brings about Zampanò's redemption, just as Christ's death and resurrection redeem fallen humanity. Moreover, as Adam's descendant, Zampanò returns to an original state of innocence and purity before the fall at the end of the story.

Such a specifically theological conclusion must have seemed too restricting to Fellini, who sought to produce poetic effects through visual images rather than argue a weighty thesis. The shooting script removes

---

[72] Fellini and Pinelli, "La strada," Pinelli MS. 7 (Box 3, IIA), pp. 101–2.

a number of such elements from the original story, concentrating on a
literary evocation of Zampanò's state of mind without attempting to
define it too precisely:

> Around him there reigns a profound silence. The sound of the backwash
> of the waves fills the night. Zampanò's heavy breathing subsides little by
> little. A kind of ponderous calm replaces the excitement of his drunken-
> ness. He looks slowly around. He sees nothing but the darkness, and in
> the darkness the white crests of the waves on the breakers. Now, Zam-
> panò is almost no longer breathing. Desperate, he is becoming aware of
> the confusing terror which has mysteriously disturbed him during the
> entire day. He slowly raises his gaze up, toward the sky. There is no
> moon. The sky glimmers with stars. Zampanò stares up for a long while
> with the terrified fear of a brute who for the first time views the firma-
> ment. Once again, he turns his gaze toward the sea. A sob arises in his
> breast and causes him to shake all over. Zampanò weeps. The end.[73]

Fellini's transition from story to shooting script removes the explicit
theological symbolism from the story, even though the shooting script
does not preclude a Christian interpretation of the final scene. The emphasis on existential anguish and "nothingness" is retained, since this
notion can be more easily rendered visually in a lyrical fashion. Fellini's
revisions of the original story thus emphasize his constant search for
concrete cinematic equivalents of emotions in imagery or sounds—the
ocean, Zampanò's breathing, the stars, and, most importantly, a single,
all-too-human action—Zampanò's weeping. In the final film, the conclusion produces an intensely moving emotional experience, rendered
with great economy by only two extremely sophisticated shots. The
continuity script's description of these final shots inevitably fails to
render the poetic power of Fellini's imagery in mere words:

> **744. MCU: Zampanò, exhausted and bruised from his earlier scuffle out-
> side the *osteria*. He breathes heavily for some time, remaining motion-
> less, staring into space. The profound silence is broken only by the sound
> of the backwash of the ocean waves. Zampanò slowly looks upward to-
> ward the stars. Then, in desperation, he looks around him. He begins to
> sob and tremble. He stares back toward the sea and breaks into tears.**

> **745. LS: Zampanò, prostrate on the beach, clutching the sand in desper-
> ation as he weeps. The camera pulls away from Zampanò until it reaches
> an ELS from an extreme high angle; the sound of Gelsomina's theme
> builds in crescendo. Fade out.**
> **The End.[74]**

[73] Fellini, "La Strada": Federico Fellini, Director, p. 175.
[74] Ibid., pp. 164–65.

Nino Rota's music plays a crucial role in achieving Fellini's poetic allusiveness. Originally, the central musical motif was a melody by Corelli which was, in fact, played on the set during shooting, as is frequently Fellini's practice. When an answer print was produced, however, the entire sound track was redubbed. The initial shooting script introduced this motif by an off-screen radio that Gelsomina overheard as she stood under the eaves of a house in the rain, waiting with Zampanò for a mechanic to repair his motorcycle.[75] In the final version of the film, Fellini and Rota rejected Corelli's tune for an original Rota arrangement inspired by Corelli. Moreover, the music is first introduced into the film not by an anonymous radio but by the Fool, who is playing it on his tiny violin (shot 375). It is infinitely more appropriate for the Fool to present what will later become Gelsomina's theme song, since it is the Fool who encourages Gelsomina to work in the circus and later, in the parable of the pebble, provides her with a philosophical rationalization of her existence with Zampanò.

Thus, what is traditionally known as Gelsomina's theme begins more precisely as the Fool's theme. Because of the Fool's parable, Gelsomina recognizes her vocation, and her acceptance of her mission is affirmed by the recurring melody she plays on her trumpet. The motif thus becomes *her* theme. The transformation of the musical motif continues until just before the conclusion of the film, where an anonymous woman first sings it and tells Zampanò that Gelsomina has died (shots 721–35). The tune then returns for the last time on the sound track of the film's final shot, but now it has become Zampanò's music. Through its haunting, evocative nature it manages to awaken Zampanò's deadened conscience and quite frequently has moved even the most cynical of audiences to tears. Rota's brilliant music functions here as more than a mere "static or redundant identifying tag," becoming "a true signifier that accumulates and communicates meaning not explicit in the images or dialogue."[76]

Fellini pursues his search for a poetic cinema on a number of levels— in his ambiguous characterization of the protagonists, in his imaginative creation of lyrical images, and in Rota's evocative music. Even in apparently simple shots devoid of dramatic action or complex dialogue, we can see Fellini's constant search for metaphoric expression, exactly the kind of "transpositions" that Zavattini had most feared. In a sequence of three traveling shots in ELS, each dissolving into the next, Fellini shows us first a herd of horses grazing (shot 579); then a small lake seen from a mountain road (shot 580); and finally a peaceful coun-

[75] Ibid., pp. 169–70.
[76] Claudia Gorbman, "Music as Salvation: Notes on Fellini and Rota," in *Federico Fellini: Essays in Criticism*, ed. Bondanella, p. 82.

tryside (shot 581). In another sequence of five traveling shots—three in ELS and two in LS—that also move forward by dissolves, Fellini films a valley shot from a mountain road (shot 634); a wood seen from road-level (shot 635); leafless trees in winter (shot 636); a town built into a hillside (shot 637); and finally a snowy field (shot 638).

All of the shots in both sequences reflect the perspective of Zampanò's moving caravan. Traditional cinematic narrative frequently employs such traveling shots and dissolves to indicate rapid passages through time and space. These shots certainly do serve this purpose in *La strada*, but Fellini also employs them poetically to say something of importance about Gelsomina without reverting to the spoken word. The first series immediately follows the convent sequence, in which Gelsomina learned from a young nun who befriends her that she, too, has a vocation: just as the nun is the bride of Christ and moves from convent to convent, Gelsomina is destined to live with Zampanò and to accompany him on his restless odyssey. The convent sequence thus confirms the message contained in the Fool's earlier parable. As a result, the views of nature in the first series of shots are ordered, calm, comforting, and even domestic. The second series of five shots, however, immediately follows the killing of the Fool by Zampanò. Now, the earlier view of nature is replaced by a more foreboding, wintry, threatening, and desolate landscape: even the town is an uninviting fortress-like structure which repels rather than welcomes Gelsomina. In what might have resulted in a number of insignificant shots, employed by a lesser director primarily to move the narrative forward in time or space,[77] Fellini's lyrical touch dominates every frame. In retrospect, we realize that each of these shots was a subjective shot from Gelsomina's point of view. Fellini has employed them, without the need for dramatic action or dialogue, as reflections of two dramatic developments in Gelsomina's life. Earlier, Gelsomina was content over the reconfirmation of her vocation. Later, her composure and self-assurance have been tragically destroyed by the death of the Fool.

As the concluding end titles of *La strada* run across the screen, we are left with a number of possible and equally plausible interpretations of the event we have just witnessed. Fellini's open-ended narrative, dominated by the director's personal mythology and populated by ambiguous figures deriving their meaning from their emotional impact on us and their potential symbolic significance rather than their socioeconomic status, suggests by its title alone ("the road") a picaresque, non-

---

[77] Marcus, in *Italian Film in the Light of Neorealism*, p. 148, argues that specific references to time and place are omitted in *La strada*, adding to the film's ambiguous tone.

linear narrative structure. The story line traces the journey of Gelsomina and Zampanò from one beach, where Gelsomina is purchased, to
another, where Zampanò finally senses a feeling of remorse and loss.
This literal journey on a physical road is far less important than the
figurative itinerary on a spiritual road the two characters have traveled.
The quest motif, from Homer's *Odyssey* onward, usually embodies a
journey of self-discovery, and Fellini's film follows this venerable literary pattern. Another intriguing viewing of *La strada* would construe
Gelsomina and Zampanò as a complex metaphor for the failure of communication in the modern world. Equally possible, however, is a feminist viewing of *La strada* as a condemnation of the exploitative relationships between the sexes and the emptiness many women discover
within their marriages. Fellini's Italian biographer has also noted that
Fellini first encountered Freudian psychoanalysis in the spring of 1954,
only twenty days before the shooting of *La strada* was completed, and
that this coincided with a profound personal crisis in his life that Fellini
still calls "a kind of Chernobyl of the psyche."[78] He began a few short-
lived sessions with Emilio Servadio, an Italian psychoanalyst in large
measure responsible for popularizing Freud in postwar Italy. Kezich argues that in the light of Fellini's personal crisis, *La strada* can be
viewed as a self-critical interpretation of his own relationship with
Giulietta Masina, a theory that has also been advanced to explain a
later film, *Giulietta degli spiriti*.[79] But Kezich also cautions that Giulietta Masina believes *La strada* represents three different aspects of
Fellini's own psyche and that the three very different protagonists of
the film are expressions of various aspects of Fellini's own personality.[80]

The film can also be read as a timeless and poetic fairy tale, a variant
of "Beauty and the Beast," where the Beast (Zampanò) is transformed
by the suffering of Beauty (Gelsomina). Zampanò's slow transformation
from a brutish and insensitive lout into a human being capable of shedding a tear also embodies a traditional, sentimental romance structure—the love of a good woman that changes an evil man. And, of
course, an essentially Christian interpretation of the film is equally
possible, emphasizing the parable of the pebble, Gelsomina's visual associations with the Madonna, the Fool's "angelic" message announcing
Gelsomina's spiritual vocation, and Zampanò's "salvation" through
the reception of a special form of "grace" that Gelsomina makes possible. This is the interpretation I myself prefer, especially after the man-

---

[78] Kezich, *Fellini*, p. 229.
[79] Ibid., p. 230.
[80] Ibid., p. 231.

uscripts involved in the film's creation are taken into account. But the fact that all of these different interpretations of *La strada* seem entirely plausible underlines the wealth of poetic and figurative visuals the film contains.

It is rare to discover a viewer of *La strada* left untouched by this masterpiece. Yet Fellini manages to foil critical attempts to reduce to merely discursive terms its emotional and poetic appeal. Perhaps Peter Harcourt summed up this irreducibly lyrical and poetic quality better than anyone else when he wrote that the most moving sequences of *La strada* are "essentially dumb" and "defy confident interpretation"; unless the viewer remains open to what he calls "a subliminal level, a level largely of images plus the complex association of scarcely perceived sound," a viewing of *La strada* remains unsatisfying.[81] On the set of his next film, *Il bidone*, Fellini neatly summed up the essential point of view of *La strada* and, at the same time, replied to the critics who interpreted his film as a betrayal of his neorealist origins: "Zampanò and Gelsomina are not exceptions, as people reproach me for creating. There are more Zampanòs in the world than bicycle thieves, and the story of a man who discovers his neighbor is just as important and as real as the story of a strike. What separates us [Fellini and Marxists] is no doubt a materialist or spiritualist vision of the world."[82]

Fellini experienced serious difficulties in making *Il bidone* even after the incredible international success of *La strada*, confirming a general rule governing the director's relationships with various producers. Dino De Laurentiis, the producer of *La strada*, refused to touch the script, and it passed through a number of hands before being accepted by Goffredo Lombardo of the Titanus Studio. Fellini has often complained about the lack of imagination of producers. Even after a successful film, they fear risking money on the director's subsequent film unless it is a sequel:

> After *La strada* I had scores of offers. To make *Il bidone*, which I was then planning? No. To make *Gelsomina on a Bicycle* or anything with Gelsomina in the title. They didn't realize that in *La strada* I had already said all I wanted to say about Gelsomina. They all wanted Gelsomina. I could have earned a fortune selling her name to doll manufacturers, to sweet firms; even Walt Disney wanted to make an animated cartoon

[81] Peter Harcourt, "The Secret Life of Federico Fellini," in *Federico Fellini: Essays in Criticism*, ed. Bondanella, pp. 241, 247; also cited in Fellini, *"La Strada": Federico Fellini, Director*, pp. 240, 246.

[82] Cited in Dominique Delouche, "Journal d'un bidoniste," in Geneviève Agel, *Les Chemins de Fellini* (Paris: Éditions du Cerf, 1956), pp. 128–29.

about her. I could have lived on Gelsomina for twenty years! Why this insistence on sequels? Have they so little imagination?[83]

Il bidone, like *Le notti di Cabiria* to follow, continues the central metaphor of conversion adopted from traditional Christian theology that lies at the center of *La strada*'s narrative. But unlike *La strada*, *Il bidone* lacks any touch of sentimentalism, and what one of Fellini's collaborators has called a "cutting aridity of style" dominates the entire film and sets it apart from the other two films in Fellini's trilogy of grace or salvation.[84] *Il bidone* also marks the beginning of Fellini's departure from the familiar provincial settings and characters of his early works. The film's merciless dissection of moral corruption and materialism in the capital city of Rome represents Fellini's first portrait of a modern Babylon that will find its fullest expression in *La dolce vita*, *Fellini Satyricon*, and *Roma*. And like *La dolce vita*, *Il bidone* is a meditation on death and human solitude.

Il bidone means "the swindle," and the main character of the film is a *bidonista*, or confidence man, named Augusto Rocca who performs his characteristic confidence game while disguised as a priest. The script was originally designed as a vehicle for Humphrey Bogart, an actor Fellini has always professed to dislike.[85] But Bogart was ill during the casting, and Fellini finally decided to offer the part to Broderick Crawford when he happened to see his face on a poster advertising *All the King's Men* in Piazza Mazzini. Crawford was chosen exclusively for his expressive features: "What a huge magnificent face Broderick Crawford had! Absolutely sensational testimony to the film photographer's art: he had only to raise an eyebrow and there was a story in it. Those little eyes sunk in those fat cheeks seemed to be looking at you from behind a wall, like two holes in a partition."[86] However, Crawford (like Bogart) was associated by audiences everywhere with Hollywood gangster pictures, and by casting an American actor associated with this traditional genre, Fellini no doubt also wished to underline his unorthodox and personal departure from the boundaries of a conventional Hollywood genre.[87]

[83] Fellini, *Fellini on Fellini*, pp. 87–88.

[84] Rondi, *Il cinema di Fellini*, p. 142.

[85] In Fellini, *Comments on Film*, p. 151, Bogart is included in a long list of things Fellini says he dislikes. In Zanelli, *Nel mondo di Federico*, Fellini explains his negative attitude toward not only Bogart but also Jean Gabin, an actor with similar mannerisms on the screen: "people who are pissed off from the beginning to the end of a film, like Humphrey Bogart is, have always irritated me" (p. 134).

[86] Fellini, *Comments on Film*, pp. 131–32.

[87] The original manuscript of *Il bidone* is conserved in the Lilly collection: Federico Fellini, Tullio Pinelli, and Ennio Flaiano, "Il bidone: soggetto e sceneggiatura di

Fellini's confidence man represents a variation of the Christian story of the good thief, the character near Christ on the cross to whom Christ promised a place with him in paradise after death. Fellini expands the traditional treatment of the gangster figure and uses Augusto to explore dimensions of human anguish, solitude, grace, and redemption as he had done in a somewhat more sentimental and accessible manner with Gelsomina in *La strada*. The film's plot traces Augusto's descent into a personal hell through five days of confidence games during which Augusto feels a growing sense of remorse for his crimes, even though he continues to commit them, driven by some inexplicable compulsion. The film's structure thus resembles that of *La strada* in its picaresque meandering from one sequence to another through what becomes an arduous journey of self-negation toward Augusto's death at the film's conclusion. Instead of the five performances of the circus routine by Zampanò and Gelsomina, each one reflecting a different stage in the relationship between the two players, five swindles performed by Augusto and his cronies—Roberto (Franco Fabrizi), Picasso (Richard Basehart), and Baron Vargas (Giacomo Gabrielli)—underline various stages in Augusto's infernal descent. The film's opening sequence presents what constitutes Augusto's characteristic signature as a swindler. After burying some old bones and what seems to be a fortune in gold and jewels under a tree on a provincial farm, Augusto (dressed as a Catholic priest) and his henchmen tell the gullible peasants who own the farm how, during a deathbed confession, a thief reported that he had stolen a fortune, murdered his partner, and buried the body and the money on their farm. Seeking to make amends for his crimes, the thief wants the people owning the land to have the merchandise on the condition that they pay for 500 masses to be said for his soul (at a total cost of 500,000 lire). Faced with what they believe to be a fortune, the peasants scrape together 425,000 lire, Augusto gives them a discount on the masses in the name of Christian charity, and he and his cronies divide the profits.

Federico Fellini, Ennio Flaiano, Tullio Pinelli," Pinelli MS. 6 (Box 3, IF). It differs in few critical respects from the Italian script published in Fellini, *Il primo Fellini*. A translation of the Italian script may be examined in Fellini, *Three Screenplays*, but the description of the film's ending in both the Italian and the English script is inaccurate. The essential criticism on *Il bidone* may be found in the following essays or books: Rondi, *Il cinema di Fellini*, pp. 232–43; Fava and Viganò, *I film di Federico Fellini*, pp. 75–80; Bondanella, *Italian Cinema: From Neorealism to the Present*, pp. 134–37; Kezich, *Fellini*, pp. 232–43; Geneviève Agel, "*Il Bidone*," in *Federico Fellini: Essays in Criticism*, ed. Bondanella, pp. 66–79; and Edward Murray, *Fellini the Artist*, 2d ed. rev. (New York: Frederick Ungar, 1985), pp. 84–97. A detailed account of the filming of *Il bidone*, the first of many such hagiographic accounts of Fellini's working procedures, may be found in Dominique Delouche's "Journal d'un bidoniste," pp. 98–157.

Immediately after this successful sting, Augusto begins to have doubts about his life of crime and enters into what may accurately be described as a mid-life crisis at the age of forty-eight. In addition to his personal crisis, after years of neglecting his daughter, Augusto must now worry about helping her make a life for herself.

Augusto's existential anguish increases through each successive trick, most of which are based on exploiting the ignorance of his impoverished victims. All of his swindles are genuine confidence games, stratagems Fellini learned in conversations with a swindler friend known in the Roman underworld as Lupaccio. Posing as a representative of the public housing authority in the second swindle, Augusto collects the down payments for nonexistent apartments from dozens of homeless families. The third swindle takes place during a party at the home of a master swindler named Rinaldo: Picasso tries to sell a fake De Pisis painting without success, while Roberto is caught red-handed as he attempts to lift a gold cigarette case from one of Rinaldo's guests. Rinaldo and his friends represent the elite of Augusto's profession, and the ignominious failure of Augusto's colleagues neatly and economically shows what a small-time criminal Augusto really is. The frenzied activities at Rinaldo's party, highlighted by a strip-tease and stark, expressionistic lighting to emphasize Augusto's anguish and solitude, foreshadow several famous sequences of *La dolce vita*. A fourth swindle consists of buying gas without having money to pay for it and leaving a coat supposedly worth 50,000 lire (but actually costing 2,000) with the service station attendant in exchange for 10,000 lire in cash.

Before the fifth and final swindle, which leads to Augusto's death, Fellini inserts an important sequence into the film that recalls De Sica's neorealist classic *Ladri di biciclette*. As Augusto and Patrizia are seated in a café, Patrizia tells her father that she needs 300,000 lire to post a bond for her new job as a cashier. As Augusto promises his daughter the money, he is recognized by one of his former victims to whom he had sold some fake medicine that almost cost the victim's brother his life. Augusto is arrested in front of his humiliated daughter (who only now discovers her father's true profession) in a scene recalling a similar sequence in De Sica's film, in which the unemployed father's attempt to steal a bicycle after his own bicycle has been stolen results in his apprehension under the horrified eyes of his frightened son. De Sica ended this scene, and the film, on a positive note: as Bruno extends his hand to his embarrassed father, the film offers a bit of solace for human solitude within the comforting confines of the family. Augusto's arrest reveals the essential corruption of his character: although he feels genuine affection for his daughter, he is willing to endanger the life of another person in order to carry out his confidence games.

With the fifth confidence game that takes place after Augusto's release from prison, the plot makes a circular return to the first swindle:
disguised again as a priest, Augusto attempts to repeat his usual swindle. By this time, however, his self-doubt and personal anguish have
reached a climax, and the plot's apparent repetition serves primarily to
emphasize the change that has at least apparently transformed Augusto, who now seems to take his role as a priest seriously. The victim's daughter suffers from polio, which has left her crippled for many
years, and the money Augusto must extort from her parents has been
carefully saved to buy an ox to support the farm. Trapped in his role as
a priest, Augusto is forced to speak to the young crippled girl in this
capacity, and he is obviously moved by her innocent purity and fervent
belief in miracles, a belief Augusto cannot share. As he leaves, he tells
the girl in a sincere voice: "You don't need me. You're much better off
than a lot of other people. Our life . . . the life of so many people I know
has nothing beautiful in it. You're not losing much, you don't need me,
I have nothing to give you."[88]

Augusto's moment of truth is now at hand. After he and his accom-
plices drive off to divide the loot, Augusto informs them that he could
not take the family's money because he felt compassion for the poor
cripple. Augusto's friends refuse to believe that Augusto could enter-
tain such a sentiment, even though Fellini has by this time convinced
the spectator that Augusto has, indeed, reformed after speaking to the
crippled girl. One of them strikes him on the head with a stone, and
Augusto falls, breaking his back. As the thieves search through Augusto's clothes, they discover the 350,000 lire. What was apparently a sentimental act of kindness by a repentant sinner is revealed to be a double
but unsuccessful swindle! Unlike in *La strada*, there is not even the
hint of a sentimental treatment of Fellini's protagonist: Augusto is rot-
ten to the core and lacks the redeeming activity of some external source
of grace, as Zampanò was privileged to have in Gelsomina. Yet, it is
precisely at this lowest point in his degradation that Fellini transforms
this inveterate sinner into a secular saint. Augusto's suffering and anguish have finally qualified him for redemption. As Augusto painfully
crawls up an arid, rocky hill, alone like Zampanò at the conclusion of
La strada, he is now almost as paralyzed as his young victim. We hear
church bells on the sound track as a small procession of peasants and
children pass by on the road above him. Augusto tries to attract their
attention but fails. As the film ends, the camera slowly draws away
from this inverted Christ figure, this confidence man who has experienced an existential hell during the entire film. The camera movement

is a benediction, "a short, gentle movement, one that seems to confer upon the dead man a peace that perhaps only those who have faith can truly comprehend," as one critic has noted.[89]

The precedent for Augusto's miraculous redemption after a life of vice that the last camera movement implies is not to be found in the cinema but, rather, in the poetic masterpiece of Catholic literature, Dante's *Divina commedia*. In the Ante-Purgatory, Dante the Pilgrim encounters Count Buonconte da Montefeltro, one of the souls who delayed his repentance until the last moment, just as Fellini implies Augusto has done. Buonconte is saved from eternal damnation by merely uttering the name of the Virgin Mary in his dying breath. As one of the

14. *Il bidone*: just before death at the end of the film, Augusto struggles to join the procession on the road above him

[89] Murray, *Fellini the Artist*, p. 97.

devils who fought over his soul with an angel and lost it complained, only "a measly tear" (*Purgatorio* 5.107) is sufficient for man's salvation.[90] And that "measly tear" suffices for Augusto as well.

We have already seen how the ending of *La strada* was radically modified from the original story through the screenplay to the final film in an attempt to produce an open-ended, ambiguous conclusion that suggested the possibility of Zampanò's redemption, yet did not force a single interpretation upon the viewer. Dominique Delouche's day-by-day account of Fellini's work on the set of *Il bidone* reveals that Fellini aimed at a similar effect in that film. He wrote three different solutions for this final scene and held off making a choice between them until the last possible minute in his shooting.[91] The first conclusion is the one published in the Italian and English screenplays: a close-up of Augusto as he whispers his final words to the people in the procession on the road above him: "Wait for me . . . I'm coming . . . I'm coming with you."[92] This solution presents Augusto as a traditional tragic figure, abandoned in his spiritual isolation with no hope of redemption. Fellini rejected this ending even before shooting his final scene. Two other possibilities were actually filmed, with the final selection of one of them taking place during the editing process. Mario Serandrei (Fellini's editor) preferred the version in which a young boy in the procession responded to Augusto's anguished cry for help, approached Augusto, and in close-up said: "I can't do anything for you now, but nothing is lost; who knows if in millions of years we won't meet each other again."[93] The close-up of the young boy would set childish innocence in relief against Augusto's mature corruption and solitude. Fellini wisely preferred the third solution, a subtle camera movement following Augusto's dying remarks away from the protagonist up toward the road and the procession that suggests, but does not demand, the possibility of his redemption and absolution. Fellini's "good thief," whose character has been purified by an odyssey through a personal calvary of emotional pain that traditional notions of dramatic structure do not fully explain, achieves his final visual presentation within a conclusion whose poetic ambiguity parallels that which Fellini employed in the closing shot of Zampanò.[94] Fellini obviously felt that a bit of Augusto

[90] Dante, *The Divine Comedy—Volume II: Purgatory*, trans. Mark Musa (New York: Penguin, 1981), p. 52.

[91] Delouche, "Journal d'un bidoniste," p. 154.

[92] Fellini, *Three Screenplays*, p. 252. As is so often the case, the published screenplay of *Il bidone* was taken from the original manuscript and did not take into account changes and modifications during the shooting of the film.

[93] Delouche, "Journal d'un bidoniste," p. 154.

[94] I cannot agree with Burke, who maintains that Augusto's death represents a

was to be found in his own personality, and his sense of complicity prevented any hint of moral condemnation in the final shot. With his subtle camera movement, Fellini leaves open the possibility that Augusto may well join the people on the road, at least in a metaphoric sense, after his painful death.

The presentation of *Il bidone* at the 1955 Venice Film Festival was a disaster, a complete reversal of the positive reception of *La strada* by many critics and international audiences. This unsettling experience would keep Fellini away from Venice for over a decade, until he finally agreed to release *Fellini Satyricon* outside of the competition there in 1969. His absolute refusal to yield to any sentimental conclusion in his portrayal of the film's central figure no doubt played a large part in the film's negative reception: both critics and audiences would have preferred a comforting and unambiguous apotheosis. In addition, a good deal of the negative critical comment on *Il bidone* was motivated by a jealous desire to settle accounts with a director who had achieved the height of international fame with *La strada*. Italian critics have always shown a marked tendency to punish any native director successful abroad, dismissing foreign accolades for his or her work as a sign of superficiality, while praising minor works by American directors as if they were masterpieces.

Le notti di Cabiria, the final film in the trilogy of grace or salvation, marked Fellini's triumphal return to both critical and commercial success. The brilliant performance by Giulietta Masina as the plucky prostitute Cabiria Ceccarelli earned her the prize for Best Actress at the Cannes Film Festival and was in large measure responsible for Fellini's second Oscar for Best Foreign Film.[95]

"kind of empty 'martyrdom' in response to the futility of his life" or that the final shot of the film represents "yet another meaningless renewal or enlightenment, an ascent lacking in any spiritual significance" (*Federico Fellini*, p. 63).

[95] The original manuscripts of both the story and the screenplay of this film are preserved in the Lilly Library: Fellini, Pinelli, and Flaiano, "Le notti di Cabiria: sceneggiatura," Pinelli MS. 8 (Box 3, IIB); and Fellini, Pinelli, and Flaiano, "Le notti di Cabiria: soggetto," Pinelli MS. 9 (Box 4, IIB-1). As was mentioned in note 8 in Chapter 2, Fellini incorrectly claims in the published Italian screenplay that this original story either was lost or never existed. No English version of the screenplay has been published, but a good deal of provocative criticism has been devoted to the film: Rondi, *Il cinema di Fellini*, pp. 158–98; Fava and Viganò, *I film di Federico Fellini*, pp. 81–86; Kezich, *Fellini*, pp. 244–63; Bondanella, *Italian Cinema: From Neorealism to the Present*, pp. 137–41; and two key articles by Claudia Gorbman and André Bazin reprinted in *Federico Fellini: Essays in Criticism*, ed. Bondanella, pp. 80–102. For information about the creation of Cabiria, see a number of brief articles by Fellini, Masina, Pinelli, and Pasolini in Fellini, *Le notti di Cabiria*; Faldini and Fofi, *L'avventurosa storia del cinema italiano . . . 1935–1959*, pp. 374–76; Fellini, *Comments on Film*, pp. 125–30; Fellini, *Fellini on Fellini*, pp. 64–66; and Fellini, *Fare un*

The character of Cabiria had been gestating for some time in Fellini's imagination. What would become the second major sequence of *Le notti di Cabiria* (Cabiria's night out with Alberto Lazzari, a famous actor, played by one of Fascist Italy's matinee idols, Amadeo Nazzari) was first offered to Anna Magnani (who rejected it) as one of two possible stories for Rossellini's *L'amore*. As mentioned earlier, Giulietta Masina appeared briefly in *Lo sceicco bianco* as a prostitute named Cabiria who meets Ivan Cavalli at night in a deserted piazza. During the filming of *Il bidone*, Fellini met an unusual prostitute about to be evicted from her shanty home, and after the woman had conquered her initial reticence, she recounted to the director a number of real and invented episodes related to her work.[96] The script met with the usual stiff resistance from producers, and some eleven or twelve of them rejected the story. Finally, Dino De Laurentiis, the producer of *La strada*, read the story one night by the headlights of his enormous black Cadillac in the Roman countryside and surprised Fellini by immediately accepting the project.[97] The stumbling block was not so much the failure at the box office of *Il bidone*, although this was certainly a factor, but rather Fellini's insistence on treating the subject of prostitution during a time when a furious battle to ban legalized prostitution in Italy was taking place, ultimately resulting in the famous Merlin law of 1958 that finally closed the state-inspected brothels. One of the many producers who turned down the story told Fellini that the subject was a dangerous one. He added that Fellini had first made a film on homosexuals (supposedly the theme of *I vitelloni*), another on dirty Gypsies (*La strada*), and yet another on swindlers, and now he was about to tackle whores. At this point, the producer wondered, what would his next film treat? Fellini immediately replied: "Producers!"[98]

While *Le notti di Cabiria* shares many thematic and stylistic characteristics with the other two films in the trilogy of grace or salvation, it is a far more complex film. As Giulietta Masina remarks, Cabiria (unlike Gelsomina) is no helpless victim; instead, she is a courageous, self-reliant woman who practices her trade without any hint of sentimental guilt or remorse even though she would naturally prefer to lead a normal life.[99] Masina's representation of Cabiria required an even

film, pp. 61–65. It is worth noting that Fellini's *Le notti di Cabiria* inspired an American musical written by Neil Simon and directed by Bob Fosse called *Sweet Charity*. Fosse directed a film version of the musical with the same title in 1969 and used another Fellini film, *8 1/2*, as the basis for his best-known work, *All That Jazz*.

[96] See the Introduction to Fellini, *Le notti di Cabiria*, pp. 5–9.

[97] See "Undici produttori," in ibid., pp. 133–40 (no author listed).

[98] Ibid., p. 134.

[99] Giulietta Masina, "Io e Cabiria," in ibid., p. 141.

more sensitive performance than her portrayal of Gelsomina in *La strada*, a character often superficially compared to Cabiria. As Fellini has admitted, the interior foundations of both female protagonists are deceptively similar. But Gelsomina is a unique and exceptional figure, and the interpretation of her function in *La strada* is ultimately governed by the ambiguous structure of the film's plot, which clearly offers Gelsomina to the audience as part of a fable or parable. On the other hand, Cabiria is more human and identifiable as a part of our everyday world: she is the personification of a state of mind, a "creature who loves and wants to be loved," as Fellini puts it, and the fact that she is a prostitute only reflects what Fellini calls his "taste for extreme exemplification."[100] Thus, while his superficial producers thought Fellini intended in *Le notti di Cabiria* a somewhat realistic denunciation of prostitution that continued the neorealist tradition he had already abandoned, the filmmaker was actually far more interested in representing the inner resources of the sympathetic and resilient character he had created for his wife's sensitive performance. Unlike *La strada*, in *Le notti di Cabiria* there is no Zampanò figure juxtaposed to Cabiria. Zampanò's role is taken up by Cabiria's hostile environment and by Oscar.[101] However, a simpleminded lay brother appearing for only a brief moment in the film echoes the Fool's message when he tells Cabiria that she should work to be in God's grace, since that is the most important thing in life.

An examination of the plot of *Le notti di Cabiria* also reveals structural affinities with Fellini's two preceding films. In *La strada*, Zampanò performed his feats of strength five times, each of which reveals an essential change in Gelsomina's relationship to the strongman. In *Il bidone* Augusto works five confidence games during the course of the film, providing us with a background against which we can assess his spiritual decline. In *Le notti di Cabiria*, there are five major sequences, all focusing upon successive moments in Cabiria's life when she seems at the brink of achieving happiness but each of which ends in failure. I am not inclined to believe that there is any special significance in the number five here. Rather, Fellini simply realizes quite well how long the succession of parallel sequences, usually ranging between ten and thirty minutes each, should last before it begins to seem repetitious to an average audience. Infinitely more important than the number of major sequences in each of the films that make up the trilogy of grace or salvation, however, is each plot's essentially circular, repetitious struc-

---

[100] Cited in Faldini and Fofi, *L'avventurosa storia del cinema italiano . . . 1935–1959*, p. 375.
[101] Ibid.

ture. In *La strada*, for example, while critics unanimously remark on the meandering, picaresque quality of the plot, they have too often overlooked the fact that within this succession of loosely related episodes, not logically connected by any cause-and-effect progression, Fellini has countered the film's picaresque aimlessness by setting it within a circular framework. There is an opening and a concluding scene at the same location (the seaside), with a finale that demands of the spectator a critical interpretation. Similarly, *Il bidone* wanders through successive episodes that can be accurately described as equally episodic or picaresque. Yet, once again, such narrative units are framed by a relentlessly circular plot structure that begins and ends with the same confidence game. The film's conclusion undermines the episodic suggestiveness of the narrative by emphasizing that something singular and unique is happening to the film's protagonist. Thus, while the loose succession of sequences connected like a string of short stories and essentially unrelated by either dramatic or logical assumptions gradually leads the audience to expect no dramatic resolution at the close of the film, the strong sense of closure that surprises the viewer during Augusto's dying moments works in an entirely different direction to counteract, retrospectively, the sense of aimlessness that the picaresque organization of Fellini's story initially implies. The possibility that a conversion or an apotheosis has taken place during the final scene is further suggested by the return of the action to the swindle that opened the film.

The major sequences in *Le notti di Cabiria* follow this same narrative pattern, juxtaposing an episodic and picaresque progression of the action with a sharp shift in direction created by the surprising sense of resolution in the conclusion, which is set in an environment reminding the viewer of the film's opening sequences. In order to fashion a protagonist closer to prostitutes he had encountered in real life than to the kind of ethereal figure he employed in his fable *La strada*, Fellini took great pains to make Cabiria's environment believable, including hiring Pier Paolo Pasolini as an expert on Roman low life to contribute dialogue to the screenplay. Pasolini has argued that a specific means of linking character to environment occurs in every major sequence of *Le notti di Cabiria*: a silent long shot of a location, somewhat deformed or stylized with respect to the norm of "reality," is followed by another long shot of Cabiria entering this environment.[102] Cabiria's physical appearance or attitude stands in sharp contrast to her surroundings. In a

---

[102] Pier Paolo Pasolini, "Nota su *Le notti di Cabiria*," in Fellini, *Le notti di Cabiria*, p. 152. Pasolini incorrectly implies that this technique is employed in *every* major sequence, but it occurs frequently enough in the film to make it one of the distinctive traits of Fellini's style.

setting exuding luxury and ostentation, she is poorly dressed; amidst corruption, she is innocent; and so forth. The contrast is a moral one, implying a social judgment of Cabiria's surroundings by Fellini, even if such judgments never constitute harsh condemnations. At the same time, the juxtaposition of such a threatening setting with the courage and persistence of the protagonist underlines Cabiria's resilience and resolution.

The five major sequences continue the apparently picaresque structure of the other two films in Fellini's trilogy of grace or salvation. In the first, Fellini introduces Cabiria in a long shot as she enters a field (also revealed by another long shot) with Giorgio, a man she has known only briefly but who she is convinced loves her. It is a sentimental, old-fashioned image of romantic love that we have seen hundreds of times on the screen. Our previous film experiences lead us to expect a payoff shot of a kiss by the riverbank, but Fellini deflates the romantic expectations of both his protagonist and the audience with an abrupt reversal. Giorgio grabs Cabiria's purse and the 40,000 lire it contains, pushes her into the Tiber, and runs off, leaving the luckless prostitute struggling in the water. Since Cabiria cannot swim, this sequence almost ends in tragedy, but she is rescued by some young boys swimming nearby. Their reward for having saved her life is to be told to mind their own business! The structure of the action within each major sequence is immediately established here, and in the next four parts the film undergoes a sudden reversal from illusory hope to misfortune and despair. Immediately after this sequence, a brief scene of transition linking the first two sections shows Cabiria walking the streets at the Passeggiata Archeologica. Fellini returns four times to Cabiria's workstation, and in each instance, he stresses the fact that Cabiria differs substantially from the traditional "whore with the heart of gold" figure in film and literature, usually used in order to arouse our compassion and patronizing pity. Quite the contrary, as André Bazin was the first to point out years ago in his brilliant essay on the film, Cabiria has no real connection with the prostitute figures of traditional melodrama "because her desire to 'get out' is not motivated by the ideals of bourgeois morality or a strictly bourgeois ideology. She does not hold her trade in contempt."[103] In the first brief view we have of her work, Cabiria dances an exuberant mambo, battles with an enormous prostitute who teases her about losing Giorgio, and drives off with another prostitute and her pimp in a new Fiat toward Via Veneto and her next adventure. Cabiria is not pictured melodramatically; she is an individualized and com-

[103] André Bazin, "*Cabiria*: The Voyage to the End of Neorealism," in *Federico Fellini: Essays in Criticism*, ed. Bondanella, p. 96.

pletely believable character, fiercely proud of the fact that she owns her own shanty home some eighteen kilometers outside the city limits, and unwilling to compromise her freedom by taking on the protection of a pimp.

In the second episode, opening with a long shot of a city street into which Cabiria enters (repeating the pattern of relating Cabiria to her environment that opens the film), Cabiria meets a famous actor outside the Kit Kat Club, who has just had a fight with his blond girlfriend. The actor picks Cabiria up, drives off with her in an enormous De Soto convertible, and takes her to the Piccadilly Club, where the two dance and witness an exotic African floor show of the kind that Fellini later creates in *La dolce vita*. Cabiria is taken to the actor's elegant home, where she dreams of a sexual encounter that will be the envy of all the girls on the streets, but at the last minute the actor's girlfriend returns, and the lovers patch up their differences and make love all night, forcing Cabiria to hide in the bathroom with a small, whimpering puppy. In this particular episode, Cabiria's ridiculous costume (bobby socks and a short fur coat that seems to have been lifted directly from the back of some nondescript animal) stands in sharp contrast to both the actor's posh residence and the kitsch pseudo-elegance of the nightclub.

In a third section, the progression from romantic illusion to disillusionment again takes place, and once again, a brief transitional scene to the third episode returns to Cabiria's station on the Passeggiata Archeologica, where the other prostitutes tease the protagonist about her night out with the actor and invite her to come with them to the shrine of the Divino Amore. The action then shifts to Cabiria's pilgrimage to the shrine, a popular sanctuary on Via Ardeatina founded in 1744 on the spot where a miraculous image of the Virgin Mary saved a passerby from a pack of wild dogs in the fourteenth century. The immediate excuse for the pilgrimage is to take the crippled uncle of one of the pimps there in the hope of a cure, but all of the prostitutes share an emptiness in their lives, Cabiria most of all, that moves them to go along for reasons of their own. At first skeptical of miracles, Cabiria is moved by the religious fervor of the other pilgrims, and she prays to the image of the Virgin, begging her to change her life. It is here that Fellini's critique of institutionalized religion reveals how incorrect leftist critics were when they denounced him as a Catholic director with a traditional theological message in *La strada*. As the crippled uncle casts aside his crutches and attempts to walk, he falls flat on his face! Fellini's rejection of such mechanical miracles in the lives of his characters is more emphatic in the Italian print than in that released in America, for the traditional intermission at the end of the *primo tempo* begins just after the uncle collapses. Cabiria's prayers for a miraculous change in her life are naturally left unanswered, and her response is to drink too much and to scoff at a group of pilgrims marching off into the distant fields, asking them if they are going out to look for snails.

The fourth section of the narrative unfolds inside a variety theater in which Cabiria reluctantly takes part in a magician's performance, and it allows Fellini to introduce his familiar world of show business into the film. In a hypnotic trance, Cabiria reveals to the audience all her hidden desires: a new life, marriage, children, a normal home. The magician presents Cabiria to an imaginary character named Oscar who asks to marry her, but when Cabiria wants to know if Oscar really loves her, the magician breaks her trance as if to suggest that illusion may allow us to express our secret desires but cannot bear a confrontation with reality or supply us with a permanent source of happiness. Cabiria leaves the theater with the audience's cruel laughter ringing in her ears, bringing this brief but crucial section to a close.

The fifth and longest episode begins immediately outside the theater, where Cabiria encounters a man named Oscar—a name identical to that of the imaginary character in her hypnotic trance. In contrast to the insensitive audience, Oscar (François Périer) convinces Cabiria that he has been moved by the confessions of her pure and innocent desires and asks to see her again. Thus, in a Pirandellian twist to a plot that has primarily stressed Cabiria's harsh environment, reality begins to imitate the world of art and illusion: a figure from Cabiria's psyche materializes before her very eyes. Cabiria soon falls in love with Oscar, who offers to marry her and take her away to a small town in the Roman hills to work in a shop. During Oscar's courtship, Fellini shows Cabiria twice back at her work, but now she is so much in love that she ignores the passing customers who beckon to her. She also encounters a slightly crazy lay brother, characterized by the same otherworldly insouciance that was typical of the Franciscans in Rossellini's *Paisà* or *Francesco*. Brother Giovanni asks if Cabiria is in God's grace, and when she responds negatively, the friar tells her to get married and raise a family. For Cabiria, however, her impending marriage to Oscar is miracle enough: selling everything she owns, she raises a dowry of some 400,000 lire. Yet, by now the spectator has been trained to expect disaster to strike each time Cabiria catches a glimpse of happiness, and the fact that Oscar's polite and benign manner is only a false mask to beguile the unwary prostitute is underlined almost too clearly by the dark glasses he has now begun to wear.[104] Oscar takes Cabiria to a cliff over-

---

[104] In fact, Bazin criticizes this detail as "the one prop that Fellini has used to a point where it has become a gimmick" (ibid., p. 99), but Fellini will continue to employ sunglasses in his male characters to underline their guile and deceitfulness

15. *Le notti di Cabiria*: under the hypnotist's spell, Cabiria reveals her secret ambitions to a jeering audience

looking a large lake to watch the sunset. Once again, as in *La strada* and *Il bidone*, Fellini's protagonist is returned for the film's climax to a setting recalling the opening sequence: Cabiria's misadventures had begun near a river; she is now robbed of her life's savings, and her romantic illusions are destroyed yet another time near another body of water.

Cabiria's story might well have ended here if Fellini had aimed for a realistic analysis of prostitution and its deleterious effects on the lives of those who practice the trade. But Fellini adds to the film a brief coda that magically elevates Cabiria's impasse to an entirely different aes-

in future films, such as *8 1/2*, in which the "gimmick" is employed with great effectiveness in characterizing Guido as a liar in the grand tradition of Pinocchio.

thetic and philosophical dimension. As Cabiria leaves the lake and returns to a nearby road, she first hears music and then encounters a group of young boys and girls singing, dancing, and playing the accordion. The music played is a variation on the earlier religious music accompanying the choirboys' chant ("ora pro nobis") during the pilgrimage at the shrine of the Divino Amore.[105] At first Cabiria is hesitant to encounter this merry group, but after one of the young people wishes her a cheerful "buona sera," Cabiria walks boldly into the spontaneous and exuberant procession, one of many such symbolic parades in Fellini's films. In the process of joining other human beings, her despair is transformed once again, as if by magic, into renewed hope. Music serves Fellini as a metaphor for salvation, for its presence is completely gratuitous, spontaneous, and unexpected. And the director visualizes Cabiria's transformation with one of his most brilliant, yet simple and economical, shots: in a close-up of Cabiria's face, her gaze turns toward the camera (violating the unwritten but conventional grammar of traditional filmmaking) and crosses that of the audience. As André Bazin so sensitively described this final shot, "here she is now inviting us, too, with her glance to follow her on the road to which she is about to return. The invitation is chaste, discreet, and indefinite enough that we can pretend to think that she means to be looking at somebody else. At the same time, though, it is definite and direct enough, too, to remove us quite finally from our role of spectator."[106] Moreover, during this final shot, the musical motif that has accompanied Cabiria throughout the film is transferred from an initially diagetic source (the musicians in the procession) to an extradiagetic one with an orchestrated crescendo. As Cabiria's glance turns to meet the camera, the music swells to underline the narrator's control of the closing shot, joining Fellini's perspective to that of his fictional creation Cabiria and uniting both of these points of view with that of his audience.

As in the other films from Fellini's trilogy of grace or salvation, the ending coda of *Le notti di Cabiria* juxtaposes an episodic and picaresque narrative with a finale that closes the circular movement of the film and suggests a religious experience transcending the complex of various adventures preceding it. But Fellini is careful only to *suggest* such a religious interpretation in each of these films. In a letter to a Jesuit priest describing his view of the world, for example, Fellini provided this evaluation of his artistic intentions in ending the film as he

---

[105] This and other remarks on Nino Rota's musical contribution to this film I owe to Claudia Gorbman's "Music as Salvation: Notes on Fellini and Rota," pp. 80–94.

[106] Bazin, "*Cabiria*," p. 102; almost every critical analysis of this film focuses on the same shot (Burke, *Federico Fellini*, p. 82; Rondi, *Il cinema di Federico Fellini*, p. 198), as does Fellini in his comments on the work.

did: "A lyrical, musical outburst, a serenade sung in the woods ends this last film of mine (which is full of tragedy), because in spite of everything Cabiria still carries in her heart a touch of grace. We must not try to discover just what is the nature of this grace; it is kinder to leave Cabiria the joy of telling us, at least, whether this grace is her discovery of God."[107]

While the trilogy employs religious symbolism and develops concepts taken from Christian tradition (parabolic discourses; religious symbolism and imagery; allusions to biblical narratives, such as the good thief, the Virgin, the Angel Gabriel, or Mary Magdalene, the holy prostitute; the key notion of conversion), Fellini consistently avoids offering any doctrinaire Christian interpretation of his protagonists. Zampanò, Augusto, and Cabiria each must experience an existential crisis that is caused primarily by a spiritual poverty. A single tear seems to transform Zampanò's brutish nature into a more human form, as he experiences genuine emotion for the first time in his life as the result of the redemptive presence of Gelsomina. A pitiless swindler's infernal descent into an emotional abyss concludes with the hope of some kind of redemptive transformation after his death. And the smile on a prostitute's face signals to us that "grace" or "salvation" may finally have been achieved by one of Fellini's embattled characters in the trilogy. While each of these characters moves within a setting informed by images and concepts owing something to Christian tradition, his or her odyssey toward a moment of transcendence at the close of each of these films ultimately depends on the inner resources of the individual rather than any outside or otherworldly source.[108] In *Le notti di Cabiria*, Fellini quite emphatically rejected the possibility of a traditional Christian notion of miraculous grace in the Divino Amore sequence. In fact, before the release of the film, *Le notti di Cabiria* encountered stiff censorship motivated not only by the film's subject matter (prostitution) but also by its secular reinterpretation of traditional religious themes. In an effort to save *Le notti di Cabiria* from mutilation by the state censors, Fellini used the intercession of a Jesuit friend, Father Angelo Arpa, to arrange a private showing of the film for Cardinal Giuseppe Siri, then the youngest cardinal in the hierarchy and a priest not known for his opposition to cinema. Siri viewed the film after midnight in a dreary projection room near the seedy dock area of Genoa, and after he had seen it, he uttered only a single sentence to Fellini: "Poor Cabiria, we ought to do something for her!"[109] As if by magic, the threat of state

---

[107] Fellini, *Fellini on Fellini*, p. 66.

[108] Burke, in *Federico Fellini* (p. 82), also claims that any redemption that occurs in this film is clearly a secular redemption, a growing sense of *self*-creation.

[109] Fellini, *Comments on Film*, pp. 127–28.

censorship evaporated, providing an unintentional proof of the close
ties between Church and State in the regime controlled by the Christian Democratic party at the time.[110] But Fellini viewed his deference
to Cardinal Siri as merely a necessary and practical step to ensure the
release of his film. However, the director was forced to pay what appears in retrospect to be a small price for Siri's support: he was asked
to delete a scene picturing the lay charity of a figure known in the
screenplay as "the man with the sack."[111] Apparently, the Church
could not tolerate the fact that private acts of Christian charity were
unauthorized by the hierarchy and uncoordinated by existing religious
organizations. The final film actually profits from the deletion of this
sequence, since it adds nothing significant to the themes Fellini had
already developed elsewhere in the narrative.

Given Fellini's intentional poetic ambiguity in the conclusions of
these three films, the spectator may never know with any assurance
whether his three protagonists finally find God. But any such purely
religious interpretation of the trilogy of grace or salvation must first
reckon with the even more important psychological changes that take
place in these characters. Of these three figures, only Cabiria actually
joins the symbolic procession down a metaphoric road that affirms life
and offers renewed hope in the future. But all three films celebrate the
triumph of Fellini's lyrical and symbolic vision over a material world
that constantly threatens to annihilate his characters. Such a life-affirming vision is almost out of place in a period characterized by existential despair. Even Fellini was unable to sustain such an optimistic
perspective in his next work, *La dolce vita*, a film that would depart in
a number of fundamental respects from the aesthetic and thematic
foundations of his first two trilogies, leading toward an increasingly

[110] Marxists such as Guido Aristarco and leftist writers such as Alberto Moravia
were appalled by this demonstration of the power of the Catholic hierarchy; see Aristarco, "Guido Aristarco Answers Fellini," in *Federico Fellini: Essays in Criticism*,
ed. Bondanella, pp. 63–64, or in Fellini, *"La Strada": Federico Fellini, Director*, pp.
208–210.

[111] See Fellini, *Le notti di Cabiria*, pp. 66–73, for the section of the screenplay that
was removed from the film by Fellini. The episode pictures a man, unrelated to the
official Church, distributing clothes and food to the needy who gives Cabiria a ride
one day. Fellini based the character on a real person named Mario Tirabassi (Kezich,
Fellini, p. 247), just as he used his encounter with a prostitute named Wanda during
the shooting of *Il bidone* to construct Cabiria. The episode can still be viewed, either
in a later work, *Block-notes di un regista*, made for NBC, or in an important documentary on Fellini's works shot by Gianfranco Angelucci for Italian television entitled *Zoom su Fellini* (in the segment called *Fellini nel cestino*). Angelucci's film is
available in Italy as a two-volume cassette, distributed under the title *Omaggio a
Fellini*.

personal and introspective cinematic world of his own imaginative creation.

More than a major step forward in the evolution of Fellini's cinema, *La dolce vita* also summarizes an entire historical period in postwar Italy. Its lush fresco of the "sweet life" of Rome, focusing on the celebrities who frequented Via Veneto and were relentlessly pursued by gossip columnists and photo-reporters in search of a scandalous scoop, seemed to epitomize the moral atmosphere in Italy after the poverty of the immediate postwar period of reconstruction had finally ended. The country was beginning its economic boom, and its first confrontation with an emerging consumer society produced the inevitable plethora of the newly rich seeking a place in the much older aristocratic society of Rome. While today the film can finally be seen for what Fellini originally intended it to be—a bittersweet but essentially comic panorama of life in the fast lane of the time—*La dolce vita* created a scandal of historic proportions, reversing the positions of the protagonists in the polemical debate over *La strada*. Church groups, representatives of the Roman nobility, and right-wing politicians who had praised *La strada* demanded that the film be banned as morally outrageous or even obscene, while critics, intellectuals, and political parties from the center to the left of the political spectrum applauded *La dolce vita* for what they felt was Fellini's realistic panorama of the corruption and decadence of Italy's bourgeoisie. Needless to say, such a debate guaranteed the film an enormous audience, and its performance at the box office broke all Italian records. A ticket cost an unheard-of 1,000 lire, and within a few years the film had grossed over 2.2 billion lire against a total cost of around 600 million lire, also a record for Italian films of the time.[112] The polemics over *La dolce vita* in the popular press did little, however, to influence the almost completely positive critical reaction to the work, which earned dozens of international awards, including the Grand Jury Prize at Cannes. More than any other single film, *La dolce vita* was responsible for the creation and dissemination of the Fellini myth—the director as superstar. After *La dolce vita*, Fellini's public persona attracted almost as much attention as his work and sometimes even threatened to eclipse it, as apocryphal tales of lavish production budgets willfully overrun, extravagant and eccentric working procedures on the set, and the like began to circulate and to be transformed into legend. *La dolce vita*'s popularity was also not limited to Italy. Years after the film's release, thousands of tourists in Rome

---

[112] Kezich, in *Fellini*, pp. 292–93, lists these figures and gives an interesting account of the film's reception. Federico Fellini, *La dolce vita* (Milan: Garzanti, 1981), pp. 161–220, provides an appendix to the Italian screenplay that includes many of the negative reactions expressed when *La dolce vita* appeared.

still flocked to Via Veneto and to the Trevi Fountain because they had seen these locations in Fellini's film.[113]

La dolce vita emerged from a process of elimination; after *Viaggio con Anita*, a script echoing Fellini's own journey to Rimini in 1956 on the death of his father, was rejected, a number of literary adaptations were considered but set aside, including those of Boccaccio's *Decameron*, Casanova's *Memoirs* (eventually done in 1976), and Mario Tobino's novel *Le libere donne di Magliano*. Finally, Fellini and his scriptwriters (Pinelli and Flaiano, assisted by Brunello Rondi) returned to the story written earlier as a sequel to *I vitelloni—Moraldo in città*.[114] When the writers examined this old project, they immediately realized that in the late 1950s, such a provincial atmosphere retained little interest for them or their audience.[115] Inspired by the many changes in Italian popular culture that had taken place since the appearance of *I vitelloni*, such as the advent of photo-reporters in the capital city, or new fashions in women's wear, Fellini wanted to attempt a completely different and modernist approach to plot in cinematic narrative: "So I said: let's invent episodes, let's not worry for now about the logic or the narrative. We have to make a statue, break it, and recompose the pieces. Or better yet, try a decomposition in the manner of Picasso. The cinema is narrative in the nineteenth-century sense: now let's try to do something different."[116]

Critics have always commented on the extravagant costumes worn by the women in *La dolce vita*, *8 1/2*, and *Giulietta degli spiriti*, but few of them realized that a particular fashion style was actually at the origin of Fellini's idea to paint a sweeping fresco of contemporary Italy.

[113] The shooting of the Trevi Fountain sequence is re-created by Ettore Scola's *C'eravamo tanto amati* (1976), where it is employed to symbolize Italian society in the late 1950s. So many tourists flooded Via Veneto after seeing the location Fellini re-created in his studio that in a brief time, the café society Fellini immortalized in the film moved elsewhere.

[114] For the English translations of the stories of both *Viaggio con Anita* and *Moraldo in città*, see Fellini, "Moraldo in the City" and "A Journey with Anita."

[115] "We realized immediately that this didn't work any longer. It spoke of a Rome of another time, the one I discovered arriving from Florence. Today [1958], a bohemian life in the sense of that period no longer exists. There is no community of artist-types living from day to day by skipping their meals altogether. Today, there is journalism, photo-reporters, motorization, the branch of café society. Another world." (Kezich, "Fellini e altri: bloc-notes per *La dolce vita*," in *Il dolce cinema* [Milan: Bompiani, 1978], pp. 24–25). Kezich's journal of the making of *La dolce vita* is the second such treatment of Fellini's films, following Dominique Delouche's account of the making of *Il bidone*. Faldini and Fofi, in *L'avventurosa storia del cinema italiano . . . 1960–1969*, pp. 3–17, also republish a great deal of important material relating to the film's production.

[116] Cited in Kezich, "Fellini e altri: bloc-notes per *La dolce vita*," p. 25.

As Brunello Rondi has explained, "*La dolce vita* was inspired in him then by the fashion of women's sack dresses which possessed that sense of luxurious butterflying out around a body that might be [physically] beautiful but not morally so; these sack dresses struck Fellini because they rendered a woman very gorgeous who could, instead, be a skeleton of squalor and solitude inside."[117] During the genesis of *La dolce vita*, the primacy of visual image over story line continued the practice of the director's earlier masterpiece, *La strada*, the original inspiration for which first came from an image Fellini had of Gelsomina which he sketched out and to which was joined an opposing image of Zampanò.[118] Once again, at another important turning point in Fellini's career, it was a visual image taken from popular culture that gave Fellini the key to a new way of *looking* at his world. Only later grasping the visual foundation of *La dolce vita* did Fellini and his scriptwriters turn to producing a script to embody his inspiration within a narrative framework.

Fellini's reference to Picasso is of great importance. Fellini had just met Picasso at the Cannes Film Festival during the screening of *Le notti di Cabiria* but never really had a chance to speak with him. For Fellini, who has dreamed of Picasso on a number of occasions in moments of artistic uncertainty, the Spanish painter represents "the eternal embodiment of the archetype of creativity as an end in itself, with no other motive, no other end, than itself—irruptive, unarguable, joyous."[119] Picasso's cubist revolution in painting helped to shift the focus from representation of reality to a decomposition of that reality into its many facets and perspectives. In like manner, with *La dolce vita*, Fellini wanted to create a new kind of cinematic narrative that would abandon the traditional emphasis on plot and story line and concentrate on supporting the narrative by visual images and narrative rhythm. Fellini's debt to Picasso is underlined by the fact that he dedicated a drawing of Sylvia (Anita Ekberg), the Scandinavian movie star who plays such an important role in *La dolce vita*, to Picasso after the completion of the film. The bizarre costume for Sylvia's public relations visit to Saint Peter's is appropriately modeled after a priest's habit, but the actress's enormous breasts so overshadow any religious intent in the sketch that the drawing may well be seen as emblematic of Fellini's aesthetic aims in *La dolce vita*. Beginning with an initial inspiration from the world of fashion and popular culture, and enriching his ideas by a personal

---

[117] Cited in Faldini and Fofi, *L'avventurosa storia del cinema italiano . . . 1960–1969*, pp. 4–5.

[118] For Fellini's complete explanation of how the *image* of Gelsomina and Zampanò preceded any story of their adventures, see Fellini, "The Genesis of *La Strada*," in Fellini, *"La Strada": Federico Fellini, Director*, pp. 181–84.

[119] Fellini, *Fellini on Fellini*, p. 147.

16. *La dolce vita*: Fellini's sketch of Anita drawn for Pablo Picasso, a major influence on the aesthetic structure of the film

investigation of events actually taking place on or near Via Veneto in the company of the Roman paparazzi, Fellini set out to create an expressionistic fresco that would distort such commonplace realities, creating characters and images so far removed from their normal representation that they found their proper setting only in the extravagant studio sets that the director's imaginative fantasy inspired.

Because of *La dolce vita*'s impact on Italian society, this film received detailed contemporary documentation, including a day-by-day diary written by Tullio Kezich.[120] The thousands of still photographs generated during its mammoth production have recently been reprinted in a beautiful volume edited by Fellini's collaborator Gianfranco Angelucci to commemorate the thirtieth anniversary of the film's release.[121] *La dolce vita* also influenced our language. "Dolce vita" became synonymous even in English with the hedonistic and superficial pursuit of pleasure in reconstructed Europe, thereby acquiring a specifically negative or moralistic connotation that Fellini never intended. Extravagant images in the cinema soon were dubbed "Fellinian," and Fellini's name became synonymous with free creativity in the cinema, much as Picasso's was in the figurative arts. One of Fellini's characters, a photo-reporter named Paparazzo (Walter Santesso), who made a living by capturing celebrities in compromising situations on or around Via Veneto, gave birth to the English and Italian word for photo-reporter that is still used today.

It is impossible to analyze either the style or the content of *La dolce vita* without some understanding of these paparazzi. The origin of the word in Italian has raised some questions. While it is indeed an Italian family name, the word is probably a corruption of the word *papataceo*, a large and bothersome mosquito. Ennio Flaiano, one of the film's scriptwriters, reports that he took the name from a character in a novel by George Gessing.[122] A sketch of Paparazzo which Fellini gave to the actor playing the role underlines the relentless, irritating, mosquito-like quality the photo-reporters possessed in the film. To create the vast mosaic of Italian society that *La dolce vita* represents, Fellini's preparatory sketches and drawings were crucial, and the director's reliance on them became an integral part of his attempts to move away from the relatively mimetic world of his early films to a visual universe derived primarily from his imaginative fantasy. Such an artistic design necessitated constant visual cues to Fellini's collaborators for makeup, set construction, and the like, and it is thus not surprising that many more sketches and designs have been conserved from this period of Fellini's career than from his previous work.

Fellini did not invent the paparazzi or the café society in which they thrived, although *La dolce vita* did much to publicize their exploits and misadventures. During the financial crisis in the American film industry of the mid-1950s, many important American productions moved to

[120] Kezich, *Il dolce cinema*, pp. 1–116.

[121] Gianfranco Angelucci, ed. *"La dolce vita": un film di Federico Fellini* (Rome: Editalia, 1989).

[122] Andrea Nemiz, *Vita, dolce vita* (Rome: Network Edizioni, 1983), pp. 110–11; see also Bertelli and De Santi, *Omaggio a Flaiano*, p. 90.

a walter santos
"Paparazzo"

17. *La dolce vita*: the insectlike paparazzo in a sketch by Fellini

Rome during a decade known as "Hollywood on the Tiber."[123] Three celebrated "media events" preceded Fellini's film and made the paparazzi who filmed them famous. In the summer of 1957, Anita Ekberg waded in the Trevi Fountain late one night in the company of Pierluigi Praturlon, who immortalized the event in a photo service syndicated around the world. This would provide the inspiration for the famous Trevi sequence in *La dolce vita*. On the night of 18 August 1958, the photographer Tazio Secchiaroli was attacked not once but twice on the same evening by two people he was photographing—Farouk, the former

[123] For an entertaining history of this decade, see Hank Kaufman and Gene Lerner, *Hollywood sul Tevere* (Milan: Sperling & Kupfer, 1982); Nemiz, *Vita, dolce vita*, contains the most complete record of the paparazzi available, including their most scandalous photographs.

king of Egypt, and Anthony Franciosa in the company of Ava Gardner. Fellini refers to this incident in *La dolce vita* when his protagonist, Marcello Rubino (Marcello Mastroianni), is attacked by Sylvia's boyfriend Robert (Lex Barker) after the Trevi Fountain sequence. Later in November of the same year, a Turkish dancer named Aichè Nanà did a striptease at a Roman restaurant called Il Rugantino, an event to which Fellini certainly alludes with the insertion of the famous striptease dance by Nadia (Nadia Gray) into the Fregene "orgy" sequence. Just as Fellini had spent a great deal of time investigating the seamy world of Roman prostitution before the shooting of *Le notti di Cabiria*, the director spent several months with paparazzi (in particular with Pierluigi Praturlon and Tazio Secchiaroli, the most famous of the group), exploring the world of Via Veneto in preparation for *La dolce vita*. In fact, the two photographers became his set photographers on a number of his later films, with Praturlon actually shooting the still photographs for *La dolce vita*. The escapades of such figures as Ursula Andress, Jayne Mansfield, Raquel Welch, Ava Gardner, Orson Welles, and the South American playboy Baby Pignatari were captured by the paparazzi's photographs and were syndicated by pulp magazines around the world, associating Via Veneto with a particular kind of ostentatious nightlife populated by movie stars, starlets, confidence men, journalists, public relations representatives, idle playboys, and that nebulous contemporary phenomenon, the "celebrity." The high water mark of paparazzi reporting was reached during the scandalous love affair between Elizabeth Taylor and Richard Burton during the Roman production of *Cleopatra* in 1962. *Cleopatra* also signaled the end of the era of Hollywood on the Tiber, for the Taylor/Burton liaison was exploited to such an extent by the mass media that the public eventually lost interest in the Via Veneto scene entirely.[124]

Although Fellini began the preparation for *Le notti di Cabiria* and *La dolce vita* with a personal investigation into the "reality" of the worlds of Roman prostitution and nightlife, a faithful and realistic representation of these worlds was the furthest thing from his mind. Nowhere is this more apparent in *La dolce vita* than in the representation of the street in question, Via Veneto. Few viewers are aware of the fact that all scenes located on Via Veneto in the film were shot inside a studio and do not represent the actual Roman street. Fellini has noted:

> In my film I invented a non-existent Via Veneto, enlarging and altering it with poetic license, until it took on the dimensions of a large allegorical fresco . . . Piero Gherardi, the designer, started taking measurements and

[124] For Fellini's discussion of Via Veneto, see Fellini, "Via Veneto: dolce vita," in *Fellini on Fellini*, pp. 67–83.

built me a large slice of Via Veneto on Number 5 stage at Cinecittà. . . .
The Via Veneto which Gherardi rebuilt was exact down to the smallest
detail, but it had one thing peculiar to it: it was flat instead of sloping.
As I worked on it I got so used to this perspective that my annoyance
with the real Via Veneto grew even greater and now, I think, it will never
disappear. When I pass the Café de Paris, I cannot help feeling that the
real Via Veneto was the one on Stage 5, and that the dimensions of the
rebuilt street were more accurate or at any rate more agreeable. I even
feel an invisible temptation to exercise over the real street the despotic
authority I had over the fake one. This is all a complicated business
which I ought to talk about to someone who understands psychoanalysis.[125]

While the content of La dolce vita remains closely connected with
the everyday world around Fellini and has not yet taken the decisive
step beyond representation of "real" public events to the representation
of Fellini's private, inner fantasy world that will mark his films after 8
1/2, the important move from films based primarily on location shooting to productions utilizing the complex studio facilities of Rome's Cinecittà that will mark his greatest and most artistically demanding
films begins with La dolce vita. Before La dolce vita, Fellini searched
Rome, Ostia, and the countryside of Lazio and Umbria for unusual but
authentic locations with poetic possibilities and built relatively few
sets on sound stages. During the production of La dolce vita and afterward, however, Fellini's cinematic style becomes completely dependent on artificial and purposely fantastic sets constructed at Cinecittà
or other studios. For Fellini, the most conducive spot for artistic creativity is "Theatre 5 in Cinecittà when it's empty. Total emotion, trembling, ecstasy is what I feel there in that empty studio—a space to fill
up, a world to create."[126] Fellini prefers a studio because it represents a
challenge to create from chaos or nothingness, like the God of the Old
Testament, using only his own imagination without the mediation of
the outside world. In La dolce vita, Gherardi's brilliant set designs, for
which he earned a well-deserved Oscar, were the result of a felicitous
marriage between Fellini's imagination and Gherardi's symbiotic comprehension of exactly what Fellini had in mind after the director presented the designer with preliminary sketches and drawings. Fellini
never conceived of a single character in the film as an abstract definition within a literary narrative. Instead, each of the dozens of figures in

[125] Ibid., pp. 67, 81.
[126] Fellini, Comments on Film, p. 102. More recently, Fellini has repeated this remark in a 1987 BBC documentary entitled "Real Dreams: Into the Dark with Federico Fellini," and he visualizes the same idea in the first sequence of Intervista.

18. *La dolce vita*: Via Veneto as Fellini reproduced it inside Cinecittà's studios in Rome

La dolce vita was immediately visualized (like Gelsomina or Zampanò before them) as a combination of facial expression, costume, and ambience within a scenographic space.[127] Gherardi's account of the creation of the more than eighty locations in the film reveals how Fellini constantly rejected real locations for those artificially constructed in the studio. In almost every instance, Fellini would take Gherardi with him on madcap nocturnal car rides in and outside of Rome, pretending that he had discovered a location suitable for the film. The search for the right villa in which to shoot the orgy sequence at the film's conclusion resulted in the examination of over twenty homes, but this search (like all the others during the production of the film) was in completely bad faith, for Fellini finally concluded: "It's useless, Piero. By now, we have invented everything, let's invent this one as well."[128] Thus, not only was Via Veneto reconstructed, but dozens of other seemingly real locations were created as well, including the dome of Saint Peter's and numerous nightclubs—one supposedly in the Baths of Caracalla; a second reflecting the period style of 1925, that of Marcello's father; and a third resembling a club Gherardi had seen in Hong Kong.

Equally original aesthetic decisions governed the film's photography. Otello Martelli has paid tribute to Fellini's ingenious resolution of technical problems, a feat reminiscent of Fellini's precocious earlier suggestions to Martelli on the set of Rossellini's *Paisà* years before. According to Martelli, it was Fellini's intuition to employ 75-, 100-, and 150-mm lenses (those usually selected for close-ups) in tracks and pans rather than the 50-mm lens "required" in the Cinemascope process. Most directors would have avoided this choice to prevent the distortion of the characters' backgrounds, particularly during camera movements. When Martelli informed Fellini of this problem, the director's response was simple: "What does that matter to us?" And, Martelli modestly admits, Fellini was entirely correct, for his transgression of the traditional technical practice resulted in a particular visual style for *La dolce vita*. It caused a highlighting of figures inside a frescolike framework with a slight distortion of their environments, a photographic mannerism that emphasized the thematic focus of the entire film.[129]

With its dozens of sets and hundreds of actors, *La dolce vita* was a mammoth undertaking always in danger of running out of control. Clemente Fracassi, Fellini's production director, was faced with unexpected and constant changes from the screenplay on the set, and the screenplay was itself continually modified during the process of shoot-

[127] Faldini and Fofi, *L'avventurosa storia del cinema italiano . . . 1960–1969*, p. 10.
[128] Cited in ibid., p. 12.
[129] Martelli is cited in ibid., pp. 10–11.

ing from day to day (usually by Brunello Rondi). While Tullio Pinelli has reported that both *La dolce vita* and *8 1/2* began with "iron-clad screenplays,"[130] the products of months and months of collaboration between Fellini, Pinelli, Flaiano, and Rondi, and that there was never anything "improvised" in the strict sense of the term in either production, Fellini nevertheless would often remain undecided about exactly how to shoot a particular scene until the last moment, requiring several different sets of props, set designs, and the like. Overnight decisions to modify the script demanded equally drastic changes in the production. For example, Pinelli notes that the famous scene at the aristocratic palace in Bassano di Sutri where Maddalena (Anouk Aimée) tells Marcello she loves him in an echo chamber that transmits her voice from one room to another was originally planned as a face-to-face conversation that Fellini changed the night before shooting. Fellini's decision forced Pinelli to rewrite the scene before the next day, and it also required immediate revisions of the physical set.[131] Gherardi remembers that in one of their many visits to various locations around Rome, he told Fellini about a similar room in the Farnese palace in Caprarola but had the feeling that Fellini was not listening; instead, it was this real location that gave birth to the modified scene and, consequently, the newly constructed set.[132]

In like fashion, Fellini treated his actors as faces and potential images rather than performers. His casting was, as always, based on the actor's image on the screen rather than any special dramatic talent. Fellini insisted that the relatively unknown Mastroianni be given the leading role, while the producer argued forcefully for an American star such as Paul Newman to ensure that his investment would not be squandered. But Fellini wisely realized that Mastroianni's completely plastic face was capable of almost any kind of expression, and that this versatility was needed over the film's three-hour development as the character he portrayed evolved on the screen. Fellini was careful to keep the script away from the actors, however, not only because their dialogue would eventually be dubbed after shooting, but also because the director was guided more by the visual image of what he wished to create in his mind than by a pedantic notion of faithfulness to the written text. Anita Ekberg, accustomed to the Hollywood system of accepting a role only after reading a complete script, at first thought Fellini was not even a serious director when he told her (quite falsely) that there was no script for her to read. It was her agent who signed the contract for

[130] Author's unpublished interview with Pinelli, 8 October 1987.

[131] Ibid.

[132] Gherardi, cited in Faldini and Fofi, *L'avventurosa storia del cinema italiano . . . 1960–1969*, p. 12.

her part in *La dolce vita*, while the actress continued to believe that Fellini wanted to sleep with her after seeing her drive around Rome in her red Mercedes convertible![133] When Mastroianni asked to see a script, Flaiano gave him a stack of blank pages that contained only a drawing by Fellini of a man swimming in the sea with a gigantic penis, reaching to the ocean floor, surrounded by mermaids. Too embarrassed to object, Mastroianni agreed to do the film.[134]

La dolce vita presents such a kaleidoscopic assemblage of major and minor characters, locations, and themes that it is no wonder critics have tried to arrange its disparate elements into tidy patterns. The most common interpretation of the film's story line divides it into an introductory prologue, seven major episodes interrupted by an intermezzo; and a concluding epilogue as follows:

Prologue: Marcello appears in a helicopter carrying a statue of Christ over an ancient Roman aqueduct.

   1. Marcello meets Maddalena, and the two go to a prostitute's home, where Maddalena insists they make love.

   2. Marcello meets Sylvia, the Swedish-American actress; they visit Saint Peter's, hold a press conference, and go to a nightclub in the Baths of Caracalla; running away from the group, Sylvia takes her famous wade into the Trevi Fountain with Marcello following her into the water.

   3a. Marcello encounters Steiner (Alain Cuny), an intellectual friend, in a church where he plays the organ.

   4. Marcello goes with his fiancée Emma (Yvonne Fourneaux) and Paparazzo to the outskirts of town, where two small children claim they have seen the Madonna; that night in a downpour, the event is broadcast over Italian radio and television, and in the ensuing scuffle, one of the pilgrims is killed.

   3b. Marcello takes Emma to a party at Steiner's home, where a group of ridiculous intellectuals listen to sounds of nature captured on a tape recorder.

Intermezzo: Marcello meets a beautiful and innocent young girl from Perugia named Paola (Valeria Ciangottini), whom he describes as resembling one of the angels in Umbrian painting.

   5. Marcello meets his father (Annibale Ninchi) on Via Veneto; they go with Paparazzo to the Cha-Cha-Cha Club, where they are joined by a dancer named Fanny (Magali Nöel), but when Fanny takes Marcello's father to her apartment, he becomes ill and returns to his hotel.

   6. Marcello meets a group of people at Via Veneto and goes with them

[133] Anita Ekberg, cited in ibid., pp. 8–9.
[134] Mastroianni, cited in ibid., p. 8.

to an aristocratic castle outside of Rome at Bassano di Sutri; there, Maddalena tells him in an echo chamber that she loves him, but then goes off with another man; Marcello then makes love to Jane, a seductive American heiress (Audrey MacDonald).

3c. Marcello learns that Steiner has committed suicide after killing his two children and goes to Steiner's home with the police to wait for Steiner's wife to return home.

7. At a villa on the coast near Fregene, Marcello presides over what passed for an "orgy" in 1959; Nadia does a striptease to celebrate her divorce, while Marcello humiliates a young woman by dressing her up like a chicken and riding drunkenly around the room on her as she crawls on her hands and knees.

Epilogue: Leaving the party at dawn, the group discovers a monster fish some local fishermen have netted from the ocean; Marcello looks across an eddy and sees Paola, but the words they exchange are drowned out by the sound of the waves; the film concludes with a close-up of Paola's smiling face.[135]

Viewed in this manner, *La dolce vita* becomes a symbolic narrative or even an allegorical narrative based on the number seven (evoking the seven deadly sins, the seven sacraments, the seven virtues, the seven days of creation, and so on). This numerological approach to the film may well be intellectually appealing, but it is, in fact, based on a false description of the film's structure. To arrive at the total of seven "major" sequences, it is necessary to pretend that a number of important sequences are something else (a prologue, an intermezzo, an epilogue). In addition, the parts of the film devoted to Steiner must arbitrarily be called a single sequence in three parts, when in fact they represent a number of different sequences. Such a critical fascination with the number seven demonstrates the critics' attempts to reduce the complexity and variety of Fellini's narrative to a structure that the film itself set out to avoid. In a sense, their response to the film's structure underlines how revolutionary Fellini's narrative, inspired by Picasso's example in the figurative arts, really was, for critics felt obliged to return Fellini's unorthodox narrative to a more traditional *literary* plot in order to discuss it.

La dolce vita, running some 165 minutes, was one of the longest Italian films ever produced. While the critical fascination with seven major episodes plus prologue, intermezzo, and epilogue does focus our atten-

---

[135] This division into seven episodes was originally suggested by John Russell Taylor, *Cinema Eye, Cinema Ear* (New York: Hill and Wang, 1964), pp. 38–44; his suggestion seems to be repeated by Kezich (*Fellini*, p. 281) and Costello (*Fellini's Road*, p. 35), to mention only two of the most important interpreters of the film.

tion on major turning points in the narrative, it is certainly neither an accurate count of the film's sequences nor a completely convincing description of the film's plot. Fellini's screenplay merely divided the script into 104 separate scenes. Employing the usual definition of a sequence in a film as a related series of shots, any critic of *La dolce vita* not mesmerized by the magic number seven will find it almost impossible to organize the numerous sequences on a strictly numerological basis.

If there is a literary antecedent to the bewildering complexity of the narrative in Fellini's *La dolce vita*, it may well be, as has been suggested by several critics, Dante's *Inferno*.[136] But the Dantesque element of Fellini's film does not reside in any numerological structure (an element of key importance to Dante's medieval poetics). Instead, it is to be found in the parallel between Dante the Pilgrim, the protagonist of the epic poem, and Marcello Rubini, Fellini's errant journalist figure. Like Dante's pilgrim in the afterlife, Marcello wanders through a corrupt world teeming with characters (the script identifies 120 of them by name). These successive encounters build up a cumulative impression that finds resolution only at the conclusion of the film.[137] Many critics have also seen an ordering principle at work in the film in the recurrent movement from evening to dawn, a device Fellini had already employed in his earlier films. In *La dolce vita*, such moments are invariably linked to Marcello's encounters during the downward spiral of his moral descent.

The originality of *La dolce vita* lies in what Robert Richardson has called "an aesthetic of disparity," a new form of film narrative that negates continuity and suppresses explanations or cause-and-effect logic and that plays one image off of another to render "that overpowering sense of the disparity between what life has been or could be, and what it actually is."[138] As a result, the film's "message," if we can call it that, is embodied less in the film's content than in its aesthetic form. The moral decadence and lack of purpose characterizing Marcello as he moves through a number of strange settings and encounters an enormous body of characters stand in sharp contrast to the director's exuberant creativity released in large measure by his abandonment of tra-

[136] For this approach to *La dolce vita*, actually an introduction to her analysis of *8 1/2* in terms of Dante's *Purgatorio*, see Barbara K. Lewalski, "Federico Fellini's *Purgatorio*," in *Federico Fellini: Essays in Criticism*, ed. Bondanella, pp. 113–15.

[137] John Welle has analyzed Marcello's encounters in terms of Dantesque "greetings" in "Fellini's Use of Dante in *La Dolce Vita*," *Studies in Medievalism* 2, no. 3 (1983): 53–65.

[138] "Waste Lands: The Breakdown of Order," in *Federico Fellini: Essays in Criticism*, ed. Bondanella, p. 111.

ditional plot and a conventional notion of "character development."
Perhaps most important is the increased freedom that Fellini allows his
camera in this film—it has the ability to be "anywhere and everywhere" and serves as a constant reminder to the viewer of the director's
creative energy.[139] While the final apotheosis of the film director must
await Fellini's *8 1/2* and the metacinematic films of recent years, *La
dolce vita* already suggests the next giant step in Fellini's evolution.

Reportedly, Fellini once considered calling this film *2000 Years After
Jesus Christ*, or, alternatively, *Babylon 2000*. The image of contemporary society that emerges from the film—life defined as all facade and
masquerade—is summarized neatly in the remark of one of the transvestites at the "orgy" near Fregene when he tells Marcello, "Last night
I looked so pretty all made up . . . and now I feel all sticky."[140] *La dolce
vita*'s portrayal of modern Rome implies a negative comparison to its
ancient and more noble past and forms only the first part of Fellini's
treatment of Roman mythology.[141] The film's major images show us
life based on public relations stunts, meaningless intellectual debates,
empty religious rites, and sterile love affairs. One of the dominant visual motifs of the film is light in a variety of completely modern
forms—the relentless flashbulbs of the paparazzi in search of their
meaningless stories; the spotlights of the garish nightclubs of the city;
the endless processions of cars with their headlights burning in the
dark; and the arc lights set up for the television broadcast of the "miracle." These lights are more blinding than they are illuminating, and
the lack of vision on the part of many of the protagonists of the film
itself becomes a thematic concern as many of them (especially Marcello and Maddalena) wear dark glasses as if to objectify their lack of
insight. Marcello's gradual downward spiral toward absolute degradation at the film's conclusion may be predicted by the presence of a stairway in virtually every episode of the film.[142]

Fellini's concern with spiritual poverty lay at the heart of his trilogy
of grace or salvation. *La dolce vita* therefore continues a theme that
was already familiar in Fellini's films. But now the director emphasizes
the *failure* of his protagonist to experience a conversion and leaves his
audience with none of the ambiguous resolutions the trilogy contained.

[139] Burke, in *Federico Fellini*, p. 113, argues that the freedom of Fellini's camera in
La dolce vita constitutes the film's most original feature.

[140] Federico Fellini, *La Dolce Vita* (New York: Ballantine, 1961), p. 268.

[141] I deal with Fellini's place in the history of Roman mythology in *The Eternal
City: Roman Images in the Modern World* (Chapel Hill: University of North Carolina Press, 1987).

[142] Costello, in *Fellini's Road*, p. 40, has very perceptively discussed the visual motifs of lights and stairways.

Religion, once offered to Fellini's characters as a possible means of escaping the meaninglessness of their anguished lives, is now represented by a series of empty images and activities and provides no solutions. The opening shot of the statue of Christ carried aloft by a helicopter finds its parallel in the dead monster fish (a parody of the traditional symbol of Christ) at the film's conclusion. Christian mythology no longer conveys any meaning in a world of press conferences where starlets have replaced priests as status symbols, a fact underlined by Sylvia's visit to Saint Peter's in clerical garb. The thirst for a religious miracle that was so important a theme in *Le notti di Cabiria*, a work finally concluding with an even more amazing *secular* miracle, that of Cabiria's renewed hope in the future, receives in *La dolce vita* a far more negative treatment. In fact, the scene in which the two young children claim to have seen the Madonna is a movie set rather than a place of private devotion. A director organizes the evening show, crowds of actors and extras are on hand to practice their performances, and the children and all of their parents are interviewed constantly as if they were celebrities. The entire performance is illuminated by the blinding arc lamps of a film set. While Catholic ritual is always spectacular, in Fellini's film it has been reduced to the status of mere spectacle, devoid of any ethical content. *La dolce vita* marks Fellini's pessimistic rejection of any hope of religious intervention in contemporary life. The only miracle possible for Fellini will be that produced by the mystery of artistic creation in *8 1/2*, an event which will take place in a setting very much like the location from which the broadcast of the "miracle" in *La dolce vita* is scheduled to take place.

If religion, the traditional answer to the quest for meaning in life, offers no solutions to Marcello or his colleagues, sexual adventures—the major preoccupation of the habitués of the sweet life—also lead nowhere. Emma, Marcello's neurotic fiancée, suffocates him with unreasonable emotional demands and exaggerated maternal attention. Maddalena's decadent sexuality can only be expressed through role-playing, as occurs when she becomes sexually excited and sleeps with Marcello in the basement apartment of a common prostitute. Sylvia, the sex goddess and movie star, whose animal energy overwhelms Marcello's jaded sensibility, is transformed into a water nymph during her famous dip in the Trevi Fountain. Paradoxically, this blond bombshell actually personifies the very essence of spontaneous and innocent sensuality, but when Marcello joins her in the fountain, it mysteriously ceases to flow, a clear sign of his spiritual impotence. Paola, the naive and innocent Umbrian angel Marcello meets at the beach, never represents a possible means of escape from Marcello's meaningless existence but serves, instead, as an image of his own lost innocence. The film does conclude

with a long close-up of Paola, underlining Fellini's belief that such innocence is a state of grace well worth seeking, but Marcello's decline
by the end of the film makes it impossible for him to believe in any
possibility of a spiritual renewal for himself. As Paola's words to him
are drowned out by the noise of the ocean's waves, Marcello is clearly
set apart from the protagonists of the trilogy of grace or salvation.

The final blow to Marcello's attempts to become an authentic writer
and to turn away from the tawdry world of gossip columns, photo-reporters, and pulp journalism is delivered by the frightening suicide of
his mentor, Steiner. The archetypal intellectual, Steiner reads Sanskrit
grammars and is at home with both modern jazz and Bach. He thrives
within a social circle of intellectuals and expatriates and seems completely happy with his wife and two small children. But Steiner believes
one has to be detached from life in order to succeed—an idea completely alien to Fellini's preference for a healthy irrationality. Steiner
can enjoy the sounds of nature (rain, thunder, wind, bird songs) only
after recording them mechanically, and his inexplicable murder of his
two children and subsequent suicide preclude any possibility of Marcello's ever following this false prophet.

La dolce vita reveals religion, sexuality, and sterile intellectual pur-
suits as ultimately failing to provide meaning in life. Marcello abandons his literary pretensions and, in the orgy sequence, accepts his role
as a public relations man, a manipulator of images and empty slogans
in a world dominated by mass media that only communicate empty
messages. Most of the film's almost three-hour narrative argues for a
chilling rejection of the sense of potential that Fellini's trilogy of grace
or salvation suggested. Yet, true to his technique of never offering defin-
itive conclusions, Fellini's last image, the shot of Paola in the distance
that remains for an unusually long amount of time on the screen, offers
us the faint hope of some escape from this dreary emotional, sexual,
and intellectual impasse.

La dolce vita marks the end of one phase of Fellini's career and opens
an entirely new one. If the seven films preceding *La dolce vita* are characterized by the director's discovery of lyrical and poetic moments in a
relatively realistic environment always instantly recognizable as the
same world inhabited by the spectator—and thus, not yet that completely artificial universe which Fellini will create in his later films—
the fresco of contemporary life and mores revealed to the audience by
La dolce vita begins a major shift from the world of the Lumières toward that more phantasmagorical universe of Méliès, in which the depiction of various forms of spectacle (beauty pageants, circuses, press
conferences, masquerade balls, the cinema, the variety hall) will even-

tually yield to a cinema based on the spectacular, displacing reality with dream, imagination, and memory.[143]

In one of the most original analyses of *La dolce vita* ever written, an essay entitled "The Catholic Irrationalism of Fellini," Pier Paolo Pasolini argues that *La dolce vita* belongs to the great productions of European decadence. Pasolini's Marxist ideology cannot accept Fellini's repudiation of reason and dialectic, nor can Pasolini agree with the essentially Catholic ideology Fellini embraces, which views life from the "non-dialectical relationship between sin and innocence" that is regulated by grace. Yet, Pasolini paradoxically proclaims the film "the highest and most absolute product of Catholicism of these last years":

> Look at the Rome that he describes. It would be hard to imagine a world more completely arid. It is an aridity that takes away life, that torments. We see pass before our eyes a river of mortifying characters in a mortifying cross-section of the capital. They are all cynics, all wretches, all egoists, all spoiled, all presumptuous, all cowards, all servile, all frightened, all silly, all miserable, all *qualunquisti*. . . . And they bring there a gust of wind that in its way is pure and vital . . . there is not one of these characters that does not emerge as pure and vital, always presented in his moment of almost sacred energy. . . . Everyone is full of energy in managing to survive, even if burdened by death and insensitivity. I have never seen a film in which all the characters are so full of the joy of being.[144]

Pasolini quite rightly identified Fellini's "inexhaustible capacity for love" as the quality that sets him apart from other directors.[145] His singular refusal to assume the tone of the indignant moral reformer that the decadent nature of his subject matter would seem to require enables Fellini to accept his fantastic re-creation of contemporary society and to present it with bemused detachment. Fellini's representation of modern life, viewed "not as a trial seen by a judge but rather by an accomplice,"[146] embodies the Olympian perspective of a great comic genius whose point of view precludes any tragic approach to his world or his work.

---

[143] See Barthélemy Amengual, "Fin d'itinéraire: du 'côté de chez Lumière' au 'côté de Méliès,' " *Études cinématographiques* 127–30 (1981): 81–111. Amengual's essay is the most brilliant exposition of the theory that Fellini's career after *La dolce vita* completely transcends his early work.

[144] Pasolini, "The Catholic Irrationalism of Fellini," pp. 70–71.

[145] Ibid., p. 71.

[146] Cited in Budgen, *Fellini*, p. 99.

CHAPTER FOUR _____

Dreams
and Metacinema

LE TENTAZIONI DEL DOTTOR
ANTONIO, 8 1/2, BLOCK-
NOTES DI UN REGISTA, I
CLOWNS, ROMA, E LA NAVE
VA, GINGER E FRED, AND
INTERVISTA

Remember that this is a comic film.[1] _____

Well, in my film everything happens . . . ok? I'm putting everything in. . . . I have really nothing to say. But I want to say it anyway.[2]

I am very fond of all these characters who are always chasing after me, following me from one film to another. They are all a little mad, I know that. They say they need me, but the truth is that I need them more. Their human qualities are rich, comic, and sometimes very moving.[3]

I thought I would begin the opening of this little film with a dream, the classic dream where one seems to fly. . . . Now, then in the dream I found myself in a dark and troublesome environment, but one which was at the same time also familiar . . . I was moving slowly . . . the darkness was profound . . . and my hands touched a wall that never ended. In other films, in dreams like this one, I freed myself by flying away, but now who knows, a little older and a little heavier, I lifted myself from the ground with great difficulty. . . . Finally I succeeded, and I found myself freed at a great height, and the landscape I saw through pieces of clouds, down there on the ground, what was it? The university campus, the hospital . . . ? It looked like a penitentiary, an atomic bomb shelter. . . . Finally, I recognized it, it was Cinecittà.[4]

AFTER *LA DOLCE VITA*, Fellini's cinema abandons any real interest in the mimetic representation of everyday reality and turns inward toward the expression of the director's personal fantasy world. Quite frequently, Fellini places such oneiric

---

[1] Note attached to Fellini's camera during the shooting of *8 1/2*. Federico Fellini, *Un regista a Cinecittà* (Milan: Mondadori, 1988), p. 50.

narratives within a metacinematic framework. In his turn toward a self-reflexive cinema in the 1960s, Fellini once again anticipated a cultural trend that literary and film historians have only begun to explore fully in the last decade as a key element in contemporary architecture, fiction, and cinema.[5] Although the abrupt break in Fellini's cinema after *La dolce vita* has autonomous sources in the director's artistic evolution and can be seen germinating even in his earliest films, Fellini's encounter with the ideas of Carl Gustav Jung at this crucial point in his career must be given some credit for the change in his narrative techniques. Fellini was introduced to Jung's thought by a Jungian analyst named Ernest Bernhard who lived on Via Gregoriana near Fellini's Via Margutta apartment in Rome. Given Bernhard's telephone number by a director friend (Vittorio De Seta), Fellini contacted Bernhard around the time of the filming of *La dolce vita*, and while the director never actually underwent serious analysis, he was guided by Bernhard in the reading of Jung's writings and in discussing his own active fantasy life and dreams.[6] Fellini not only read a number of Jung's writings very closely, but he also made a pilgrimage to Jung's home in Zurich in 1965. In 1972, Fellini described what Jung had meant to him:

[2] Fellini, *"8 1/2": Federico Fellini, Director*, ed. Charles Affron (New Brunswick, N.J.: Rutgers University Press, 1987), pp. 130, 132 (shots 460, 469). Subsequent references to *8 1/2* will be to this continuity script and will be given by shot number rather than page number.

[3] Fellini's voice-over at the end of *Block-notes di un regista*. Cited from the sound track of the American print by Joseph McBride, "The Director as Superstar," in *Federico Fellini: Essays in Criticism*, ed. Bondanella, p. 160.

[4] Fellini's voice-over at the beginning of *Intervista*. Federico Fellini, *Block-notes di un regista* (Milan: Longanesi, 1988), pp. 78, 79–80.

[5] For discussions of cinematic narrative and metacinema, I have found the following studies most useful: Robert Stam, *Reflexivity in Film and Literature: From Don Quixote to Jean-Luc Godard* (Ann Arbor, Mich.: UMI Research Press, 1985); William Skska, "Metacinema: A Modern Necessity," *Literature/Film Quarterly* 7, no. 4 (1979): 285–89; Edward Branigan, *Point of View in the Cinema: A Theory of Narration and Subjectivity in Classical Film* (Berlin: Mouton Publishers, 1984); and David Bordwell, *Narration in the Fiction Film* (Madison: University of Wisconsin Press, 1985). Contemporary literary criticism has dedicated a great deal of attention during the last decade to metafiction, and a number of such specifically literary studies shed light on parallel developments in the cinema. See Linda Hutcheon, *Narcissistic Narrative: The Metafictional Paradox* (New York: Methuen, 1984), as well as her more recent *A Poetics of Postmodernism: History, Theory, Fiction* (New York: Routledge, 1988); Patricia Waugh, *Metafiction: The Theory and Practice of Self-Conscious Fiction* (New York: Methuen, 1984); Lucente, *Beautiful Fables*; and Kathryn Hume, *Fantasy and Mimesis: Responses to Reality in Western Literature* (New York: Methuen, 1984).

[6] For Fellini's relationship with Bernhard, see Kezich, *Fellini*, pp. 302–7; or Alberto Carotenuto, *Jung e la cultura italiana* (Rome: Astrolabio, 1977).

It was like the sight of unknown landscapes, like the discovery of a new way of looking at life; a chance of making use of its experiences in a braver and bigger way, of recovering all kinds of energies, all kinds of things, buried under the rubble of fears, lack of awareness, neglected wounds. What I admire most ardently in Jung is the fact that he found a meeting place between science and magic, between reason and fantasy. He has allowed us to go through life abandoning ourselves to the lure of mystery, with the comfort of knowing that it could be assimilated by reason.[7]

Fellini has always believed that there is "no dividing line between imagination and reality,"[8] and Jung helped to convince him that the dreams and fantasies he had experienced since childhood and that he had considered an infantile manifestation of adult immaturity were, instead, a means of gaining access to an imaginative world of far greater significance, that of Jung's "collective unconscious," common property of all human beings. To communicate on a subliminal level with his audience by means of films expressing a symbolic world rather than representations of reality might therefore be possible. Specifically, Fellini's encounter with Jung convinced him that his cinema could be opened up to the broader possibilities of intuitive creativity: "I have always thought I had one major shortcoming: that of not having general ideas about anything. The ability to organize my likes, tastes, desires in terms of genre or category has always been beyond me. But reading Jung I feel freed and liberated from the sense of guilt and the inferiority complex that the shortcoming I touched upon always gave me."[9]

Fellini recognized the intellectual power of Jung's rival Freud, but Freud's severity and doctrinaire approach to the unconscious struck Fellini as uncongenial, paternally authoritative, and somewhat threatening, while Jung's fascination with the cultural and poetic aspects of symbols in the life of the psyche was both more permissive and more suggestive: "Freud with his theories makes us think; Jung on the other hand allows us to imagine, to dream and to move forward into the dark labyrinth of our being, to perceive its vigilant, protective presence."[10] The key factor in Fellini's preference for Jung over Freud as a mentor in the exploration of his own unconscious was their very different pronouncements on the symbolic role of imagery, a crucial consideration in Fellini's own artistic creativity. For Fellini, Freud's approach to symbolic imagery was reductive. Freud's symbol "substitutes for something

---

[7] Fellini, *Fellini on Fellini*, p. 147.
[8] Ibid., p. 152.
[9] Fellini, *Comments on Film*, p. 164.
[10] Ibid., p. 167.

else which should be done away with and therefore is better forgotten than expressed"; it was "a way of hiding what is forbidden to express," while, in contrast, Jung viewed the symbol as an expression of an intuition and as "a way of expressing the inexpressible, albeit ambiguously."[11] Examining his fertile imagination through Freud's perspective, in Fellini's opinion, would condemn the director to a "cure," since Freudian psychoanalysis construed Fellini's dreams and fantasies as evidence of psychic repression, while Jung's approach to the symbol as an archetypal image of humanity's collective unconscious suggested, instead, Fellini's privileged role as a creator of images that lent themselves to artistic expression on an emotional rather than a rational or logical level. As Jung's most popular interpreter notes, "dreams, in Jung's view, are the natural reaction of the self-regulating psychic system and, as such, point forward to a higher, potential health, not simply backward to past crises."[12] Moreover, Fellini has always maintained that his personal life was filled with strange, inexplicable coincidences that Jung had studied seriously in an essay entitled "On Synchronicity."[13] Jung's scientific approach to these kinds of psychic phenomena encouraged Fellini to explore the connections between the psychic and the material world in his own synchronic experiences and to believe that they might lead him beyond the restrictions of logic and reason toward an imaginative universe.

In short, Jung provided Fellini not with a philosophical system or a tightly constructed psychology of the unconscious but, instead, with the intellectual justification the director needed to expand his own initially reluctant reliance upon his private resources of fantasy and imagination. Even as a child of seven or eight, Fellini's imagination was apparently extraordinary. He named the four corners of his bed after the four cinemas in Rimini (Fulgor, Opera nazionale balilla, Savoia, Sultano), and each night when the young Fellini went to bed, he had strange visual experiences. Closing his eyes, a phantasmagoric spectacle would pass before him, "a galaxy of luminous points, spheres, shining circles, stars, flames, colored glass, a nocturnal and sparkling cosmos that first presented itself immobile, then in a movement ever more

[11] Ibid.

[12] Joseph Campbell, "Editor's Introduction" to *The Portable Jung* (New York: Penguin, 1976), p. xxii.

[13] See *The Portable Jung*, pp. 505–18, for the text of Jung's essay. In Fellini, *Comments on Film*, pp. 11–14 and 168–70, Fellini notes that a number of concrete decisions in his life have resulted from such synchronic experiences, including his selection of an actor in *E la nave va* and his decision to abandon the film project entitled *Il viaggio di G. Mastorna*. Kezich's biography of Fellini also notes that a synchronic coincidence Fellini experienced even foretold the death of the analyst Bernhard in 1965 (*Fellini*, p. 304).

vast and encompassing, like an immense vortex, a dazzling spiral."[14] The phenomenon would repeat itself as many as three or four times during the evening. These experiences gradually became less frequent as adolescence replaced them with what Fellini calls "much more concrete" and presumably sexual preoccupations.[15] As an adult artist, Fellini felt compelled to recapture this easy access to a world outside everyday reality denied to him after adolescence, "to rediscover on the level of consciousness the visionary faculty."[16]

Jung helped Fellini come to grips with his "visionary faculty" from childhood through an encounter with his adult dreams. One immediate result of the meeting with Bernhard was Fellini's compilation of private dream notebooks beginning in late 1960, only a few pages of which have been published to date.[17] While reading Jung and discussing his works with Bernhard, Fellini began to record sketches of the visual content of his dreams with the dates of their occurrence and the director's comments on what they seemed to signify in a number of large notebooks. These sketches are rendered in the visual style typical of Fellini's caricatures or his preparatory drawings for films. In many cases, the illustrations in these notebooks resemble comic strips that set dialogue in bubbles and employ the bright colors typical of such popular publications. One of the earliest of these illustrated dreams is dated 12 November 1961. In a Florentine square recalling Giorgio De Chirico's metaphysical paintings, or Fellini's nocturnal piazzas in his early films, Fellini is seen in silhouette as a frightened schoolboy, his anxiety rendered visually by drops of sweat typical of comic strip figures under pressure. Forced to take an examination without adequate preparation, Fellini finds himself at a total impasse, paralyzed with fear. In contrast, his assistant Brunello Rondi (the figure illuminated under the streetlamp) has already completed the assignment without difficulty, further increasing the discomfort and guilt Fellini feels. The dream uses a common situation from everyone's childhood memories to express the adult dreamer's far more serious doubts about his creative powers. Another, much later but undated, dream sketch contrasts Fellini's flattering view of himself in his dreams (he is a young man, viewed from

[14] Fellini, *Fare un film*, p. 87.

[15] Ibid., p. 88.

[16] Ibid.

[17] See, for example, Ornella Volta, "Le journal des rêves de Federico Fellini (dessins et propros recueillis par Ornella Volta)," in *Federico Fellini*, ed. Gilles Ciment (Paris: Éditions Rivages, 1988), pp. 14–21 (including black-and-white illustrations); several color illustrations in De Santi, *I disegni di Fellini* (illustrations 292–93, 296); and especially Federico Fellini, "Fellini oniricon," ed. Lietta Tornabuoni, *Dolce vita* 1, no. 3 (1987): 29–44 (numerous color illustrations).

19. Fellini's dream notebooks: a dream of 12 November 1961 reveals an anxious Fellini taking an examination in a De Chirico–like square in Florence

20. Fellini's dream notebooks: Fellini as he dreams of himself (thin and with a bushy head of hair) and as he is (balding and gaining weight)

behind with a healthy head of hair) with an image of the older, somewhat stockier, and balding man he has become late in life.[18] This sketch
underlines how Fellini's dreams are not merely expressions of wish fulfillment but also contain critical self-images as well. An even more
interesting record of another dream, dated December 1974, shows a
young Fellini flying in a balloon with Pope Paul VI. The pontiff points
toward a huge woman whose exclamation, "Oh," produces the white,
fluffy clouds in the sky around the two figures. As a cardinal in Milan
years earlier, Pope Montini had severely punished a group of Milanese
Jesuits who defended *La dolce vita* by disbanding their group, transferring their leader to Bangkok, and forbidding the author of the favorable
review of Fellini's film from writing on the cinema for twenty-five
years![19] For Fellini, Paul VI always represented paternalistic authority,
moralistic judgment, and a refusal to communicate. But in this dream
Fellini also finds a positive meaning in the pope's presence, for Montini's warning that the huge woman represents the "great fabricator and
dissolver of clouds" underlines the woman's ambivalence: she can both
facilitate and impede the director's contact with reality. Fellini identified the woman as a lawyer his father had hired years earlier in a suit
for war damages, and he only remembers that he was so attracted to her
that he almost fainted.[20]

It is difficult to make confident assessments of Fellini's dream notebooks, since the vast majority of the images they contain have never
been published. From the several dozen images I have been able to examine, however, it seems clear that they reflect the normal range of
unconscious phenomena uncovered by psychoanalysis. They are visually intriguing and complex and deal not only with the usual sexual
fantasies one might expect but also with problems of anxiety, insuffi-
ciency, and artistic blockage, preoccupations of all artists. Most of the
few published sketches from the dream notebooks cannot be identified
as *direct* sources of any specific images from Fellini's works, although
a thorough examination of the hundreds of such images in Fellini's jeal-

[18] The drawing has previously been published in Fellini, "Fellini oniricon," p. 30. I
came upon the original copy of this sketch from Fellini's dream notebooks when I
was examining one of the manuscripts obtained from Fellini by the Lilly Library:
"Prova d'orchestra: chiaccherata sul filmetto che avrei in animo di fare," Fellini MS.
5 (Box 1). Fellini had apparently inserted the sketch into the manuscript by mistake.
This manuscript contains a version of the film's soggetto that varies slightly from
the published version in Fellini, *Prova d'orchestra* (Milan: Garzanti, 1980).

[19] Fellini, in "Fellini oniricon," p. 31, discusses the director's relationship with the
then Cardinal Montini. This work contains an earlier dream sketch dated 15 April
1961 that grew out of Fellini's meeting with Montini in an unsuccessful attempt to
help his Jesuit friends. The article also contains Fellini's explanation of this dream.

[20] Ibid., p. 38.

21. Fellini's dream notebooks: Fellini and Pope Paul VI in a hot-air balloon before "the great fabricator and dissolver of clouds"

ously guarded record of his psychic life might well uncover many specific connections between his dreams and particular shots or sequences. At any rate, Fellini's encounter with Bernhard, his enthusiastic reading of Jung's works, and his resulting dream notebooks most certainly explain in large measure why, subsequent to *La dolce vita*, Fellini frequently abandons causal relationships and logical connections in his story lines in favor of a freer interplay between fantasy and reality and an increasingly self-assured reliance on the expressive potential of symbolic imagery typical of the dream state.

The first of Fellini's films to reflect his preoccupation with dreams, *Le tentazioni del dottor Antonio* also responds to the moralistic attacks from segments of Italian society and the Church against the alleged obscenity and defamatory character of *La dolce vita*.[21] Produced as one part of an episodic film entitled *Boccaccio '70*, including contributions by Visconti, Monicelli, and De Sica, this intriguing film, although not a major work in the Fellini canon, nevertheless provided the director with the perfect vehicle for experimentation in a new cinematic style employing color photography that joined Fellini's constant search for new narrative forms with his personal interest in dreams and psychoanalysis.[22] In *Le tentazioni del dottor Antonio*, Fellini shows the deleterious effects upon a bigoted puritan named Doctor Antonio Mazzuolo (Peppino De Filippo) of a billboard poster advertising milk that contains an enormous and sexually suggestive image of Anita Ekberg. In the Christian tradition, Saint Anthony is celebrated as a monk who triumphed over a number of sexual visions and temptations—he is for Fellini the perfect model of the Catholic repression he was attempting to exorcise in his own personality and which found vocal expression in many of the moralistic attacks on *La dolce vita*. But in contrast to his Christian namesake, the visions that Fellini's Doctor Antonio experiences destroy his middle-class respectability by releasing destructive sexual drives that had been meticulously repressed until his encounter with the billboard. The resulting conflict between his strict morality

---

[21] Published scripts of *Le tentazioni del dottor Antonio* must be used with care, given their omissions of changes made in the final version of the film. See Federico Fellini, *"8 1/2" di Federico Fellini*, ed. Camilla Cederna (Bologna: Cappelli, 1965), pp. 165–66 (soggetto) and pp. 169–90 (sceneggiatura); and, in English, Fellini, *Three Screenplays*, pp. 253–88 (only the script).

[22] A number of critical analyses of *Le tentazioni* underline its role as a transitional film from the early, representational works to Fellini's later and highly subjective narrative style. See Rondi, *Il cinema di Fellini*, pp. 298–300; Rondi finds the film flawed in a number of respects but underlines its importance as a key to Fellini's subsequent development; Barthélemy Amengual, "Une mythologie fertile: *Mamma Puttana*," in *Federico Fellini*, ed. Ciment, who sees *Le tentazioni* as the turning point in Fellini's cinema; or Burke, *Federico Fellini*, pp. 114–25.

and his unconscious desires ends in madness. The film contains an unusual narrator, representing Eros or Cupid, whose infantile voice provides ironic commentary on Antonio's psychic battles with his sexual temptations and sings the sexually suggestive advertising jingle accompanying the billboard, exhorting the public to drink more milk.[23]

Such a relatively simple story line allows Fellini almost unlimited freedom to explore the conflict between Antonio's sexual repression and the unrestricted expression of Eros symbolized by the buxom figure of Anita Ekberg on the billboard. Desire and repression make up the film's explicit theme, but the role of the cinema as a psychic screen or mirror of the audience's mediated desire certainly constitutes a secondary and perhaps even more interesting topic. The billboard poster is consciously constructed in the exact shape of the Cinemascope screen on which Fellini's own film is projected.[24] Fellini underlines his implicit treatment of the role of cinema as a mirror of the audience's sexual desires with a query addressed by a German seminarian to a member of the construction crew assembling the poster: "Cinema?" The seminarian receives the ambiguous reply, "No, milk."[25] The fact that the billboard is equipped with a sound system to broadcast its own "sound track," a loudspeaker delivering the advertising jingle, furthers the link between the billboard and a movie screen. As the billboard photograph of Anita Ekberg steps down from the poster and begins to move, it becomes literally a "moving picture." When the gigantic Ekberg picks up Doctor Antonio in her huge hand, Fellini makes one of his very infrequent references to the history of the cinema—an obvious allusion to the celebrated scene in *King Kong* in which, in an inverse situation, the massive gorilla captures the girl.[26] The contrast of Anita's enormous size and the puny figure of Doctor Antonio was produced by the use of special effects—scale models of the buildings in the EUR district of Rome that recall the techniques employed in similar scenes in *King Kong*.

However, Fellini's narrative owes a greater debt to the unconscious than to cinematic history, as the story line of *Le tentazioni del dottor*

[23] "Bevete più latte, il latte fa bene, il latte conviene ad ogni età" ("Drink more milk, milk is good for you, milk is suitable for every age"). Both the Italian and English scripts fail to print the entire jingle.

[24] See Burke, *Federico Fellini*, pp. 114–25, for a discussion of Fellini's metacinematic intent in this film.

[25] This key episode is omitted from both published scripts of the film and was probably inserted into the story later in the filming process during the dubbing.

[26] In Zanelli, *Nel mondo di Federico*, p. 130, Fellini calls the original version of *King Kong* (1933) one of his favorite films. Dino De Laurentiis tried repeatedly but without success to convince Fellini to direct his remake of this American classic.

Antonio imitates the disjunctive, discontinuous state of a dream. Groups of figures appear and disappear without any logical motivation; they are dressed in the bizarre costumes we associate with Fellini's later color films. Fellini employs color photography for the first time in his career in this film. This was not an aesthetic choice but one imposed on him by the producers, since the other episodes were to be shot in color.[27] Even though he would return to black-and-white photography for *8 1/2*, Fellini's subsequent conversion to color photography after *8 1/2* would allow him to employ color to evoke the dream work in his narratives. For most of the film, the camera's point of view reflects the hallucinations of Doctor Antonio, as the surfacing of his repressed sexual desires stimulated by the vision of the billboard begins to disorient his superficially normal personality. When Anita finally becomes irritated with Antonio's silly reaction to her presence on the poster, she begins to strip naked, responding to his repressed desires. On three occasions, Antonio breaks the cardinal rule of conventional representational cinema by rushing toward the camera and ordering the audience not to look at the screen, thus highlighting the metacinematic subtext of the film. As Anita drops her last garment, the narrative suddenly cuts to Antonio, now dressed in the armor of a Saint George fighting the dragon, a theme suggested in a painting shown earlier on an office wall. Antonio throws his phallic lance at Anita; it lodges in the stomach of the figure on the billboard just beneath the actress's breasts; and the film suddenly cuts to a dream sequence of a funeral procession in which all of the characters in Antonio's life appear, chanting "Hurray for Mazzuolo the Liberator." This funeral sequence has affinities with the conclusion of *8 1/2*, but the very different mental condition of Doctor Antonio turns this fantasy into a nightmare rather than a triumph of psychic integration. Antonio's fruitless battles with the dragons of his subconscious destroy this comic figure, and as an ambulance arrives the next morning to carry him away, he is found "draped over the

---

[27] In "The Long Interview," in Fellini, *Federico Fellini's "Juliet of the Spirits,"* p. 32, Fellini told Kezich that *Boccaccio '70* offered him the opportunity to play with color without too much aesthetic commitment, whereas in *Giulietta degli spiriti*, the use of color became a major aesthetic preoccupation. Fellini also notes that colors are an integral part of dreams and that *Boccaccio '70* had also demonstrated the difficulty of making a subtle color film. In the scenes of the buildings in the EUR district, for example, the film was designed to contrast Antonio, dressed in black, with the starkly white marble buildings, but when the film was developed, the marble took on a bluish tint due to reflected light (p. 34). In the same interview, Fellini rejects as romantic and reactionary an often cited statement of his on the use of color in the cinema—"there are only two colors you can use in the cinema—black and white" (p. 35).

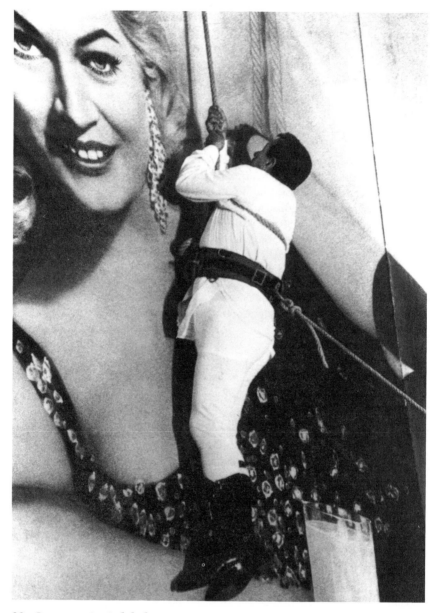

22. *Le tentazioni del dottor Antonio*: Dr. Antonio's secret passions are aroused by the billboard poster of Anita outside his window

poster in a comic parody of intercourse."[28] Antonio's demise provides a
direct response to the bigoted attacks on Fellini's *La dolce vita* and a
warning against the negative effects of repressing normal human sexuality. Who but a repressed fool such as Doctor Antonio, Fellini asks his
audience, would refuse to drink more milk when milk is associated
with such attractive and imposing distributors as those of Anita Ekberg?[29]

Le tentazioni del dottor Antonio remains one of Fellini's minor
films, but a minor film of great suggestive power. Not only does it pre-
figure the revolutionary developments in Fellini's style that arise from
his encounter with Jung, but it also incorporates Fellini's interest in the
unconscious within an implicitly metacinematic discourse on the role
of sexual desire and audience response in the cinema. Such questions
have become a central concern of film theory during the last decade,
and while Fellini's films are not intended to provide a systematic investigation of them, critics who continue to interpret Fellini as an anti-
intellectual director with little of critical importance to offer contemporary film theory would do well to remember that *Le tentazioni del
dottor Antonio* touches on such theoretical concerns long before they
became fashionable in the critical literature.[30] Fellini's views on the
subject of cinematic desire finds comic expression in the film's closing
shot as the impish narrator, Cupid or Eros, who is perched on the ambulance that carries Doctor Antonio away to the insane asylum, repeats
Doctor Antonio's earlier infraction of the cardinal rule of representational cinema by sticking out her tongue directly at the spectator and
the camera eye. Her final narrative "statement" challenges us to con-
tradict Fellini's visual assertion that the triumph of Eros over sexual
repression is not only inevitable but desirable.

Although the interval separating *Le tentazioni del dottor Antonio*
from *8 1/2* is brief, the leap taken by Fellini's imagination between
these two works is truly staggering.[31] More successfully than any of

[28] Burke, *Federico Fellini*, p. 120.
[29] Amengual, "Une mythologie fertile," p. 34.
[30] For a discussion of such theories relating to spectatorship and the notion of desire in the cinema, represented by the work of such theorists as Christian Metz,
Jacques Lacan, and a host of others, the best general treatment may be found in Dud-
ley Andrew, *Concepts in Film Theory* (New York: Oxford University Press, 1984),
esp. chaps. 8–9.
[31] As might be expected from the work's important place in the history of the cinema, the criticism on *8 1/2* is voluminous. Two detailed discussions of the film's
production exist: Camilla Cederna's essay, "La bella confusione," in Fellini, *"8 1/2"
di Federico Fellini*, pp. 15–85; and Deena Boyer, *The Two Hundred Days of "8 1/2"*
(New York: Garland, 1978). Three essential guides to the analysis of the film should
be consulted: Fellini, *"8 1/2": Federico Fellini, Director*; Ted Perry, *Filmguide to "8*

Fellini's other works, *8 1/2* joins a dreamlike narrative form to a self-reflexive analysis of cinematic creativity. Fellini outlined his initial ideas for the film in a letter to his collaborator Brunello Rondi in October 1960. A man of undefined profession must interrupt his confused and complex life for a two-week visit to the baths at Chianciano for a rest cure. He would be described on two levels, the "real" one of his time spent at the spa and another "fantastic level of dreams, imaginings, and memories, that assail him."[32] At this point in the film's evolution, many of the most famous episodes were already envisioned: the harem sequence; the visit to a bishop (later changed to a cardinal); the mistress; the vision of the Ideal Woman, Claudia Cardinale; La Saraghina; the telepath. Fellini worked with Pinelli, Flaiano, and Rondi to create a script that was rewritten three or four times; then Fellini and Pinelli locked themselves in a pensione outside of Rome to rewrite one final draft, producing the document that was eventually published as the shooting script. Additional changes were made during production on the set (usually by Rondi or Fellini), especially in the finale of the film. Originally written to end in a dining car, the script was revised drastically to create the famous carousel ending that became the trademark of Fellini's entire cinematic production. At the last minute, however, even after actors had been selected and advanced work had started on the many sets of the film, Fellini experienced a crisis of confidence and inspiration. Shutting himself in his office, he began writing a letter to his producer to call off the entire project because the film no longer made any sense to him. At that moment, the chief machinist invited Fellini to celebrate the beginning of *8 1/2* with a glass of champagne on the set:

> The glasses were emptied, everybody applauded, and I felt overwhelmed by shame. I felt myself the least of men, the captain who abandons his crew. I didn't go back to the office where my half-written copout letter was waiting for me, but instead sat down, blank and emptied, on a little bench in the garden in the middle of a great coming and going of workers, technicians, actors belonging to other working troupes. I told myself I was in a no exit situation. I was a director who wanted to make a film he no longer remembers. And lo and behold, at that very moment every-

1/2" (Bloomington: Indiana University Press, 1975); and Albert E. Benderson, *Critical Approaches to Federico Fellini's "8 1/2"* (New York: Arno Press, 1974). Other major treatments of the film include an entire issue of the French journal *Études cinématographiques* (nos. 28–29, 1963); my own *Federico Fellini: Essays in Criticism*, which includes widely cited essays by Christian Metz, Barbara Lewalski, and Timothy Hyman; Rondi, *Il cinema di Fellini*, pp. 301–33; and Costello, *Fellini's Road*, pp. 79–147.

[32] Fellini, *"8 1/2": Federico Fellini, Director*, p. 227.

thing fell into place. I got straight to the heart of the film. I would narrate everything that had been happening to me. I would make a film telling the story of a director who no longer knows what film he wanted to make.[33]

The sudden revelation to Fellini of his real theme, unconsciously avoided until he had his back against the wall, was no doubt encouraged by Fellini's growing reliance upon his subconscious as a result of his encounter with Jung and the analysis of his own dreams. The film's strange numerical label, after Flaiano's suggestion of *La bella confusione* had been rejected, underscores the personal nature of *8 1/2* and refers to the total number of films Fellini had produced up to that time. Fellini arrived at this total by considering his first codirected film with Lattuada, *Luci del varietà*, and the two episodes produced with other directors (*Un'agenzia matrimoniale* and *Le tentazioni del dottor Antonio*) each as half of a film for a subtotal of one and one half. This subtotal added to the six previously completed films plus the one in progress came to a total of 8 1/2 films. The fact that its protagonist, Guido Anselmi (Marcello Mastroianni), was a film director like Fellini and even wore the same kind of hat and black suit Fellini habitually wore during the period prompted critics to interpret the film as purely autobiographical. Fellini categorically denies this, maintaining instead that the films that seem to be his most autobiographical narrate completely invented stories.[34]

If autobiographical approaches to Fellini's films lead toward a critical reductionism that Fellini quite understandably detests, there is no doubt that the narrative structure of *8 1/2* reflects Fellini's interest in the dream state. The film opens with a nightmare (shots 1–18): Guido is trapped in a car inside a tunnel, while all around him strange individuals are sitting inside other cars blocked in a traffic jam, including a woman we later discover to be his mistress Carla, who is being fondled by an older man. Guido seeks to escape from the car and suddenly rises high above the clouds in a classic flying fantasy until he is pulled down to earth abruptly by a man later identified as the press agent for Claudia, an actress Guido has called to the set of his projected film. Sexual anxieties (flying, his mistress's betrayal) in Guido's life are thus neatly

[33] Fellini, *Comments on Film*, pp. 161–62.

[34] In *Un regista a Cinecittà*, Fellini notes: "But it is not true that Marcello is me, my cinematographic double, an alter ego . . . I put my hat on his head not to identify him with me but to give him a trace, a suggestion . . . I seek to make him similar to me because this is the most direct way for me to see the character and the story" (p. 52).

joined to the film's major theme, Guido's attempt to escape responsibility in his work and his life.

Fellini abruptly moves from the nightmare to a waking state in Guido's hotel room at the spa (shots 19–31), which we are now invited to construe as the "real" world and in which Guido receives his first harsh criticism from his doctor and his French scriptwriter. Just when we have been reassured that there are clear demarcations between illusion and reality in Fellini's narrative, we move to the important scene in Guido's bathroom (shots 32–33) that undercuts our facile confidence. The bathroom sequence now emphasizes the *cinematic* quality of everything we have just witnessed, with the intrusive presence of studio arc lamps and the warning buzzer of a sound stage. Neat boundaries between fantasy and reality collapse as both kinds of visual experience are subsumed under the overriding category of cinematic illusion.

A second major jump from "reality" to Guido's subconscious occurs in a transition from Carla's hotel room (shots 93–104) to Guido's dream of a country cemetery (shots 105–16). In his lovemaking with his mistress, Guido "directs" Carla, ordering her to play the role of a whore. Later, while he sleeps as Carla reads a comic book in bed, Guido's mother, dressed in black, enters the room, triggering Guido's second dream. The dominant emotion of this sequence is guilt—Guido's father criticizes the grave that his son should have made higher and more beautiful; his producer appears to reprove Guido's artistic hesitations; and when Guido kisses his mother, she turns into his wife Luisa. The link between Guido's wife, mistress, and mother suggests not only that the protagonist suffers from a classic oedipal complex but that he is attempting to extract from the different women in his life a complex and impossible synthesis of maternal, wifely, and whorish qualities. The origin of Guido's specific form of sexual desire will become clearer through the narrative's subsequent revelation of other dreams and fantasies.

All of Guido's dreams and fantasies are not negative, however. During an evening performance at the spa, Guido meets the telepath Maurice (Ian Dallas), who correctly reads the strange phrase Guido has in his mind: "Asa . . . Nisi . . . Masa." The significance of the phrase is immediately explained in the complex farmhouse sequences (shots 226–47), which show Guido as a young boy finding total security and well-being in the care of his nannies and his grandmother, who bathe him in a huge wine vat and carry him off to bed in warm blankets. After the adults leave the children, a young girl tells Guido not to sleep, since that night they will see the eyes move in a portrait hung in the room by reciting the magic words "Asa Nisi Masa." The telepath had thus tapped into the adult Guido's subconscious and recalled a childhood experience that still governs his relationships with women in the present. The magic words come from a children's word game much like our own "pig Latin" that transforms the Italian word *anima*, meaning soul, spirit, conscience, even consciousness. There is little doubt that Fellini refers here to the "anima" Jung defines in discussing the usually unconscious feminine aspect of male personality in the essay "Marriage as a Psychological Relationship" (1926), also an important influence on *Giulietta degli spiriti*. In it, Jung declares that most of what men say about women's emotional life or their eroticism derives from their own anima projections and is accordingly distorted. Furthermore, Jung argues that certain kinds of women seem to attract such masculine anima projections:

> The so-called "sphinx-like" character is an indispensable part of their equipment, also an equivocalness, and intriguing elusiveness—not an indefinite blur that offers nothing, but an indefiniteness that seems full of promises, like the speaking silence of a Mona Lisa. A woman of this kind is both old and young, mother and daughter, of more than doubtful chastity, childlike, and yet endowed with a naïve cunning that is extremely disarming to men.[35]

While the farmhouse sequence explains Guido's adult search for the security he knew fleetingly as a child, his first encounter with the cardinal at the spa is interrupted by the sight of a woman's leg that triggers an abrupt cut to the famous sequences devoted to Guido's school days and his traumatic encounter with La Saraghina (Edra Gale), a huge prostitute who practices her trade in an abandoned pillbox on the beach near the school. This flashback will explain the origins of Guido's adult views on sexuality and women. Guido and his friends pay La Saraghina to dance, and the woman pulls Guido into the dance with her just before the priests from the school interrupt the scene and capture Guido in a comic chase that employs speeded-up motion typical of the jerky manner in which silent comedies are projected on a contemporary fixed-speed camera (shot 371). The priests then subject the young boy to a cruel interrogation, fixing forever in Guido's mind the repressive equation of woman with sin and the devil. After praying for forgiveness before a statue of the Virgin, the young Guido nevertheless returns to see La Saraghina (shots 390–92); he is still fascinated by her strange appeal. Here Fellini inserts a brilliant dissolve (shot 389 to 390) from the face of the Virgin, whose image is identical to that of the Beautiful Unknown Woman (Caterina Boratto), who appears from time to time in Guido's adult life without being identified, to La Saraghina's pillbox.

---

[35] *The Portable Jung*, p. 174.

Once again, Fellini combines an implicit reference to the cinema with the exploration of Guido's psyche, for Caterina Boratto was a famous actress popular during Fellini's childhood, and her mysterious appearances throughout the course of *8 1/2* underscore the subliminal presence of cinema throughout Fellini's metacinematic narrative. Despite the cruel punishment Guido receives in school, leading to his identification of feminine sexuality with evil, the experience has only confused Guido. As an adult, he will always be condemned to separating women into two groups—virgins and whores. He will consider sexual desire "dirty" with women he loves and respects (such as Luisa) and appropriate only with "bad" or "fallen" women such as La Saraghina or Carla. Unable to imagine a woman as a complete person, as both a free subject *and* an object of desire, Guido is condemned to search guiltily for the Ideal, a nonexistent woman whom the adult Guido eventually ejects from the concluding circle of the carousel after he comes to terms with his personal problems.

We now understand in retrospect why Fellini's narrative jumps from Guido's first visit with the cardinal to his traumatic encounter with La Saraghina, since the cardinal symbolizes the institution that produced the original sense of sexual guilt in the young boy. By this time Guido is desperately trying to reconcile all of his conflicting ideas about sexuality and women, and when his mistress Carla appears in the public square and sits near Guido, Luisa, and their friend Rossella, the protagonist's frantic reaction is to imagine a friendly encounter between his wife and mistress—surely the height of male wish fulfillment! The narrative then cuts abruptly to the memorable harem sequence (shots 509–74). Here, in Guido's fantasy, all of the women in his life are reconciled in a manner similar to the meeting between Luisa and Carla that Guido has just imagined. Guido's harem fantasy is set in the same farmhouse kitchen where the young Guido was bathed by his nannies (shots 226–47) and where he found a fleeting moment of paradisiacal security in their arms. It is thus not a sensual garden of earthly delights as we might expect but, instead, a womblike refuge where women cuddle him after his bath, pander to his every childish desire, and rebel against his tyranny only with a make-believe revolt that gives Guido the opportunity to prove his manliness without having to do so in bed. There, according to one remark by Jacqueline Bonbon (Yvonne Casadei), the French dancer whose forced retirement to the attic when she reaches her twenty-sixth birthday is the pretext for the women's revolt against Guido's male chauvinism, Guido is all talk and no action. All of the women in Guido's life, assembled in the harem, represent aspects of Guido's anima, and, as Jung noted, they are therefore distortions of a fully expressed and free feminine character.

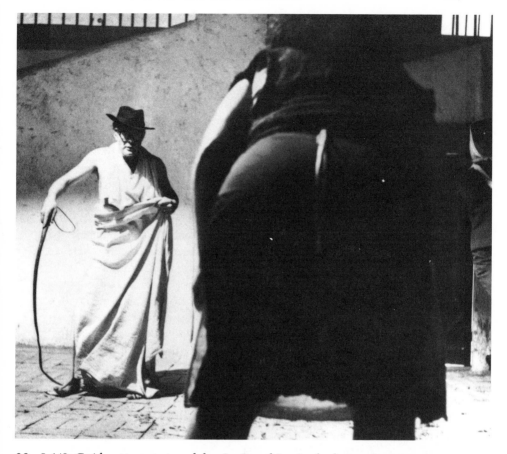

23. *8 1/2*: Guido attempts to subdue La Saraghina in the harem fantasy sequence

8 1/2 contains some forty major episodes of various sequences with a total of fifty-three major characters and a host of minor ones.[36] With its huge cast and numerous imaginative set constructions, avoiding whenever possible shooting in outside locations, the film recalls the equally mammoth production of *La dolce vita*. The essential difference between the loosely constructed episodic narratives of the two films lies in *8 1/2*'s use of dreams and fantasy sequences to link the mass of visual material together. Almost everything in *8 1/2* contradicts the traditional seamless story line of the conventional Hollywood film. But now the peculiarly Fellinian technique of stringing together a large number of loosely related sequences becomes a stream-of-consciousness narra-

[36] For convenience, I accept Perry's count in *Filmguide to "8 1/2,"* pp. 2–9.

tive with the intrusive presence of dreams, waking fantasies, and imaginative visual creations on the screen that represent the subjective
perspective of the protagonist-director. Rapid jumps between Guido's
"reality" at the spa, his dreams or nightmares, and his projected fantasies visualized for our examination destroy any traditional sense of
time. Our natural desire to pinpoint the time of the narrative is frustrated to some degree by Fellini's confusion of costumes, which juxtaposes characters dressed in the style of the 1930s (the era in which both
Guido's and Fellini's childhood took place) with those of the present
(1962) in the same scenes. The film's editing further disorients and dis-
locates our conventional perspectives. Traditional establishing shots
are avoided to deny us any confidence in our sense of space and place.
Without such establishing shots, the constant jumps in the narrative
flow between "reality," Guido's waking fantasies, and flashbacks to
Guido's past or privileged insights into his dreams and nightmares are
even more disconcerting than they might otherwise be. Even backgrounds from shot to shot of the same sequence, particularly in shots
reflecting Guido's subjective stream of consciousness, may change
without notice. As a result, transitions from one shot to the next do not
match, producing the same puzzling sensation we often experience during a dream. This is particularly striking during the presentation of the
confessionals that should be a stable part of the background for a number of shots depicting Guido's traumatic punishment by the priests for
visiting La Saraghina (shots 384–88). The confessionals actually change
both position and shape from shot to shot.[37] Such devices that underline the dreamlike nature of the narrative and its function as a reflection of the protagonist's subjective states of mind are added to camera
techniques that further emphasize the spectator's sense of uneasiness.
Guido's major concern is to escape responsibility—his professional responsibility to complete a film he is incapable of conceiving; his moral
responsibility to his wife Luisa (Anouk Aimée), whom he betrays with
his sultry mistress (Sandra Milo); his intellectual responsibility to remain open to the devastating critiques of his future film provided by
the French intellectual Daumier (Jean Rougeul); his apparently neglected obligations to his deceased parents and to his friends and colleagues, who depend on him and his authority for their livelihood. Even
the theme of the science-fiction film that he cannot bring to a conclusion deals with escape—the launching of a rocket ship from earth after

---

[37] An extremely detailed analysis of this entire sequence may be found in a pam-
phlet by Marilyn Fabe, "8 1/2": The Saraghina Sequence (Mt. Vernon, N.Y.: Macmillan Films, 1975).

a thermonuclear disaster.[38] Guido's sense of imprisonment and his inability to elude responsibility find perfect expression in the director's photography. Whenever the camera does not embody Guido's subjective point of view, it consistently traps Guido within its restrictive frame while other characters are paradoxically able to move easily in and out of the frame as they make their strident demands of Guido.[39] While Guido attains freedom of movement through the creative power of his imagination, he is never able to shake off the prison of Fellini's camera.

As we watch Guido's narrative unfold and attempt to untangle the interrelated projections of his perceptions of the "real" world around him from his flashbacks, dreams, and fantasies, a second and even more complicated theme develops within the consistently oneiric atmosphere of *8 1/2*'s story line: a metacinematic discourse on Guido's *inability* to produce his science-fiction film—a discourse that paradoxically constitutes the content of Fellini's *completed* film. Throughout Guido's story, a number of strange sounds and lights puzzle the spectator. When Guido enters his hotel bathroom after a physical examination (shot 33), a humming sound is followed by a bright, overexposed light and a buzzing noise. The same buzzing is repeated on the sound track on numerous occasions: in Guido's hotel lobby (shot 117) and the lobby of the spa (shot 129); while Luisa leaves the theater during the projection of Guido's screen tests (shot 630); and intermittently during shots 603 and 643–48 as the screen tests are being projected. The last shots of the screen tests also contain the intensified sound of a film projector in operation on the sound track. Spectators familiar with a sound stage will recognize the first humming noise as that produced when arc lamps are lit, while such buzzer noises warn people on a set that shooting is about to begin. With such simple but effective self-reflexive devices, Fellini constantly reminds the careful viewer that Guido's story is a film in progress and that the true intent of *Fellini's* film is to recount Guido's inability to make the science-fiction film. The incomplete sets of the space platform visited by Guido and his colleagues underline the fact that Guido's film never materializes, while the film we are watching, that by Fellini, is moving confidently toward

[38] Kezich reports that immediately after the conclusion of *Giulietta degli spiriti*, Fellini actually signed a contract with Dino De Laurentiis for a film entitled *Assurdo universo*, the Italian title of a science-fiction novel by Frederic William Brown published in 1949 as *What Mad Universe*, a film Kezich sees as having some affinities with what he calls the "fantacoscienza" film entitled *Il viaggio di G. Mastorna*, the mythical film on the passage between life and the afterlife that Fellini never completed (*Fellini*, pp. 357–58).

[39] Perry, *Filmguide to "8 1/2,"* p. 21.

completion. As Christian Metz has noted, *"we never see the film that Guido is to make; we do not even see extracts from it, and thus any distance between the film Guido dreamt of making and the film Fellini made is abolished: Fellini's film is composed of all that Guido would have liked to have put into his film—and that is precisely why Guido's film is never shown separately."*[40]

The episode of the screen tests (shots 575–655), in which members of the production team, Luisa, and some family friends and relatives gather to help Guido select actresses to fill various roles in the science-fiction film, displays the sophisticated mirroring of art and reality, life and cinema, that takes place in *8 1/2*. The screen test sequences also provide an extremely complex key to the aesthetic principles underlying the entire work. At first, we are puzzled by the striking absence of any screen tests for the most obvious protagonist—the main character in Guido's science-fiction film. Eventually, we realize that no protagonist of the projected science-fiction film exists, since that film does not exist. Guido, on the other hand, does exist, but only as the protagonist of the film we are observing in progress. It will soon dawn on the viewer of *8 1/2*, although probably not after only one viewing of the film, that the roles presented during the screen tests have nothing whatsoever to do with the science-fiction film of which we never catch a glimpse. Instead, they are figures from Guido's past or present *life* and not *characters* in a projected film. Earlier, in shot 130, we learned that a French actress (Madeleine LeBeau, actually a French actress) had been summoned by Guido to play the role of a mistress. But all of the women who appear in the screen tests for the role of the mistress identified in the film as "Miss Olimpia" are look-alikes of Carla, Guido's mistress in real life, just as the actresses testing for the part of a wife resemble Anouk Aimée or those of La Saraghina resemble Edra Gale. The link between the screen tests and Guido's projected film has been suddenly broken as Fellini mingles screen tests for Guido's projected but never visualized science-fiction *film* with tests that seem to cast actresses to play characters in Guido's *life*. Neither the mistress nor the wife nor La Saraghina could conceivably have anything to do with a science-fiction film about the aftermath of nuclear war. The frequent noise of the soundstage buzzer, mentioned previously, occurs incessantly during the screen tests as a cue that Fellini's own film in progress has begun to supplant the film Guido is unable to complete.

The fact that the character represented in Guido's life by Carla is identified in the screen tests as "Miss Olimpia" actually refers to Fel-

---

[40] "Mirror Construction in Fellini's *8 1/2*," in *Federico Fellini: Essays in Criticism*, ed. Bondanella, p. 133; also in Fellini, *"8 1/2": Federico Fellini, Director*, p. 264.

lini's own screen tests just prior to the making of *8 1/2*. Deena Boyer's day-by-day account of the production of the film notes that the screen test sequence was the first part of *8 1/2* Fellini shot. On that first day of production (9 May 1962), the first actress to portray Carla in the screen tests was a woman named Olimpia Cavalli, who wore the same costume that Sandra Milo wore only a few days earlier on 7 May for the real screen test that won her the role of Carla.[41] The interpenetration of various levels of "reality" in the narrative underlined by the strange congruency between the screen tests Fellini shot to establish his actors for *his* film and the screen tests Guido used to define characters in his life rather than in his projected film has already been suggested implicitly throughout the film by the fact that a large number of the film's characters retain the names of the actors who interpret them. This technique, also used in *La dolce vita*, throws our normal perceptions of the clear distinctions between actors and the characters they play off ever so slightly.[42] Guido's three production assistants, Bruno Agostini, Cesarino, and Conocchia, all retain their names in the film. Rossella Falk (Luisa's friend who plays the critical "cricket" to Guido's Pinocchio), Nadine Sanders (the airline hostess), and Mario Pisu (Guido's friend with a young mistress named Gloria, played by Barbara Steele) are called, respectively, Rossella, Nadine, and Mario in the film. Claudia Cardinale appears both as an actress named Claudia summoned by Guido to audition for his film (who eventually discovers that there is no film and therefore no part for her) and as the ideal vision of feminine beauty Guido finally omits from the concluding carousel at the film's finale.[43]

Throughout the course of *8 1/2*, Guido is constantly assailed by criticisms of his weak personality, his failure to complete his projected film, his pessimism, and his intellectual inconsistency. When Guido is examined by a doctor at the spa just after the nightmare opening the film, the doctor asks him if he is preparing another film without hope (shot 20). The French intellectual Daumier then enters the room and informs Guido that the script he is reading contains no central idea or

[41] Boyer, *The Two Hundred Days of "8 1/2,"* p. 17; the complicated significance of the screen test sequence was first explained thoroughly by Costello, *Fellini's Road*, pp. 130–34, although Perry, *Filmguide to "8 1/2,"* pp. 56–58, is also quite useful in making sense of this important episode. The exact schedule of the production of *8 1/2* by individual sequences may be examined in Fellini, *"8 1/2": Federico Fellini, Director*, pp. 235–37.

[42] See Costello, *Fellini's Road*, pp. 83–88.

[43] Costello, in ibid., pp. 85–86, sees four levels of meaning in the presence of Claudia Cardinale: as Guido's Ideal; as a character in Guido's film; as an actress named Claudia hired by Guido to play the role of the museum curator's daughter; and finally as the real Claudia Cardinale hired by Fellini to interpret all these roles.

problematic (shot 54). Mario's young mistress (shot 59) did not like Guido's last film. After Claudia's first appearance as the Ideal at the spa handing Guido a glass of pure water in his fantasy, Daumier attacks this scene as the worst in the entire script (shots 64–65). One of two young girls introduced to Guido in the production office by Cesarino as his "nieces" (but obviously sleeping with him) remarks that Guido cannot create a real love story (shots 287–88). Conocchia (shot 295) is angry because Guido has not told him what his film is about. After Guido's first meeting with the cardinal, which results in a flashback to Guido's childhood and the central sequence with La Saraghina explaining Guido's sexual fixations, Daumier mercilessly attacks the episode (shots 392–95), accusing Guido of departing from an initial denunciation of Catholic consciousness and concluding as the Church's accomplice (a frequent criticism aimed at Fellini himself). Guido's producer, Pace (Guido Alberti), attacks Guido's lack of clarity (shot 401) and orders him to choose the actresses during the screen tests (shot 590). Claudia even says that Guido is afraid of constructive criticism and that his artistic impasse has been caused by his failure to know how to love (shots 684–86). Guido's paranoia and fear of creative blockage, fed by such incessant attacks, finally lead to his imagined suicide during the press conference, where he is hounded by reporters and paparazzi, one of whom declares in English that Guido has nothing to say (shots 690–736). Finally, immediately before the famous ending that brings 8 1/2 to a resounding conclusion, Daumier once again intervenes, praising Guido for canceling the projected film, since intellectuals must remain lucid even when that necessitates refusing to create (shots 738–54). Daumier also cites Mallarmé's famous remarks about the blank page, as well as Rimbaud's view that true perfection lies in nothingness, to justify Guido's creative failure.

During the screen tests, Guido reacts to Daumier's incessant negativism by imagining that the critic is hanged by his production assistants (shots 577–86). This particular scene, as well as all of the others portraying Guido's critics as grotesque, comic characters, may well represent Fellini's imagined revenge upon his detractors. More importantly, however, by including all of the conceivable attacks on Guido's unrealized film in the narrative, Fellini also managed to incorporate into 8 1/2 all of the possible attacks on *his* completed film. The film thus not only presents a complex visual experience but, at the same time, invites the spectator to undertake a self-conscious analysis of the limitations of that visual experience. And in the constant movement back and forth between the magic visualizations of Guido's potential script and Daumier's petty attacks on it that follow, the irrational creative powers of the artist clearly prevail over the logical and rational discourse of the intellectual.

The one significant Italian literary precedent that exists for Fellini's brilliant exploration of the unconscious within a metacinematic framework is Luigi Pirandello's trilogy of the theater: *Sei personaggi in cerca d'autore* (1921); *Ciascuno a suo modo* (1924); and *Questa sera si recita a soggetto* (1930). In addition to these three dramatic works, Pirandello also composed two early short stories from which his revolutionary inquiries into the nature of drama originally departed ("La tragedia d'un personaggio," 1911; and "Colloqui coi personaggi," 1915), as well as important explanatory prefaces to the entire trilogy of the theater and to *Sei personaggi*.[44] We have already noted how Pirandello's move away from realism in the theater anticipates Fellini's own transition from neorealism to the creation of his unique poetic cinema during the 1950s. Now, the Sicilian dramatist seems to have provided Fellini with a model for transcending representational discourse entirely, moving toward metacinema much as Pirandello revolutionized the theater with his metadramatic plays.

Pirandello's preface to *Sei personaggi* describes the characters from his imagination as if they had an independent existence as real people. One day, he claims, six of them came to his home and demanded to be given artistic form on the stage. In what Pirandello calls "a spontaneous illumination of the fantasy,"[45] he decided to ignore their rather melodramatic tale and give them, instead, another artistic form—they would represent six characters eternally unable to express themselves in the dramatic form of their own choosing. While they believe their destiny lies in the production of the melodrama, which is *una commedia da fare*—a play in the making—Pirandello's drama, unlike their projected play, achieves artistic completion and constitutes the dramatic staging of the characters' failure to achieve artistic expression in a play of their own. There is thus a direct and very obvious parallel between the *unrealized* drama of Pirandello's six characters or the *unshot* science-fiction film planned by Guido, on the one hand, and the *completed* play or film by Pirandello and Fellini, on the other hand. The content of *Sei personaggi* and *8 1/2*, respectively, dramatizes or visualizes a failure of artistic expression, and this projection of the failure of artistic expression paradoxically becomes a self-reflexive artistic creation itself.

A number of significant parallels between *8 1/2* and *Sei personaggi* confirm the affinity between these two masterpieces. Pirandello's play

[44] For the texts of the three plays and the two prefaces, see Luigi Pirandello, *Maschere nude* (Milan: Mondadori, 1958), vol. 1; the short stories are in Pirandello, *Novelle per un anno* (Milan: Mondadori, 1978), vols. 1 and 2.

[45] Pirandello, *Maschere nude* 1:39.

constantly emphasizes its own metadramatic nature by unfolding on an empty stage during a dress rehearsal, just as Fellini's film underlines the fact that its subject is a film in progress by showing us not only incomplete sets (such as the launching pad) but numerous locations that are so fantastic that they could be found only on a movie set. Pirandello's play avoids the classic division of the dramatic text into scenes or acts, just as Fellini interrupts the traditional smooth flow of narrative by confusing various levels of consciousness. Both works contain the entire range of negative commentary that could possibly be addressed to them: the director and the actors called to stage the melodrama of the six characters fulfill the metacritical function that the French intellectual carries out in *8 1/2*. When we finally catch a glimpse of the traumatic event that has shaped the tragedy of the six characters, it is the classic primal scene of incest so central to Freudian psychoanalysis. The melodrama that the six characters wish to stage is the moment at which the father makes advances toward his stepdaughter, but before we discover whether or not the act of incest was consummated, the characters' play is interrupted. The failure to complete the psychodrama proposed by the frustrated six characters provides the content for Pirandello's completed play. The screen test sequences in *8 1/2*, with their confusion of life and art, may be compared to scenes from *Ciascuno a suo modo* in which actors on the stage and real people in the audience argue over the drama being presented as a *pièce à clef*. The constant refusal to separate fiction and reality in Fellini's film also occurs in two "Choral Intermezzi" of *Ciascuno a suo modo*, in which the action on the stage is transferred to the foyer and corridors of the theater itself, destroying the conventional division between stage and audience.

Perhaps most importantly, however, both *Sei personaggi* and *8 1/2* present a crucial dramatization of the moment of artistic creation. In *Sei personaggi*, this occurs when the six characters assemble to present their psychodrama. As if by magic, their attempt to stage their melodrama causes the materialization of a seventh character—Madama Pace, the procuress-owner of the "dress shop" in which the father makes his fatal assignation with his stepdaughter. Pirandello specifically calls this event "my fantasy in the act of creation."[46] There is no rational explanation for the presence of the seventh character: she is not in search of an author like the other six figures but simply shows up because her presence is required to complete the scene. The implication is that in the endless attempts of the six characters to stage their melodrama, all of which must fail since Pirandello has defined them as

[46] Ibid., 1:44.

incomplete characters, Madama Pace will automatically show up in their midst each time they do so.

In Fellini's film, an even more moving representation of artistic creativity in process takes place during the justly famous finale, in which Guido reconciles himself with his past and begins once again to act as a film director. At the same time, Fellini himself asserts his complete mastery over the bewildering collection of characters and interwoven story lines that have alternated between reality and fantasy throughout the film. As Daumier drones on and on about how intellectuals must sometimes reject artistic creation, the telepath Maurice announces to Guido: "We're ready to begin" (shot 743). From this point until almost the end of the film (to shot 770), Fellini visualizes Guido's sudden realization that acceptance represents the key to all of his psychological and professional problems. Every character in Guido's life, now dressed in white to signify his reconciliation with each of them, marches down the staircase off the launching pad in a carousel celebration around a circuslike circle: Carla, his mother and father, his coworkers and friends, the Beautiful Unknown Woman, La Saraghina, and all the rest are there. Conspicuously absent, however, from the final assembly are Claudia, the Ideal, and Daumier the critic. The Ideal Woman is now superfluous since Guido has ceased to make distinctions between Carla and Luisa. And Daumier's negativism has been rendered ridiculous by the very act of creation taking place on the screen in front of our eyes. Guido's solution is beguilingly simple: acceptance brings reconciliation. Guido no longer has to choose; he is freed from the paralyzing effects of choice and responsibility. All in the same breath, he can now kiss the ring of the cardinal (shot 768), arrange an assignation with Carla on the following day (shot 768), and come to an understanding with Luisa (shot 770), who finally accepts his invitation to join the others in the dancing circle. As one perceptive critic of Fellini's Catholic conditioning has put it, the rejection of choice at the conclusion of Guido's story represents the achievement of a world without sin.[47] Guido is finally at peace with himself and with others, but he undergoes no apotheosis or conversion either in the traditional Catholic sense or even in that more specialized sense of a secular and personal change of character that typified Fellini's trilogy of grace or salvation. Now, it is the world of Art that redeems Guido, not an act of will or a moral conversion.[48] After Guido steps into the magic circle with the rest of the

---

[47] Nicole Zand, "The Guilty Conscience of a Christian Consciousness," in Fellini, "8 1/2": Federico Fellini, Director, pp. 278–79.

[48] Branigan, in Point of View in the Cinema, pp. 161–63, finds four different resolutions at the conclusion of 8 1/2: (1) Guido's suicide, a negative transcendence; (2) Guido's acceptance of his contradictions; (3) Guido's subsequent return to action as

figures from his confused life, the last shot of the film (772) takes place in the dark of the night, which also represents the dark of the movie theater. The young schoolboy Guido marches backward and forward with the four circus clowns who accompany his fife with their instruments. The clowns march off, leaving Guido in the spotlight. The spotlight is turned off, Guido exits, and the rest of the ring lights are extinguished. The music continues as the credits begin at the end of the film. Guido, the adult director, had been in control of the ending until he stepped with his wife into the magic circle of his experiences. At that point, the young schoolboy Guido took the adult's place. Now, with the disappearance of young Guido from the screen, Fellini the director reasserts his presence and his ultimate control over Guido's story. The finale, which began as a celebration of Guido's acceptance of life, an attitude that allowed the adult director to begin his work and to rediscover a fresh creative power, now becomes a celebration of the triumph of Fellini's own artistic creativity. Fellini's ending may have been intended originally to serve as a trailer, an advertisement for the film's "coming attraction." Concluding the metacinematic discourse of *8 1/2* with such a sequence, what one critic has recently termed a "representation of a representation" or a "presentation *prior* to representation"[49] stands as the most subtle of the many metacinematic elements of this masterpiece.

Almost all of Fellini's works after *8 1/2* contain some metacinematic references.[50] However, a self-reflexive examination of the nature of cinema as an art form becomes the *major* theme in six specific films. Four of these works—*Block-notes di un regista*, *I clowns*, *Roma*, and *Inter-*

---

an author, a director, as a result of his acceptance; and (4) a final transcendence presenting Art as the ultimate mediation between reality and fantasy.

[49] Charles Affron, "8 1/2 What?" in Fellini, "8 1/2": Federico Fellini, Director, p. 17. Almost every critic of this moving ending (Kezich, Costello, Affron, and Perry, to mention only a few), as well as Fellini himself, notes that the original ending of the screenplay concluded in a dining car of a moving train. There is no question that the emotional and artistic power of Fellini's final choice was, indeed, the best choice. Moreover, the fact that the final ending was originally intended to be an advertising trailer for the film is a generally accepted fact. However, in an unpublished interview with Tullio Pinelli (8 October 1987), Fellini's collaborator informed me that the ending was *not* intended to be a trailer. Instead, Pinelli claims he convinced Fellini to change the ending because the movement and action in the carousel would be more effective than the static railroad scene and would underline the element of fantasy so crucial to the entire film.

[50] For instance, *Prova d'orchestra* is a pseudodocumentary; *Amarcord* and *La città delle donne* make interesting statements about cinema as the reflection of the spectator's desire; and *Toby Dammit* treats the role of the actor. However, I have discussed these films in different chapters, since the metacinematic themes of these works are less important than other arguments.

vista—form a coherent group, since Fellini appears in each film as himself. To put it more precisely, the director Fellini becomes the actor named Fellini playing the role of a character called Fellini who is a director of the films in question. Fellini's presence in these films thus serves to confuse what is generally a clear distinction between the functions of character, actor, and director.[51] Two other films—*E la nave va* and *Ginger e Fred*—touch on the history of the cinema as an art form and juxtapose the cinema with the other mass medium of our century, television. The four films in which Fellini appears as himself, as well as *E la nave va*, all call into question the usually clear distinction between fiction and documentary film, and to some extent they parody the conventions of documentary, a genre Fellini has generally disliked during his entire career and which he attacked in *Un'agenzia matrimoniale*. Two of these four self-reflexive films—*Block-notes di un regista* and *I clowns*—were also made for television, a medium Fellini distrusts even more than documentary film as a means of expressing the individual artistic signature of an auteur.

Block-notes di un regista, produced for the American NBC television network, was, in Fellini's words, a "conversational" sort of program that the director could assemble without concerning himself with its sketchy nature, but Fellini was surprised by the pleasure such an unpretentious project gave him after his initial reluctance to work in the new medium of television.[52] Moreover, placing himself in the role of a documentary filmmaker (even if only to parody the pretentious assumption that such works capture the "truth" or "reality" of their subject matter) forced Fellini to reconsider the entire question of film's relationship to reality. Fellini concluded, not surprisingly, that "the only documentary that anyone can make is a documentary on himself. 'The

[51] Italian scripts for the two television films are included in Federico Fellini, *Fellini TV: "Block-notes di un regista"/"I clowns,"* ed. Renzo Renzi (Bologna: Cappelli, 1972), which contains, in addition to the scripts for the first two works, Fellini's important statement on films for television ("Come non detto," pp. 209–13), which appears in English as "Fellini on Television" in *Federico Fellini: Essays in Criticism*, ed. Bondanella, pp. 11–16. The complete script in Italian for *I clowns* as well as an extremely important historical account of clowning may be found in a larger and more profusely illustrated edition: Fellini, *I clown*, ed. Renzi. For *Roma*, see Federico Fellini, *"Roma" di Federico Fellini*, ed. Bernardino Zapponi (Bologna: Cappelli, 1972), which includes the "sceneggiatura letteraria" that Fellini had in hand when he shot the film (pp. 93–209) as well as a partial continuity script derived from a moviola analysis done *before* mixing on the film was completed. For the continuity script of *Intervista*, see Fellini, *Block-notes di un regista*. This edition also contains a number of soggetti for projected films—*Viaggio a Tulun*, *L'Opera*, *Il cinema Fulgor*, *Cinecittà*, and *L'America*.

[52] For Fellini's remarks on his approach to the film, see Fellini, "Why Clowns?" in *Fellini on Fellini*, p. 116; or Fellini, *Fare un film*, p. 110.

only true realist is the visionary,' who said that? The visionary, in fact, bears witness to happenings which are his own reality, that is, the most real thing that exists."[53] Twenty years later during the preparations for the production of *Intervista*, a film with important thematic and narrative similarities to *Block-notes*, Fellini expressed the same view on the supposedly documentary tendency of the cinema and its relationship to "reality": "The equivocation arises from the fact that people think the cinema is a camera full of film and a reality, outside, already prepared to be photographed. Instead, you only put yourself in front of the camera lens. Otherwise, the cinema can only offer contradictory information."[54]

First broadcast in America in 1969 by NBC as *Fellini: A Director's Notebook* and retransmitted a number of times with great success in the United States, *Block-notes di un regista* has remained practically unknown in Italy. Only recently was it released in public showings in Rome, but the film was screened primarily in revival houses and apparently no Italian print of the work has ever been produced (the print first shown in Italy in 1989 was a worn-out English print from the British Film Institute that lacked Italian subtitles or dubbed dialogue).[55] Fellini made *Block-notes* just after his recovery from a serious illness and an artistic crisis resulting in his decision to abandon the project of *Il viaggio di G. Mastorna*. In the *Mastorna* project, Fellini had planned to examine the afterlife with a script written in collaboration with the novelist Dino Buzzati. *Block-notes* opens with a shot of the meadow of Dino De Laurentiis's studio (called Dinocittà to distinguish it from the better-known Cinecittà, where Fellini has made most of his recent films), upon which abandoned constructions from the set of *Mastorna* are slowly becoming covered with weeds and dust. The scene is introduced by a voice-over provided by Fellini himself in his somewhat faltering English. Amidst the false cathedral of Cologne and the skeleton of a jet airliner lives a group of hippies. One of them recites a poem, rather insultingly entitled "Mastorna Blows," that underlines Fellini's

---

[53] Fellini, *Fellini on Fellini*, p. 120; or Fellini, *Fare un film*, p. 113.

[54] Fellini, "America," in *Block-notes di un regista*, p. 62. Fellini makes this remark in discussing the impossibility of his ever making a film in America.

[55] It is thus no surprise that the two most important critical essays on this film are in English: Joseph McBride, "The Director as Superstar," in *Federico Fellini: Essays in Criticism*, ed. Bondanella, pp. 152–60; and A. J. Prats, "The New Narration of Values—*Fellini: A Director's Notebook*," in *The Autonomous Image: Cinematic Narration and Humanism* (Lexington: University Press of Kentucky, 1981), pp. 1–37, plus the appendix on p. 158 outlining the film's thirteen major narrative sequences. In my own references to the sound track of this film, I refer to the English version of the film and not the published Italian script that reprints an Italian translation of the original.

failure to bring his project into existence by calling the film a "fool's dream." Suddenly, Fellini's camera begins to make a series of zooms and reverse zooms onto the abandoned sets, and as the roar of a plane landing is heard on the sound track, the opening scene of the *Mastorna* project materializes amidst the skeletal remains of the set: a plane with engine trouble lands in the square opposite the Cologne cathedral, and out of it emerges the protagonist Mastorna, a cello player.

The sudden eruption of Fellini's creative powers out of what seems to be an artistic impasse portrayed by this opening scene will be repeated on numerous occasions during the exposition of the loosely constructed plot of *Block-notes*. In the process, Fellini examines not only his abandoned project, but past work (*Le notti di Cabiria*) as well as work in progress or planned for the future (*Fellini Satyricon, Roma*). But the transitions between these various subjects show little or no logic and certainly do not claim to give the spectator a historically accurate idea of the development of Fellini's cinema. For example, another voice-over (an English journalist) notes that Fellini's new project, *Fellini Satyricon*, represents a voyage in time and that the director is looking for parallels between modern Rome and the Rome of Nero: the film cuts to a view of the Colosseum shot with a red filter as we wander among the ruins of this edifice, peering furtively at the whores and transvestites who inhabit the site at night; the reference to the Colosseum apparently reminds Fellini of the episode he cut from *Le notti di Cabiria* (the "Man with the Sack" episode that the Church found objectionable), and now the narrator suddenly becomes the director's wife, Giulietta Masina, who describes the origin of the scene cut from *Le notti di Cabiria*. First, we see the "real" man with the sack in a sequence shot in color at the Colosseum during the "present" (the time Masina is speaking); then we jump to the original black-and-white sequence that was cut from *Le notti* many years previously.

In a remark that serves to reject the sequence shot in the distant past, Fellini announces suddenly with another voice-over that *his* memories of the ancient Romans are still dominated not by ruins such as the Colosseum but rather by those images he saw at the cinema when he was a young boy. The narrator's reference to the past produces a scene of a provincial movie theater in which one such silent Roman historical costume drama is being shown to an audience including a young child. We immediately assume the boy is the young Fellini, although this assumption is never confirmed in the sequence itself. When the spectator notes that the silent film being shown in the theater is tinted in color,[56]

[56] It is, of course, true that silent films were not entirely black and white; many of the most important silent films (Pastrone's *Cabiria*, for example) employed hand-

it becomes immediately clear that Fellini's fantasy, and not his desire to reproduce the historical "facts" from his adolescence, is the ultimate source of this screening. The silent film narrates the conspiracy of a Roman empress against the emperor, and during the unfolding of the plot, the wanton conspirator not only licks her lips in a lascivious fashion that has become the hallmark of sexually promiscuous women in Fellini's late films, but also looks directly into the camera eye and winks at us during her performance. This violation of the convention of traditional cinema that feigns to ignore the presence of the camera becomes an increasingly common stylistic feature of Fellini's metacinematic works, reappearing a number of times in the other self-reflexive films we shall analyze.

The fantastic evocation of the Romans in the silent cinema introduces a number of equally puzzling ancient presences in the modern world. In one sequence, Fellini takes scriptwriter Bernardino Zapponi, script girl Marina Boratto, and a clairvoyant named Genius to the Appian Way to search for spirits of the ancient Romans. Genius is partially successful, for he claims to see three dead brothers from the Republican period, and the camera shows us three shrouded images. Subsequently, Fellini takes a subway ride with a professor of archaeology through the various substrata of ancient Rome that lie under the modern city buildings. Suddenly, the subway stations become populated with ancient Romans speaking the incomprehensible dialects Fellini will employ in *Fellini Satyricon*. The mythical past of ancient Rome has begun to invade and overcome the historical present time of the documentary.

Another sequence is introduced with a voice-over by script girl Marina Boratto, the daughter of the actress (Caterina Boratto) who played the Beautiful Unknown Woman in *8 1/2*. Marina's voice-over announces that "if you use a little imagination," the modern prostitutes who meet their clients beside bonfires in the outskirts of Rome will easily be transformed into their ancient counterparts. Four such women are first shown in their modern garb; a subsequent shot reveals them suddenly dressed in red Roman togas; in like manner, four modern Roman men arrive in a red truck and are suddenly transformed into Roman legionnaires. Underlining the fact that it is Fellini's cinematic fantasy producing such creative transmutations, while romping in the field with a prostitute one of the legionnaires looks straight into the camera and winks at us, repeating the action of the empress from the earlier Roman potboiler film. When the four men drive away in their

---

tinted film in crucial parts of the narrative. Nevertheless, the silent cinema was predominantly black and white, and Fellini's use of a tinted silent film is intended to underline its fictive, nonhistorical character.

truck (not a chariot), they are nevertheless still dressed in their ancient armor. This obvious anachronism underlines the triumph of Fellini's fantasy over the mundane requirements of documentary realism, which could never allow such an incorrect combination of objects from different historical eras. A similar transformation, produced by the haunting presence of the ancient Roman past within the modern present, occurs as Fellini takes his crew to the Roman slaughterhouse to locate extras to play Roman soldiers for *Fellini Satyricon*. When Caterina Boratto visits her daughter at the slaughterhouse and watches the butchers dressed as soldiers fight in mock combat, the modern actress suddenly turns into a wanton Roman matron (complete with ancient costume) who derives obvious sexual delight from the violence in the ring.

During the course of this brief television documentary, Fellini's visualization of the power of the ancient Roman past to shape the modern imagination has captured, with this parody of the documentary film genre, the expressive fantasy of Fellini's imaginative cinematic images rather than any important "truths" about the past. In a concluding sequence in Fellini's casting office, the director (never shown except for his hands) encounters a huge group of grotesque and eccentric characters who, like the six characters of Pirandello's play, demand to be given artistic form by the director. Fellini acknowledges in a voice-over the fact that he needs them more than they need him, and thus he sets the stage for the concluding scene of *Block-notes*: an image of a now silent Fellini on the set of *Fellini Satyricon* directing his next film. As Fellini (an actor playing the role of the character, the director Fellini) disappears, we witness artistic creativity in progress. It is fitting that for the first time in the film, the authoritative voice-over falls silent, as rational discussions and explanations have been replaced by active image-making.

While *Block-notes di un regista* has been largely ignored in most critical discussions of Fellini, its unpretentious nature as a television film designed for a broad, commercial audience should not obscure the originality of its narrative style, aspects of which will surface again in other, more substantial, metacinematic films. Along with his other brief work during the same period (the episodic film *Toby Dammit*), *Block-notes di un regista* helped Fellini to rebound from the psychological damage caused by the abandonment of the Mastorna project through a return to work on a film set in a minor key. *Block-notes* marks an important step in Fellini's development of a self-reflexive cinema, since the director himself begins to play a leading role (as himself) in this film. Fellini's next two films will combine the director's interest in metacinema with two topics of the greatest importance: a definition of the clown, a central figure in Fellini's cinema; and a personal portrait of Rome, a special city in the Western imagination that plays a crucial role in Fellini's art.

With *I clowns*,[57] Fellini produced a masterful presentation of several of his key themes. This television documentary on the nature and history of the clown not only provides an enormous amount of factual information about clowning but also parodies the very idea of such a documentary investigation, thus providing a new and far more complicated expression of Fellini's metacinema than was possible within the limited and unpretentious *Block-notes*. In addition, Fellini's consideration of the nature of the clown encouraged him to develop a useful theory of comedy and comic types, based upon clowning, that this and other subsequent films embody. But perhaps most important of all, *I clowns* fulfills the promise of *8 1/2* and reveals a brilliant emphasis on cinematic imagery that, liberated from the shackles of tightly constructed plots, now finds free and highly original expression in a film that develops in three narrative sections: (1) the re-creation of circus experiences from the director's childhood (the realm of memory); (2) the analysis of the present condition of clowning in the modern world (the realm of documentary and a parody of this genre); and (3) a finale that resurrects the institution of the dead clown by the power of the director's artistic fantasy (the realm of the imagination that triumphs over reality while being nourished by memory). In the first section of *I clowns*, we hear Fellini's adult voice on the sound track as we see a young actor playing the part of the adolescent Fellini as he visits the circus for the first time and sees the clowns there and, later, all around him in his hometown. In the film's second and central section, the young Fellini is replaced by the adult director making a documentary film on the history of clowns that reveals the clowns to be almost extinct in our time. Fellini's investigation of the history of clowning gradually turns into a parody of the documentary genre as the section progresses. In the final third of the film, Fellini transcends the search for historical "truth" or "facts" in his documentary; with his creative imagination nourished by memories from the past, the director provides not one but two different versions of an ending by resurrecting the art of clowning, which the documentary section of the film had already pronounced dead.

The opening scene of *I clowns* shows a young boy waking up in the

[57] For major interpretations of this work, see A. J. Prats, "Plasticity and Narrative Methods: *The Clowns*," in *The Autonomous Image*, pp. 122–57; William J. Free, "Fellini's *I clowns* and the Grotesque," in *Federico Fellini: Essays in Criticism*, ed. Bondanella, pp. 188–201; and Mireille Latil-Le Dantec, "Le Monde du cirque et le monde comme cirque: *Les Clowns*," *Études cinématographiques* 127–30 (1981): 49–64.

24. *I clowns*: a young boy recalling the comic strip "Little Nemo" sees the circus for the first time

night and going to the window to see a circus tent being erected. While the director's voice leads us to believe that this figure represents the visualization of his own past experiences, it should also not be forgotten, as previously mentioned, that this particular scene recalls a specific comic strip, "Little Nemo" by Winsor McCay, whose drawings Fellini kept by his bedside during the production of *I clowns*.[58] The next morning, the young boy asks what he saw. He is told by the family maid that the circus has come to town, and that, if he is not a good boy, those Gypsies will carry him off. Afraid but still curious, the boy goes to investigate the tent. Eventually, he is taken to see the circus that evening. *I clowns* then re-creates a series of clown acts, all shown as if from the young boy's subjective perspective (indeed, they are often photographed over his shoulder). On several occasions, the clowns wink at him (and us) by looking directly into the camera eye, alerting us to the

[58] See Chap. 1.

metacinematic nature of the narrative to follow and underlining the
fictive and *cinematic* nature of the scenes we are watching.

Fellini has defined the clown as an expression of "the irrational aspect of man; he stands for the instinct, for whatever is rebellious in
each one of us and whatever stands up to the established order of
things. He is a caricature of man's childish and animal aspects, the
mocker and the mocked. The clown is a mirror in which man sees himself in a grotesque, deformed, ridiculous image. He is man's shadow."[59]
Fellini divides clowns into two comic types: the Auguste clown, the
eternal rebel, drunkard, adolescent misfit; and the authoritarian white
clown who is the Auguste's constant companion. As Fellini puts it,
"they are two psychological aspects of man: one which aims upwards,
the other which aims downwards; two divided, separated instincts."[60]
This same division can be found in the most famous Hollywood comedy teams, such as Laurel and Hardy, Martin and Lewis, Burns and Allen, Harpo and Groucho Marx, Abbot and Costello. The two kinds of
clowns also function rather well as psychological profiles of two immediately recognizable kinds of human personalities: the white clown
stresses duty and authority and generally represses his natural instincts; on the other hand, the Auguste clown remains free of repressive
guilt and constantly breaks all the conventional rules of behavior, just
like the children who immediately identify with him.

Fellini's view of the clown not only explains the dynamics of circus
acts but also has applications to human personality outside the circus
ring. The opening scenes of the clown acts viewed through the perspective of Fellini's adolescence establish a simple pattern of clowning:
clown acts usually imitate or parody other, more traditional, circus acts
in a grotesque fashion. Thus, the strongman act of Robor, who balances
a canon on his back catapulted there by another strongman, is immediately parodied by two clowns, one of whom catapults a lighted cigar
into the other's mouth. A knife-thrower's act is immediately carica-
tured by a midget clown, who plants a hatchet into the head of his colleague, and so on. The film's opening sequences thus establish the fact
that one of the clown's key features is his inevitable parody of the "reality" around him. But the various characters the young Fellini views
for the first time in the circus ring have another metacinematic dimension as well, for they also recall themes or characters in films produced
by the adult director: the two gigantic female wrestlers, Miss Matilde
and Miss Tarzan, cannot help but remind us of La Saraghina in *8 1/2*
(especially as the Wagnerian music employed in that film accompanies

[59] Fellini, *Fellini on Fellini*, p. 123.
[60] Ibid., p. 124.

them here); the ringmaster's warning before Robor's performance that those in the audience without strong hearts should take care seems taken directly from Zampanò's routine in *La strada*; in the final procession that closes this section of the film, the famous music of the finale of *8 1/2* by Nino Rota can be heard. While the initial vision of the circus reproduces the young boy's puzzled and frightened reaction, this same vision also anticipates his future by including images from the films he will create as an adult.

Fellini then demonstrates that clowns inhabit our everyday world, not just circus rings. In fact, according to the director's voice-over that is now heard for the first time in the film, the young Fellini was terrified not by the clowns but by the fact that these grotesque figures had counterparts in his everyday reality. The evocation of Fellini's childhood during his first visit to the circus is now joined to the adult director's recollections of how the typology and actions of the clowns shaped his view of his provincial world. Fellini's jump back in time reveals a town not unlike that pictured in more detail later in *Amarcord*: it is populated with individuals who have the same traits as the two kinds of clowns that Fellini has identified with the circus. Augustes appear in a number of comic characters: the lecherous Giannone making suggestive gestures at the bemused peasant women; the drunken husband whose wife transports him home in a wheelbarrow; the slightly demented Giudizio, who plays soldier in the town streets and obscenely deflates the amorous postures of the local vitelloni who worship a sexy German tourist, anticipating the subsequent appearance of Anita Ekberg, also dressed in white fur, during the second section of the film; the vulgar coachmen outside the station whose arguments and scuffles reproduce the chaos of the arrival of the clowns in the circus. In contrast to these sympathetic figures are the local white clowns identified with authority: the midget nun who reappears in *Amarcord* and whose size recalls the dwarf clowns; the mutilated Fascist war veteran in his wheelchair with his companion, Signora Ignes, who knows Mussolini's speeches by heart, a comic type that appears not only in *Roma* but also in *Amarcord*; and, most important of all, the stationmaster humorously named Cotechino (the name of a type of boiled pork sausage popular in Fellini's Emilia-Romagna). Cotechino's authority is undercut by the insulting raspberries of the young boys who leave town on the local commuter train until, on the following day, Cotechino brings another, even more powerful, white clown to the station, a Fascist *gerarca*, or party official, whose presence provokes not a raspberry but an almost equally amusing parody of the Fascist salute delivered by all of the boys as the train pulls away from the station.

A sudden cut to a black-and-white still photograph brings us abruptly back from Fellini's recollections of his past to the present; we have now entered the second and documentary segment of *I clowns*. For the first time in the film, Fellini's actual physical presence joins his voice on the sound track as we see him in his office preparing his documentary film and his trip to Paris. Fellini's manner is unusually abrupt and authoritarian, typical of the white clown.[61] But inevitably, in the presence of a white clown (in this case, the director of the film who is playing the role of himself), the Auguste clown must appear. In the documentary section of *I clowns*, the inept and bumbling Auguste types come from Fellini's fictive crew: Maya, his secretary; the carpenter Gasperino; his grip Alvaro; Lina, Alvaro's mother and Fellini's seamstress and hairdresser; and Roy, the English cameraman. Several of these characters have already appeared as "real" people in *Block-notes*, but even if a knowledge of Fellini's earlier pseudodocumentary, in which these same characters pretend to be "real people" rather than actors, has not sufficiently prepared the viewer for the parody of documentary filmmaking that will follow, we have already seen both Lina and Alvaro in the first section of the film, where they play Zig Zag and Signora Ignes, the constant companions of the Fascist war veteran sitting by the seaside in his wheelchair. The same kind of confusion between actors, characters, and "real" people marked *Block-notes*: for example, one of the modern Roman prostitutes who turns into an ancient Roman whore with the arrival of the truck drivers reappears as one of the "ordinary people" who populate Fellini's casting office toward the end of the film. Such simple devices in both films serve to obscure the boundary lines between fact and fiction, art and reality, while at the same time underlining the essentially cinematic reality that is each film's subject.

As the documentary section of *I clowns* unfolds, supposedly seeking the historical "truth" about the demise of the clown in the contemporary world, we realize that we are actually in the midst of another clown show. Fellini's crew bump into each other, drop photographs, tear up paper when removing it from a typewriter, and generally reflect the incapacity to deal with the material world typical of the Auguste. Even the initially imperious white clown that Fellini represents at the beginning of his search for historical truth gradually becomes trans-

---

[61] As Fellini has noted, his own personality represents a combination of both clown types: "when I imagine myself as a clown, I'm an Auguste. But a white clown too. Or perhaps I'm the ringmaster. The lunatics' doctor, himself a lunatic!" (ibid., p. 130). The irresponsible adolescent who runs away from commitment and moral choices, as the protagonist of *8 1/2* did, thus represents one side of the authoritarian figure of the film director, who must be in complete control of everything and everyone on the set.

formed into the Auguste type, as Fellini's investigation reaches one dead end after another. Fellini is derisively identified as "Mr. Bellini" by one of the employees at the French television station where the troupe goes to see a documentary film containing footage devoted to Rhum, one of the greatest of all Augustes. When the motion picture projector at the home of one of the great clown families of the past, the Fratellini brothers, fails to function and reveals nothing but a burnt and imageless film, Fellini, Italy's greatest filmmaker, protests that he would like to help out but understands nothing about movie projectors! Forced to take on the authoritarian characteristics of the white clown in his role as film director, Fellini nevertheless turns into an irreverent and inept Auguste when confronted with the documentary's uncomfortable preoccupation with historical truth and facts.

During the second section of *I clowns*, the documentary film on the clowns in Paris is interrupted five separate times by re-creations of important clown acts from the past: (1) the death of Jim Guillon, the greatest Auguste, after leaving his hospital bed to watch the clown act of his colleagues Footit and Chocolat; (2) the "cake baked in the hat" routine made famous by Antonet and Beby, a famous Auguste and white clown duo; (3) a fashion parade of numerous white clowns famous for their fastidious and sumptuous dress, set in contrast to the sloppy and slovenly costumes worn traditionally by the Auguste type, an anticipation of the equally dazzling parody of an ecclesiastical fashion show in *Roma*; (4) the evocation of the acts by the three Fratellini brothers in orphanages, army hospitals, and insane asylums; and (5) the concluding routine of Bario, the famous clown that Fellini and the troupe visit in retirement at the end of the second section of the film.

While the *dialogue* of the film's second section insists that the circus and the clown are dead institutions, out of step with the contemporary world, the film's *action* (particularly the bungling efforts of the clownish film crew commanded by the director, a clown of a different order) parodies the documentary's arrogant pretensions to uncover any such "truth." In fact, the exuberant tone of the five re-created clown acts stands in marked contrast to this lugubrious, funereal pessimism. Implicitly, the "message" of *I clowns* has already been delivered, even though the film's conclusion will make it ever clearer: the director's artistic fantasy possesses the capacity for reviving the comic essence, if not the historical "reality," of this moribund institution. Interestingly enough, both views of the clown—the pessimistic and the optimistic—reflect different aspects of the director: his reason and logic lead him to believe that the clown has been transcended (a fact that his voice-over narrative emphasizes), while his fertile artistic fantasy, the realm of the irrational and the unconscious, works to counter this pessimistic vision with clowns that are living images.

The transition from part two (documentary and parody of documentary) to the third and final section of I clowns is, in fact, announced by Fellini's voice-over as he reacts to his failure to learn anything from the brief silent film on Rhum at the French television studio: "Perhaps the clown is definitively dead," he wonders. Immediately after, there is a sudden cut from Fellini's "reality" in Paris to a funeral for a clown that acts as a direct response to Fellini's question. The funeral is for Fischietto, an Auguste whose demise is announced by his white clown colleague. Here, a number of details underline the *filmic* nature of the death and eventual resurrection of this clown figure. Both Lina and Gasperino (originally part of Fellini's troupe in the documentary) now turn up at various moments during the clown funeral, revealing their true nature as clowns and abolishing the now nonexistent distinction between the world of documentary "reality" and that of the circus. The notary who reads Fischietto's last will and testament uses a hammer to hit everyone's head, and after striking all the clowns in the scene, he turns directly toward the camera and hits its lens as well, as the noise of breaking glass is heard on the sound track. In *Block-notes*, several actors winked at the camera eye to remind us that we are watching a film. Now a clown parodies even this metacinematic clue by including the camera eye in his clown act. Fellini's constant emphasis on the presence of the camera serves to establish the fact that in his films, the world of art triumphs over that of reality. The metacinematic nature of I clowns is nowhere more humorously visualized than in a single shot of one part of the clown funeral. In the same frame, we see (1) the cameraman of the film we are watching, who is shooting (2) the fictional cameraman of Fellini's crew, who is shooting (3) a clown taking a picture of other clowns. The shot is even more complex than this description implies, for there is, of course, a fourth cameraman shooting everything we are seeing on the screen. Thus, the "real" cameraman within the frame is yet another actor.

Metacinematic works usually contain self-reflexive critiques, what might be termed metacriticism. In the narrative structure of 8 1/2, Fellini included all of the possible attacks on the work that he could imagine. I clowns also contains diagetic metacriticism, but, as one might expect in a film about clowns, such material serves to provide a hilarious caricature of critical discourse. A journalist seated near Fellini during this extravagant clown funeral asks the director what the "message" of his television special is. When Fellini begins to provide an answer to the question, assuming the officious tone of a white clown, an empty bucket suddenly drops over his head, drowning out his fictitious answer but actually providing the director's authentic answer; the bucket over the director's head is soon followed by another bucket over the head of the journalist. In *8 1/2*, Fellini had poked fun at the hapless Daumier with the triumph of the director figure, Guido. Now, both critic and director are dismissed as inadequate critics of the marvelously vivacious clown acts taking place around them. Faced with the mysterious and continually fascinating comic appeal of these clown figures, even the director's explanations seem out of place and presumptuous.

The funeral procession begins in a circular manner reminiscent of the finale of *8 1/2*, but the pace accelerates to such an extent that many of the old clowns are forced to drop out from fatigue. In spite of our desire to believe that clowns will live forever, everything about the clown funeral has underlined its artificial, artistically created nature and its distance from any historical reality. The funeral is an act staged by a film director rather than an activity that is spontaneous and alive. Death may be mocked, but as the final reality of clowning, as well as of life itself, it seems that it cannot be denied. Once again, the director's voice-over assumes the persona of the authoritative white clown when he suddenly brings the entire funeral scene to a halt: "You can turn off the lights. It's over."[62]

Fellini's *conscious* attempts to resurrect the dying institution of the clowns have thus apparently ended in failure. Death triumphs at last over the clown even as the clown mocks his own fate. But Fellini adds an epilogue to *I clowns* that obviates such a pessimistic conclusion. Fumagalli, one of the old clowns who left the whirling funeral procession because of his fatigue and old age, tells Fellini about a circus number he once performed with his partner Fru Fru. The two clowns *pretended* that Fru Fru was dead while Fumagalli searched for him, calling him on the trumpet. As Fumagalli's voice-over explains the routine, Fellini's *camera* now dominates the narrative, moving purposefully through the paper streamers hanging down around the set left over from the funeral celebration and heading toward the door of the circus. There follows a dissolve to the empty circus from Fellini's childhood, *not* the one re-created on the movie set in parts two and three of the film. A pair of clowns—a white clown and an Auguste—call to each other with their trumpets, playing "Ebb Tide." They gradually descend from the bleacher seats of the circus to the center of the ring, where they play, illuminated in the spotlight, then disappear into nothingness on the screen as they walk out of the ring together. As Fellini notes in his essay on clowns, the final meeting of the two clown types and their dis-

[62] Fellini, *Fellini TV*, p. 203.

appearance together moves us "because the two figures embody a myth which lies in the depths of each one of us: the reconciliation of opposites, the unity of being."[63]

While the conclusion of *I clowns* ends Fellini's search for the "truth" about clowning on a hopeful note, emphasizing the power of the imagination to triumph over mere facts, this moving finale also contains a number of clear references to Fellini's own films. The trumpet number recalls a series of similar moments in earlier works: not only Giudizio's playing of the trumpet in the first part of *I clowns*, which showed us Fellini's memories of the "clowns" in his provincial hometown, but also the famous trumpet music played by Gelsomina in *La strada*, or Polidor's trumpet solo that magically caused a group of balloons to vanish from the nightclub into which Marcello had brought his father in *La dolce vita*. Ultimately, however, the final image of *I clowns* evokes the magic moment of comic acceptance and the dramatization of artistic creativity that concludes *8 1/2* in a similar circus ring. The main theme of *I clowns* thus develops an idea suggested first in *8 1/2*. Only artistic imagination, informed by memory and intuition, will serve to give life to the dying institution of the clown. After Fellini accepts the absurdity of his obsession with a phenomenon revealed by the documentary to be a dead institution, the director laughs at his mania, and in the process he accomplishes the impossible, resurrecting the dead clowns in a "world beyond reality," which is the same artistic realm in which Guido's apotheosis has taken place in *8 1/2*.[64] With its virtuoso imagery rather than a logical or rational argument, Fellini's self-reflexive "documentary" on the demise of clowns and clowning in the modern world has revealed only a single "truth": the supreme clown of the cinema is Fellini himself, and only his comic vision has succeeded in resurrecting the image of the figure that has for centuries embodied a shadow image of our common humanity.

As a result of the new techniques that Fellini adopted subsequent to *8 1/2* in his metacinematic films, reflecting the impact of dreams on his narrative style, there is an increased reliance in his cinema on the expressive power of the autonomous image. Judged by conventional standards, *I clowns* represents a film with relatively little internal logic or traditional narrative structure. Yet, the pseudodocumentary character of the film and the fact that Fellini's view of clowns is informed by a coherent theory of clowning provide a minimal narrative structure within which Fellini moves back and forth between memories of the past, the present documentary in progress, and imaginative re-creations

[63] Fellini, *Fellini on Fellini*, p. 124.
[64] Free, "Fellini's *I clowns* and the Grotesque," p. 201.

of clowning. With *Roma*, on the other hand, there is simply no internal logic guiding Fellini's highly subjective collection of episodes and images reflecting his memories or opinions of the Eternal City. Individual images within the various episodes stand alone, supported entirely by their inherent expressive power, and the diverse sequences are held together only by the fact that they all ultimately originate from the director's fertile imagination.

Extant archival materials from *Roma*'s soggetto underscore the director's interest in privileging image over narrative even in the film's initial conception. In fact, rather than a traditional soggetto, the preliminary documents related to this film, now conserved in the Lilly Library, consist of six separate illustrated notebooks, each of which treats a major sequence of the future film.[65] Fellini's earlier film for the American television network, *Block-notes di un regista*, had conceived of the pseudodocumentary as a reflection of the director's notebooks in order to justify its episodic structure. Now the soggetto of *Roma* begins literally with notebooks and sketches, and the unique feature of this particular collection of notebooks is that the images in each folder are clearly designed to take precedence over the relatively insignificant written outline of a future script. Thus, the entire narrative structure of each projected sequence revolves around the development of a dominant image sketched on the original manuscript, while the written script serves primarily an informational function.[66] Naturally, changes occur between the completion of the soggetto, with its illustrative drawings, and the shooting and editing of the final film, but the major changes involve *additions* of new sequences to those projected in the six folders rather than deletions of the topics first conceived as images there. Notebook 1 ("Inizio Roma") introduces the opening of the film with a color sketch of Zeus, the school headmaster, who is chasing a young schoolboy dressed in a sailor suit. The young boy represents a continuation of the pseudoautobiographical figure from *I clowns* who observed the circus in his provincial hometown. Zeus and the boy do, in fact, dominate the initial section of *Roma*, which re-creates Fellini's memories of his childhood and the role that Rome played in them.[67]

[65] The materials are catalogued in the Lilly Library as Fellini MS. 10 (Box 2, folders 1–6).

[66] Some critics point to an earlier film, *Fellini Satyricon*, as that in which the image first takes on such an autonomous character. But in *Fellini Satyricon*, Fellini always has a narrative story line based on the admittedly fragmentary original literary text upon which to base his imagery. In *Roma*, on the contrary, everything in the film originates from Fellini's own imagination.

[67] Zeus appears four times in the film: he leads a group of children over a ridiculous little stream identified as Caesar's famous River Rubicon; he rants and postures in the classroom before pictures of various authority figures of the regime (king, pope,

Notebook 2 ("Arrivo a Roma") opens with a color sketch of a buxom woman and a cuirassier; the notebook's text suggests the outline of the second part of *Roma*, that which traces the arrival of a young provincial to the capital city. While the cuirassier plays a minor role in the sequence eventually filmed (appearing only for a few moments at the Stazione Termini), the buxom woman represents a character type that the young man meets repeatedly; she suggests sexual availability. Notebook 3 ("Raccordo anulare") offers a color caricature of an enormous woman, the kind of prostitute who generally plies her trade along the autostradas outside of Rome, with an important note to Danilo Donati (Fellini's set designer) about constructing the autostrada entirely at Cinecittà rather than using a real highway: "The belt road is to be reconstructed on the meadows of Cinecittà—500 meters, half a kilometer, are sufficient."[68] This comment serves as a reminder that Fellini has continued the practice, begun during *La dolce vita* and *8 1/2*, of re-creating virtually everything in his films inside the studio complex of Cinecittà in order to obtain complete control over the light and the images he films and to avoid any hint of representational realism in his work. Notebooks 4 ("Defilé") and 6 ("Gli aristocratici e il defilé") are devoted to the justly celebrated ecclesiastical fashion parade. They contain not only a number of suggestions from Fellini to Donati for the priests' incredible costumes, but one interesting page also explains the surprising source of the dominant image of the entire sequence—the appearance of Pope Pius XII. Notebook 5 ("I casini") treats the brothels of Fellini's youth and contains the drawing of a huge prostitute coming down a flight of stairs, an image that will dominate the brothel sequence when filmed.

Fellini's reliance on imagery rather than story line in *Roma* produces one of his most brilliant and original films. The final film contains seven major sequences, representing an expansion of the original five general topics initially suggested by the soggetto by including a sequence re-creating a variety show performance at the Barafonda theater and another sequence examining the excavation of a Roman subway amidst the ruins of the city's ancient past. The film's opening sequence

---

and Mussolini); he is present during the slide show that ends in a suggestive vision of a nude woman; and he once again appears in the cinema and has a violent argument with one of the spectators. The young boy in the sailor suit, usually interpreted as the young Fellini (although he is never identified in this way in the film) appears in a number of scenes: the camera zooms up to his delighted face during the sexually suggestive slide show at the school; he stares at the dentist's wife in the movie theater, who is described by the narrative voice-over as "worse than Messalina"; and he appears in the last vignette of the segment on the provinces staring at trains departing for the capital city.

[68] Fellini MS. 10 (Box 2, folder 3), p. 1.

anticipates *Amarcord* and offers a series of brief vignettes portraying Fellini's first impressions of Rome and Roman history as a young boy in the provinces before he moved to the capital. The same young boy in a sailor suit employed in the opening sequences of *I clowns* seems to represent the young Fellini (although this is never specified in the film), and a narrative voice-over that is not Fellini's provides the minimum of information needed to move the story forward.[69] The boy's experiences serve primarily to effect a visual link between the idea of Rome and that of sexuality and the cinema. In school, a pious slide lecture on Roman monuments is interrupted by the insertion of a sexy slide of a partially dressed woman, and the camera zooms to the obviously delighted boy's face as his discovery of the opposite sex and the Eternal City are connected in his psyche. Later he is taken to the movie theater by his family, and the Roman historical film he sees is even more unusual than the one Fellini inserted in the opening section of *I clowns*. The film is not silent, since we hear dialogue on the sound track when it begins, but the characters *act* as if they are in a silent film. Moreover, the Christian heroine, joined in the Colosseum by her patrician Roman lover, who decides to share her fate, is quite obviously a young girl from the 1970s whose hairstyle and manner have nothing to do with either ancient Rome or the 1930s (the era in which the film that the boy is watching was supposedly made). Once again, an obvious anachronism (employed earlier in Fellini's metacinematic films) calls attention to the artificial, cinematic quality of the work of art we are watching. In the theater, the young boy sees the rapacious dentist's wife (described by the voice-over as "worse than Messalina") who usually came to the movies to be touched in the dark by the young men. At that point, Fellini cuts to the kind of sudden re-creation of a link between past and present that we have already seen in *Block-notes*: the dentist's wife is literally transformed into Messalina, a lascivious Roman empress in a red toga, who services a number of men waiting in line behind her modern convertible. Later in a bar, one of the local vitelloni announces with pompous authority that Roman women all have enormous rear ends.

Given the young boy's precocious experience linking Rome with sexuality, it is no wonder that he connects the two topics in his psyche and that, as a young adult, this association will continue to dominate his thinking about the Eternal City. The connection between Rome and the existence of sexuality of a specific and defective kind is a central concept in Fellini's view of the city's influence on Italians. In a number

[69] With the exception of *Block-notes di un regista*, I refer to the original Italian prints, and not those distributed in the United States, as the basis of my remarks.

of different articles and interviews, Fellini has identified Rome as a completely feminine city, combining qualities of the ideal mother and the mistress.[70] The maternal side of Rome, its indifference, explains why the city never obliges the child to grow up. Romans are thus never neurotic, but they also never become adults. Fellini locates the primary cause of such chronic infantilism in the Catholic church, since the ultimate mother figure centered in Rome is, of course, the Madonna. The brothels that occupy such an important place in *Roma* must be understood from Fellini's particular point of view: the people who frequented the state-controlled brothels did so, according to Fellini, not merely to achieve sexual release but primarily because they wanted to remain attached as long as possible to a generous and maternal figure who would remove their doubts and responsibilities and, above all else, not cause them problems. Their ritualistic visits to the brothels represented a "return to the maternal lap" that indefinitely delayed their growth into mature adults.[71]

The second sequence of *Roma*, which traces the arrival of a young provincial (Peter Gonzales) to Rome's Stazione Termini and his subsequent introduction to life in a Roman boardinghouse and an outdoor trattoria, provides a portrait of this kind of sexual environment. While most critical treatments of *Roma* assume that this young provincial, like the boy in the sailor suit before him, represents Fellini, there is no such positive identification in the film itself. The boardinghouse and its grotesque population of strange individuals were suggested by the drawings of Attalo, a famous cartoonist for *Marc'Aurelio* whom both Fellini and scriptwriter Bernardino Zapponi knew before the war.[72] The landlady of the household is a grotesquely obese woman (first employed by Fellini in *Fellini Satyricon*) who is confined to her bed with an "inflammation of the ovaries" and who warns her new boarder not to "profane" the household. Her effeminate son curls up against this enormous mass of feminine flesh in a fetal position. Fellini suggests with this freakish mother and son that such gigantic Earth Mothers who spend their lives spoiling their male children only succeed in hindering their healthy development into mature heterosexuals. Later, eating outside with the rest of the neighborhood in the open-air trattoria entirely constructed for Fellini by Donati inside Cinecittà's enormous Teatro 5, the young provincial encounters several vulgar but obviously sexually

[70] See, for example, Fellini, *Fare un film*, pp. 144–50; Fellini, *Un regista a Cinecittà*, pp. 100–105; or Fellini, *"Roma" di Federico Fellini*, pp. 69–73.

[71] Fellini, *Un regista a Cinecittà*, p. 100.

[72] See Olivieri, *L'imperatore in platea*, pp. 70–71, for a reproduction of the kind of drawing Fellini recalls in this sequence; or Fellini's description of such a distasteful environment as "la mia casa ideale" in Fellini, *"Roma" di Federico Fellini*, p. 39.

available women. As the sequence ends later that night amidst the statues and ruins on the Appian Way, an enormous prostitute stands aggressively by the ancient road, waiting for her clients. Through a succession of related but not logically connected images, Fellini has not only visually presented his belief that Rome is predominantly a female city but has also dramatized the inevitable results of the kind of psychological environment Rome provides for the young male: the permissive and indifferent maternal figure leads her son inexorably toward furtive liaisons with prostitutes as his habitual means of expressing his sexuality, or toward homosexuality. Neither result represents for Fellini a healthy form of adult sexual development.

An abrupt cut follows, shifting the film's action to modern Rome, where Fellini and his film crew are shown organizing their entry into the city on the autostrada. While the voice-over introducing this section is not that of Fellini, Fellini himself takes part in this sequence, playing himself. The young provincial's entrance into the Eternal City had been marked by constant sexual overtones. The mature director's entrance into the city, in like manner, represents a phallic journey toward the womb of the city, with the crew's crane functioning as an almost too obvious symbol of the male sexual organ.[73] The same phallic imagery reflecting the director's masculine pretensions to "penetrate" the feminine mysteries of the Eternal City also characterizes the fifth sequence, devoted to the construction of the Roman subway system. A phallus-shaped mechanical device called a "mole," which resembles a dildo or a vibrator far more than a real construction drill, reveals to Fellini's crew (this time in the director's absence) an ancient Roman home. Its frescoes disintegrate on contact with the modern air. The autostrada and the subway sequences are also the most clearly self-reflexive parts of *Roma*, and, like the central documentary segment of *I clowns*, they draw our attention to the fact that what we are watching is a film, a work of art rather than a completely credible effort to grasp the "truth" about Rome through documentary techniques. Both of these sequences with documentary pretensions end in complete failure. The infernal traffic jam that traps the film crew and director at night by the Colosseum (a Colosseum completely fashioned at Cinecittà, as is the autostrada), the ancient frescoes that fade away before the horrified eyes of the camera crew during the subway sequence, all point to

[73] Several critics have underlined the phallic suggestiveness in this sequence and in the later subway sequence: see Walter C. Foreman, "Fellini's Cinematic City: *Roma* and Myths of Foundation," *Forum Italicum* 14 (1980): 78–98, the best analysis of the film, to which my own discussion is indebted; and Aldo Tassone, "From Romagna to Rome: The Voyage of a Visionary Chronicler (*Roma* and *Amarcord*)," in *Federico Fellini: Essays in Criticism*, ed. Bondanella, pp. 261–88.

the presumptuousness of a male director who attempts to fathom the mysterious feminine presence of the Eternal City with the phallic instruments of the camera and the drill. By linking such phallic symbols to the documentary sequences and to his own failure to gain any important information about Rome from such a "realistic" approach, Fellini also seems to imply that he must transcend his own upbringing, since it causes him to equate Rome with a woman who must be sexually mastered in order to be understood. In fact, quite different implements must be employed to gain access to Rome's secrets.

It comes as no surprise after viewing *I clowns* and considering the way in which Fellini treats the relationship between fact and fiction in that earlier metacinematic film that the sequences of *Roma* linked to the production of a documentary film result in failure and creative blockage, whereas sequences based on Fellini's imaginative re-creation of his past memories or fantasies of Rome—such as the episode of the variety theater (sequence 4), the brothels (sequence 6), or the ecclesiastical fashion parade (sequence 7)—constitute the most brilliant sections of this unusual movie. The re-creation of the variety theater in Rome at the beginning of the war follows a conversation between some Roman students who demand that Fellini present an "objective" portrait of the city, and the director himself, physically present in the film, is also active on the sound track voice-over for the first time in the film. It is the sudden sound of Fellini's voice (and not the unidentified speaker who has provided the narrative commentary in the film up to this point) that signals Fellini's response to the students' request—a completely *subjective* and imaginative re-creation of a Roman avanspettacolo that constitutes one of the most entertaining sequences Fellini has ever created in any of his works. The Barafonda theater sequence is also one of greater complexity than the clown acts of *I clowns*, since in the theater sequence, the performances on the stage are equalled and sometimes even surpassed by the "performances" in the audience. One of the most important Futurist manifestos, entitled "The Variety Theater," argued years earlier (1913) that the variety hall theater conventions should replace those of traditional drama.[74] Fellini agrees with the Futurists that vaudeville theater is the prototype for a new kind of spectacle. Moreover, Fellini demonstrates the appeal of such an aesthetic not only in the variety hall sequence but also with the earlier chaotic entrance into the city on the autostrada, in the parade of women in the brothel sequence, and in the ecclesiastical fashion show. Each of these other sequences is organized along the same aes-

[74] See Filippo T. Marinetti, *Marinetti: Selected Writings*, ed. and trans. R. W. Flint (New York: Farrar, Straus and Giroux, 1972), pp. 16–22, for the text of this manifesto.

thetic lines as a variety show, and thus they all dramatize and visualize
the narrative structure of *Roma* itself: extremely discontinuous but
highly entertaining individual sequences characterized by autonomous
imagery that propels the narrative visually rather than verbally according to a literary story line. Like the Futurists before him, Fellini accepts
the diversity and the apparent chaos of the variety theater as a positive
model to juxtapose with the classical notions of order, balance, sym-
metry, and proportion that traditional theatrical performances or cinematic narratives embrace.

Perhaps no single sequence of *Roma* relies so completely on the
autonomous image as that of the ecclesiastical fashion parade. Fellini
was conscious of the fact that his presentation of the entire spectrum
of clergy—nuns, country priests, cardinals, bishops, even the pope—
within the satirical environment of a fashion parade represented hyper-
bolic excess that reached and very nearly went beyond the outer limits
of acceptable satire.[75] Fellini has always rebelled against certain repressive aspects of his Catholic upbringing (especially in *8 1/2* and *Giulietta
degli spiriti*), but there is also no doubt that the director requires an
authority such as the Church as a target against which to open fire.
Moreover, as an artist, Fellini has a great deal of sympathy for church
ritual:

> I like the choreography of the Catholic church. I like its unchangeable
> and hypnotic representations, its precious productions, its lugubrious
> chants, its catechism, the election of a new pontiff, its grandiose mortu-
> ary apparatus. The merits of the Church are those of any other creation
> of thought that tends to protect us from the devouring magma of the
> unconscious. . . . Then there is in me a bedazzled interest in the Catholic
> church that has been the most extraordinary creator of artists, a watchful
> and generous commissioner of masterpieces.[76]

In the original manuscripts of *Roma*'s illustrated soggetto, the fashion
show and, in particular, the spectacular appearance of Pope Pius XII, the
pontiff who embodies the conservative views of Rome's "black aristoc-
racy" (the fashion show's sponsor), receive careful attention. One page
of drawings and instructions offers Danilo Donati important visual
clues for the extravagant costumes of various prelates: "Remember:
one cardinal like a *pinball machine*, one cardinal like a *cuttlefish bone*;
one cardinal (invisible?) that is *only an electric light*."[77] The examples
of the images Fellini wanted to achieve, each of which tends to dehu-

[75] Fellini, *Un regista a Cinecittà*, p. 100.
[76] Ibid., p. 105.
[77] Fellini MS. 10 (Box 2, folder 4), title page (Fellini's emphasis).

25. *Roma*: Fellini's directions to Danilo Donati for the creation of various unusually shaped cardinal's uniforms from the original manuscript of the *soggetto*

manize the cardinals, were rendered brilliantly by Donati's consummate skill as a designer. Even more interesting in terms of identifying the mysterious sources of Fellini's specific inspiration for an individual image are the remarks directed to Donati that discuss his idea of how the final appearance of the pope at the end of the sequence should look. In one long note, Fellini underlines the fact that *"everything has to be*

26. *Roma*: Donati's realization of Fellini's directions, resulting in invisible cardinals composed only of light

invented" (his emphasis) in this sequence and tells Donati he has found exactly the kind of image he wants to conclude the sequence: "For the appearance of the pope at the end, I noticed the advertising for something I don't remember the other evening in a bar, but which consisted of two enormous disks that were revolving, giving the impression of a sparkling of unstoppable rays. I shall have a photo of the thing made for you."[78] Fellini's note to Donati also contains a small circular diagram of the shape the director borrowed from popular advertising, and he sketches the same shape again in a larger diagram on the page of the soggetto that describes the pope's appearance.[79]

In the completed film, the pope's appearance against this strange, circular background constructed entirely of glittering, revolving lights in the form of a superilluminated halo constitutes the ultimate moment in *Roma* when image completely dominates traditional narrative story line and becomes itself the "content" of the film. In his recent photographic memoir of Cinecittà, Fellini recalls that the atmosphere on the set during the filming of this scene was extraordinary. His film crew, normally the most cynical, disrespectful group of people imaginable, suddenly fell silent and stood in awe before the Neapolitan extra playing the pope. Even Fellini found himself unconsciously lowering his voice while he directed, as "the figure of the pope, so hieratic and unreachable, so sumptuous and inhumanly regal, acted with the occult force of an archetype, imposing upon us, even within its artifice, a kind of hypnotic, enchanted subjection."[80]

Fellini appears briefly as himself in the final sequence of *Roma*, which takes the director and his crew to visit the annual Festa de Noi Antri in the bohemian section of Rome, where, among other events, the cameraman has his camera stolen. It is appropriate that the closing sequences of a metacinematic film on Rome should examine a "metafestival," for the Festa de Noi Antri is a celebration by the residents of Trastevere of "themselves," just as Fellini's *Roma* celebrates not merely the image of the Eternal City but also that of his own artistic creativity. The actress Anna Magnani suddenly appears walking in the evening. A narrative voice-over (this time clearly Fellini's voice) identifies the actress and, in a mixture of intellectual pretentiousness and self-deprecating irony, makes the following statement about the woman with whom he had starred years earlier in *Il miracolo*: "She could also be, in a way, the symbol of the city, a Rome seen as whore and vestal virgin, aristocratic and threadbare, gloomy, and clownish—I could go on until tomorrow morning." When Fellini's voice continues, asking permission of Magnani to direct a question to her, the actress immediately replies: "Federi', go to bed. . . . Go on. . . . No, I don't trust

[78] Fellini MS. 10 (Box 2, folder 5), title page.
[79] Fellini MS. 10 (Box 2, folder 4), p. 20. The drawing is accompanied by a note to Donati ("inside an enormous revolving wheel").
[80] Fellini, *Un regista a Cinecittà*, p. 105.

VOCE
Le mitrie... La tiara... Il ca_
mauro...

46. a 60 a·disposizione regia.
Ed ecco apparire, abbaglianti,
maestosi, vescovi e cardinali,
con immense vesti rosse, e al-
tissime mitrie, carichi di col
lane, tempestati di diamanti,e
anelli; alcuni sono altissimi
e ischeletriti, altri tozzi,
grassissimi come rospi, grotte
schi fra gli ornamenti splendi
di. Il coro aumenta di podero-
sità; fra l'incenso e i vesti-
ti così vistosi, s'è creato per
incanto un clima di alta cerimo
nia religiosa; sembra di assi-
stere a una messa solenne, o a
qualche altro grandioso rito
in San Pietro.

61.
Alla fine, su una portantina
portata a spalle da quattro sa-
cerdoti e circondata da chieri-
ci coi flabelli, entra un vec
chissimo cardinale che tiene ab
to...

27. *Roma*: the geometric shape Fellini wanted to create during the appearance of the pope, from a sketch on the original manuscript of the *soggetto*

you! . . . Ciao! . . . Good night!"[81] In both *I clowns* and *Roma*, the narrative voice-over loosely linking together the films' episodic sequences always reflects the rational, authoritative, inquisitive side of Fellini's function as a documentary director—the "white clown" aspect of artistic creativity, to continue the typology Fellini developed in *I clowns*. Invariably, Fellini demonstrates the limitations of this purely rational approach to filmmaking, limitations that can be transcended only by the creative power of fantasy. Thus, in *I clowns* the historical "fact" of the demise of clowning, which Fellini not only does not deny but emphasizes in his documentary, is not so much resolved as it is transcended by a clown extravaganza that paradoxically dramatizes the death of clowning. In like manner in *Roma*, the Eternal City comes completely alive only in sequences directly indebted to the director's fantasy or memory—the opening sequence representing Fellini's provincial origins; the arrival in Rome; and the three variety acts in the Barafonda theater, the brothel parades, and the ecclesiastical fashion show. The purely documentary sequences only visualize obstacles to artistic creativity: the gigantic traffic jam at the Colosseum, on the one hand, and the disintegrating frescoes underneath the city's surface, on the other.

Anna Magnani's allegation of Fellini's unreliable and untrustworthy nature is directed primarily at his narrative voice and his rational search for the documentary "facts" about Rome. The implication of her remarks is that the reliable aspect of Fellini's character resides in the subjective power of his expressive imagery created through his boundless fantasy. The celebration of the director's fantasy and imaginative power, in fact, becomes the key to the finale of *Roma*, which no longer attempts to provide rational arguments to explain or authoritative narrative commentary to accompany the director's cinematic images. The finale is completely devoid of voice-over commentary and relies entirely on camera movement and imagery. It pictures a group of motorcyclists, initially suggesting a modern expression of the ancient barbarian invaders of the Eternal City, as they race through the city past its most celebrated architectural landmarks on the Capitoline Hill, the Forum, and the Colosseum, where they eventually converge. Previously, in their attempts to enter Rome by the autostrada, Fellini and his crew

[81] I cite directly from the sound track of the *Italian* version of *Roma*, since the published script (Fellini, *"Roma" di Federico Fellini*, p. 365) reflects the state of the film before final dubbing. My remarks here and elsewhere on *Roma*'s narrative voice-overs are based on the Italian version of this film, not the half-dubbed, half-subtitled American print that changes quite radically the relationship of the film to narrative voice. See Foreman, "Fellini's Cinematic City," esp. note 10, for a fuller discussion of the sound track of the American print.

had been trapped at precisely this point, but now the cyclists pass the spot without difficulty and roar out into the night on Via Cristoforo Colombo (an avenue appropriately named after the discoverer of a new world). The shot framing the motorcycles speeding down the center line of the road toward the Colosseum and beyond it changes perspective, and we suddenly become aware of the fact that it is Fellini's *camera* that is speeding down the highway, not the motorcycles. The energy and restless movement of these new barbarians have now been incorporated by the director into a triumphant celebration of his own creative energy.[82]

Fellini's Roman trilogy—*La dolce vita, Fellini Satyricon,* and *Roma* —makes a unique contribution to the history of Roman mythology, one of Western culture's most important and persistent concentrations of images, ideas, and myths.[83] In each of these films, but especially in *Roma*, where he consciously sets out to elevate imagery and imagination over plot, Fellini uses the backdrop of ancient and modern Rome to demonstrate that for him, mythmaking and image-making are universal human activities and that an artist's exhilaration in the act of creativity is the ultimate human freedom. It may come as something of a surprise that Fellini associates the moving camera eye, the symbol of the triumph of his creative imagination, with a new breed of modern barbarians on motorcycles. But Fellini rejects the sterile lamentation of the passing of old mythologies and old images. Instead, he affirms that the artist's task is to use the past to rebuild new and more up-to-date imagery and ideas, much as earlier barbarian invaders modified what they found amidst the ruins of the city they had destroyed to fashion for themselves a more vital culture.

With *Intervista*, a film awarded the Grand Prize at the Moscow Film Festival and the Special Jury Prize at Cannes, where it was applauded by a standing audience for almost a half-hour, Fellini creates a unique synthesis of all of the metacinematic themes in his work from *8 1/2* to the present. *Intervista* is what he calls a "filmetto"—an unpretentious and intimate little film celebrating the personal, artisan-like quality of his brand of cinema in an era when special effects and elaborate electronic technology seem to have taken over the silver screen, leaving

---

[82] For a more complete analysis of *Roma* from this perspective, an essay that has obviously influenced my own viewing of this conclusion, see Foreman, "Fellini's Cinematic City."

[83] In this book, I have preferred to discuss these three films within a different context from that of the development of Roman mythology. However, for a history of this venerable tradition and a specific analysis of how Fellini's Roman trilogy uses and shapes it, see my *The Eternal City: Roman Images in the Modern World.*

little room for the sensitive "minimalism" of a film such as this one.[84]
Upon first examination, *Intervista* appears to be a more complicated
version of *Block-notes di un regista*, a relationship suggested not only
by the same title on the original manuscript—later changed to *Intervista*—but also by a number of similar structural devices in the two
films. *Block-notes* presented to the spectator of Fellini's television special a number of different films: (1) an abandoned project, *Il viaggio di
G. Mastorna*, as well as a new film, *Fellini Satyricon*; (2) a Roman *peplum* costume drama Fellini remembered from his childhood; (3) a past
film, *Le notti di Cabiria*; and (4) the documentary film being made by
NBC showing Fellini at work at Cinecittà.[85] *Intervista* shares a number
of the themes of these works. We see Fellini preparing sets and shooting
screen tests for an adaptation of Kafka's *Amerika*. But, unlike the two
films mentioned in *Block-notes*—*Fellini Satyricon* and *Mastorna*—the
references to *Amerika* in *Intervista* exist for the sole purpose of presenting an unmade film. Like Pirandello's six characters or Guido's science-fiction film in *8 1/2*, Fellini's *Amerika* will never achieve artistic
fulfillment because its function in *Intervista* is to serve, paradoxically,
as a film without an author.[86] In the second place, *Intervista* contains a
number of "autobiographical" elements, as Fellini re-creates his memories of his first visit to Cinecittà, the explicit subject of the film.[87] This
section of *Intervista* recalls parts of *Block-notes* as well as sequences
from *I clowns*, *Roma*, and *Amarcord*. Parallel to the brief clip from *Le
notti di Cabiria* in *Block-notes*, Fellini presents a moving sequence
from *La dolce vita* in *Intervista* and screens the sequence in the pres-

[84] Fellini's characterization of *Intervista* as a "little film" may be found in the published continuity script: Fellini, *Block-notes di un regista*, p. 69. The original manuscript of a provisional and incomplete version of *Intervista*'s script may be examined in the Lilly Library: "Block notes di un regista: appunti di Federico Fellini
(prima versione provvisoria)" (Fellini MS. 2, Box 1). The most important interpretations of *Intervista* may be found in Gianfranco Angelucci, "Un'intervista tutta da
vedere," *Intermedia Journal* 1, no. 5 (1987): 36–39, 41; articles and interviews by
Olivier Curchod, Vincent Amiel, Ornella Volta, and Jean A. Gili in *Federico Fellini*,
ed. Ciment, pp. 168–83; and Zanelli, *Nel mondo di Federico*, pp. 2–25.

[85] Curchod (" 'J'écris *Paludes*,' " in *Federico Fellini*, ed. Ciment, pp. 168–69), is the
only European critic to have remarked on the link between *Block-notes* and *Intervista*. The lack of critical discussion in Europe reflects the fact that the film (distributed in America as *Fellini: A Director's Notebook*) was not even screened in Italy
until 1989.

[86] Kafka has long been one of Fellini's favorite authors, and the director did, at one
time, consider such an adaptation. But by the time he made *Intervista*, this project
had already been discarded. For Fellini's remarks about making a film on America,
see Fellini, "L'America," in *Block-notes di un regista*, pp. 61–65.

[87] For Fellini's views on Cinecittà, see "Cinecittà," in ibid., pp. 58–60; or the co-
piously illustrated text in Fellini, *Un regista a Cinecittà*.

ence of the now much older actors who gained international fame from their performances in the work—Marcello Mastroianni and Anita Ekberg. Then, there is the documentary film in progress, now a familiar element in all of Fellini's metacinematic creations. Here, a group of Japanese journalists interview Fellini while he prepares *Amerika*. Finally, and most important of all the films in *Intervista*, there is the film that Fellini shoots under the spectator's nose, *Intervista* itself, a film that subsumes all of the other films listed above and gives them meaning in a new metacinematic context.

Intervista is thus a self-reflexive film that presents itself to its audience during the process of its very creation. For this reason, Fellini calls it a "live" film ("un film in diretta"), and has compared it to *8 1/2* rather than to the simpler *Block-notes*.[88] Fellini's description of *Intervista* makes the work's artistic intentions clearer: "This pleasant chat among friends represents the ultimate result of my way of making cinema: where there is no longer a story or a script, and not even a feeling, unless it is the feeling, precisely, of being inside a kind of creativity that refuses every preconceived order."[89] In *Intervista*, Fellini wants his audience to experience the exhilarating sense of creation that he, as the director, experiences. If *8 1/2* portrayed the complex processes going on in the mind of a film director undergoing a personal crisis, *Intervista* depicts an equally complex creative process, but there is no longer the mediating figure of an imaginary director between the film and the audience: the film we see in the process of being made in *Intervista* is the completed film *Intervista*, just as Guido's inability to complete a film in *8 1/2* provides Fellini with the raw material that is the subject of *his* film. Kafka's *Amerika* is a pretense in Fellini's *Intervista*, just as Guido's science-fiction film served as the pretense for the release of Fellini's creative powers in *8 1/2*.

Like events in a dream, the narrative of *Intervista* reflects the stream of consciousness of its creator. In fact, in discussing this work, Fellini declared that a creator is "a person who materializes a dream."[90] Fellini underlines the importance of dreams for his work with an opening sequence in Cinecittà at night without any title credits to introduce the beginning of the film. Fellini and his crew assemble in the interior of Cinecittà to photograph the famous Teatro 5 from a high crane shot as

---

[88] Cited by Zanelli in *Nel mondo di Federico*, pp. 12, 14; Zanelli also notes (p. 14) that Fellini's collaborator on the script, Gianfranco Angelucci, calls *Intervista* "un 8 1/2 più leggero." For a discussion of Angelucci's relationship to Fellini, see Rocco Fumento, "Maestro Fellini, Studente Angelucci," *Literature/Film Quarterly* 10, no. 4 (1982): 226–33.

[89] Cited in Zanelli, *Nel mondo di Federico*, p. 14.

[90] Cited in ibid., p. 9.

if seen in a dream from above, surrounding the buildings of the studio complex with what Fellini identifies as a "lunar light" and the mysterious smoke made from gunpowder, naphthalene, and magnesium that Fellini consistently uses to produce a dreamlike, phantasmagoric atmosphere in his films. There is a moment of total silence as the enormous crane takes on the characteristics of a prehistoric monster, photographed against the background of the lunar light and the strange, misty smoke.

This hauntingly beautiful shot of the mechanical apparatus that is being used to construct the film we are seeing is but the first of a long series of shots in *Intervista* that concentrate not on any narrative story line but, instead, on revealing the *means* by which film is created. This emphasis on the technical aspects of filmmaking not only serves to distance *Intervista* from any possibility of realistic documentary, but it also underlines Fellini's view that cinema must be the personal expression of an artist, not simply a reflection of the latest cutting-edge technology, because, in fact, most of the "tricks of the trade" Fellini shows to us are as old as the cinema itself. Immediately following the scene of the crane illuminated at night, Fellini portrays his dream of Cinecittà, the description of which is given in the final epigraph to this chapter. Much later in the film, we are shown the interior of the set designer's office, and only then do we realize that the dream we saw was produced not by the crane shot but, instead, by photographing a small-scale model of Cinecittà. This same emphasis on the superiority of the illusion of cinematic "reality" over the "reality" of the everyday world is evident in the preparation of Fellini's sets. Fellini's crew visits the site of the Casa del Passeggero, the station from which Fellini used to take the tram as a young man to go to Cinecittà, and discovers that it has fallen into a state of neglect. However, the crew finds another location, the garage of the tram company, and transforms this false location into one more "real" and convincing than the actual site itself.

The tram also provides Fellini with a means of stressing the creative power of cinematic art. Two halves of a single tram are fixed upon two truck beds so that they can drive through the city toward Cinecittà, simulating the motion of an actual tram on a track. Dividing the tram into two parts provides room for a camera crew to work in each section, creating the illusion that our gaze can encompass both ends of this artificial vehicle while it is in motion. Having carefully revealed to the spectator this mechanism for producing the illusion of a tram ride, Fellini then proceeds to use it in his reenactment of his first trip to Cinecittà as a young journalist, sent to interview a female star. During the trip to the magic capital of the cinema, a number of strange sights are seen from the tram: a waterfall, elephants by the seashore, and Ameri-

28. *Intervista*: Fellini directs the preparations for the scale model of Cinecittà that will appear in his dream vision opening the film

can Indians standing guard on the bluffs overlooking the tram. Naturally, none of these sights could possibly be found near Rome, but in the cinema, Fellini is informing us, anything the mind can imagine is possible. At one point in the tram ride, the two halves of the artificial tram are mysteriously united into a whole, as if linked together during the re-creation of the fantastic voyage to Cinecittà by the power of the imagination. Later, in the back lot of the studio where one of the last sequences of *Intervista* takes place, the attentive spectator will see the now discarded two sections of the tram used by Fellini to create his illusory jump back into his past. The fact that the artistic means used to create the illusion is now part of the junk pile of Cinecittà emphasizes the ephemeral quality of all cinematic artifice.

In a recent BBC documentary film on his work, Fellini described his profession as "precisely a total, cynical vocation of puppet master,"[91]

[91] Transcript of "Real Dreams: Into the Dark with Federico Fellini" (BBC television program, 1987), p. 13. I am indebted to Gianfranco Angelucci for this transcript and for a videotape of the documentary.

and *Intervista* constantly stresses the director's function as master manipulator, as the master illusionist behind all the artificial images projected on the screen. Fellini does this by first luring the spectator into
accepting one of his illusions, for the moment, as the film's focus. This
generally involves a scene re-creating a memory from Fellini's past.
Then, Fellini suddenly breaks the spell of credibility that sequence has
created with an abrupt intrusion of his authoritative presence, thereby
disclosing the artifice involved in the preceding sequence. The best and
most amusing examples of this procedure take place during Fellini's re-
creation of his first visit to Cinecittà. There he observes the filming of
an adventure movie starring the *diva* the young Fellini has come to
Cinecittà to interview. As this preposterous swashbuckler of a film,
with its exotic location (India during the British Raj) reconstructed inside Teatro 14, unfolds, an unnamed director of the 1930s has an irrational fit of anger over the way a scene is being shot. The papier-mâché
elephants on the set lose their tusks during the shooting, and, incensed
over the producer's cheap attempts to avoid renting real elephants, the
director knocks over a whole row of fake elephants and threatens to go
to Germany to work. Suddenly, Fellini breaks into the sound track with
an address to the director, reminding us that the director on screen is
only an actor playing a director in the adventure film. Fellini then
walks onto the set and into the frame, and he demonstrates how the
actor should have done the scene, knocking over the remainder of the
flimsy animals. On another occasion, we see the actor playing the
young Fellini (Sergio Rubini) go to interview the diva inside a small
trailer parked on the lawn of Cinecittà. As the actor playing the role of
the young Fellini enters this trailer, the film cuts to the inside of a studio sound stage, where a much more elaborate set of a similar trailer is
being constructed resembling the one Rubini has just entered. Sitting
near this second trailer on the set, Fellini discusses the making of
Amerika with his actual assistants, Maurizio Mein and Fiammetta Profili (played by themselves), and then he turns toward the omnipresent
Japanese television crew shooting their documentary on his cinema and
says: "Now we have seen our young journalist enter the trailer . . . and
now he is inside all alone in there waiting to meet the actress that
causes him so much disturbance. Rubini, can you hear me?"[92] The re-
creation of the interview that Fellini had with the star follows. On another occasion, we hear Fellini's voice on the sound track prompting an
actor on the screen with his lines, dutifully repeated by the actor following the director's cue. This small but significant detail reveals the
usual manner in which Fellini shoots a scene. He speaks continuously

[92] Fellini, *Block-notes di un regista*, p. 121.

to the actors, telling them what to say, where to move, and how to express their emotions as the camera is rolling. But this simple demonstration of Fellini's habitual working practices on his set also reminds us once again that we are watching a film and is only one of the many constant distancing devices that Fellini employs in *Intervista* to disabuse us of any mimetic or representational expectations we might have while watching the film.

A first viewing of *Intervista* can be a confusing experience. Since the initial fiction of the film is that the spectator is following a Japanese crew doing a documentary film on Fellini's work while the director is preparing his own feature film, an adaptation of Kafka's *Amerika*, we are not surprised when we see the screen tests or preparations for Fellini's projected film. In addition, after *I clowns* and *Roma*, re-creations of Fellini's memories and experiences from the past, abruptly inserted into the narratives of what are pseudodocumentaries, come as no complete surprise. But what puzzles the viewer in *Intervista* is that, unlike in *I clowns* or *Roma*, we also see the preparations for these flashbacks to the past (the construction of the Casa del Passaggero or the tram to Cinecittà; the dialogue between the actor playing the young Fellini in the actress's trailer and the older Fellini on the set) as well as the preparations for the *Amerika* project. In short, while we are prepared to see the preparations for one film, we are astonished to see, instead, preparations for two of them. The impact of this initially puzzling situation completely demolishes the boundaries between art and reality, fact and fiction, film and metafilm, even set and location. Fellini means for us to understand that everything in *Intervista* is completely invented, artificial, fictional. After seeing *Intervista*, Alberto Moravia remarked that for the director of the film, the past and the present were the same thing. When asked his opinion of Moravia's remark, Fellini replied that the lack of any dividing line between past and present was the key not only to all his films but to his entire life.[93]

More than any film since *8 1/2*, *Intervista* compares Fellini to a *Deus artifex*:

Film is a divine way of telling about life, of paralleling God the Father! No other profession lets you create a world which comes so close to the one we know, as well as to unknown, parallel, concentric ones. For me the ideal place—I have said this many times—is Theater 5 in Cinecittà when it's empty. Total emotion, trembling ecstasy is what I feel there in that empty studio—a space to fill up, a world to create.[94]

[93] Both Moravia's remark and Fellini's reaction are cited by Ornella Volta in "Federico Fellini: l'interview d'*Intervista*," in *Federico Fellini*, ed. Ciment, p. 177.
[94] Fellini, *Comments on Film*, p. 102.

The concluding scene of *Intervista* provides a simple but moving visualization of these ideas. Unlike the relatively unreliable, pretentious, or smugly rationalistic voice-overs that Fellini's earlier metacinematic films employed, the director's voice now tells us that *Intervista* "should end here" and that, in fact, it is over. He then recounts an anecdote about one of his producers, who complained that Fellini's works always ended without a bit of hope. "Give me at least a ray of sunshine," the producer would beg Fellini during his screenings.[95] Fellini's voice-over continues: "A ray of sunshine? Well, I don't know, let's try."[96] The lights in Teatro 5 are lowered, except for a single zone of light that is framed by a camera suspended in the darkness. A man walks into the illuminated space and signals a take with the usual board. The image freezes and the titles appear over the image.

With *Intervista*'s conclusion—a camera capturing a beam of light— Fellini celebrates the primordial raw material of cinema. Fellini has constantly stressed that light represents for him the essence of the cinema: "For me, in fact, the cinema is this—images. Light comes even before the theme, even before the actors selected for the various roles. Light is really everything: it is substance, sentiment, style, description. It is everything. The image is expressed with light."[97] But, as Gianfranco Angelucci, collaborator on the script of *Intervista*, has quite rightly noted, Fellini's desire to photograph light, the primordial matter of the created universe, also shows the director in competition with God in creating his own universe of puppet characters and artificial locations within which he is the supreme master.[98] Fellini's homage to the art of the cinema ends on this noble image of the film director— that of the divine artificer creating matter from light in the image of the Divine Creator of the Book of Genesis. But such a dignified and somewhat pretentious estimation of the film director's vocation must be balanced against the lighter, humorous, and self-deprecating tone of the entire film that has preceded this conclusion. In discussing clowns, Fellini once cited an ancient Chinese saying of Lao Tse, reshaping it to reflect his theory of the two clown types: "Lao Tse says: 'If you make a thought (= the white clown), laugh at it (= the Auguste).'"[99] Lao Tse's philosophy may well provide a key to all of Fellini's works, as one per-

[95] According to Kezich, the producer who said this to Fellini was Angelo Rizzoli, in reacting to *La dolce vita* (*Fellini*, p. 276).

[96] Fellini, *Block-notes di un regista*, p. 182.

[97] Fellini, "Fellini on Television: *A Director's Notebook* and *The Clowns*," in *Federico Fellini: Essays in Criticism*, ed. Bondanella, p. 14.

[98] Angelucci, "Un'intervista tutta da vedere," p. 39.

[99] Fellini, *Fellini on Fellini*, p. 125.

ceptive French critic has noted.[100] In one of his most interesting statements on the nature of film, which he made to Gianfranco Angelucci after a visit to Turin's Museo del Cinema, Fellini defines this art form in the following way: "the cinema has always been the same thing: a rickety camera with someone behind it filming a clown moving in front of it!"[101] Fellini's magic in *Intervista* and the film's conclusion, stressing the role of the primordial element of the universe, light, in producing a film, offer a picture of the director as a creator in God's image. Yet, the fact that Fellini placed himself in front of his camera also identifies the director with the clown. It is the paradoxical combination of these two highly unlikely vocations that represents, for Fellini, the magic formula of the cinema.

Block-notes di un regista, I clowns, Roma, and *Intervista* are self-reflexive films whose main purpose is the exploration of the dimensions of cinematic art and a concrete definition by Fellini of his own vocation as a film director. *E la nave va* and *Ginger e Fred*, on the other hand, examine two very different art forms, grand opera and television, but in the process of representing these other means of artistic communication, Fellini also says something of importance about the nature of cinema. Grand opera interests Fellini because of its ritualistic, conventional nature and becomes in *E la nave va* a metaphor for any type of artistic expression. Fellini examines the world of television in *Ginger e Fred* because it is diametrically opposed to the cinema he loves.[102]

E la nave va presents a portrait of the passing of ritual in modern life and, by implication, in the cinema as well. The film's explicit story line

[100] Jacqueline Risset, "La notte sperimentale del cinema," in Fellini, *Block-notes di un regista*, p. 189.

[101] Angelucci, "Un'intervista tutta da vedere," p. 41.

[102] The continuity scripts for both films have been published: Fellini, *E la nave va;* and Fellini, *Ginger e Fred*. The Lilly Library Fellini archives contain a number of interesting manuscripts: (1) "E la nave va: soggetto di Federico Fellini e Tonino Guerra," Fellini MS. 8 (Box 2), the original copy of the story for the film (subsequently published in the Longanesi edition above), which includes a splendid color drawing of the Austrian battleship seen in the film; (2) "Ginger e Fred: soggetto e sceneggiatura di Federico Fellini e Tonino Guerra con la collaborazione di Tullio Pinelli," Pinelli MS. 13 (Box 4, IIE), the original copy of the script eventually published in the Longanesi edition above with the story (this MS. does not contain the soggetto, even though the title indicates that it does); (3) an unpublished English translation of the dialogue of *Ginger e Fred*, Fellini MS. 4 (Box 1), prepared by Fellini's production office. A very important consideration of Fellini's sketches and preparatory materials for *E la nave va* may be found in Raffaele Monti and Pier Marco De Santi, eds., *L'invenzione consapevole: disegni e materiali di Federico Fellini per il film "E la nave va"* (Florence: Artificio, 1984). The most useful critical analyses of the two films are several articles or interviews by Ornella Volta, as well as essays by Gérard Legrand and Robert Benayoun, in *Federico Fellini*, ed. Ciment, pp. 138–67.

follows the funeral ceremonies for Edmea Tetua, a famous diva of Italian grand opera. Representatives from the musical world (singers, directors, critics, friends, and former lovers of the singer), as well as a group of important representatives of the Austro-Hungarian Empire, set forth from Naples on a cruise toward the singer's birthplace, the island of Erimo, to scatter her ashes in the ocean. This unusual voyage on the Italian liner *Gloria N.* takes place at approximately the time the Sarajevo incident ignites the conflagration of the Great War. During the voyage, a group of Serbian refugees are taken on board the ship; a menacing Austrian battleship then appears and orders the Italian captain to give up his Serbian passengers. After a confusing explosion, both ships are sunk. Fellini has included in *E la nave va* a number of themes that are relatively unusual for his cinema. By setting the film on the eve of a world war and including some of the political tensions that prefaced this great conflict, he provides a relatively unusual historical framework for the film. Second, he fills the film with representatives from grand opera, an art form Fellini had always professed to dislike and fail to understand.[103] Third, the narrative story line of *E la nave va* appears to reflect a more traditional linear development than was typical of Fellini's other metacinematic works, which delight in moving back and forth between different levels of illusion and reality, fact and fiction.

In spite of the film's relatively traditional narrative structure, *E la nave va* continues Fellini's now familiar metacinematic critique of the realistic pretensions of documentary film and broadens it into a satirical attack on the intrusive nature of contemporary journalism. In fact, Fellini has called the film a "little fable on hyperinformation."[104] By this, Fellini means to imply that, far from possessing too little information, today the average person has too much of it and is, in fact, bombarded by mass media to the point where an authentic relationship with reality or an intelligent separation of the good and useful information from the "static" is no longer possible. Fellini combines his portrait of the world of grand opera with his critique of mass media by including among the passengers a bothersome and bungling English journalist named Orlando (Freddie Jones), whose feeble attempts to report the "facts" of what occurs during the confrontation between the *Gloria N.* and the Austrian battleship end in disaster and demonstrate how ambiguous supposedly objective reporting really is. Even with Or-

---

[103] In *L'opera*, one of the four sketches for possible films included in Fellini, *Blocknotes di un regista* (pp. 46–54), Fellini discusses his lack of real appreciation of opera and his failure to sit through an entire performance of an opera until relatively late in his life. In this discussion, he repeatedly defines opera as an Italian collective ritual.

[104] Fellini, *E la nave va*, p. 158.

lando and a cameraman on the spot as eyewitnesses taking silent news-
reels of the disaster, the cause of the sinking of the two ships remains
a mystery. Orlando offers several plausible explanations. It is first suggested that a young Serbian terrorist tossed a bomb into the battleship's
cargo bay after leaving the *Gloria N.* But this seems unlikely since the
young man has just fallen in love with a girl on board who has chosen
to leave the ocean liner with him. The first explanation thus also includes a melodramatic element typical of grand opera: the juxtaposition of love and duty. It is then suggested that the firing of the Austrians' cannon ignited the powder magazine of the battleship. A third
alternative is also mentioned—that the Austrians began shelling the
Gloria N. on purpose, looking to provoke an international incident. We
are also shown the incident not once but twice, and in slow motion,
but no amount of detail or different perspective resolves the mysterious
tragedy.

The Orlando's reliability as an objective witness to any events is continuously undercut during the film. His journalistic techniques invariably
fail to uncover important truths. When he is granted an interview with
the Grand Duke of Herzog and inquires about the state of the international situation, the Duke's metaphoric reply ("We are sitting on the
edge of a volcano") is garbled in translation into an incomprehensible
phrase, "We are sitting on the mouth of a mountain." This mistake
produces a comedy of linguistic errors in Italian, German, and Hun-
garian, during which Orlando, the Grand Duke, his interpreter, and
the Grand Duke's entourage argue over the meaning of a single word. If
we cannot agree on a single word, Fellini seems to be saying, it is unlikely that we shall reach any consensus about other important issues
through an examination of the "facts." On another occasion, Orlando
stands in front of the movie camera with the captain of the ship like
any good television correspondent during the evening news, but his
bumbling attempts to deliver the facts about the ocean voyage are undermined by his inability to report correctly even the captain's name or
his birthplace. Perhaps the most damning proof of Orlando's inability
to reveal any important information to us is given when he watches the
Russian baritone Ziloev hypnotize a chicken with the force of his voice.
Alone of all the onlookers, Orlando is hypnotized as well, an almost
too obvious comment on the journalist's similarity in brain power, gul-
libility, and lack of critical distance to the unfortunate fowl.

The most striking characteristic of grand opera as Fellini presents it
in *E la nave va* is its highly ritualistic and conventional quality, the
essence of its divorce from artistic realism. What could be more unlike
a representation of everyday life than a group of people who communicate by singing to each other? The many unusual characters of *E la*

nave va from the world of opera react to events in their lives in exactly the same manner as on the stage—they sing. On two separate occasions—during the boarding of the *Gloria N.* in Naples, and during the confrontation between the Italian liner and the Austrian battleship— Fellini allows all of these comic figures to assemble and sing together in the grand tradition of a Verdian chorus. While we recognize the music immediately, since it is composed of a medley of the most famous themes by Verdi, Fellini has had the lyrics changed to suit his own story by his friend Andrea Zanzotto, one of Italy's greatest living poets and an earlier contributor to *Casanova.*[105] As the passengers form a chorus and protest the Austrians' capture of the Serbian refugees, the majestic music they are singing magically transforms their ridiculous posturing into a moving metaphor of how artistic expression is inevitably opposed to the tyrannical exercise of power. Perhaps nowhere else in the film does Fellini demonstrate so dramatically how strong an emotional appeal an essentially irrational art form can exercise over even the most cynical of audiences.

Because of its highly mannered nature as an art form, in *E la nave va* the world of grand opera becomes transformed into a metaphor for the kind of cinema that contemporary Italian audiences have abandoned. The film's opening sequences present an encapsulated history of the technical development of the cinema. Fellini has often expressed the desire to have entered his profession during the early years of its existence:

> I would have liked to have been born twenty years earlier and made films with the pioneers, with Za-la-Mort, Za-la-Vie and Polidor, in that traveling-players atmosphere with the setting sun as a curtain. To participate in the birth of the movies would have been much more gratifying to my temperament than to arrive when specific film rules were imposed: structuralism, semiology. Inevitable things which keep you posted on artistic and cultural conditions but deprive you of that uproarious and disquieting atmosphere, that somewhat savage joy that linked the cinema to the circus and made it feel like a symbolic essence of life's intrigues.[106]

The opening sequences of *E la nave va* are black and white, and the only sound to be heard is the noise of an old silent projector. After a

---

[105] During the departure scene, Fellini employs passages from *La forza del destino*: act 2, scene 5; act 3, scene 6; act 4, scene 5; plus the recurrent "Fate" motif from the overture. As the singers face the battleship and protest the enforced capture of the Serbian refugees, Fellini uses passages from other Verdi masterpieces: *Aida* (act 1, "Battle Hymn"; act 2, scene 2); *Nabbuco* (act 2, scene 2); and *La traviata* (act 3, finale). Zanzotto's lyrics can be examined in Fellini, *E la nave va*, pp. 36–37, 134–36. I am indebted to Rebecca Bowles for identifying the musical passages for me.

[106] Fellini, *Comments on Film*, p. 181.

few moments, the black-and-white tone shades into a sepia color typical of old films exhumed from dusty film archives. With the beginning of music on the sound track as the singers prepare to board the *Gloria N.*, the film's tones finally move from sepia to color, completing Fellini's brief survey of the major technical advances of film art. *E la nave va* was shot entirely in Technicolor, then discolored in the developing process to create the black-and-white or sepia tones and the grainy texture typical of film in the pre-color era. Orlando's first appearance during these initial sequences is accompanied by the familiar silent-film titles in place of dialogue. Thus, the opening of *E la nave va* begins with a scene paying homage to the early work of the Lumière brothers, here the departure of an ocean liner instead of their celebrated sequence of the arrival of a train in a station. The fantasy of Méliès soon overtakes any documentary insistence on realism, as the rest of *E la nave va* celebrates the creative possibilities of Cinecittà's Teatro 5 and the potential of Fellini's imagination. The film's conclusion stresses not the explanation of the sinking of the *Gloria N.*, which remains confusing and mysterious, but instead the world of cinematic illusion. First Fellini provides a comic shot of the silent cameraman trying to maintain his balance and his tripod while working upon the sinking, slanting deck of the *Gloria N.* During this heroic effort to document for posterity the "facts" of the terrible disaster at sea, passengers and crew try to escape by running toward the side of the ocean liner. A subsequent cut reveals that the ship is actually an elaborate movie set. There is a camera on a crane shooting the entire scene, surrounded by special-effects technicians filling the air with smoke, while other workmen shake the plastic sheets that form an artificial ocean. The huge deck of the *Gloria N.* is actually a gigantic hydraulic construction in Cinecittà's Teatro 5, capable of supporting the weight of 250 people and 170 tons of material. Fellini's crew built it to simulate the rolling and pitching of a real ocean liner on the high seas.[107] The camera through which we witness this scene now frames another camera with an individual sitting behind it peering into this camera, which is pointed directly at us. Earlier, Orlando had attempted, with comic results, to determine the "facts" behind the sinking of the *Gloria N.* But now, with Fellini's final revelation of his artistic artifice, we are confronted with the only "truth" that matters for him—that of artistic illusion. Fellini's celebration of cinematic artifice here has been anticipated throughout the film by his use of sets designed to expose their own blatantly contrived nature. The shots of the *Gloria N.* and the Austrian battleship on the water are obviously produced with tiny models set upon a plastic ocean. At one

[107] See Ornella Volta, "Quelques notes en plus, prises au cours du tournage," in *Federico Fellini*, ed. Ciment, p. 144, for details about the hydraulic construction.

29. *E la nave va*: Fellini's technicians prepare the scale model of the Austrian battle-ship that will sail upon a plastic ocean

point in the narrative, a singer turns to another as they stare, enraptured, at a horizon of tinfoil and plastic that reflects the rays of an even more obviously fabricated sun and declares, "Ah . . . how marvelous! It seems imaginary!"[108] In another director's works, they would have expressed astonishment at how "real" such a sight appeared. Indeed, all of the scenes of the ocean voyage of the *Gloria N.* were produced inside the studio, except for the ship's departure from the port of Naples: that sequence was created by painting the wall of a Roman pasta factory to resemble the sides of an ocean liner and then employing camera movements to simulate the ship's departure.[109]

As Fellini's camera tracks into the lens of the camera operated by the unidentified individual in Teatro 5, the earlier black-and-white tone of the opening sequences suddenly returns. Now Orlando delivers an ironic parody of the last stage in the "history" of the cinema according

[108] Fellini, *E la nave va*, p. 57.
[109] See Volta, "Quelques notes en plus," p. 144.

to Fellini—the advent of television and commercial spots. Orlando, whose name Fellini chose after he happened to see it on a billboard advertising ice cream near the Rome airport,[110] has been set adrift in a life raft with the lovesick rhinoceros in the ship's hold as his only companion, and he has survived only by drinking the animal's milk. Orlando's last line is a rhetorical question, delivered in a manner that is unmistakably like hundreds of testimonials to the superior qualities of endless products promoted by television commercials: "Do you know that the rhinoceros gives an excellent milk?"[111] At this point, the screen frames Orlando and his rhinoceros companion through a filter that makes it appear as if they were being shot through a port hole. But this "small screen" implicitly reproduces the reduced visual field of the television screen. Fellini's history of the cinema in *E la nave va* thus concludes on an unsettling note. Films for commercial advertising shown on the small and aesthetically limited television screen may have superseded the creative expression of the individual director, whose many illusory tricks of the trade Fellini has just revealed to us.

Television's relationship to the cinema, the dramatic differences between a traditional film audience and a television audience, and the damaging effects of commercial interruptions of a director's film when screened on television are all themes that have become almost an obsession with Fellini in the past decade. As early as 1969 and 1970, when he made *Block-notes* and *I clowns*, Fellini had very clearly expressed his negative views on the theoretical differences between the two media.[112] From a technical point of view (the perspective that interested Fellini most when he first wrote about the subject), the smaller size of the television screen precludes any real artistic use of extra-long shots, and the relative clarity of the television image inhibits Fellini's ability to express his imagery in an ambiguous visual fashion. For Fellini, television is primarily a means of communication rather than of artistic expression, and it possesses a different and simplified visual syntax. When he produced films for television, Fellini actually paid little attention to the fact that they would be broadcast on the smaller screen. As far as he was concerned, these films were created the same way as his other works destined for the movie theaters.

As the power of television in Italy has steadily grown to the point where the public and private television networks have become the major source of capital for Italian film production, Fellini and other Italian

[110] Fellini, *E la nave va*, p. 160.

[111] Ibid., p. 144. Millicent Marcus has suggested to me that Fellini may also be referring to his earlier advertising jingle about milk in *Le tentazioni del dottor Antonio*.

[112] Here I paraphrase Fellini's arguments from "Fellini on Television," pp. 11–16.

directors have become increasingly concerned with the social changes
in audiences, which have produced an entirely different kind of film
spectator. One particular sequence of *Intervista* portrays this threat in
a humorous fashion, showing Fellini's film crew at Cinecittà besieged
by a band of Indians. The sequence begins in the familiar fashion we
have all come to recognize from having seen dozens of American west-
erns, but it concludes by revealing that the lances of the attacking Indians are actually television antennae, the symbol of the cinema's nem-
esis. But with fewer and fewer people willing to pay to see films in
movie theaters, and more and more of them staying at home to watch
films on television, many traditional features of the Italian audience
have been fundamentally altered. Television's impact on cinema in Italy has thus ceased to be a laughing matter:

> I too think that the cinema has lost authority, prestige, mystery, magic.
> The giant screen that dominates an audience devotedly gathered in front
> of it no longer fascinates us. Once it dominated tiny little men staring
> enchanted at immense faces, lips, eyes, living and breathing in another
> unreachable dimension, fantastic and at the same time real, like a dream.
> Now we have learned to dominate it. We are bigger than it. See how we
> have reduced it: here it is the size of a cushion between the library and
> the flower pot. Sometimes it's even in the kitchen, near the refrigerator.
> It has become an electric domestic servant and we, seated in armchairs,
> armed with remote control, exercise a total power over those little im-
> ages, rejecting whatever is unfamiliar or boring to us. . . . We wipe out
> the images that don't interest us. We are the masters. What a bore that
> Bergman! Who said Buñuel was a great director? Out of the house with
> them. I want to see a ball game or a variety show. Thus a tyrant spectator
> is born, an absolute despot who does what he wants and is more and
> more convinced that he is the director or at least the producer of the
> images he sees. How could the cinema possibly try to attract that kind of
> audience?[113]

Television represents a threat to the creative expression of the individual artist, in Fellini's opinion, not merely because it employs an impoverished technological language (which it does), but, more importantly,
because it destroys the ritualistic nature of cinematic experience, the
sense of attending a church where images rather than words are communicated in a dreamlike language that projects our fantasies onto the
silver screen in a fantastic and voyeuristic environment that we experience as a group rather than in the privacy of our homes. The destruc-
tion of the ritualistic quality of the cinematic experience deprives the

---

[113] Fellini, *Comments on Film*, pp. 207–8.

directors of their traditional control over the audience and dissolves the dreamlike character of the artistic expression that the viewers share. In addition to the general deleterious effects of showing a film (a work of art) on television (a medium of communication rather than of expression), there are the particularly damaging effects of interrupting a film with commercials.

Over the last decade, commercial television has begun to compete aggressively with the three state-owned television networks, which screen feature films without commercial interruption except for the intermission between the primo tempo and the secondo tempo, a division that screenings in movie theaters also follow. In contrast, commercial networks interrupt films constantly and often in a far more intrusive manner than is typical even of American television. For some time, a number of Italian directors, including Fellini and Ettore Scola, have supported making such commercial interruptions more difficult or even prohibiting them entirely on the grounds that an author's right to have his or her work of art screened by the public includes the right to have that product viewed in an integral form. As Fellini has indignantly declared, "the insolence, aggression, and massacre of television publicity inserted within a film! It is like violence committed against an artistic creation."[114] Italian private networks have agreed to some reasonable guidelines designed to avoid the interruption of a film at a crucially dramatic moment but have naturally refused to ban commercials completely. This is their only source of revenue, while public television networks have access to the governmental budget and yearly payments by Italian citizens to cover expenses. They can therefore be more generous about screening films without too frequent commercial interruptions.

What concerns Fellini is the fact that television commercials and their disruption of the narrative structure of serious films, which have their own peculiar rhythms and cadences, may have created an entirely different kind of spectator from that which once populated the provincial theaters of Fellini's youth: "perhaps we are creating a sort of conditioning with television advertising, a conditioning composed of approximation, lack of attention and concentration. The maximum expression of bad manners, therefore, a kind of slap at culture, at the personality of the author, the sentiment of his fable, and the sense of the message that always exists when somebody is telling you a story."[115] When the major private channel in Italy, Silvio Berlusconi's Canale 5, broadcast a number of Fellini's works, interrupting them with the usual

---

[114] Fellini, *Ginger e Fred*, p. 75.
[115] Ibid.

number of commercials, Fellini indignantly protested. Not owning the rights to the films, which generally belong to the producer, Fellini could of course do very little to prevent this commercial exploitation of his work. He did publicly apologize, however, for the disturbance his films caused when they interrupted Berlusconi's advertising! More recently, in a polemical debate between Berlusconi's network and Ettore Scola, Fellini has intervened on Scola's behalf against what he has termed the "disgraceful, vulgar, hoodlumlike, stupid interruption of films with publicity spots."[116] Fellini has, as I noted earlier, produced several commercials himself. In addition, his most recent films have been financed by public and private television networks. But his opposition to commercials is not hypocritical. He is not opposed to commercials themselves but, rather, their constant interruption of the rhythm of a film's narrative on television. Fellini's feelings are so strong on this issue that he insisted on an unusual contract for his most recent film, *La voce della luna*. Even though the bulk of his financing for the film came from a company ultimately dependent upon the archenemy, Silvio Berlusconi, Fellini insisted on a clause in the contract that would prohibit Berlusconi from broadcasting the film on his own commercial network. Thus, Fellini used his reputation to force Berlusconi to pay for a film that only the public television network could ever broadcast!

Given Fellini's strong feelings about the topic of television and its relationship to the cinema, it was inevitable that he would eventually treat television in one of his films. *Ginger e Fred* provides a humorous and highly critical view of television from behind the scenes of a television studio. Its comic vision of the organization and broadcasting of a variety show underlines the negative aspects of television in an implicit comparison to theatrical productions and similar productions immortalized by the cinema. Fellini shows us television at its worst while the medium broadcasts a butchery of a variety show, a genre Fellini has long admired and that appears in important parts of a number of his works (*Luci del varietà*, *Le notti di Cabiria*, *Roma*). For this reason, *Ginger e Fred* may be legitimately considered along with the other more obviously metacinematic films analyzed here.

Fellini's notes for the film, published with the screenplay, reveal that

---

[116] Bruno Blasi, "Spot teppisti: intervista con Federico Fellini," *Panorama* 27 (5 November 1989): 55. This debate is of some importance, since Scola is also the shadow minister of culture for the opposition Communist party, while Silvio Berlusconi, the owner of the private network, supports the Socialist party of Bettino Craxi, one of the Communist party's chief opponents. Fellini's position is based strictly on aesthetic grounds, however, and he has no connection with any specific political group in Italy. But Fellini is indirectly involved in the controversy on a personal level, since Berlusconi's financing produced *La voce della luna*.

he had apparently considered opening the film with an image from an extremely well known classic (he suggests something from Chaplin's *City Lights*, Eisenstein's *Battleship Potemkin*, or even the Trevi Fountain sequence from his *La dolce vita*) that would be decomposed and disintegrated by an electronic computer. His notes provide the following definition of television, which fits its image in *Ginger e Fred* perfectly:

> Note: The abnormal, the monstrous, the delirious, the alienated, the exceptional reproposed by TV as [if it were] the most obvious, normal, familiar, and customary aspect of daily life; and, on the other hand, the banality, the insignificant, the informal, the collective, the undifferentiated, presented with solemnity, trumpet flourishes, reflectors, choreography, and the rhythms of a sacred ceremony.[117]

The film's relatively simple plot rejects the unconventional, nonlinear structure typical of the other metacinematic films for a relatively straightforward and simple story about the nostalgic encounter of two former dancers from the variety theater of the 1940s, Ginger (Giulietta Masina) and Fred (Marcello Mastroianni). Their stage names recall the celebrated dance team of Fred Astaire and Ginger Rogers whose tap-dancing routines from Hollywood films they imitated. Separated for decades, the two are reunited for a brief appearance together on a television variety program called "Ed ecco a voi" ("We Proudly Present").

While Fellini's cast includes the now familiar collection of individuals who have been selected to appear in the film because of their physical appearance rather than their professional status as actors, the three prominent actors in *Ginger e Fred* evoke past Fellini films. The unctuous and patently insincere master of ceremonies is played by Franco Fabrizi. The superficiality and insignificance of his personality in *Ginger e Fred* cannot help but recall his earlier roles as the unreliable Fausto of *I vitelloni* or the con artist of *Il bidone*. Giulietta Masina, of course, always represents for Fellini what he calls the "projection of wounded and triumphant innocence," while Mastroianni may be said to reflect Fellini's desire to evade responsibility and maturity.[118] Once again, as in *8 1/2*, Mastroianni wears one of Fellini's hats as part of his costume. Together in the film, Masina and Mastroianni evoke some of the most famous moments in all of Fellini's cinema.

The other dozens of characters are the most unusual assortment Fellini has ever created. What Fellini dislikes most about television is its reduction of everything it presents to the same mass level of insignifi-

---

[117] Fellini, *Ginger e Fred*, p. 33.
[118] Ibid., p. 57.

30. *Ginger e Fred*: Ginger and Fred are presented to the television audience of *Ed ecco a voi!* by the master of ceremonies

cance. Unlike the various routines in the traditional variety hall theater Fellini loves, television imitates the *variety* of the variety hall but completely distorts the individuality of the separate routines. Moreover, everything becomes part of the entertainment world. A sampling of the people to appear with Ginger and Fred gives some idea of this grotesque mass media freak show. There is a transvestite who claims that her vocation is to bring love (that is, sex) to the inmates of Italian prisons; an engineer who holds the record for the longest time spent in captivity by kidnappers and the highest ransom paid, whose finger was cut off and sent to his relatives during the negotiations with his captors; a woman who abandons her family because she falls in love with an extraterrestrial. Then there is the man who can impregnate a woman with only his glance, the maker of edible underwear, a Mafioso complete with police escort, a cow with fifteen teats, and last but not least, twenty-five dwarf dancers called "Los Lilliputs."

Besides these eccentric figures, there are a number of look-alikes of famous people or show business personalities who constantly roam around the television studio, including a Ronald Reagan figure from Rome, a Queen Elizabeth with an accent from Puglia, a Marcel Proust from Sicily, and a host of others who recall Clark Gable, Franz Kafka, Marlene Dietrich, Liza Minelli, Woody Allen, Betty Davis, Marty Feldman, and Telly Savalas. These look-alike figures serve a very important purpose, for even more than the grotesque and freakish people who will appear on the program because of something unusual they have done, the look-alikes underline television's "profoundly anticultural operation," as Fellini puts it, its approximation, its secondhand nature: "here is the question of the look-alikes: somebody that appears like someone else, just as television would like to resemble the cinema, chronicle, reality."[119]

Along with the cultural leveling of the television program itself, there is, in addition, a constant barrage of commercials selling products that not only characterizes television broadcasting but has also permeated the world around the film's characters. When Ginger arrives in Rome at the Stazione Termini, and later when both Ginger and Fred say farewell at the same station, the enormous building is dominated by a gigantic zampone sausage, just one of the many products offered to the public by Cavalier Fulvio Lombardoni.[120] Lombardoni's firm also offers the Pasta Scolamangi—pasta that is supposed to make the eater lose rather than gain weight. But the most humorous commercial is undoubtedly that for Betrix watches. It opens with the famous tercet of Dante's *Divina commedia* about the pilgrim's confused state in the middle of the journey of his life, then adds a second tercet that brags about how a Betrix watch (the brand name an obvious reference to Beatrice, Dante's muse), complete with compass, will always help you find your path. The journey to God and salvation in Dante's poem has been supplanted by blatant consumerism. It is precisely this kind of kitsch culture—typified by the use of references to Western civilization's greatest epic poem to sell a compass watch—that Fellini identifies with television and its commercials.

Ginger e Fred parades an endless stream of these superficial and shallow characters before us. Only during the appearance of Ginger and Fred do we sense any genuine emotion or feeling from the participants in the television program. Just before they begin their routine, all the studio lights go off because of some technical failure. Huddling together

[119] Ibid., p. 76.

[120] This mythical industrialist of gastronomic delicacies in *Ginger e Fred* probably refers to Cavalier Pietro Barilla, the owner of one of Italy's most famous food companies, and the man who commissioned Fellini to do his celebrated spot on Barilla pasta analyzed in an earlier chapter.

in the dark, Fred tells Ginger that it is not so bad in the dark, since it is just like being in a dream, far from everything. When the lights return and they begin their tap-dance number, any note of poignant nostalgia is shattered when Fred falls because of the passing of the years and his lack of practice. The two old hoofers nevertheless make it through their number and win a round of applause, but the demands of the television program for ever more unusual but momentary surprises continue unabated. An admiral is wheeled out on the stage even as the applause dies down, and the variety show rolls on relentlessly with its interminable procession of eccentric characters. While we have been emotionally touched for a brief moment by the nostalgic appearance of Ginger and Fred, Fellini also leaves us with the rather bitter realization that entertainers like Ginger and Fred and the old-fashioned but authentic kinds of routines they performed are as completely out of place in the contemporary world as buggy whips or plastic collars.

Fellini's metacinematic works stand in sharp contrast to the films he produced through *La dolce vita*, for they abandon the representation of reality in order to depict, with increasing confidence, the *process* of artistic representation. In all of these films, the impact of Jung and Fellini's own understanding of the dream work have moved Fellini's cinema far away from the essentially literary plots that dominated his early works and closer and closer to a self-reflexive narrative style that privileges the autonomous image over plot, dialogue, or story line. These films parody documentary film's sometimes arrogant pretensions to capture "reality." And each of these metacinematic works deconstructs the very concept of artistic illusion by constantly revealing Fellini's technical artifice to his audience.

CHAPTER FIVE

Literature and Cinema

TOBY DAMMIT

AND *FELLINI SATYRICON*

Everything that connects the cinema with literature is the result of laziness and sentimental whim, when it is not actually due to brutal calculation. It is a case of doing something arbitrary and unnatural, like sticking four car wheels on to a horse, or cutting a steak into the shape of a cod-fish.[1]

AFTER THE COMPLETION of *Giulietta degli spiriti* in 1965, Fellini had originally intended to film *Il viaggio di G. Mastorna*, a script he wrote in the summer of 1965 with Dino Buzzati, whose novels and short stories have often been compared to the works of Franz Kafka, one of Fellini's favorite writers.[2] While Fellini was making his preparations to begin work on *Mastorna*, a number of crises and misfortunes suddenly overtook him and radically altered his plans. Most shattering of these events was Fellini's sudden physical collapse in 1967. While he languished in the hospital, receiving anxious telegrams from friends and dignitaries all over the world (an experience which quite naturally convinced him he was on the brink of death), his condition was eventually diagnosed, at what seemed to be the last moment, as the rare Sanarelli-Schwarzmann syndrome. One of the positive

---

[1] Fellini, *Fellini on Fellini*, p. 156. I limit my discussion of Fellini and literature to *Toby Dammit* and *Fellini Satyricon*, because these films are the only works that are based on writers universally recognized as major figures. *La voce della luna* will be discussed in the conclusion of this book. *Casanova* will be treated in a more appropriate forum, a chapter on Fellini and sexuality. The sheer size of Casanova's memoirs makes them difficult to consider as a strictly literary work, and Fellini's *Casanova* represents more an interpretation of the protagonist rather than a true adaptation of the literary form of the memoirs Casanova wrote.

[2] For discussions of Fellini's life during this crucial period that marks his first interest in adaptations of literary texts, see Kezich, *Fellini*, pp. 357–97; Liliana Betti, *Fellini: An Intimate Portrait*, trans. Joachim Neugroschel (Boston: Little, Brown, 1979), pp. 120–53; or Alpert, *Fellini: A Life*, pp. 190–212.

effects of Fellini's enforced convalescence was his completion of his autobiographical essay, *La mia Rimini*, which was published in 1967 and
then reissued along with a number of splendid photographs of his
hometown.[3]

During this crucial period in his life Fellini pondered a number of
different films. The *Mastorna* project, originally the property of Dino
De Laurentiis, was purchased by Fellini's new producer, Alberto Grimaldi, for several hundred million lire. The already constructed set reproducing the Cologne cathedral in *Mastorna* was eventually employed
during the opening sequences of *Block-notes di un regista* for American
television. By the time Fellini had shifted from De Laurentiis to Grimaldi, he was uncertain about his ability to tackle *Mastorna* and finally
agreed, after considering Boccaccio's *Decameron* and Ariosto's *Orlando
Furioso*, to begin work on Petronius's *Satyricon*. But before that highly
ambitious film was begun, Fellini completed not only his brief metacinematic *Block-notes*, which concludes with a shot of his preparations for
Fellini Satyricon, but also another brief but much more significant adaptation of a short story by Edgar Allan Poe, *Toby Dammit*. Fellini was
convinced to do this film by a French producer, Raymond Eger, who had
commissioned a number of important European and American directors to submit proposals for Poe adaptations.[4]

Fellini has described the *Mastorna* project as "a journey, imagined or
dreamed, a journey into memory, into repression, into a labyrinth that
has an infinity of exits but only one entrance, and that therefore the
real problem is not to get out but to get in."[5] *Mastorna* may well represent the Ur-film of Fellini's subconscious, a collection of images and

---

[3] Federico Fellini, *La mia Rimini*, ed. Renzo Renzi (Bologna: Cappelli, 1987); the
text of the essay without the photographs can be found in Fellini, *Fare un film*, pp.
3–40; or in English as "Rimini, My Home Town," in Fellini, *Fellini on Fellini*, pp. 1–
40.

[4] According to Ornella Volta, "Come é nato *Tre passi nel delirio*," in *"Tre passi
nel delirio" di F. Fellini, L. Malle, R. Vadim*, ed. Liliana Betti, Ornella Volta, and
Bernardino Zapponi (Bologna: Cappelli, 1968), Eger examined scripts from Joseph Lo-
sey, Roger Vadim, Fellini, Louis Malle, Orson Welles, and Luchino Visconti before
selecting the three scripts by Fellini, Malle, and Vadim. This same volume also contains a detailed discussion of the creation of *Toby Dammit* by Liliana Betti ("Alla
ricerca di Toby Dammit," pp. 31–59), as well as the Italian script for the film (pp. 71–
96). For an English version of Betti's essay, see her *Fellini: An Intimate Portrait*, pp.
130–53. No English script of *Toby Dammit* exists, although the Lilly Library con-
serves the original manuscript of the director's shooting script, which differs in some
important respects from the script published by Cappelli as well as from the completed film: Federico Fellini and Bernardino Zapponi, " 'Toby Dammit' dal racconto
di Poe 'Non scommettere la testa col diavolo': riduzione di Fellini & Zapponi," Fellini MS. 11 (Box 2).

[5] Fellini, *Comments on Film*, p. 171.

narrative situations that has remained with him since the project's conception in 1965 and whose influence has, by Fellini's own testimony, nourished many of his other films, including *Fellini Satyricon*, *Casanova*, *Prova d'orchestra*, *La città delle donne*, and *E la nave va*: "Perhaps it serves the same function as those tugboat operators who pull transatlantic liners out of port: something, in sum, born not to be made but to permit others to be made. A kind of inexhaustible creative uranium."[6] But Fellini made this somewhat self-confident description of the positive benefits of *Mastorna* quite recently. During his life-threatening illness, when he abandoned the project in desperation and turned to his short television film and the two adaptations from Poe and Petronius, Fellini experienced a serious crisis of confidence that called into question his hitherto inexhaustible capacity to bridge the gap between his fantasy and the mundane requirements of reproducing his fantasy in a concrete cinematographic form. His preoccupation with dreams, the subconscious activity Fellini has always considered the secret sanctuary of his genius, only seemed to heighten his concerns over his imaginative powers, for many of the dreams he had during this time pointed toward worrisome subconscious doubts about his creative capabilities.[7] The crisis of confidence Fellini experienced would remain fixed in his memory, looming over him as an ominous and recurring possibility each time he would begin a new film in the future. It also marked the director's awareness of his middle-aged status and his growing concern with death and mutability, as he was forced to come to grips with his own mortality in the hospital.

I have provided a brief outline of Fellini's life during the period that led to the filming of *Toby Dammit* and *Fellini Satyricon* because it is impossible to understand his decision to employ literary texts as the bases of his scripts without some consideration of his biography. Although Fellini's biographers have surveyed the various aspects of his crises and have provided an account of the vagaries of the different projects dating from this period, they have failed to explain satisfactorily why Fellini suddenly turned not once but twice to literary sources for inspiration. This question remains a crucial issue for students of Fellini's cinema, since Fellini has consistently opposed adaptations or trans-

---

[6] Ibid., p. 169.

[7] See Fellini, "Fellini oniricon," for color reproductions of three such dreams. The first two date from 1966 and underline the impossibility of realizing *Mastorna*; the last dates from 1978 and was apparently provoked by Fellini's seeing a suitcase in the Amsterdam airport with the name "J. Mastorna" written on a luggage tag. It contains a scene of Fellini in bed gazing at the character of Mastorna on a screen in front of the bed, an image that recalls the scene of the young boys in bed masturbating before a movie screen in *La città delle donne*.

positions of literary works by Italian directors and is perhaps the most
vehement supporter of *original* screenplays as the basis for a serious
cinema arising from an auteur's personal artistic expression. During
this period, some of the most important Italian films were based on
highly original and personal literary adaptations: Antonioni's *Blow-Up*;
Pasolini's *Medea, Oedipus Rex*, and *Il decameron*; Visconti's *Il gatto-
pardo* and *Morte a Venezia*; and Bertolucci's *La strategia del ragno* and
Il conformista. Fellini was certainly aware that his own opposition to
adaptations was outside of the mainstream during the decade. When
questioned about persistent demands from producers or critics that he
produce a version of Dante's *Divina commedia*, Fellini explained his
reluctance to turn to literature for inspiration:

> A work of art has its own unique expression. Those transpositions from
> one art form to another I find monstrous, ridiculous, off the mark. My
> preferences are for original subjects written for the cinema. I believe the
> cinema doesn't need literature, it needs only film writers, that is, people
> who express themselves according to the rhythms and the cadences in-
> trinsic to film. Film is an autonomous art form which has no need of
> transpositions to a level which, in the best of cases, will always and for-
> ever be mere illustration. Each work of art thrives in the dimension
> which conceived it and through which it is expressed. What can one get
> from a book? Plot. But plot itself has no significance. It is the feeling
> which is expressed that matters, the imagination, atmosphere, illumina-
> tion, in sum, the interpretation. Literary interpretation of events has
> nothing to do with cinematic interpretation of those same events. They
> are two completely different methods of expression.[8]

In turning to Poe and Petronius, Fellini employed an entirely different approach to literary texts from what would normally be used in
filming an adaptation. During the production of these two films, Fellini's cast of collaborators underwent changes, some of which reflected
the various crises in his life. The death of Gianni di Venanzo, the magical director of photography of *8 1/2* and *Giulietta degli spiriti*, in 1965
forced Fellini to turn to another great technician, Giuseppe Rotunno,
who continued to work with Fellini, with the exception of *Block-notes*
and *I clowns* (done by Dario di Palma), until he was himself replaced
on *Ginger e Fred* by Tonino Delli Colli, who has continued to be Fellini's director of photography ever since. When Ennio Flaiano ceased to
work with Fellini after *Giulietta degli spiriti* because of a fundamental
difference of opinion, ending a close collaboration that stretched back
to *Luci del varietà*, Tullio Pinelli also broke off an even longer collab-

---

[8] Fellini, *Comments on Film*, p. 28.

oration that had begun during the years Fellini worked with him as a scriptwriter. The break with Pinelli was merely a professional one and did not affect their friendship, unlike that with Flaiano, and collaboration between Fellini and Pinelli was renewed again with *Ginger e Fred* and *La voce della luna*. To replace these scriptwriters who had parted company with Fellini precisely because their own sensibilities were not in harmony with the director's new style, Fellini struck up a friendship and an artistic collaboration with Bernardino Zapponi, whose *Gobal*, a collection of short stories, impressed Fellini very much. Fellini even proposed to the French producer the substitution of several of Zapponi's stories for the tale from Poe, a proposal that was obviously rejected given that the thematic unity of the projected film depended on sources from Poe's works.[9] When Fellini received the ultimatum to work with the tale of the American writer or abandon the project, he was finally forced to return to Poe.

The manner in which Fellini selected the specific story to film is quite extraordinary. According to the testimony of his trusted assistant Liliana Betti, Fellini actually refused to read Poe's stories, relying instead on summary outlines of the short stories provided by either Betti or Zapponi. As ever a believer in Jungian synchronic experiences, Fellini was confirmed in the belief that Zapponi would be the ideal collaborator by the coincidence that his office and Zapponi's home were located on the same street. Now, the choice of the story to film from Poe's collection would be determined by a similar incident. Returning from supper with Zapponi one night, Fellini saw the Ariccia bridge that had collapsed a few months before and connected it with the bridge in the short story "Never Bet the Devil Your Head: A Tale with a Moral."[10]

Poe's story is not among his most important and is very infrequently anthologized. It is not difficult to understand why. In an article on Poe and the cinema published with the Italian version of the script of *Toby Dammit*, Zapponi identified the reason for the popularity of Poe's most famous stories: "Poe's tales have the fixity of dreams; there is a sense

[9] Bernardino Zapponi, *Gobal* (Milan: Longanesi, 1967). According to Kezich (*Fellini*, p. 378), Fellini was initially struck by "C'é una voce nella mia vita," the monologue of a psychotic murderer who hears his victim's voices through a disconnected telephone receiver; when he learned that an option on this story had already been bought by another director, Fellini proposed another of Zapponi's stories, "L'autista," a tale about a chauffeur who begins to hate his master's car so much that he eventually dismantles it and pushes it into the ocean.

[10] See Betti's account of the evolution of the script in *"Tre passi nel delirio,"* pp. 45–50. For the original version of the story, see *Collected Works of Edgar Allan Poe: Tales and Sketches 1831–1842*, ed. Thomas Ollive Mabbott (Cambridge: Belknap Press, 1978), 2:619–34.

of horror in concentric circles, in a spiral, in a vortex. There is a lack of air, of time; the perspectives are deformed as in nightmares. Poe refuses conventional schedules, classical approaches; he possesses a mathematics all his own that is dumbfounding and that only the force of his imagination renders credible."[11] Zapponi goes on to say that the many Poe adaptations by Roger Corman starring Vincent Price are excellent films in their own right, but their style is completely foreign to Poe's stories, which only served to provide Corman's titles. In his opinion (and, we must presume, also Fellini's), transferring Poe to the screen intact is almost impossible, since the structure of his tales and that of the cinema do not share the same rhythm and aesthetics: "Poe can provide stimuli, not stories; he can set off in the director a mechanism that produces a neurotic twinship. With his anxieties, he can influence the author of the film, suggest to him visions, ideas, nightmares, or characters. He can initiate a creative process in a receptive mind. Shadowy and delicate, he cannot stand being confronted directly."[12] The most famous of Poe's stories—"The Fall of the House of Usher," "The Tell-Tale Heart," "Murders in the Rue Morgue," "The Mask of the Red Death," "The Pit and the Pendulum"—have direct links with popular genres, such as the detective or horror story, and these stories have been adapted for the cinema over and over again. But "Never Bet the Devil Your Head" is anything but a typical horror story. It is an ironic monologue by a narrator who recounts the decapitation of his friend Toby Dammit, whose habitual swearing and betting is explained by the fact that his mother beat him with her left hand. Toby was in the habit of offering to bet the devil his head that he could do something, primarily since this would, he felt, cost him nothing. One day, however, in front of a covered bridge, Toby declared that he could jump over a turnstile, making his usual wager with the devil. At that moment "a little lame old gentleman of venerable aspect" says "Ahem!"[13] This gentleman accepts Toby's wager, assuring the brash young man that the leap will be an easy one but neglecting to warn him of a flat iron bar concealed from his view. After Toby's leap results in his decapitation by the bar, the old man (now revealed to be the devil under this innocuous disguise) runs off with Toby's head.

The plot outline of "Never Bet the Devil Your Head" makes the tale sound like a possible candidate for the Roger Corman variety of Poe adaptation, but it is precisely the presence of Poe's ironic narrator that

[11] Bernardino Zapponi, "Edgar Poe e il cinema," in *"Tre passi nel delirio,"* ed. Betti et al., p. 15. Zapponi's article also contains a list of adaptations from Poe for the cinema up to 1968, most directed by the same Roger Corman who distributed *Tre passi nel delirio* in the United States.

[12] Ibid., p. 19.

[13] Poe, *Tales and Sketches 1831–42,* 2:627.

completely changes the mood of the tale from a potential horror story
to a literary game, a satire of the Transcendentalist tradition in American literature that was so crucial a movement during the time the story
was written. When the narrator first reports Toby's usual wager—"I'll
bet the Devil my head"—he says that there was something "queer"
about Toby's statement, a remark, in his view, that "Mr. Coleridge
would have called mystical, Mr. Kant pantheistical, Mr. Carlyle twist-
ical, and Mr. Emerson hyperquizzitistical."[14] The narrator constantly
refers to literary journals, reviews, and arguments of the time, and the
devil even tells Toby that he is confident Toby will make the jump
"handsomely, and transcendentally." After Toby's decapitation, the
narrator sends the bill for the funeral expenses to the Transcendentalists, and when they refuse to pay it, he has Mr. Dammit dug up and
sold for dog's meat![15] As one discussion of the story concludes, Poe's
"serious meaning is that the Transcendentalists are to blame for the
narrator's loss of head. Lost in a mystical maze of transcendental meaning, the narrator has lost sight of common sense matters . . . the figurative loss of head in Poe is that of a narrator who has chosen to ally
himself with a school of critics who lose sight of the obvious in their
search for the profound."[16]

[14] Ibid., p. 625.

[15] Ibid., pp. 629, 631.

[16] Frederick Bohne, "Fellini's *Toby Dammit*: An Original Adaptation," *Film Criticism* 1, no. 1 (1976): 28. Bohne argues that both Poe and Fellini are concerned with
the absurd effects of a mindless critical doctrine on an artist. But Bohne never specifies the "mindless critical doctrine" that is supposedly Fellini's target in the film.
Other critical discussions of Fellini's version of Poe suffer from the same attempt to
find a strict correspondence between Poe and Fellini. Michael Begnal, in "Fellini &
Poe: A Story With a Moral?" *Literature/Film Quarterly* 10, no. 2 (1982), claims that
Poe rejects the "so-called social purpose of nineteenth-century American fiction, just
as Fellini was to reject the neo-realism of the then contemporary Italian cinema" (p.
130), whereas *Toby Dammit* has nothing to do with this particular moment in Italian film history.

Walter C. Foreman, in "The Poor Player Struts Again: Fellini's *Toby Dammit* and
the End of the Actor," in *1977 Film Studies Annual: Part One*, ed. Ben Lawton and
Janet Staiger (Pleasantville, N.Y.: Redgrave, 1977), pp. 111–23, stretches a point in
arguing that acting and Fellini's rejection of stars constitute Fellini's major theme.
This view results from Foreman's focus on Dammit's drunken rendition of a passage
from *Macbeth* at the awards ceremony. Dammit's decapitation thus symbolizes for
Foreman the death of the actor as well as the birth of the director's creative powers.
While this is an intriguing thesis and one that anticipates a similar (and much more
convincing) argument that Foreman makes elsewhere concerning *Roma*, Foreman's
proof here is less convincing. Fellini has never abandoned the use of stars, and few of
his films lack the usual mixture of one or two well-known stars along with a host of
lesser-known actors. But most importantly, from the film's inception, one of Fellini's
major concerns was precisely the selection of the star to portray Toby. The original
manuscript of the script Fellini and Zapponi developed from the synopsis of the story's plot contains the question "Peter O'Toole? Terence Stamp?" on its cover. (Fellini

Little in Poe's mildly humorous satire of nineteenth-century American literary movements could possibly have interested Fellini, Zapponi, or the French producers, who had quite naturally chosen a trilogy of works from Poe with very different goals in mind. In fact, the script that Fellini and Zapponi produced is more like a radical transformation than an adaptation. In their hands, Toby Dammit becomes a drunken, drug-addicted Shakespearean actor down on his luck who comes to Italy to make a Catholic western. His primary motivation in accepting the role is the production company's promise of the use of a new Ferrari during his stay in Italy. While the script retains the disreputable character of Poe's Toby Dammit, the ironic narrative voice of the story is completely absent in Fellini's film. The few times on the sound track that a narrative voice-over appears, it is Toby's voice, and his English in the original Italian print stands in sharp contrast to the Italian used elsewhere in the film, except for some important conversations between Toby and his Italian hosts.[17] In the original manuscript, Fellini and Zapponi have retained Poe's wager with the devil. In a drunken stupor, Toby leaves the awards ceremony and races around the outskirts of Rome in his Ferrari until he comes to a bridge that has collapsed. Warned by a little man who sticks his head out of a window when he hears the racing motor of Toby's Ferrari that the bridge has collapsed and that Toby will have to take a detour, Toby makes his fatal wager.[18] This reference to Toby's wager with the devil was cut from the

---

and Zapponi, " 'Toby Dammit' dal racconto di Poe," Fellini MS. 11 (Box 2), front cover of manuscript). Peter O'Toole was eventually selected first, but after an initial agreement, the English actor withdrew because he did not want to have his image compromised by such a disreputable protagonist as Toby Dammit had become in Fellini's script. Terence Stamp was substituted at the last minute. An interesting anecdote about this cover reveals Fellini's complete disrespect for archival problems. When I was examining this manuscript (a document Fellini had apparently not looked at since the production of the film) with Fellini in 1988 for the Lilly Library, Fellini looked at two caricatures on the cover, and, finding them not to his liking, canceled them with his pencil before I could object that they were of value to scholars!

See also Steven Kovács, "Fellini's *Toby Dammit*: A Study of Characteristic Themes and Techniques," *Journal of Aesthetics and Art Criticism* 31 (1972): 255–61, a useful study of the film that emphasizes Fellini's opposition to the Catholic church.

[17] The original manuscript in the Lilly Library and the published script reprint all dialogue in Italian. Both documents are thus misleading, for while Toby's opening statement is in Italian, the rest of his lines are delivered in English in the original Italian print of the film.

[18] Little Man: "A leap, you say? . . . How'll you do it? You'll never make it!"

Dammit: "Listen, I'll pass over there; I want to pass over. I'll bet my head, do you understand? My head!"

published shooting script, which retains only one reference to Toby's habitual betting during his television interview.[19] But in the completed film, all references to bets with the devil are suppressed.

Nothing of Poe remains in Fellini's film except the tale's central character and his death by decapitation. Fellini's grotesque picture of the state of Italian cinema during Toby's visit to Rome to make his western, however, may be seen as an up-to-date equivalent of Poe's satire of the contemporary literary scene. As Toby drives from the Rome airport to the city in a state of delirium, Fellini produces the same kind of infernal traffic that he will later employ for his own entrance into the Eternal City in *Roma*. He is accompanied by Padre Spagna (Salvo Randone), a priest who explains to Toby that the western they will make presents a Catholic reinterpretation of the genre with Christ returning to the frontier. The style of the film will involve simple shots with elemental and eloquent imagery: "syntagms, as my [friend] Roland Barthes would say . . . something between Dreyer and Pasolini with a touch of Ford, of course."[20] The directors in the car tell Toby that the film will treat the decadence of the capitalist system, following the theories of Lukàcs; a singer with "generous breasts" will represent the "illusory refuge into the irrational," while "the prairie is the region of earth 'without history' "; even the buffalo have a symbolic function in this unbelievable film that the priest hopes will reconcile Piero Della Francesca with Fred Zinnemann![21]

Toby's interview at the television station and the subsequent awards ceremony for the "Lupa d'oro" film prizes at a nightclub continue Fellini's satire of similar media events in earlier works. Most of the actresses receiving awards obviously have no acting talent and are being recognized only for their physical attractiveness. As the camera shows a close-up of a pair of enormous breasts and then a woman's bottom, the voice-over of the master of ceremonies pompously announces: "Lupetta d'oro to Marilú Traversi: for having revealed during her debut a

---

Little Man: "Your head? Mamma mia . . . and with whom will you bet your head? I won't accept, I don't want your head . . ."
Dammit: "I'll bet my head with the devil."
(Fellini and Zapponi, " 'Toby Dammit' dal racconto di Poe," Fellini MS. 11 [Box 2], p. 72).

[19] In the published shooting script, Toby is asked at the television studio if he often wagers; he replies that he does, and when he is asked why he does it, he says: "I'll bet you can't guess" (Betti et al., "*Tre passi nel delirio*," p. 82). In the final film, these lines are redubbed as a question and answer about Toby's experiments with LSD: in them, Toby declares that he takes dope when he wants to return to normal!

[20] Betti et al., "*Tre passi nel delirio*," p. 75.

[21] Ibid., pp. 76, 77.

temperament that testifies to a sincere vocation."[22] The entire awards
ceremony unfolds in this vein. Obviously drunk, Toby is presented to
the audience and delivers part of the monologue from *Macbeth* concluding with the famous description of life as a "tale told by an idiot,
full of sound and fury." At this point he breaks down, confesses to the
audience that he is a failure as an actor, and eventually leaves the stage
to drive his Ferrari off to his death.

Every aspect of Fellini's style in *Toby Dammit* underlines Toby's
progress toward his final confrontation with the bridge that had originally inspired Fellini's interest in Poe's story. The narrative aims at reproducing Toby's highly hallucinatory and unbalanced state of mind.
Long tracks at the airport lobby show us strange and unusual figures
staring into the camera as we feel what it must be like to be a film star
at the mercy of the public's gaze. The bright lights of flashbulbs from
the crowds of paparazzi constantly blind Toby, continuing a theme introduced with *La dolce vita*. At the airport, Toby had performed what
the script describes as an "absurd mime act" at the top of an escalator,
as if he saw something that was invisible to everyone else there. Later,
after a Gypsy outside the car going into Rome demands to read his palm
and then suddenly refuses to tell him what she sees, Toby remembers
his vision at the airport. The earlier "absurd mime act" is now explained for us. A young girl throws Toby a large white ball as the scene
is reenacted in its entirety, reflecting the thoughts in Toby's mind. During the television interview, Toby declares that he does not believe in
God but does believe in the devil. When asked whether the devil looks
like a goat, bat, or black cat, Toby answers, now revealing to the viewer
the identity of the young girl at the airport: "No . . . I'm English, not
Catholic. To me the devil is cheerful, agile. He looks like a little girl."[23]
An abrupt cut again reveals the girl on the screen from Toby's subjective point of view.

When Toby finally reaches the fallen bridge, we share his vision of
the blond girl on the other side with her white ball. He races the engine
of the Ferrari and roars into the abyss in what is now the suicide of a
demented actor rather than the thoughtless wager that was contained
in Poe's tale. Suddenly, there is a silence on the sound track rather than
the expected violent crash. As Fellini's camera slowly tracks toward the
bridge, we first hear the noise of what is revealed to be a wire bouncing
up and down; the tracking shot continues even closer to reveal a wire
with blood on it. In a series of several brief cuts, the mystery is now

---

[22] Ibid., p. 89.

[23] I cite from the sound track of the Italian print, since the published script provides this dialogue in Italian.

disclosed: first the white ball bounces noiselessly until it reaches To-by's severed head; then the girl stoops down, replacing the ball with Toby's head; a final shot shows the bridge as dawn approaches. The credits are projected over an old photograph of Edgar Allan Poe, who wears the same kind of foulard tie Toby sported during the entire film and whose physical features are remarkably close to Terence Stamp's makeup.

As this description of the film's conclusion makes clear, Fellini's interest in the Poe tale was primarily directed toward the expressive power of the final scene, evident as early as the composition of the original script, which contains a beautiful color drawing of the bridge, the wire, and Toby's head.[24] This stark image of an abyss into which the troubled actor plunges desperately to end his psychological suffering may well represent Fellini's attempts to exorcise the demons in his own psyche during this troubled time in his career. Poe's tale thus offered Fellini an excuse to return to his fantasy world of cinematic imagery and never represents a sincere attempt to create a faithful adaptation. Fellini himself has noted that the film was intended to parody and exasperate his own style to the point of the grotesque "in order never to be able to turn back."[25] Fellini had indeed sensed a "neurotic twinship" in Poe's tales, and the stimuli of a single image in one of Poe's stories rekindled the creative process in his receptive mind. The abyss he created in the studio with the collapsed bridge that decapitates Toby must also be taken as a nightmarish vision of a psychic abyss the struggling director had to cope with in his own life. Tullio Kezich's biography of Fellini reports an interesting dream Fellini had on 21 August 1967, just before he turned to shooting *Toby Dammit, Block-notes,* and *Fellini Satyricon.* In the dream, Fellini saves certain children but is decapitated at the steering wheel of a car.[26] In re-creating Toby's decapitation, Fellini did, indeed, begin to restore his creative powers, thus saving his future "children"—his subsequent films. And this therapeutic operation would reach an even more successful conclusion with Fellini's encounter with Petronius.

Fellini's approach to Petronius's *Satyricon* involved an infinitely more complicated and lengthy process of preparation and thought than the much shorter (37 minutes) *Toby Dammit.* Now, Fellini's irreverent attitude toward literary adaptation that had resulted in the radical transformation of Poe was directed toward a far more imposing target.

[24] The sketch is on p. 75 of " 'Toby Dammit' dal racconto di Poe," Fellini MS. 11 (Box 2).

[25] Cited in Faldini and Fofi, *L'avventurosa storia del cinema italiano . . . 1960–1969,* p. 284.

[26] Kezich, *Fellini,* p. 371.

238

. 75

cavo di acciaio ~~uscito dall'~~
~~interno del fanale,~~ gli ha
troncato netta la testa.

31. *Toby Dammit*: Fellini's sketch of Toby's decapitation from the original manuscript of the script

Fellini had first read Petronius years earlier during his collaboration on *Marc'Aurelio*, when he had worked at least two nights on adapting the work for a music hall show intended to include his friend Aldo Fabrizi.[27] After the war was over, an editor had requested from Fellini and another artist friend in his caricature shop on Via Nazionale a sketch to use for the cover of a new edition of the Latin classic, but Fellini's sketch was never published. After completing *I vitelloni* Fellini read a complete edition of Petronius and toyed with the idea of making it into a film. At that time in his life, Fellini identified the text with his own nostalgic memories of treatments of ancient Rome in the silent cinema associated with Rimini's Cinema Fulgor. Fellini has always claimed that the film he remembers best from his childhood was Guido Brignone's *Maciste all'inferno* (1926), one of a series of films with an ancient Roman backdrop that employed the strongman protagonist made famous by Giovanni Pastrone's *Cabiria*, perhaps the greatest of all silent films with an ancient Roman setting.[28] Fellini has included references to his encounter with Brignone's film as part of his metacinematic discourse in both *I clowns* and *Roma*.

Petronius had often been suggested to Fellini as a possible source of a film, one of the titles (along with Dante's *Inferno*, Casanova's *Memoirs*, *The Decameron*, and *Orlando Furioso*) he promised producers to make ever since the time of *I vitelloni* in exchange for funding to do films that really interested him. However, during the convalescence after his illness in 1967, Fellini reread Petronius and was fascinated by an element he had not noticed before: the missing parts, the blanks between one episode and the next.[29] What intrigued Fellini most about Petronius's text was precisely the text's fragmentary nature, the huge gaps that existed between the small part of the book that remained extant and that mysterious remaining part forever lost to us. Completely disregarding the traditional approach to the ancient world in the cinema, which most often involves a complex attempt to re-create the past accurately through elaborate costumes and "authentic" sets, following the best historical scholarship available, Fellini saw his task as that of an archaeologist who is forced to reconstruct the form of an

[27] Federico Fellini, *"Fellini Satyricon" di Federico Fellini*, ed. Dario Zanelli (Bologna: Cappelli, 1969), pp. 16–18, contains a discussion of Fellini's familiarity with Petronius before the film was made.

[28] See Federico Fellini, "Amarcord Maciste," in *Gli uomini forti*, ed. Alberto Farrassino and Tatti Sanguineti (Milan: Mazzotta, 1983), p. 182. For another discussion of ancient Rome's impact on the history of the cinema in English, see the exhaustive treatment in Jon Solomon, *The Ancient World in the Cinema* (Cranbury, N.J.: A. S. Barnes, 1978), or the briefer discussion in my own *The Eternal City: Roman Images in the Modern World*, which focuses on Fellini's contribution to this topic.

[29] Fellini, *Comments on Film*, pp. 171–72.

ancient work of art from only a few remaining shards.[30] And just as the dream state had suggested important narrative techniques to Fellini from *8 1/2* onward, Fellini found the key to his adaptation of Petronius in dreams.

In a certain sense, all of Fellini's cinema after *8 1/2* attempts a representation of the director's dreams. To be more precise, Fellini wishes the spectator to experience during the projection of *Fellini Satyricon* the visual imagery the director himself experiences in his dreams. Most dreams are highly personal experiences, and to explain them one must know something about the dreamer's private life. With *8 1/2* and *Giulietta degli spiriti*, Fellini had presented many of his own private obsessions and fantasies. But this completely personal approach to dream narrative seemed to reach a dead end with the failure to realize *Mastorna*. Now the challenge would be to create an "objective" oneiric narrative that had no direct connection with Fellini's private life. And Petronius suddenly seemed to provide the perfect occasion to do so, for his *Satyricon* offered Fellini the possibility of creating

> sparse fragments, in large part repressed and forgotten, made whole by what might be called a dream. Not by a historical epic reconstructed philologically from documents and positively verified but by a great dream galaxy sunken in the darkness and now rising up to us amid glowing bursts of light. I think I was seduced by the possibility of reconstructing this dream with its puzzling transparency, its unreadable clarity.[31]

In discussing Jung's influence on Fellini, we have already noted Fellini's desire to combine the ease of access to the world of dreams he enjoyed as a child with the adult artist's need to "rediscover on the level of consciousness the visionary faculty."[32] Fellini believed he could enlist Petronius's help in reviving his connection to the unconscious by making a film that would reproduce a dream's puzzling and contradictory qualities of simultaneous transparency and clarity where everything had to be invented by his "passion of the fantasy,"[33] then objectified in order to make a work of art. *Fellini Satyricon* aimed, therefore, at a narrative that would embody two seemingly contradictory characteristics of the dream state: the strange, disconcerting, and oneiric sensation of unfamiliarity (since the dream takes place in an atemporal setting and breaks all the realistic conventions of mimetic representation); and the enigmatic transparency of familiarity (since the dreamer senses that the unfamiliar images of his dreams are nevertheless linked

[30] Fellini, *Fare un film*, p. 104.
[31] Fellini, *Comments on Film*, pp. 172–73.
[32] Fellini, *Fare un film*, p. 88.
[33] Ibid., p. 105.

in some mysterious way to his own personality). Fellini's task was "to eliminate the borderline between dream and imagination: to invent everything and then to objectify the fantasy; to get some distance from it in order to explore it as something all of a piece and unknowable."[34]

Quite clearly, therefore, Fellini selected Petronius not as a substitute for a personal narrative of his own but as a challenge to his inventive powers, which, he feared, might be on the wane. And the complex process between this momentous decision, the creation of the scenario treatment, the elaboration of the screenplay from the scenario, and the final realization of the film as a succession of visual images points to a constant search, on the director's part, for a nonliterary and completely visual narrative, similar to that in a dream. There are a number of indications of this search for an essentially visual language in *Fellini Satyricon*, not unlike the sketches on the original manuscripts of *Roma* that underline Fellini's similar design in that subsequent film. One indication of the primacy of the image in *Fellini Satyricon* is, in fact, the existence of a larger-than-normal number of preparatory sketches and drawings, many of which have been published, and all of which aim at the precise evocation of the expressive quality of the images in question.[35] Fellini's preparatory sketches dramatically increase in number precisely during a period in his life when he was extremely interested in dreams and was recording them in his dream notebook. Perhaps most revealing, however, is an examination of the evolution of the film from scenario to screenplay to its final cinematic form, made possible by the fact that both the scenario and the screenplay have been published.[36] Appendixes 1, 2, and 3 to this chapter contain in outline form, for ease of rapid consultation, the twenty-four chapters of Petronius's *Satyricon* in its standard American translation by William Arrowsmith; the twelve sections of Fellini's original treatment; and the eight major sequences (themselves divided into numerous and asymmetrical numbers of scenes) eventually employed in the final edited print of the film. The literary text confronted Fellini with a wide variety of literary

[34] Fellini, *Comments on Film*, p. 173.

[35] See plates 66–81 in De Santi, *I disegni di Fellini*; or, more importantly, Liliana Betti, ed., *Federico A. C.: disegni per il "Satyricon" di Federico Fellini* (Milan: Libri Edizioni, 1970), containing dozens of these sketches.

[36] Fellini, *"Fellini Satyricon" di Federico Fellini*, contains both scenario and shooting script in Italian; an English translation may be found in Federico Fellini, *Fellini's "Satyricon,"* ed. Dario Zanelli (New York: Ballantine, 1970). Unfortunately, the Lilly Library materials do not contain any original documents from this film. I have, however, been able to study the original shooting script now in the possession of Norma Giacchero, but it differs in very few respects from the script published in Italian. The published Italian script does not correspond exactly to the completed film, as is usually the case with Fellini's works.

styles (Greek romance, Milesian tales, mock epic, parodies of tragedy), all joined together in a loose narrative structure that contemporary critics would call picaresque. The wanderings of the book's protagonist, Encolpius, as he is hounded by the wrath of the god Priapus, who has caused his impotence for reasons unclear from the extant remains of the book, are described from a subjective perspective by a first-person narrator. Throughout the book, or what remains of it, Petronius takes great pains to parody and deflate various myths (especially those of Ulysses and Circe), comparing Encolpius humorously and unusually unfavorably to these majestic figures from classical antiquity. In the scenario treatment, Fellini drastically alters the original, in particular eventually curing the impotence of Encolpio (Martin Potter) not with a male lover, as was the case in the original, but with a symbolic coupling with Enotea (Donyale Luna), an Earth Mother figure and sorceress. He places Eumolpo (Salvo Randone) at the celebrated banquet of Trimalcione (Mario Romagnoli), whereas in Petronius the poet Eumolpus was not present. He tells the story of the Matron of Ephesus at the banquet rather than on Lica's boat, abandons Gitone (Max Born) in midnarrative, and decapitates Lica (Alain Cuny) instead of having him drown at sea as the Lichas of Petronius does.[37] Furthermore, he adds to Petronius a number of original episodes: the brothel scene in the Suburra (II); the theater sequence (III, although its main figure, the actor Vernacchio [Fanfulla], is not named in the treatment); the collapse of the Insula Felicles (IV); the murdered emperor (VII); the villa of the suicides (VIII); and the hermaphrodite (IX).

While Petronius's Oenothea was a rather comic figure whose "cure" was less successful than that offered Encolpius by a man, Fellini greatly expands the role of his Enotea, so that her presence spans two separate episodes: IX, where a dwarf with a permanent erection tells her story; and XII, where she finally cures Encolpio of his impotence. But Petronius's manuscript ends in midsentence without any hint of a final journey. Its focus is, in fact, Eumolpus and his strange last testament, while both Ascyltus and Encolpius are not mentioned; Giton dropped out of Petronius's narrative even earlier. Fellini's scenario treatment concludes with the image of Encolpio wandering on the seashore after Ascilto (Hiram Keller) is murdered. Eumolpo and his strange bequest are completely ignored.

The scenario represents a drastic transformation of the original text. But, more importantly, whereas Petronius's book was *accidentally* frag-

---

[37] In order to avoid confusion, in this chapter and its appendixes I use the Italian names of the characters in discussing Fellini's film and Arrowsmith's anglicized Latin names to refer to the figures in the literary text.

mentary and is interrupted at arbitrary and usually puzzling places, Fellini's scenario—the intermediate phase of his adaptation—has transformed the jumble of narrative material into a smoothly flowing, quite readable narrative with clear and logical transitions between the twelve proposed sequences, resulting in a document that reads more like a traditional short story than the fragmentary literary source. In the hands of a more traditional director, this scenario could well have produced exactly the kind of film Fellini attempted to avoid, a costume drama filled with togas, bulging biceps, chariot races, and gladiator contests, the kind of *peplum* epic so typical of Italian film production in the mid-1960s. Moreover, Fellini has focused attention on Encolpio's sexuality in the treatment and has changed, in important respects, its polymorphous character, moving his protagonist toward the ultimate encounter with the essence of feminine sexuality, Enotea. The treatment's narrative is surprisingly traditional in style, given the highly nontraditional character of its source, for it avoids the many lacunae in the original by filling in the gaps, adding interpretative scenes, characters, or adventures, and in general smoothing over the missing narrative elements with material of Fellini's own invention.

In the transition of *Satyricon* from scenario to screenplay and its filming, there are a number of major transformations that may be conveniently divided into two categories: (1) essentially *cinematic* qualities are added to the story to enhance the sense of unfamiliarity and detachment Fellini wished to convey in his narrative, thus embodying aspects of the dream state; and (2) several key additions or modifications are made to the final sequence and the ending. In the first category may be placed all those characteristics of the film that have traditionally occupied most analyses of it by critics and historians. Almost all of the film's sequences are reproduced in the spacious studios of Cinecittà, even many locations that *seem* to have taken place outside. With the film's more than eighty changes of set, this extravagant use of elaborate scenography alone constituted an important contribution to the film's oneiric quality. Exterior locations are extremely rare. This not only results in a sense of confinement typical of the dream state but also permits Fellini to play with exotic and unusual combinations of typically oneiric, non-natural, and evocative colors. Fellini's colors are usually far removed from so-called natural colors, since for him, the more one approaches reality mimetically, the more one falls into imitation rather than expression.[38]

Perhaps equally important to Fellini's evocation of a dream state in the narrative is his rejection of a traditional concentration on character

[38] Fellini, *Fare un film*, pp. 94, 96.

or its development for an almost completely original focus on a chromatic development and its generative potential.[39] As Stephen Snyder has demonstrated, Fellini's film aims at producing a dominance of different colors throughout. With the use of color filters, particular film stocks, and special lighting, the narrative (in what Snyder calls its "assimilative pattern") moves from a predominance of blue, associated with water in the Vernacchio sequence; to red, linked to fire, in the Trimalcione sequence; then to white, associated with air, in segments devoted to Lica and the hermaphrodite; and this tint turns to a brown earth color that first appears in the Festival of Mirth and continues through the Enotea sequence. Even more original, however, is the "generative pattern" Snyder discovers in the film, as Fellini exploits the metaphoric qualities of actual color generation in the narrative: a combination of primary or subtractive colors (red, yellow, blue) yields black, while the combination of additive primaries (green, red, blue) produces white. Such a generation of color occurs three times in the narrative: from the film's opening through the Trimalcione episode; from the appearance of Lica through the theft of the hermaphrodite; and, finally, from the Festival of Mirth to Encolpio's departure. In each case, the color generation accompanies the protagonist's decision to affirm life and to experience personal growth.

There is also a very rich literature devoted to the actual creation of the film that testifies to the primacy of the autonomous, dreamlike image at every step of its development.[40] Peter Ammann, a Swiss psychoanalyst of the Jungian school who assisted Norma Giacchero, Fellini's scriptgirl, with continuity, noted that Fellini constantly attempted to distance himself, to detach himself from his narrative material.[41] Fellini's director of photography, Giuseppe Rotunno, added that this same kind of cold detachment was the goal in both the camera work and the lighting.[42] Zapponi remarked that Fellini employed a strange, jerky, and incomprehensible form of dubbing, aiming at a feeling of estrangement in his audience by deliberately causing the lips of his actors to move out of synchrony with their dialogue.[43] Rino Carboni, director of makeup, commented that Fellini had directed him to aim for hal-

[39] I owe this point to an important article by Stephen Snyder, "Color, Growth, and Evolution in *Fellini Satyricon*," in *Federico Fellini: Essays in Criticism*, ed. Bondanella, pp. 168–87.

[40] Detailed discussions of the making of *Fellini Satyricon* are to be found not only in Betti, *Federico A. C.*, but also in Fellini, *Fellini's "Satyricon"*; and especially in Eileen Lanouette Hughes, *On the Set of "Fellini Satyricon": A Behind-the-Scenes Diary* (New York: Morrow, 1971).

[41] Hughes, *On the Set of "Fellini Satyricon,"* p. 38.

[42] Ibid., p. 73.

[43] Ibid., p. 91.

lucinatory, spectral, and haunting effects, an appearance supported by
most of Fellini's preparatory sketches.[44] Set and costume designer Danilo Donati was directed to produce surroundings and clothes that con-
veyed a timeless and unreal quality.[45] And finally, Nino Rota's musical
compositions were guided by Fellini's order to provide music that explained nothing and that avoided, above all else, sentimentality and
emotional involvement.[46] Rota's musical score aims at a dream atmosphere with metallic sounds produced electronically, an almost completely unrhythmic, atonal music combining three kinds of instruments: electronic ones, Afro-Asiatic traditional ones, and conventional
orchestral ones whose sounds are distorted electronically.[47]

If, as most critics of Fellini believe, the filmmaker's characteristic
shot is a pan that simulates the turning of a character's gaze from right
to left (or the reverse) and therefore forces the spectator to share the
protagonist's perspective and to identify with him or her, in *Fellini Satyricon* the director relies more frequently on tracking shots of a special
kind, not usually employed in his other films. As Stuart Rosenthal has
pointed out, the typical Fellini tracking shot evoking empathy and
identification becomes a colder, more objective system of tracking in
Fellini Satyricon.[48] In the famous track through the Lupanare brothel,
as Encolpio and Gitone return home after their experiences in Vernacchio's theater (sequence II, scene 5), for example, the camera constantly
shifts perspective: sometimes it follows the two actors; sometimes it
moves parallel with them; sometimes it even moves in front of them,
constantly changing position during the presentation of this grotesque
spectacle of human sexuality. But at all times it refuses to share their
subjective perspective (as is typical of Fellini's tracks and pans), and as
a result, the two characters become part of a bizarre landscape rather
than sympathetic figures with whom we are emotionally engaged. Fellini's decision to shoot *Fellini Satyricon* in Cinemascope resulted in a
wide but severely flattened image underscoring the fact that Fellini's
characters are "just passing through" the succession of tableaux the director presents for our delectation, without engaging our emotions.[49] In
many instances, characters enter Fellini's static frames first as shadows, then as full bodies (for example, Encolpio's appearance in the first
few shots of the film). The frame itself is employed by Fellini as a com-

[44] Ibid., pp. 121–22.

[45] Ibid., p. 227.

[46] Ibid., p. 180.

[47] Pier Marco De Santi, *La musica di Nino Rota* (Rome: Laterza, 1983), pp. 132–
33.

[48] Rosenthal, *The Cinema of Federico Fellini*, p. 82.

[49] Ibid., p. 80.

pletely flat, totally delimited space not unlike that of an ancient or Renaissance fresco. In other films of the same decade (*Block-notes, I clowns, Roma, Amarcord*), Fellini frequently employs a narrative voice-over that provides the spectator with a perspective from which to evaluate the visual information on the screen. Of course, as we have seen in the metacinematic works of Fellini, this narrative voice may often be far from reliable. In *Fellini Satyricon*, however, such narrative cues are almost completely absent, except for the first and last scenes of the film. And the concluding voice-over ends in midsentence in homage to the fragmentary remains of its literary source.[50]

Of even more interest are the original sequences Fellini invented and added to the final screenplay as filmed. The most important of these represents a battle between Encolpio and the Minotaur in the Labyrinth during the Festival of Mirth (sequence VIII, scene 51). Here Fellini does more than alter the mythological references and their parodies that he encountered in Petronius. As appendix 1 shows, Petronius frequently juxtaposed Encolpius to Ulysses and his picaresque journey to that of the *Odyssey*. In the Minotaur scene, Fellini reverses this association, linking his character Encolpio to Theseus and the rescue of Ariadne. However, Fellini's Encolpio is defeated ignominiously by the Minotaur, who seems to be destined to become another of his male lovers, moved to pity by Encolpio's desperate declaration that he is merely a humble student and not a professional gladiator. Encolpio's role as a heroic Theseus is immediately undercut, however, when he reveals his impotence as he is forced to make love with Arianna in full view of the cheering crowd. Fellini probably found the suggestion for this particular scene in Apuleius's *The Golden Ass* (book 3), where Lucius is subjected to a mock trial at the Festival of Risus, God of Laughter.[51] But Fellini had more in mind than a mere classical footnote. The physical shape of the Labyrinth set, as well as the strange and enigmatic manner in which the battle is filmed, also presents the spectator of the film with a classic dream image of the psyche. And Theseus's journey into the Labyrinth in search of Ariadne constitutes one of the most famous mythological metaphors Western culture has produced of an interior search, a journey into the depths of the mind to discover new dimensions of the unconscious. When Encolpio emerges confused and impotent from this dreamlike structure, Fellini has now prepared him (and the spectator) for his eventual transformation, which occurs after his lovemaking

[50] Joseph Markulin, in "Plot and Character in Fellini's *Casanova*: Beyond *Satyricon*," *Italian Quarterly* 23 (1982): 68, makes this point.

[51] Bernard F. Dick, "Adaptation as Archaeology: *Fellini Satyricon* (1969)," in *Modern European Filmmakers and the Art of Adaptation*, ed. Andrew Horton and Joan Magretta (New York: Frederick Ungar, 1981), p. 151.

32. *Fellini Satyricon*: Fellini's sketch of the labyrinth and its Minotaur, a visual metaphor for the unconscious

with the Earth Mother, Enotea. Here, in what seems to constitute the film's most symbolic and significant image, Fellini not only treats his mythological material ironically and humorously but goes even further to reveal the "powerlessness of the ancient tale to regenerate the hero."[52] Encolpio emerges from the oneiric complex of the Labyrinth physically defeated and, more importantly, emotionally drained. Only an act of grace can now save him. Many earlier Fellini films suggest similar moments of self-revelation and employ the notion of religious conversion as a metaphor for character development and as a convenient narrative means of concentrating the action at the film's conclusion. In the trilogy of conversion, for example, a number of main characters (Zampanò, Augusto, Cabiria) enjoyed privileged moments of

[52] A. J. Prats, "The Individual, the World, and the Life of Myth in *Fellini Satyricon*," *South Atlantic Bulletin* 44 (1979): 49.

self-awareness which, although clearly and quite intentionally far removed from traditional Catholic notions of spiritual grace, nevertheless
suggest secular and personal epiphanies. Such a miraculous change is
denied to Marcello in *La dolce vita*. In *8 1/2* and *Giulietta degli spiriti*,
these moments of self-discovery form part of the protagonists' encounter with their subconscious, their dreams, and their fantasies, to which
we are given special access through a series of subjective flashbacks
or oneiric visions. Reflecting Fellini's own voyage into his personal
dreamworld, the conclusions of both *8 1/2* and *Giulietta degli spiriti*
equate freedom and psychological growth with mental wholeness and
acceptance of a past that formed his protagonists into the adults they
have become.

When Encolpio makes love to Enotea, he does not possess her. Enotea
possesses him, releasing Encolpio from the deadly verbal myths and
rhetoric to which he and his companions (especially Eumolpo) are all
too tightly bound.[53] And as Encolpio is finally released into the world
to act autonomously for the first time in the film, he now wisely refuses Eumolpo's inheritance—not just the poet's possessions but, more
importantly, words themselves, which he had bequeathed to his young
friend earlier in the film's fourth sequence. While Petronius's *Satyricon*
ends with the image of Eumolpus being eaten by his would-be heirs,
Fellini's treatment had abandoned Encolpio to his aimless wanderings
after he buried his friend Ascilto. At the conclusion of the scenario
treatment, Fellini describes the projected film as "this vast and incomplete mosaic: a mosaic of which we have reconstructed only some episodes."[54] He then adds that the conclusion of the film will rest upon
several disparate and evocative images from the past—an old man, a
laughing soldier, girls picking olives, and so forth.

This lyrical ending was completely changed in the film's final form.
We have a hint of this future transformation in the work's first image—
an opening shot of a flat, white wall covered with incomprehensible
Latin graffiti against which Encolpio enters the film, first as a voice-
over, then as a black shadow upon the white wall, and finally as a complete figure set against the wall. The white color echoes Encolpio's
weakened capacities at the film's beginning, capacities that will eventually be strengthened during his sexual encounter with Enotea. Fellini
now returns to Petronius in the conclusion of the film with the picture
of Eumolpo's greedy heirs chewing the poet's flesh—an episode that he
had cut from the scenario. This unsettling image of spiritually dead old
men feeding on the flesh of a mediocre vendor of words is now juxta-

[53] Ibid., p. 57.
[54] Fellini, *"Fellini Satyricon" di Federico Fellini*, p. 149.

33. *Fellini Satyricon*: Enotea, the mysterious sorceress whose amorous affections cure Encolpio of his impotence

posed to a more positive and invigorating image of an odyssey that Encolpio's sexual transformation has made possible. Rather than wandering aimlessly as in the original scenario treatment, in the final version of the film Fellini shows Encolpio setting out to explore new worlds and new experiences with the other young men who refuse to take part in this grisly parody of the Christian Eucharist. And rather than close his film with several disparate images taken from the ancient world, Fellini now provides the spectator with a last shot of a number of fragmented frescoes that recall various characters and episodes in his own film rather than relics of ancient Roman painting. In particular, we see Encolpio in color against the same kind of wall that opened the film. But now the wall reflects the triumph of the director's imagination, the concrete visual embodiment of the fact that he has dominated the void presented to him by the gaps in Petronius's manuscript and has succeeded in revitalizing the powers of his own imagination.

Encolpio's release from the bonds of traditional literary culture reflects the similar release that Fellini experienced during the making of *Fellini Satyricon*. Beginning the film during what began as a physical crisis but soon developed into an artistic crisis as well, the director

turned reluctantly to a literary source in order to recharge the sources
of his visual imagination. With an objectification of his own oneiric
experiences in the film, Fellini evolved a novel and highly original cinematic style with Petronius as a springboard that abandoned many of
the characteristic features of his artistic signature as a director. Fellini
was well aware of the difficulty of the undertaking. Had it failed, he
might well have been caught up in an artistic paralysis from which he
could never have emerged:

> Certainly it is difficult to wipe two thousand years of history and Chris-
> tianity off the slate, and square up to the myths, attitudes and customs
> of peoples who came long before us, without judging them, without mak-
> ing them the object of a moralistic complacency, without critical re-
> serves, without psychological inhibitions and prejudices; but I think the
> effort will be precisely one of evoking this world, then knowing how to
> sit back, calm and detached, and watch it all unfold.[55]

Perhaps the most surprising effect of Fellini's evocation of imperial
Rome in Fellini Satyricon is that this "fresco in a fantasy key" also
manages, as Fellini points out, to present "a powerful and evocative
allegory—a satire of the world we live in today."[56] While Fellini claims
to interpret pre-Christian Rome as unfamiliar territory, more like a distant planet or a dreamworld than a historical reconstruction, his vision
of a dehumanized, chaotic, and disintegrating pagan world bears important analogies to our own world. These analogies emphasize the decadent status of the arts in imperial Rome as well as the failure of ancient
Roman mythology to provide any coherent meaning for that now distant world. In ancient Rome, the artist and his unique creations are
rarely appreciated. When Eumolpo guides Encolpio through a museum
devoted to pre-imperial art, these ancient relics put contemporary imperial Roman art to shame, and in the scenes of the museum's superficial and hurried spectators, there is more than just a suggestion of the
frantic tourists who today race through the Sistine Chapel or the Villa
Borghese in order to return to the comfort of their air-conditioned
American Express tour buses. The imperial theater is equally decadent.
In Vernacchio's theater, the drama of Sophocles and Plautus has degen-
erated into breaking wind on stage and an imitation of the bloodletting
in the Colosseum, with the hand of a slave actually cut off on the stage
to titillate the bloodthirsty audience.

Fellini's view of the Rome of Petronius brings home how the age of

[55] Federico Fellini, "Preface to Satyricon," in Federico Fellini: Essays in Criticism,
ed. Bondanella, p. 19.
[56] Ibid., p. 17.

Petronius lacked stable values and was awaiting the arrival of the new and superior mythology of Christianity. Such an implicit parallel to the counterculture atmosphere of the late 1960s is most evident in the two major sequences that, as Alberto Moravia pointed out, are those least dreamlike: Trimalcione's banquet and the villa of the suicides. The banquet scene (almost the only part of the film directly inspired by Petronius's original) shows the familiar newly rich, a forerunner of a society obsessed with conspicuous consumption, whose energetic vulgarity overwhelms world-weary men of deeper culture. And the villa of the suicides, placed in the middle of the film, illuminates the themes of decadence and corruption that precede and follow. The fate of the noble husband and wife who kill themselves rather than fall into the hands of the emperor's cruel soldiers highlights the confusion, loss of values, and instability of a world stripped of structure and republican ideals. The values of the ancient republic have vanished, and there is nowhere for a virtuous man or woman to escape the barbarity of the times except beyond the grave. Even pagan culture, so fascinating in a number of respects, is dominated less by a sense of morality or a philosophical ideal than by magic, sorcery, superstition, witchcraft, and hermaphrodites. It can offer no true solution to the moral confusion that the film depicts.

Yet, the twentieth-century spectator recognizes himself quite easily in the surrealistic imagery, the stylized makeup, and the discontinuous and fragmented, dreamlike narrative. The loss of center and the disintegration of cultural values portrayed in *Fellini Satyricon* points unequivocally to the period of the late 1960s, the time when the film was made. In fact, as Fellini notes, the premiere of the film took place in Madison Square Garden after a rock concert with an audience of some ten thousand young people, many of them hippies, amidst the odor of marijuana and hashish:

> The show was a knockout. The young people applauded every scene; many slept, others made love. Amid total chaos the film went on relentlessly on a giant screen that seemed to reflect an image of what was happening in the hall. Unpredictably, mysteriously, in that most improbable ambience *Satyricon* seemed to have found its natural site. It didn't seem mine any more in that sudden revelation of secrets understood, of subtle, unbroken links between the ancient Rome of memory and that fantastic audience from the future.[57]

Indeed, Fellini finds this atmosphere and the breakdown of old mythologies exhilarating, for such a moment also promises the arrival of a new

---

[57] Fellini, *Comments on Film*, pp. 174, 176.

mythology around which a new and more satisfying culture will be constructed in the future, just as Christianity eventually superseded the outmoded myths from classical literature that miserably failed to provide meaning for the protagonists of Fellini's film. Fellini himself has remarked:

> I feel that decadence is indispensable to rebirth. I have already said that I love shipwrecks. So I am happy to be living at a time when everything is capsizing. It's a marvelous time, for the very reason that a whole series of ideologies, concepts and conventions is being wrecked. . . . This process of dissolution is quite natural, I think. I don't see it as a sign of the death of civilization but, on the contrary, as a sign of its life. . . . The young are aware that a new world is beginning.[58]

While *Fellini Satyricon* represents more of a "spectacle for contemplation"[59] than a coherent story of conventional dimensions, it also foreshadows the potential beneficial effects of the arrival of the new barbarians that the conclusion of *Roma* celebrates.

What mattered most to Fellini in the making of *Fellini Satyricon* was not so much the evocation of the similarities between the decadence of Petronius's Rome and that of our own world, even though this parallel is an important consideration that certainly had a pronounced emotional impact on Fellini's audience when the film first appeared. Instead, as Fellini noted in his major statement on filmmaking, the ultimate *personal* significance of *Fellini Satyricon* lies in the fact that the film represented a therapeutic challenge to his seemingly exhausted creative powers, a self-imposed testing process that Fellini successfully survived: "But all these more or less convincing explanations [of the film] finally count for very little. The important thing is that in making this film, I rediscover inside a pleasure, a joyous fervor that I have feared was lost. I seem to feel that my desire to make films has not been exhausted."[60] It is ironic that while Encolpio achieved his creative freedom for action through rejecting the verbal culture of his own time, Fellini, on the other hand, liberated his essentially visual fantasy by an encounter with one of the most important literary texts that Encolpio's era produced. The literature of both Poe and Petronius thus served Fellini as restorative therapy, "curing" his weakened imaginative powers and restoring the joy in creation he felt he had lost.

---

[58] Fellini, *Fellini on Fellini*, p. 157.
[59] Markulin, "Plot and Character in Fellini's *Casanova*," p. 66.
[60] Fellini, *Fare un film*, p. 105.

Appendix 1

PETRONIUS'S *SATYRICON*[61]

I. "Among the Rhetoricians": Encolpius attacks empty rhetorical formulae (the entire narrative reflects his point of view).

II. "Giton, Ascyltus, and I": Giton recounts Ascyltus's advances; Encolpius and Ascyltus quarrel over Giton.

III. "Lost Treasure Recovered": Encolpius and Ascyltus steal a mantle, try to sell it, and recover a worthless one they had previously lost.

IV. "The Priestess of Priapus": Psyche (Quartilla's maid) confronts Encolpius and Ascyltus for their disturbance of the rites of Priapus; Quartilla suggests a sexual "cure" for her malaria; Encolpius's impotence is first mentioned; Giton deflowers Pannychis.

V. "Dinner with Trimalchio": Encolpius, Giton, and Ascyltus attend the banquet; Trimalchio's life and fortunes are described in mosaics; detailed descriptions of the banquet food and conversation are provided, while Trimalchio tells a story about witches; Fortunata (Trimalchio's wife) converses with Scintilla; Trimalchio discusses his eventual death, his tomb, and his last wishes, then quarrels with Fortunata; a band practices a death march for Trimalchio's future funeral, provoking the comic intervention of the fire brigade and the end of the banquet.

VI. "Giton, Ascyltus, and I Again": Ascyltus steals Giton's affections; the two friends divide their possessions, with Giton choosing to stay with Ascyltus; Encolpius's lament over the loss of Giton.

VII. "I Meet Eumolpus": Encolpius first encounters the poet Eumolpus in an art museum, where the poet recounts his pederastic love affair in the city of Pergamum and explains contemporary decadence as caused by the love of money; the poet's poem on the fall of Troy causes the museum guests to attack him and Encolpius to criticize his verbosity.

[61] Chapter headings are from the standard English translation by William Arrowsmith (New York: New American Library, 1959) and were not part of the original manuscript by Petronius, which was first discovered in 1663.

VIII. "Old Friends and New Rivals": Encolpius regains Giton, Eumolpus is attracted to Giton, and Ascyltus offers a reward for Giton's return, which Eumolpus wants to collect; Encolpius, Giton, and Eumolpus depart by sea to escape Ascyltus.

IX. "Lichas and Tryphaena": Encolpius and Giton discover they are on a boat commanded by Captain Lichas of Tarentum and Tryphaena, the very people they are attempting to escape; Eumolpus tries to disguise them as his slaves and notes the parallel of their voyage to that of Odysseus toward the cave of the Cyclops in the *Odyssey*.

X. "Discovered": Lichas and Tryphaena learn from dreams the true identities of Encolpius and Giton (producing a parody of the recognition scene between Odysseus and his old maid in the *Odyssey*); a rhetorical set piece of Eumolpus's defense of his two "slaves" follows; the two men threaten suicide and self-castration, forcing Lichas and Tryphaena to come to terms with their former friends and lovers.

XI. "The Pleasures of Peace": Eumolpus recounts the Story of the Matron of Ephesus after all is forgiven.

XII. "Shipwrecked": a storm at sea carries Lichas away, who drowns and is buried; Encolpius declaims a speech on human mortality.

XIII. "The Road to Croton": Encolpius, Eumolpus, and Giton reach Croton, a city of makers of wills and those who pursue the inheritances of will-makers; Eumolpus pretends to be rich to gain the citizens' favor.

XIV. "Eumolpus on the Writing of Poetry": a long digression contains Eumolpus's poem on the Roman civil wars.

XV. "Life at Croton": the three friends enjoy life in Croton but fear that Eumolpus's deception will be discovered.

XVI. "Circe": Circe calls Encolpius by the pseudonym of Odysseus ("poly-aenos" or "the much praised"), continuing the parody of mythological themes in Petronius, but Encolpius proves himself impotent with this enchantress.

XVII. "A Second Attempt": after an exchange of letters, Encolpius and Circe try again.

XVIII. "I Take Myself in Hand": Circe expresses her contempt for the impotence of Encolpius, while he contemplates death and self-castration.

XIX. "Oenothea": Oenothea agrees to cure Encolpius in return for a night in bed; Encolpius kills one of the sacred geese of Priapus; Oenothea's cure is described only in fragments of the manuscript.

XX. "Interlude with Chrysis": Oenothea's cure has apparently proved unsuccessful.

XXI. "Philomela": an inheritance-hunter of Croton, a lady with a son and daughter, offers them to Eumolpus in the hope of obtaining his inheritance; Encolpius proves impotent again with her young son.

XXII. "Restored": Encolpius's impotence is finally cured by Mercury (as he claims) through making love with a man rather than with a woman.

XXIII. "Matters at Croton Come to a Head": the imaginary ship owned by Eumolpus carrying a rich cargo of slaves never arrives, arousing the suspicion of Croton's citizenry.

XXIV. "Eumolpus Makes His Will": Eumolpus wills his nonexistent fortune to heirs willing to eat his flesh and lists historical precedents for this distasteful meal; the narrative ends in the middle of Eumolpus's description of cannibalism at the Roman siege of Numantia with no further mention of Encolpius or the other characters.

Appendix 2

I. "I sotterranei del Circo Massimo": Encolpio and Ascilto steal a woman's cloak during the games (the characters are supposed to speak a form of corrupted Latin in this sequence, thereafter shifting to Italian).

II. "Incontro con favoloso Gitone": Encolpio and Ascilto meet Gitone; the three young men pass through the Suburra and its fantastic collection of prostitutes; Ascilto and Gitone disappear.

III. "Ritrovamento di Gitone in un teatro della Suburra; Ascilto rischia di morire sgozzato in un lupanare": around closing time in the baths, Encolpio learns that Ascilto has lost Gitone in a crap game to an actor, and Encolpio goes to the theater to find Gitone (Fellini explains here that one of the performances will be a reconstruction of the life of Mucius Scaevola); Gitone appears in a girl's costume, is taken away by Encolpio, and the two walk through a brothel, during which time Gitone is led off by a prostitute; Encolpio discovers that Ascilto is in the brothel and has made love to the Empress, who is disguised as a prostitute, and he must do the same or be crucified by her.

IV. "Crollo dell'Insula Felicles; Incontro con il poeta Eumolpo tra le macerie": Encolpio, Ascilto, and Gitone are sleeping in the Insula Felicles; after a squabble, the two friends divide their property and Gitone chooses to stay with Ascilto; the building collapses and Encolpio saves Eumolpo, who tells him they will dine with Trimalcione.

V. "La cena di Trimalcione": the scenario defines Trimalcione as the classic nouveau riche who fancies opulent displays of wealth through lavish banquets and a pompous recitation of his doggerel poetry; Encolpio meets Lica and Trifena at the banquet, while Trimalcione treats his guests to a speech about the finality of death; Trimalcione quarrels with Eumolpo

---

[62] The complete text of the original scenario may be examined in either Fellini, *"Fellini Satyricon" di Federico Fellini*, pp. 111–45; or Fellini, *Fellini's "Satyricon,"* pp. 47–90. The headings are from the original Italian scenario.

when the poet (after drinking too much) refuses to praise his verse; the collapse of the balcony saves Eumolpo from Trimalcione's slaves and he escapes from the banquet with Encolpio, to whom he drunkenly bequeaths not only his poems but poetry itself, the sea, and all of nature; the next day Lica takes Encolpio and Eumolpo to his ship.

VI. "Viaggio in mare e incontro con l'imperatore": Encolpio discovers both Gitone and Ascilto on board Lica's ship, as well as Quartilla, the priestess of Priapus, who during an orgy on board ship narrates the next sequence (the first story within a story).

VII. "Storia della matrona di Efeso": Quartilla tells this famous tale from Petronius's original, then proposes a marriage between Gitone and a young girl named Pannichina; suddenly Lica's ship is boarded by soldiers attacking the young Caesar (an albino of around eighteen years of age) who murder him; snow falls on Lica's ship and, after being overtaken by a storm at sea, it sinks.

VIII. "La villa dei suicidi": Encolpio and Ascilto survive the storm (no trace of Eumolpo or Gitone can be found), and they discover Lica's corpse; they come upon a beautiful patrician villa, the owners of which have committed suicide to escape the wrath of the new emperor; they meet a slave girl and then a man preparing a wild boar to eat, who invites them to join him.

IX. "L'oracolo ermafrodito": the miraculous Hermaphrodite in the temple of Ceres is stolen by Ascilto and Encolpio but dies shortly thereafter and is burned on a funeral pyre by the two friends.

X. "La città stregata: Encolpio diventa impotente": after the two friends observe the arrival of the new emperor from Africa, we shift to Encolpio's impotence with a beautiful woman (in Fellini's treatment, this is the first time in Encolpio's life such a thing has occurred); an old crone tells Encolpio that there is a dwarf in the area who was punished in an opposite fashion with a permanent erection.

XI. "Il nano dal membro eretto narra la storia della ragazza dalla vagina infuocata": in this second story within a story, the dwarf informs Encolpio that a poet-sorcerer once punished a local woman for her arrogance and the woman eventually became the sorceress Enotea, whose private parts provide the fire for the area's hearth-fires.

XII. "La maga Enotea e i suoi incantesimi; morte di Ascilto": the two friends visit a village amphitheater to steal money for Enotea; while an old homosexual stares at Encolpio, Ascilto steals his purse, and the two go to Enotea's home; Enotea is an old peasant woman around seventy years old but still beautiful; Encolpio is finally cured of his impotence after making love to Enotea, and afterward, all around him he is aware of the entire universe (gods, fauns, nymphs) uniting in "monstrous couplings"; meanwhile Ascilto has raped a peasant girl and is killed by the girl's father, forcing Encolpio to bury and abandon his friend; by now he has already missed the boat's departure and he walks on alone; in conclusion, Fellini writes: "the story is interrupted, it breaks up and disintegrates into little fragments that are, however, the best conclusion for this vast incomplete mosaic: a mosaic of which we have reconstructed only some episodes . . . the evocation is over, the past dissolves."[63]

[63] Fellini, *"Fellini Satyricon" di Federico Fellini*, p. 145.

Appendix 3

FELLINI SATYRICON[64]

I. "Il lamento di Encolpio": (1) against a wall covered with ancient graffiti, Encolpio laments the loss of Gitone to Ascilto; (2) Encolpio and Ascilto fight in the Baths, Encolpio learning that Gitone has been sold to the actor Vernacchio.

II. "Encolpio ritrova Gitone; crollo dell'*Insula Felicles*": (3) Encolpio enters Vernacchio's theater, spots Gitone on stage, and witnesses the performance of the emperor's "miracle," as a slave's hand is chopped off and replaced with a golden hand; (4–5) after regaining Gitone, Encolpio returns home through the Lupanare (the Roman brothel), passing numerous scenes of sensual delight; (6–9) in the Insula Felicles, the Roman tenement building, Encolpio and Ascilto quarrel; they divide their property—including Gitone, who chooses to go with Ascilto, driving Encolpio to despair.

III. "La cena di Trimalcione": (10) the tenement building collapses; (11) in the art museum, Encolpio encounters the poet Eumolpo, who blames current corruption on an obsession with money; (12–13) Encolpio and Eumolpo go to supper at Trimalcione's villa, first passing a pool where numerous guests are bathing, and observe the arrival of Trimalcione, who greets Eumolpo as a brother poet; (14 cut in final print); (15) Trimalcione's dining room, where the opulent banquet begins; Eumolpo's declamation of poetry is greeted with jeers and thrown food; Trimalcione's wife Fortunata dances a frenzied and sensual dance but is then attacked by her husband and covered with food when she dares question his attentions to two young boys; (16) Eumolpo is almost thrown into the ovens by Trimalcione's slaves after he accuses Trimalcione of stealing verses from Lucretius.

IV. "La tomba di Trimalcione; un cinedo racconta la storia della matrona di Efeso": (17) the guests visit Trimalcione's tomb; (18–23) an effeminate

[64] This schematic outline is based on repeated viewings of the Italian print; titles of the various sequences are those Fellini uses in ibid. Roman numerals refer to Fellini's numbered sequences, while Arabic numbers denote scenes within each sequence. It should also be pointed out that the published scripts in both English and Italian are not complete continuity scripts, since the final dialogue was modified during the dubbing of the sound track of *Fellini Satyricon*. The scripts do, in large measure, follow the sequences and scenes enumerated here.

homosexual recounts the story of the Matron of Ephesus (cut to the story's narration from the tomb scene, the first of the stories within a story in the film); (24–25) Eumolpo and Encolpio leave the banquet, and the poet bequeaths poetry and other beautiful things to the young man in a drunken stupor.

V. "Nave di Lica; morte di Cesare": (26–31, a different version of this sequence, was eliminated); (unnumbered sequence in the modified screenplay) Encolpio, Ascilto, and Gitone are captured and taken in chains aboard Lica's ship, where they are to serve the pleasure of Lica and Trifena, but during the Greco-Roman wrestling match, Lica defeats Encolpio and falls in love with him; (33) the preparations for the wedding of Lica and Encolpio; (32) a young albino, Cesare, is assassinated by rebellious troops, who afterward board Lica's ship and decapitate him; (43 follows out of original order) the troops of the new emperor on parade during the civil war.

VI. "La villa dei suicidi": (34–42) Encolpio and Ascilto visit a patrician villa, whose owners commit suicide to escape the new emperor; they capture an African slave girl, who makes love with them until they turn to each other.

VII. "L'ermafrodito": (44–46) the two friends encounter the wagon of a nymphomaniac, with whom Ascilto makes love, while the woman's servant tells Encolpio about the hermaphrodite in the temple of Ceres; (47–50) with the aid of another man (whom they eventually murder), Ascilto and Encolpio steal the hermaphrodite, who dies of thirst in the desert.

VIII. "La città magica": (51) Encolpio, as Theseus, combats the Minotaur in the Labyrinth; the Minotaur wins but spares Encolpio's life because of his beauty, while the proconsul of the city explains that the town has played a trick on Encolpio, as is customary during the festival dedicated to the God of Laughter; Encolpio's reward is a sensual Arianna, with whom he must couple in full view of the crowd; Encolpio discovers he is impotent and is rejected with contempt by Arianna; Eumolpo suddenly appears and (52) explains to Encolpio that he will take him to the Giardino delle Delizie for a cure; (53) Encolpio is whipped by prostitutes in an attempt to cure his impotence, while the proprietor of the Giardino (in the original script it was the dwarf of the scenario) recounts to Encolpio the story of Enotea; (scenes 54–55 are suppressed); (56–60) the film cuts to the second story within a story, the tale of a sorcerer rejected by a beautiful young girl, who is eventually cursed by the sorcerer and forced to provide fires for the village's hearths from her private parts; (61–62) Encolpio, Ascilto, and a boatman head toward Enotea's home; (63–64) while Encolpio drinks a potion offered to him by an old black woman, outside Ascilto struggles with the boatman; Enotea (an old woman, more a crone than a beauty) appears to Encolpio and they make love; Encolpio emerges from this tryst cured of his impotence but discovers a dying Ascilto, whom he buries and laments; (67) Encolpio reaches the seashore where Eumolpo's ship is waiting, but Eumolpo has died, leaving his worldly goods to those willing to feast upon his flesh; while the old men partake of this gruesome meal, Encolpio accepts the captain's invitation to embark with a crew of young men who refuse to eat Eumolpo's flesh and who head out toward new shores and new adventures; while Encolpio (in a voice-over) reports that he decided to depart with them and begins to recount his adventures, his words end in midsentence just as the extant manuscript of Petronius does; the camera cuts from a shot of a distant island to a series of fragmented frescoes, all referring to characters and episodes from the film but without any discernible narrative structure.

CHAPTER SIX _____

Fellini and Politics

AMARCORD AND

PROVA D'ORCHESTRA

Especially as regards passion for pol- _____
itics, I am more Eskimo than Ro-
man. . . . I am not a political person,
have never been one. Politics and
sports leave me completely cold, in-
different.[1]

I believe a person with an artistic bent is naturally conservative and needs
order around him. . . . I need order because I am a transgressor; I even
recognize myself as one. And to carry out my transgressions I need very
strict order, with many taboos, obstacles at every step, moralizing, proces-
sions, alpine choruses filing along.[2]

Good intentions and honest feelings, and a passionate belief in one's own
ideals, may make excellent politics or influential social work (things
which may be much more useful than the cinema), but they do not nec-
essarily and indisputably make good films. And there is really nothing ug-
lier or drearier—just because it is ineffectual and pointless—than a bad
political film.[3]

What I care about most is the freedom of man, the liberation of the indi-
vidual man from the network of moral and social convention in which he
believes, or rather in which he thinks he believes, and which encloses him
and limits him and makes him seem narrower, smaller, sometimes even
worse than he really is.[4]

THE CRITICAL commonplace that
Fellini is totally uninterested in political or social problems and that,
unlike many other Italian directors, whose films quite frequently depart from clear ideological perspectives, Fellini's cinema aims only at
an egocentric representation of the director's private fantasy world is a

[1] Fellini, *Comments on Film*, p. 15.
[2] Ibid., pp. 179–80.
[3] Fellini, *Fellini on Fellini*, p. 151.
[4] Ibid., pp. 157–58.

gross misinterpretation that was first advanced during the 1950s at the height of the polemical debates surrounding *La strada* and *Le notti di Cabiria*. At that time in their attempts to direct Italian cinema toward what would surely have resulted in an artistically barren brand of social realism, leftist critics in Italy and France tried to denigrate Fellini's early films as conservative works that embodied the most reactionary aspects of prewar Italian culture.[5] And yet, over the years, Fellini's early films have endured and have been praised not only for their artistic achievements but for their sociological value as well. While many of the ideologically "correct" films leftists praised during the 1950s now seem dated and are rarely shown, such early films as *Lo sceicco bianco* and *I vitelloni* continue to garner praise not only as entertaining works of art but also as penetrating portraits of provincial life in the Italy of the period. The very films from Fellini's subsequent trilogy of conversion—*La strada* and *Le notti di Cabiria*—that evoked the most negative responses from critics on the left are now more correctly seen as among the most original cinematic expressions of the dominant philosophical issues of the postwar period, treating problems of communication and alienation identified by European existentialism within a society characterized by rapidly changing values and disruptive economic development. The thirtieth anniversary of the release of *La dolce vita* was celebrated in Italy with a number of articles and interviews that quite rightly defined this masterpiece as a brilliant fresco of a new, media-conscious society that had emerged from the sleepy, provincial culture of Italy in the 1950s and that had anticipated by at least a decade contemporary concerns over the domination of popular culture by mass media images, a theme continued and broadened in a number of Fellini's more recent metacinematic works to include what he considers to be the insidious influence of commercial television. And, in spite of the vulgar simplification that reduces Fellini's images of women to representations of grotesque whores and sexually promiscuous women sticking out their tongues at the camera to signify their availability, Fellini not only anticipated the feminist movement in Italy with his bittersweet analysis of matrimony in *Giulietta degli spiriti*, but in two other works focusing on male sexuality (*Casanova* and *La città delle donne*), he provided devastating critiques of images men have projected upon women that he and his generation inherited from

[5] Examples of these early attacks may be found in the previously cited polemics over *La strada* and *Le notti di Cabiria* in Bondanella, ed., *Federico Fellini: Essays in Criticism*, and in Fellini, *"La Strada": Federico Fellini, Director*; a more recent example of this point of view may be found in the broadside attack on Fellini's "irrelevance" in Robert P. Kolker's *The Altering Eye: Contemporary International Cinema* (New York: Oxford University Press, 1983).

Italy's traditionally male-dominated culture. As Lina Wertmüller, a director with much clearer ideological assumptions, has pointed out, in spite of Fellini's overriding interest in the representation of his own fantasy world, "Federico has given us the most significant traces and graffiti of our history in the last twenty years. He declares he is not concerned with politics and is not interested in fixed themes or ideological layouts, but he is, in the final analysis, the most political and sociological, I believe, of our authors."[6]

Thus, while Fellini's cinema does not ignore the many social and political problems that have arisen since he first began making films, the approach Fellini takes to such themes and the cinematic style with which he treats such questions differ radically from that typical of the so-called political film, which became popular in Italy during the 1960s and 1970s.[7] The dozens of such political films produced by such figures as Bernardo Bertolucci, Marco Bellocchio, Pier Paolo Pasolini, Luchino Visconti, Liliana Cavani, Elio Petri, Francesco Rosi, Gillo Pontecorvo, and the Taviani brothers usually view Italian politics from a Marxist perspective; they often contain a hybrid mixture of Marxist and Freudian social theories, and they often treat Italian fascism as a favorite topic. While the best of such films succeed in blending their ideological messages with great commercial appeal at the box office, their political content reflects a period in Italian culture when various forms of Marxist ideology dominated the thinking of Italy's intellectuals.

Numerous explanations of Italian fascism have been advanced, some based on scholarly research, others reflecting the ideological prejudices of their proponents. The most popular of these theories during the prewar period while Mussolini was still in power advanced the notions of a "moral crisis," the "intrusion of the amorphous masses into history," the idea that psychological disabilities gave birth to the movement, or the Stalinist-inspired doctrine that fascism was an instrument of the capitalists' attempt to suppress the class struggle.[8] Explanations of fascism in the Italian cinema have tended to follow theories developed *before* the fall of the Fascist regime and thus before much of the important scholarship of the postwar period based on extensive archival re-

[6] Cited in Faldini and Fofi, *L'avventurosa storia del cinema italiano . . . 1960–1969*, p. 275.

[7] For an analysis of the "political" film in Italy, see my *Italian Cinema: From Neorealism to the Present*; or John Michalczyk's *The Italian Political Filmmakers* (Rutherford, N.J.: Fairleigh Dickinson University Press, 1986).

[8] For a treatment of the various historical explanations of Italian fascism before and after the Second World War, see A. J. Gregor, *Interpretations of Fascism* (Morristown, N.J.: General Learning Press, 1974); or Renzo De Felice, *Interpretations of Fascism* (Cambridge: Harvard University Press, 1977).

search had been published and disseminated. Such cinematic treatments usually follow a combination of psychoanalytical and Marxist theories. As an economic and political explanation, Marxist thought depicts the Fascist movement as a tool of agrarian or industrial capitalism to suppress the working class. On the level of social psychology, Freudian or neo-Freudian theories depict the individual Fascist as the product of destructive influences from childhood or adolescence, usually sexual in nature.

While Fellini's works have provided audiences with significant images of Italian society in the course of representing the director's own artistic concerns over a period of four decades, *Amarcord* and *Prova d'orchestra* are unique in their *concentration* on political issues. In *Amarcord* (Fellini's last major commercial success and the winner of an Oscar for Best Foreign Film among dozens of other awards), Fellini combines a nostalgic look back at his own provincial origins with a relentless dissection of the origins of Italian fascism in a film that some critics initially defined as only a bittersweet remake of the provincial milieu of *I vitelloni*. As a portrait of the provincial world of the 1930s during Mussolini's reign, Fellini's *Amarcord* distinguishes itself from most other Italian films on the *ventennio* by its refusal to portray Italy's Fascist past through the prism of the "politically correct" Marxist or psychoanalytical ideologies so popular in the political film in Italy. That is to say, he does not give his audience the opportunity to dismiss their Fascist heritage by showing us bloodthirsty Fascists in black shirts and jackboots, like Bertolucci's Attila (Donald Sutherland) in *Novecento*, or cowardly conformists who kill in order to be accepted by their peers and to compensate for a traumatic sexual event in their past, such as Marcello in Bertolucci's *Il conformista*. Fellini believes that if the heinous crimes of such individuals can be explained away by their pathological personalities, the inevitable result of such images of fascism will be a comforting and self-congratulatory feeling on the part of the audience watching such films. Since "normal" people do not feel they share such deviant characteristics, they can consider themselves uncontaminated by their Fascist heritage:

> Fascism is not viewed, as in most political films that are made today, from (how can I put it?) a judgmental perspective. That is, from the outside. Detached judgments, aseptic diagnoses, complete and definitive formulae always seem to me (at least on the part of those of the generation to which I belong) a bit inhuman. The province of *Amarcord* is one in which we are all recognizable, the director first of all, in the ignorance which confounded us. A great ignorance and a great confusion. Not that I wish to minimize the economic and social causes of fascism. I only

wish to say that today what is still most interesting is the psychological, emotional manner of being a fascist. What is this manner? It is a sort of blockage, an arrested development during the phase of adolescence. . . . I don't wish to say that we Italians have not yet gone beyond adolescence and fascism. That would be an excessive and unjust affirmation. Things are certainly very much different from then, that is obvious. . . . And yet, . . . Italy, mentally, is still much the same. To say it in other terms, I have the impression that fascism and adolescence continue to be, in a certain measure, permanent historical seasons of our lives: adolescence of our individual lives, fascism of our national life. That is, this remaining children for eternity, this leaving responsibilities for others, this living with the comforting sensation that there is someone who thinks for you (and at one time it's mother, then it's father, then it's the mayor, another time Il Duce, another time the Madonna, another time the Bishop, in short other people): and in the meanwhile, you have this limited, time-wasting freedom which permits you only to cultivate absurd dreams—the dream of the American cinema, or the Oriental dream concerning women; in conclusion, the same old, monstrous, out-of-date myths that even today seem to me to form the most important conditioning of the average Italian.[9]

As the astute interpreter of Italian popular culture Fellini has always been, the director believes that the average Italian during the Fascist period had very little familiarity with political ideologies, and the years of popular support generated for Mussolini before foreign wars destroyed his regime cannot be explained away by positing a nation of sexual deviates, or a conspiracy theory that defines the regime as a capitalist tool to repress the working classes. Fascism dominated Italy for over two decades precisely because it exploited an archetypical Italian weakness: eternal adolescence.

The unique emotional impact of *Amarcord* on audiences all over the world—and not just those Italian spectators whose age or nationality made them especially interested in the Fascist era—is a direct result of Fellini's refusal to produce a "political" film that intends merely to denounce an embarrassing episode in Italy's history. As Fellini himself underlines above, he recognizes himself in the portrait he paints of Italy's past. *Amarcord* also seems to be Fellini's most purely autobio-

[9] Fellini, "*Amarcord*: The Fascism Within Us—An Interview with Valerio Riva," in *Federico Fellini: Essays in Criticism*, ed. Bondanella, pp. 20–21. For other discussions of Fellini and fascism, see Lester J. Keyser, "Three Faces of Evil: Fascism in Recent Movies," *Journal of Popular Film* 4, no. 1 (1975): 21–31; Peter F. Parshall, "Fellini's Thematic Structuring: Patterns of Fascism in *Amarcord*," *Film Criticism* 7, no. 2 (1983): 19–30; and Renzo Renzi, *Il fascismo involontario e altri scritti* (Bologna: Cappelli, 1975), pp. 131–81.

graphical work, since nearly all the major characters in the film are also discussed as figures from Fellini's childhood in Rimini in his essay "La mia Rimini," which has been published a number of times and even translated into English.[10] The authenticity of the regional atmosphere is further increased by the collaboration on the script of Tonino Guerra, a poet who composes verse in the dialect of Fellini's region and who is best known for other important scripts written for Antonioni, Rosi, and the Taviani brothers, as well as for Fellini.[11]

Fellini's *Amarcord* departs from the typical portrayal of fascism in the Italian cinema, for both Fellini's memoirs and *Amarcord* avoid dividing the inhabitants of this Rimini of his imagination into "good" heroes (the anti-Fascists) and "bad" villains (the Fascists). Instead, the townspeople are sketched out in masterful caricature portraits as comic types, all of whom have antecedents in Fellini's earlier works. Indeed, some of the same figures make their first appearance in *I clowns* and *Roma* in sequences devoted to Fellini's provincial origins. Instead of being sinister, perverted individuals, Fellini's Fascists are first of all pathetic clowns, manifestations of the same arrested development within the individual that all the townspeople share. Much of the film's narrative focuses on a typical family of the period, a likable group in most respects but with important defects and weaknesses. Aurelio, the father (Armando Brancia), is a relatively successful construction foreman of working-class background whose anarchist origins are not forgotten by the local Fascists whenever there is a political disturbance. A relatively gentle man, he is nevertheless capable of violent fits of irrational anger directed against his children, especially Titta (Bruno Zanin), the young man whose misadventures occupy a major portion of the film. Aurelio's wife Miranda (Pupella Maggio), the long-suffering archetype of Italian motherhood, defends her son Titta even when he deserves punishment and spoils her brother Lallo (Nandino Orfei), or "Il Pataca," as he is affectionately called by his vitelloni friends.[12] Lallo lives with his sis-

---

[10] The Italian text may be found in the following sources: Fellini, *La mia Rimini*; Federico Fellini, *Il film "Amarcord" di Federico Fellini*, ed. Gianfranco Angelucci and Liliana Betti (Bologna: Cappelli, 1974), pp. 49–86 (here reprinted with the title "Il mio paese"); and Fellini, *Fare un film*, pp. 3–40. The English version, "Rimini, My Home Town," can be examined in Fellini, *Fellini on Fellini*, pp. 1–40. There are several minor differences between these various versions of the essay. For the reactions to *Amarcord* of some of the people upon which the characters are based, see Dario Zanelli, "I riminesi di fronte ad *Amarcord*," in *Nel mondo di Federico*, pp. 71–77.

[11] For a discussion of Guerra as scriptwriter, see Questerbert, *Les Scénaristes italiens*, pp. 183–99; or Rebecca West, "Tonino Guerra and the Space of the Scriptwriter," *Annali d'italianistica* 6 (1988): 162–78.

[12] Lallo's nickname "Il Pataca" is also a slang term from Fellini's province that

ter's family without ever seeming to have to earn a living, and he may
be considered the prototype of the young male loafers Fellini made famous in his earlier film *I vitelloni*. Miranda is also capable of hysterical
fits of anger in her perennial arguments with Aurelio. Titta's grandfather (Peppino Ianigo), a likable old man whose mind is still dominated
by sexual fantasies, also lives with the family. Uncle Teo (Ciccio Ingrassia), Aurelio's brother, has been confined to an insane asylum and
is visited by the entire family in one important sequence.

The comic representation of the townspeople of *Amarcord* owes an
obvious debt to Fellini's background in cartoons and comic vignettes.
Their one or two typical tics that Fellini deftly reveals to us establish
their strange or grotesque characters as soon as they appear on the
screen. Since Fellini's purpose in sketching out the entire population of
the town is to underline the causes for the eternal adolescence of its
inhabitants, the largest group of characters comes from Titta's school.
The portraits of the pope, the king, and Mussolini hanging in the classrooms make it clear that the school's purpose is to perpetuate the ignorance and confusion Fellini believes is typical of the Fascist era. Almost nothing of any importance is taught there. Titta's classmates are
all immediately recognizable as stereotypical caricatures of truant students found in the classrooms of any society in any historical period:
Naso (Alvaro Vitali), his name emphasizing his protuberant nose; Il
Ciccio (Fernando de Felice), the class fat boy; Aldina (Donatella Gambini), the local beauty who is completely indifferent to Ciccio's attentions; Gigliozzi (Bruno Lenzi), the organizer of the practical jokes
played on the hapless Candela (Francesco Vona), a slightly effeminate
young man; and Ovo (Bruno Scagnetti), a small imp of a boy who is
incapable of pronouncing Greek syllables.

The schoolchildren seem almost normal, however, when compared
with their teachers. Zeus, the schoolmaster (Franco Magno), continues
his authoritarian manner from *Roma*. The professor of fine arts (Fides
Stagni) has breakfast during her inane lessons on Giotto's perspective.
While the professor of mathematics (Dina Adorni) tries to teach her
class the rudiments of algebra, the only things the students can think
of are her enormous breasts and her feral expression. The professor of
Italian (Mario Silvestri) bores the students with monotonous recitals of
patriotic verse by Vittorio Alfieri, trying to inspire a warlike spirit in
his pathetic pupils. The philosophy professor (Mauro Misul) delivers a

---

refers to the female sexual organ and may be translated as "cunt." Its use in the film
as a familiar term of address functions in much the same manner as the Venetian
mona ("cunt") or the Florentine *bischero* ("prick"), two other words with sexual
meanings that are also employed by Italians in informal speech and may also be used
as familiar and affectionate forms of address among good friends.

delirious parody of the Fascist philosophy of Giovanni Gentile to his
inattentive class. Don Balosa (Gianfilippo Carcano), the parish priest
and religion instructor, offers a superficial definition of the Holy Trin-
ity while wiping his glasses, as half of the class sneak out of the room
on tiptoe. Later, while confessing Titta and his friends, the priest is primarily interested in whether the boys are masturbating or not, warning
them that the saints cry when they do so.

Gradisca, the village beauty (Magali Noël), with whom the entire village is infatuated, joins other caricatures of masculine desire, such as
the nymphomaniac Volpina (Josiane Tanzilli) and the buxom tobacconist (Maria Antonella Beluzzi). Other figures include the slightly mad
Conte di Lovignano (Antoniono Faà di Bruno), the local aristocrat; the
town idiot, Giudizio (Aristide Caporale), a figure Fellini employs as
early as *I vitelloni*; and a street vendor named Biscein (Gennaro Ombra), who regales us with tall tales of sexual adventures in the harem of
a visiting Arab sheik at Rimini's Grand Hotel. A likable but rather
pompous and pedantic lawyer (Luigi Rossi) often interrupts the narrative to explain various details of the town's history to us, as do Giudizio
and Biscein. And, last but not least, Fellini also shows us various characters who represent political authority: the local Fascist gerarca (Fer-
ruccio Brembilla); and the visiting *federale* (Antonio Spaccatini), whose
histrionic gestures are modeled after the regime's public style developed by Achille Starace, head of the Fascist party for some years. A
blind accordionist, an unidentified motorcyclist who roars about the
city streets at night and on the nearby dock, and the owner of the local
Cinema Fulgor, called "Ronald Coleman" because of his physical likeness to the American movie star (Mario Liberati), round out this incred-
ibly funny population.

Given the large number of the town's inhabitants that Fellini takes
great pains to caricature, it would be accurate to speak of Fellini's
Amarcord as a "choral" film, since so much of the narrative is taken
up by the presentation of this large group of comic figures during moments in the life of the town when they interact together as a group.
This emphasis on the group begins with the first major sequence of the
film, that devoted to the celebration of the coming of spring and the
passing of winter on St. Joseph's Day (19 March) with the burning of a
witch in effigy on a bonfire called a *fogarazza*. Almost every one of the
numerous characters discussed above first appears during this celebration, and the choral nature of the film continues during other important
sequences, especially that devoted to the arrival of the Fascist federale
on 21 April, the traditional anniversary of the founding of Rome and a
holiday celebrated by Mussolini's regime; and again when the entire
town sails out into the ocean to catch a glimpse of the passage of the

Rex, the enormous ocean liner that embodied Mussolini's plans to rival other countries in all fields, especially those in which such technological advances had propaganda potential. Finally, Gradisca's wedding to a *carabiniere* officer closes the film with almost the entire village present. In addition to these four major sequences, there are numerous other aspects of *Amarcord* that underline how the destructive mythologies of Fascist popular culture have pervaded all levels of life in the provinces: in the detailed vignettes Fellini provides of misinstruction in the public schools and of misdirected piety in the church during confessions; during the squabbles at the dinner table as the large, extended family typical of Italy during the period represents a microcosm of the larger town; during the various promenades in the town square where all the people strut back and forth, looking at others and placing themselves on parade as well. As Fellini notes in discussing the federale's visit—but his argument fits all the group activities in *Amarcord*—"living in this kind of environment, each person develops not individual characteristics but only pathological defects."[13] Taken separately as individuals, these comic characters seem to have only

> manias, innocuous tics: and yet, it is enough for the characters to gather together for an occasion like this, and there, from apparently harmless eccentricities, their manias take on a completely different meaning. The gathering of April 21st, just like the passing of the *Rex*, the burning of the great bonfire at the beginning, and so on, are always occasions of total stupidity. The pretext of being together is always a leveling process. People stay together only to commit stupid acts. And when they are alone, there is bewilderment, solitude, or the ridiculous dream of the Orient, of Fred Astaire, or the myth of luxury and American ostentation. It is only ritual that keeps them all together. Since no character has a real sense of individual responsibility, or has only petty dreams, no one has the strength not to take part in the ritual, to remain at home outside of it.[14]

In Fellini's depiction of both the federale's visit to town and the passage of the *Rex*, the director employs the ritualistic behavior of the entire town to ridicule fascism as a political movement. Imitating Starace's athletic and frenetic style (employed by the regime to underline the vitalistic, energetic, youth-oriented image idealized by the movement), all of the inhabitants present themselves at the train station to greet the *federale*: he arrives in a great puff of smoke, a recurrent image which, along with fog, is an eloquent concrete metaphor for the obscurantism of the period. Unlike most of the rest of the buildings in the

---

[13] Fellini, "*Amarcord*: The Fascism Within Us," p. 21.
[14] Ibid., p. 22.

town, which were built on the grounds of Cinecittà, to film the federale sequence Fellini used the already present entrance to Cinecittà itself, constructed by Mussolini in the typically Fascist and modernist architectural style. But by using this studio complex as the backdrop for the arrival of the federale, Fellini also subtly suggests a major theme of *Amarcord*, the continuity of the psychological state of mind in Italy that once produced fascism but still exists today as "that aspect of us which is stupid, shabby, weak-willed: an aspect which has no party affiliation, of which we should be ashamed, and for the repulsion of which it is not enough to declare, 'I serve in an anti-fascist party,' because that aspect is inside of us and, already once in the past, fascism has given it expression, authority, standing."[15] A figure such as the professor of mathematics seemed only comically grotesque in her classroom. But when she stands before a symbol of the regime's power, such as the federale, her grotesque nature takes on a more ominous tone bordering on delirium, her personality magically transformed by her fascist uniform. Without a touch of the irony that the director obviously intends in his treatment of such a scene, the teacher can then declare imperiously: "It's marvelous . . . this enthusiasm that renders us young and ancient at the same time. . . . Young . . . because fascism has rejuvenated our blood with luminous ideals . . . but ancient, because never before as now do we feel we are the children of Rome!"[16] Immediately after this statement, echoing the regime's propaganda aimed at portraying Italy as both the inheritor of ancient Rome and the vanguard of a new youth cult, Lallo the vitellone, also now in uniform, delivers his own interpretation of Mussolini's significance to us while staring directly into the camera eye and employing a vulgar gesture: "Ah! I say only this . . . Mussolini has two balls this large!"[17]

Something of importance is almost always communicated whenever Fellini resorts to such a metacinematic device. Here, the causal connection between a misdirected sexuality based on an arrested state of psychological development and the pervasive fascism in the town of *Amarcord* that Lallo's exclamation suggests constitutes one of the most important themes in Fellini's film. Gradisca, the object of desire of the

[15] Ibid., pp. 22-23.

[16] Cited in Fellini, *Il film "Amarcord" di Federico Fellini*, p. 199. This published script was created from an analysis of the film on the moviola, but the final copy of the film still contains a number of important changes, forcing the scholar to use the script with the usual caution that must be employed with all of Fellini's Italian scripts. In *Federcord: disegni per "Amarcord" di Federico Fellini* (Milan: Libri Edizioni, 1974), Liliana Betti and Oreste del Buono discuss the making of the film and reprint a large number of the many sketches and drawings Fellini employed in its production.

[17] Fellini, *Il film "Amarcord" di Federico Fellini*, p. 199.

entire town, almost faints with sexual excitement as she tries to touch
the passing federale.[18] Later, when the town turns out to see the *Rex*,
Gradisca experiences a similar moment of comic sensual arousal. During the excitement following the federale's arrival, Ciccio fantasizes
about the final success of his attentions to Aldina. Standing before an
enormous face of Mussolini constructed from pink and white flowers,
he finally succeeds in his daydreams in taking Aldina as his "Fascist
bride."

Fellini believes that while fascism exploited the perennial lack of sexual maturity endemic in Italian culture, the ultimate blame for such
sexual repression and frustration tormenting the inhabitants of *Amarcord* lies with the Catholic church. The sexual exhibitionism typical of
Latin and male-dominated cultures, for Fellini, also represents a manifestation of fascism: "[sexuality] should be an emotion and, instead, it
is in danger of becoming a show, something clownish and useless, an
ugly thing which women endure passively and dumbfoundedly."[19] For
this reason, Fellini prefaces the visit of the federale and the group hys-
teria connected with the regime's symbols with the individual confessions of Titta and his classmates in church. While Gradisca will try to
"touch" the visiting Fascist official, the parish priest, in contrast, seems
interested only in making sure that the boys avoid touching themselves! But as Titta asks himself during confession, how could you not
touch yourself when you are surrounded by sexually arousing images,
such as the buxom tobacconist with the sensual voice, the amply endowed professor of mathematics, the plump peasant women with enormous bottoms seated on their bicycles, the nymphomaniac Volpina
prowling about town in search of her prey, and, most of all, Gradisca,
the woman who is the object of the entire male population's frustrated
lust? As Titta refers to each of these tempting females, the film rapidly
cuts in a succession of brief shots to each of the women.

The sequence devoted to Gradisca is the most interesting, for it develops inside the Cinema Fulgor and is the archetype of all such cinematic liaisons in Fellini's films. In his imagination, Titta follows Gradisca into the totally deserted cinema. As Titta moves from one seat to
another, closer and closer to Gradisca with each successive cut, Gradisca, as if in a trance, stares at the silver screen, which displays a close-
up of Gary Cooper from *Beau Geste*, a film made in 1939 but released

---

[18] The scene is described in this fashion in the script: "Gradisca, seized by a fit of
feminine fanaticism, makes her way among the crowd, blowing kisses and screaming
hysterically: 'Let me touch him . . . I want to touch him. . . . Viva il Duce! The
Duce is handsome! Viva!' " (ibid., p. 198).

[19] Fellini, "*Amarcord*: The Fascism Within Us," p. 22.

34. *Amarcord*: the ideal Fascist couple is married in a fantasy sequence before a huge image of Mussolini

in Italy only after the end of the war.[20] Such a conscious anachronism plays up the metacinematic intentions of the entire sequence. Titta and the rest of the village have transformed Gradisca into an object of mediated desire, since their passion for her is determined by the model of the Hollywood movie star. Gradisca relates to Gary Cooper, her own sexual fantasy, in a similar manner, searching endlessly for the equivalent of a movie star in her own life. Eventually, she will have to be satisfied with a mere officer of the carabinieri, just as the young boys will eventually be forced to marry women who cannot possibly live up to the fantasies they have known only in the movies. When Titta gazes at Gradisca through the thick cigarette smoke enveloping this female figure, as one perceptive critic has noted, the smoke (again symbolic of another of the many cultural mystifications in the town) glamorizes her as if she were seen through a soft-focus movie lens.[21] As we gaze at Titta as he gazes at Gradisca gazing at Gary Cooper, we are provided with a double vision, enabling us to experience Titta's "mystified perspective, while we judge it as the product of an inexperienced youth."[22] We are prompted to evaluate both Titta and Gradisca as characters who relate to members of the opposite sex only through a form of mediated sexuality that originates in the cinema. This brief but brilliant sequence captures the implicit link between repressed sexuality and public behavior in the popular culture of the town, but it also deconstructs and demystifies the complicated cultural operation of mimetic desire that mediates passion by means of external models from the movies.

The sequence in which Fellini presents the passage of the *Rex* expresses a similar metacinematic theme and has equally demystifying intentions. This ocean liner, which actually existed and set speed records for transatlantic crossings between Italy and New York during the era, was one of the regime's proudest achievements. Its passage provides the excuse for another gathering of the entire town. A number of complex tracking shots follow the various inhabitants to the seashore, where they all embark in small boats to sail out to meet the *Rex*. Subsequent long shots show us the boats leaving the harbor and riding on the sea, waiting for the sun to set. This first part of the sequence employs real boats on a real ocean filmed on an outside location by the sea, but as night draws nearer, we suddenly become aware that Fellini has shifted the scene from the ocean to a movie studio. The rocking of the boats in the water is obviously produced by artificial means; some boats are motionless in the background while two boats in the fore-

[20] Kezich, *Fellini*, pp. 428–29.
[21] Millicent Marcus, "Fellini's *Amarcord*: Film as Memory," *Quarterly Review of Film Studies* 2 (1977): 423.
[22] Ibid.

ground rock from side to side, instead of bobbing up and down as would be most natural. Furthermore, the sea upon which the people are floating is revealed in the final shot to be a series of black plastic sheets obviously blown by a wind machine and sprayed with water. Fellini's *Rex* is an artificial ocean liner painted on a billboard construction near the Cinecittà pool with backlighting suggesting its port holes. As Fellini simulates the ship's passage by camera movements past the stationary set construction, his *Rex* seems to flop over into the water, revealing its status as both a product of cinematic artifice and as a false and mystifying image proposed by a regime founded on equally artificial ideals. Once again, Gradisca is moved as she had been by the presence of the Fascist federale or by the image of Gary Cooper on the movie screen. In the Cinema Fulgor sequence, Fellini revealed the mechanism behind the apparatus of the cinematic image by disclosing its function as a mediator of authentic sexual desire. Now, with the *Rex* sequence, he employs similar metacinematic devices to demystify a much more sinister political myth.

The federale's visit, introduced by Titta's sexual fantasies in confession, is followed by the family's visit to the asylum to see their insane Uncle Teo. Fellini uses Teo as an extreme example of the devastating results of sexual repression. During a country excursion, Teo escapes, climbs up a tree, and, screaming at the top of his voice, exclaims over and over again: "I want a woman!" He refuses to descend until a midget nun, a grotesque representative of the repressive force of the same church that has helped to reduce Teo to such a state, orders him to do so. Teo's pitiful cry might well be taken as the emblem of the entire male population of *Amarcord*. The fact that the *Rex* sequence directly follows the Uncle Teo sequence provides a demonstration of how such destructive sexual behavior may be transferred from an individual psychological level to motivate the behavior of an entire group of people. Failing to discover a proper channel for their sexual drives, and lacking an unmediated object of sexual desire, the townspeople must either go mad or displace their stifled desires onto political symbols skillfully manipulated by the regime.

To complete the dismal picture of an entire society immersed in the "lack of information, in the lack of awareness of problems which are concretely real, in the refusal to go deeper into matters of life out of laziness, prejudice, convenience, and presumption,"[23] Fellini then follows the *Rex* sequence with a troubling sequence in which Titta's grandfather is so disoriented by the thick, smothering fog typical of the Po River region that he cannot even recognize his front door and won-

---

[23] Fellini, "*Amarcord*: The Fascism Within Us," p. 22.

35. *Amarcord*: Titta tries to seduce Gradisca in the cinema

36. *Amarcord*: the townspeople cheer the passage of the *Rex*

37. *Amarcord*: Fellini's sketch of the insane Uncle Teo screaming "I want a woman!"

ders if he has died. The fog is a poetically concrete visual metaphor for the isolation and alienation characterizing the entire town. The sense of hermetic closure and resistance to new ideas suggested by the fog bank is also emphasized by the mysterious appearance of a beautiful peacock during a snowstorm, the traditional symbol of vanity that serves as a general commentary on the entire city. Fellini's masterful interconnection of sketches or vignettes of individual comic characters with sequences that reveal the consequences of such individual behavior on a wider level is one of the most original features of *Amarcord* and provides the viewer with a coherent and persuasive portrait of Italian Fascist culture that few political films of the period can equal.

One of the most interesting stylistic features of *Amarcord*, an aspect of the film that emphasizes its choral nature, is its proliferation of narrative points of view. In the original Italian print, we discover a complex mixture of direct addresses to the camera by various characters, as well as voice-overs providing information or commentary on the film's action. In a few significant instances, the voice is that of Fellini himself, a fact that is often overlooked when viewing prints or videocassettes dubbed in English. Giudizio, the town idiot, opens the film by plucking from the air one of the puffballs (the "manine") that poplar trees give off to announce the arrival of spring in the town. Then, "with the self-assurance of the ignorant," as the script notes,[24] Giudizio proceeds to provide an officious explanation for these puffballs. As he does this, it is obvious to anyone who has ever seen Fellini shoot on location that the actor is merely reciting his lines while receiving verbal prompts from the director himself behind the camera. This is Fellini's normal procedure in shooting scenes with both professional and nonprofessional actors. As the filming is not done with synchronized sound, Fellini usually removes his voice and other extraneous sounds from the track during the dubbing process. Giudizio's awkward and unnatural manner of speech and the fact that he is speaking directly into the camera call attention to the artificial manner in which his commentary unfolds.

Moreover, the fact that Fellini has chosen the village idiot to open the film casts doubt on the reliability of the narrative. In the original shooting script, Giudizio's explanations are interrupted by two ironic questions Fellini himself addresses to him: "What do you want to tell us?" and "What sense does that make? Speak clearly!"[25] Later, when the townspeople are heading to the ocean to see the *Rex*, Giudizio peers into the camera once again and asks where they are going. Another eccentric character, the street vendor Biscein, repeats a similar operation twice. At the end of the film after Gradisca's wedding, he turns directly toward the camera and says good-bye to the audience. Earlier, after Fellini had re-created his fantastic account of his sexual adventures in the harem at the Grand Hotel, Biscein turned to the camera and counted the times he made love there. In the midst of his extravagant enumeration that by itself belies the truth of his story, another narrative voice-over, that of the lawyer, interrupts Biscein, announcing that the street vendor made love twenty-eight times! A third eccentric peasant appears during the visit to crazy Uncle Teo, giggles over Teo's desperate cries from the tree, and also stares into Fellini's camera eye. Such re-

---

[24] Fellini, *Il film "Amarcord" di Federico Fellini*, p. 122.

[25] Ibid. While these particular questions were eventually changed in the final dubbed print of the film, Fellini intervenes in the narrative of *Amarcord* on a number of occasions that will be discussed in this chapter.

peated devices throughout *Amarcord*'s narrative function to prevent
the viewer from ever relying completely on any of the various narrative
points of view expressed in the film or taking the images on the screen
as an authentic historical reconstruction of Italy's Fascist past. First and
foremost, *Amarcord* represents a fiction, but the fictitious, artificial
quality of *Amarcord*'s narrative is employed by Fellini in an original
way to say something of importance about Fascist popular culture.

Since Titta is one of the film's most important figures (not to mention that the director's memoirs of his adolescence in Rimini identify
Titta as one of Fellini's best friends), it is not surprising that *Amarcord*
reflects Titta's point of view at crucial moments in the narrative. The
confessional sequence culminating in Titta's attempts to touch Gradisca in the Cinema Fulgor after listing all the other objects of feminine
desire in the village (the buxom tobacconist, the math teacher, the peasants on the bicycles, Volpina) quite naturally is accompanied by Titta's
voice-over explanation, as the sound track reflects his stream of consciousness during his confession with Don Balosa. But two other remarks listed in the published script as delivered by Titta's voice-over—
the remark in which he wonders who is at the beach introducing a cut
to Volpina, the town nymphomaniac; and an explanation of Uncle
Teo's identity—are delivered in the completed film not by Titta but by
Fellini himself.[26]

The most complicated narrative commentary delivered in the film
comes from the pompous lawyer, who appears five times during the
film, stares into the camera eye each time, and delivers a number of
somewhat pedantic remarks. Our perception of him as an omniscient,
reliable narrator is undercut immediately upon his first appearance after the fogarazza sequence has introduced the entire population of the
town. As the lawyer tries to explain the ancient origins of the town,
citing Dante, Pascoli, and Carducci as just a few of the famous poets
who have lauded the virtues of its inhabitants, he is repeatedly interrupted by the vulgar sound of a raspberry delivered on the sound track
by Fellini himself! When the lawyer loses his patience and demands
that his tormentor come out into the open ("Show yourself! I am ready
to give you any explanation face to face!"), he receives only another
raspberry and an ironic address.[27] The lawyer later comes before the
camera to explain the architectural styles of the town, asking for the
audience's comprehension when the local madame passes by in her car-

[26] These voice-overs, labeled respectively "Voce Titta" and "Voce Titta (provvisorio)" may be found in ibid., p. 155 and p. 234.

[27] See ibid., pp. 138–39, for the script (which identifies the tormenting voice-over
as only "The Voice of a Man." In the dubbing of the film, Fellini inserted his own
voice.

riage with the newly arrived prostitutes for the brothel. He later explains the political symbolism behind celebrating 21 April, the mythical date of Rome's foundation and the day when the Fascist *federale* visits the town. Later, he discusses the sexual fantasies connected with Rimini's Grand Hotel. In connection with the Grand Hotel, the lawyer's commentary both introduces Gradisca's tryst with the prince and explains the origin of her name as a result of her celebrated invitation to the prince to join her in bed. "Gradisca" may be translated into English as "Please do"; the dubbed English print of *Amarcord* distributed in the United States renders her name as "S'il vous plâit." The lawyer then casts doubt upon Biscein's version of his endless lovemaking with the harem girls lodged in the hotel. Finally, while discussing the historic proportions of the unusual snowstorm preceding the appearance of the peacock in the town square, the lawyer is struck by a snowball thrown by some unidentified person off-camera. The lawyer declares that the person who threw the snowball was *not* one of the boys in the town, and given his disrespectful treatment by Fellini earlier, the obvious conclusion is that Fellini has also thrown the snowball at him.[28] Such an energetic interjection of the director into the action he is filming is not unusual. Gideon Bachman's documentary of the making of *Fellini Satyricon* shows Fellini taking part in throwing food at the pedantic poet Eumolpo during the filming of Trimalcione's famous banquet scene.[29]

In spite of the frequent republication of Fellini's Rimini memoirs describing a number of the major characters (Gradisca, Titta, Giudizio, "Ronald Coleman," the schoolteachers, the priest) later to appear in *Amarcord* as actual individuals from the director's past, Fellini has consistently refused to consider his films autobiographical and insists, as he puts it in his major treatise on filmmaking, that "my films from my past recount memories that are completely invented. And in the end, what difference does it make?"[30] Fellini himself is aware that his own writings about his provincial origins present the critic or historian with ammunition for the construction of a reductionist interpretation of *Amarcord* based on the director's autobiography, but he insists that this approach to the film is misguided:

I'm always a bit offended when I hear that one of my films is "autobiographical": it seems like a reductionist definition to me, especially if

---

[28] This particular part of the snowball sequence is not included in the published script and was obviously added during the shooting (see ibid., pp. 301–4, for the original version of the scene).

[29] See Gideon Bachman, *Ciao, Federico!* (1969), available on videotape.

[30] Fellini, *Fare un film*, p. 41.

then, as it often happens, "autobiographical" comes to be understood in
the sense of anecdotal, like someone who tells old school stories. So
much so that at the beginning, I felt a great reluctance in speaking about
it. I continued to say: be careful, "Amarcord" doesn't mean "I remember" at all; instead, it is a kind of cabalistic word, a word of seduction,
the brand of an aperitif: *Amarcord* . . . I felt that authorizing a viewing of
the film with an autobiographical "key" would have been a grave error.
So much so that at one moment I wanted to entitle it simply *Viva l'Italia!* Then, I thought that this would have been too mysterious or too
didactic. Another title I wanted to give it was *Il borgo*, in the sense of a
medieval enclosure, a lack of information, a lack of contact with the un-
heard of, the new. . . . Then, finally, scribbling little sketches for the title,
this word came to me—*Amarcord*; but you have to forget its origin. For,
in its mystery, it means only the feeling that characterizes the whole
film: a funereal feeling, one of isolation, dream, torpor, and of ignorance.[31]

Fellini has always provided less than completely reliable information
about his past. During his early career, a number of interesting stories
circulated about him that were either confirmed during interviews with
him or, at least, not denied: that he was born on a train; that he ran
away to join the circus in 1927, supposedly explaining his later interest
in clowns; that Guido's adventures in school as a young boy and his
encounter with La Saraghina in *8 1/2* happened to Fellini himself when
he was sent for two years to a church school in Fano. Yet Fellini's biographer Tullio Kezich denies all these famous stories, noting that all
the trains in Italy were blocked on the day of Fellini's birth (20 January
1920) owing to a national strike. He adds that Fellini's mother and all
his other relatives deny he ever ran away to join the circus, and points
out that Fellini's brother Riccardo, and not Federico, actually attended
the famous school in Fano. Much the same may be true of the supposedly autobiographical anecdotes Fellini relates in *Amarcord*. For example, Dario Zanelli's interviews of the people on whom many of the
film's characters are based suggest that there are no reliable correla-
tions between Fellini's past and the characters he has invented. In his
memoirs, Fellini offers the following account of the origin of Gradisca's
name, the same one he visualizes in a beautiful dreamlike sequence in
Amarcord: "Once, when a Prince of the blood royal had stopped in Rimini, she had been suggested to him as a woman who knew how to
behave respectfully when the occasion demanded it. When she was naked before the Prince, careful of what she had been told, she offered

[31] Fellini, "*Amarcord*: The Fascism Within Us," pp. 24–25.

herself with the word 'Gradisca!' "[32] Fellini goes on to remark that it
is he, and not his best friend Titta, who attempted without success
to touch Gradisca in the Cinema Fulgor. In interviewing the actual
woman, Gradisca Morri, Dario Zanelli discovered that her name was
given to her at birth and not as a nickname. When she was born, in
November of 1915, her father was fighting on the Italian front in the
Carso region at a place called Gradisca. Luigi Benzi, Fellini's best friend
and the model for Titta in both Fellini's memoirs and the film, told
Zanelli that many of the episodes in the film actually happened but not
necessarily to the character in the film. The sexual encounter with Volpina apparently happened to Fellini, not Titta, as did the visit to the
mad uncle. Titta's encounter with the buxom tobacconist, who allows
the young boy to pick her up in the shop and to suckle her enormous
breasts, was apparently an embellishment of the young boys' fascination with her ability to lift heavy weights.

The historical veracity of the events recorded in *Amarcord* or in Fellini's memoirs has little or nothing to do with their artistic function
in Fellini's film, as the director quite correctly hastens to underline in
almost every discussion of his work. As Fellini has declared, by re-creating his past through the fictional prism of his cinema, he has canceled
it out to the point that "now I can't distinguish what really happened
from what I made up. Superimposed on my real memories are painted
memories of a plastic sea, and characters from my adolescence in Rimini are elbowed aside by actors or extras who interpreted them in my
films."[33]

It is precisely because Fellini wishes to avoid the close identification
between his own past and the province depicted in *Amarcord* that he
uses such a complex and ironic series of narrative perspectives in the
film. The choral nature of these perspectives draws attention away
from possible sources in Fellini's biography and emphasizes their
shared origins in the culture of the period during Fellini's adolescence.
At the same time, the irreverent manner in which Fellini presents his
narrators—greeting the most important one with raspberries and snow-
balls—makes it clear that no presumptuous and authoritative interpretation of Italy's Fascist past, as has been attempted by so many other
more ideological directors, is intended in *Amarcord*. Fellini is a storyteller, not a political scientist or a historian, and the constant addresses
to the camera eye by his not completely reliable narrators also serve to
emphasize the fact that the world he has created from Italy's past is a
cinematic artefact, not a historical "fact" that is subject to historical

[32] Fellini, *Fellini on Fellini*, p. 25.
[33] Fellini, *Comments on Film*, p. 39.

proof or documentation. The intrusion of the director's voice on the sound track or his even more energetic intrusion into the action by throwing a snowball at his mouthpiece character, the pompous lawyer, also constitutes a clear admission that Fellini considers himself to be one of the Amarcordians, as ignorant and confused during his provincial years under the Fascist regime and as eternally adolescent as any of the characters he criticizes and satirizes. Without completely condemning any of them, he represents them all in the usual nonjudgmental manner typical of Fellini's portraits of Italian life since his first works appeared in the 1950s.

The extraordinary international success of *Amarcord* proved that Fellini's fictional interpretation of Italy's Fascist heritage had transcended mere historical re-creation. It obviously struck a responsive chord in non-Italian viewers who had never lived under a Fascist regime and who had probably never even heard of Mussolini. But there is something quite disturbing in *Amarcord* for any spectator of this film. While the characters in it are obviously comic types and the political regime they live under has long since vanished, the Amarcordians are nevertheless far more familiar figures than the sexually traumatized conformist Marcello Clerici in Bertolucci's *Il conformista* or the even more abnormal and monstrous Fascist killer appropriately named Attila in Bertolucci's *Novecento*. Their tics and manias are not so far removed from our own, and our bemused observation of the humorous antics of Fellini's characters never relieves us of the feeling that there on the screen, but for an accident of historical circumstance, we, too, could well be depicted. *Amarcord* stands as Fellini's most complex visual representation of a political theme, even though the ideological dimensions of the film do not exhaust its artistic achievements. Presenting a human comedy and transcending historical, ideological, or geographical boundaries, *Amarcord* speaks to our common humanity.

While delays in the preparation of *La città delle donne* stalled the production of that project in 1978, on 16 March Aldo Moro—president of the Christian Democratic party and architect of the historic compromise between the ruling Christian Democrats and the Italian Communist party led by Enrico Berlinguer—was kidnapped by Red Brigade terrorists and murdered after fifty-five days of captivity. Never before was the stability of Italy's republic so shaken or threatened by chaos or the threat of a repressive response that would undermine the country's democratic institutions. Reacting to this atmosphere of potential anarchy, Fellini agreed to produce *Prova d'orchestra* for Italian state television and quickly composed a soggetto and a script with the assistance of Brunello Rondi. The film was completed in record time—only sixteen days of shooting and a total production time of some two months (of which four weeks were required for the dubbing). As Fellini has noted, the "little film," as he called it, was perhaps far more suitable for television than his other television films. It employed a single set, an ancient oratorio reconstructed at Cinecittà. Its style concentrated on close-ups and employed relatively few of his characteristically mobile camera movements, a camera style more suitable for the small-screen format. And *Prova d'orchestra* is structured around a fictional television interview of the individual members of an orchestra during rehearsal in the oratorio, a means of communicating information for which television is particularly suited.[34] But with this brief pseudodocumentary film, Fellini raises important philosophical questions about the relationship of the individual to the society in which he lives and works.

The image of an orchestra rehearsal is a somewhat unusual metaphor for a director whose insensitivity to concerts and grand opera, in spite of his long and fruitful collaboration with composer Nino Rota, is legendary. For the first time in Fellini's long collaboration with Rota, the composer wrote the musical score for this film *before* the film was shot, since the four original musical motifs Rota provided would be used during production on the set to give some direction to the actors simulating the orchestra rehearsal. Also of significance is the fact that Fellini and Rota employed original musical tunes of great simplicity, completely alien to the more majestic classical motifs from the masterpieces of orchestral music they might well have selected. The unpretentious quality of the music on the sound track, which every viewer of the film will unconsciously compare to orchestral pieces by Mozart, Brahms, or Beethoven, helps to emphasize the gap that exists between music in the present period of cultural confusion and the imposing musical monuments from the past. This disparity between present and past music, set within the metaphor of Italian society as an orchestra out of tune, also provides an implicit evaluation of the disastrous state of contemporary society. The script of *Prova d'orchestra* is a relatively uncomplicated one, tailored to the seventy-minute television format. During the first part of the film, Fellini's voice functions as the television interviewer while the camera analyzes the individual members of the orchestra and their authoritarian conductor (Balduin Baas), providing a frightening picture of the chaos and disharmony that threatens this microcosm of Italian society. After a long discussion between the conductor and the interviewer, the orchestra's smoldering resentment against the conductor breaks out into an open revolt that is suddenly

---

[34] Michel Ciment, "Entretien avec Federico Fellini," in *Federico Fellini*, ed. Ciment, p. 113.

interrupted by a huge wrecking ball that breaks down one of the oratorio's walls, covering the scene with dust and debris. The collapse of the
wall shocks the orchestra into rehearsing for a brief moment as an integrated, harmonious group. But this magic spell is soon broken, and
the film ends on a threatening note as the conductor reverts to his native language, haranguing his rebellious charges in German.

Fellini has declared that he thought of the metaphoric possibilities of
an orchestra rehearsal long before the dramatic Moro assassination occurred:

> When I was present at the recording of the music for my films, I was
> always struck by the feeling of surprise and incredulity, and I was equally
> moved to see that each time a miracle renewed itself. Individuals who
> were very different from each other arrived in the recording room with
> their various instruments, but also with their personal problems, their
> bad humor, their illnesses, their portable radio to listen to the results of
> sporting events. And I was astonished to discover that in this context of
> disorder and approximation, and with these rebellious schoolchildren, as
> a result of repeated attempts, one arrived at submerging this heteroge-
> nous mass into a single form, even an abstract one, which is that of mu-
> sic. This operation of producing order from disorder provoked in me a
> great emotion. It seemed to me that this situation contained in itself, in
> some way and in an emblematic fashion, the image of a life in society or
> a group expression that was compatible with the expression of each in-
> dividual, each instrument retaining its own identity and its own calling
> and, at the same time, mingling in a harmonious discourse concerning
> each one of them.[35]

The comic framework of *Prova d'orchestra*, within which Fellini develops his views on the individual's relationship to society, is also not far
removed from the caricature world of the Italian provinces under fascism in *Amarcord*. Like the inhabitants of *Amarcord*, the members of
the orchestra are comic types whose personalities, tics, and physical
traits explain the instruments they have chosen to play. The musicians
characterize the piano as a mythological animal. The flute is defined as
the instrument nearest to the human voice, sweet but supernatural.
Rhythm instruments are comic instruments, played by Neapolitans.
The cello is called the pillar of the orchestra, close to the "ideal friend"
(discrete, faithful). The trombone serves both clowns and angels and is
a solitary voice. The violin is proposed as either the quintessential masculine or feminine instrument (one embarrassed female musician admits that she considers the violin a "phallic" instrument).

[35] Ibid., pp. 112–13.

In contrast to the completely chaotic group of comic characters who make up the orchestra's musicians, the conductor is a lonely, authoritarian figure, appropriately of German nationality. His relationship to his musicians is strained, at best, and when he interrupts their rehearsal on the numerous occasions he takes to correct their interpretations of the music, he vituperates the musicians mercilessly in his less than perfect Italian, as he tosses his musical score into the air in disgust: "Where are we, perhaps on a soccer field? Have you mistaken me for a referee? Too loud! Too penetrating, all of you should be castrated!"[36] His outbursts finally provoke the musicians and their union representatives to call a long break, during which time the conductor in his dressing room laments to the television interviewer (Fellini) how times have changed:

> The time of greatness is finished. Kaputt! . . . Now we are all equal. . . . You say "orchestra director," but this phrase has no meaning any longer, an orchestra director is like a priest: he must have a church with believers, with the faithful, but when the church collapses and when the believers turn into atheists. . . . Music is always sacred, every concert is a mass. . . . there used to be so much love between us musicians and a director: a love that, as you see, is now lost. My musicians and I share only a lack of confidence . . . one against the other, doubt ruins belief . . . and so we play together but we are united only in a common hatred . . . like a destroyed family.[37]

The musicians' revolt against the director is an obvious parody of the chaotic political situation in Italy at the time. Insulting graffiti are sprayed on the oratorio walls ("Hurray for Record Players," "Down with Beethoven!"). The musicians shout political slogans employing the same rhythmic chant that demonstrators of the period employed: "Time has run out, director you're screwed"; "orchestra, terror, whoever plays is a traitor"; "orchestra, terror, death to the director!"[38] The musicians place a gigantic metronome on the director's podium to overturn his authority, but even this mechanical instrument is eventually attacked by other musicians, who want all authority over the orchestra abolished. Only the collapse of the wall under the thunderous blows of the demolition ball silences this cacophonous anarchy and brings the musicians back under the control of the director for a brief moment, as he addresses them: "You are here, I am here. Everyone

[36] Cited in Fellini, *Prova d'orchestra*, p. 89.

[37] Ibid., pp. 102–3.

[38] Ibid., pp. 108–10. In the original Italian, the slogans rhyme: "Il tempo é scaduto, direttore sei fottuto!"; "orchestra, terrore, chi suona é un traditore!"; "orchestra, terrore, a morte il direttore!"

must pay attention to his instrument, we can only do that. . . . The notes save us. . . . The music saves us. Grab onto the notes, follow the notes, one after the other. . . . We are musicians, you are musicians. . . . And we are here to rehearse. . . . Don't be afraid, the rehearsal continues."[39] Now, for the first time in the film, the musicians play in harmonic unison, and one of the few long shots Fellini employs in the entire film captures them all on their feet following the director's command. But the blissful moment lasts only for an instant. The dangers of chaos and anarchy, suggested by the huge demolition ball still visible in the background, are now joined to the future threat of a repressive reaction to the disorder displayed by the musicians. The director delivers another of his vituperative speeches to his musicians, reminding them that noise is not music. As he screams "Da capo!" to them, the screen fades to black, and the director continues his tirade with a long string of orders delivered in German in a menacing tone that can only remind the viewer of Hitler.[40] The demented attitude of the orchestra conductor is captured perfectly by Fellini in a color sketch that he inserted in the original manuscript of the film's scenario treatment.

Fellini's film was premiered not on Italian television, for which it was intended, but instead at the Palazzo Quirinale, the residence of the president of the Italian Republic, in October of 1978. This screening was held at the request of then-president Sandro Pertini, and the audience included not only Fellini but also the then–prime minister Giulio Andreotti and Pietro Ingrao, the then-president of the Chamber of Deputies and a key member of the Italian Communist party.[41] This solemn setting must have amused Fellini as a bizarre forum, given the traditional Italian critical interpretation of his work as unconcerned with

[39] Ibid., p. 113.

[40] The menacing German ending was apparently a last-minute addition to the film during the dubbing, since there is no trace of it in the original manuscript. There is, however, an apocalyptic note in the original ending, for the question is posed why the Last Judgment is announced by a trumpet: "Why a musical instrument, even a trumpet, why not? It unites the heaven and the earth." (Cited in Fellini, "Prova d'orchestra," Fellini MS. 6 [Box 1], p. 69). This script, conserved in the Lilly Library of Rare Books, varies in some respects from the previously cited script published by Garzanti. The Garzanti edition also contains a version of the film's subject, the original manuscript of which may be examined in the previously cited Lilly manuscript entitled "Prova d'orchestra: chiaccherata sul filmetto che avrei in animo di fare" (Fellini MS. 5 [Box 1]). This particular manuscript contains two interesting drawings: one, on the cover page in ink, of a hand directing music; another in color and reproduced in this book, of the director.

[41] According to Kezich (Fellini, p. 475), the film was first shown in public theaters on 22 February 1979 and finally on RAI-Uno, the major state television channel, on 26 December 1979.

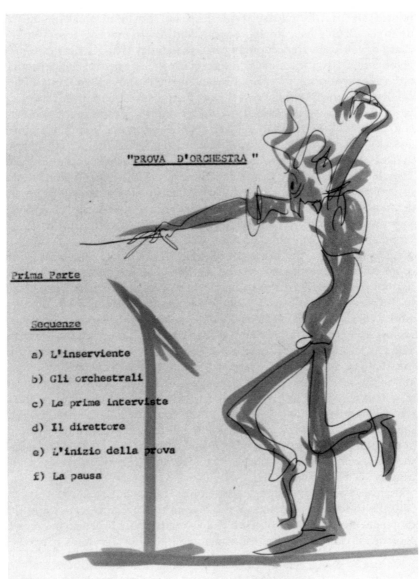

38. *Prova d'orchestra*: Fellini's sketch of the German conductor from the original manuscript of the film's *soggetto*

politics. Before the release of the film and during its final touches of
dubbing, Fellini had already confided to his friend Oreste del Buono
that he was most preoccupied by the possibility that his film would be
given a reductive, ideological interpretation.[42] Because of the particular
circumstances of its premiere in the Quirinale and subsequent polemical discussions in Italian newspapers, Fellini's fears about the reception
of the film were well founded.[43] The German voice closing the film was
construed as a warning of a future Hitler emerging from the chaotic
anarchy of an orchestra playing out of tune, symbolizing Italy. Some
viewers even applauded what they saw as Fellini's call for the return of
"Uncle Adolph" at the end of the film.[44] Fellini's protests against the
interpretation of the film as merely a political allegory represent an understandable preoccupation of the artist that his work not be reduced
to a simplistic formula. And there is, in truth, much more to *Prova
d'orchestra* than a simpleminded or reactionary political metaphor. As
a negative utopia, the image of the chaotic orchestra also offers a far
more edifying and positive vision of the possibility of another kind of
harmonious society in which the desires of its members and the needs
of the group are reconciled.[45] *Prova d'orchestra* also holds out the possibility of harmonizing the forces of reason and the demands of the instincts, the ego and the id, that seem to have run amuck in the oratorio.
The German conductor cannot but suggest the paternal authority figures Fellini attacked in *Amarcord*, reminding us that Fellini's ideas
about the relationship of the individual to society have actually been
modified very little by the specific historical circumstances of political
terrorism surrounding the release of the film. Calling the film a representation of a "collective confusion," Fellini noted that most viewers
of the film projected their own fears and frustrations onto his fable, and
the somewhat hysterical reactions to the film from both left and right
in Italy seem to confirm his view.[46]

Perhaps even more importantly, however, *Prova d'orchestra* rests on
Fellini's fundamental belief in the redemptive qualities of art and the
therapeutic possibilities of the artisan's craftsmanship. The conductor's
declaration that following the music and playing the notes may save

[42] Oreste del Buono, "Prova a Cinecittà," in Fellini, *Prova d'orchestra*, p. 5.

[43] Fellini, *Prova d'orchestra* (pp. 121–45), contains excerpts from Fellini's many interviews on *Prova d'orchestra*, almost all of which attempt to deny a simply allegorical or merely political dimension in the film.

[44] Fellini, in *Comments on Film*, pp. 211–12, reports that he was personally con-
gratulated for such an idea one evening in a Roman restaurant, an interpretation he
defines as a "monstrous" error.

[45] Lorenzo Codelli, "Orchestra et choeur," in *Federico Fellini*, ed. Ciment, p. 109,
first identifies the film as a negative utopia.

[46] Fellini, *Prova d'orchestra*, p. 134.

the musicians underlines Fellini's unshakable faith in the humanistic potential of artistic creation and in the possibility of communicating this life-affirming message to his audiences. But the figure of the conductor is the film's major weakness. While Fellini certainly does not consider his German conductor to be the reflection of his concept of the artist in *Prova d'orchestra*, he fails to provide a character who does embody the redemptive power of art. This failure to distinguish clearly between the orchestra conductor who degenerates into a parody of Hitler and the true artist with redemptive potential weakens Fellini's basic argument that the conductor's Hitlerian traits illustrate repressive, reactionary forces triggered by anarchic disorder, forces which Fellini contrasts to art's powers to liberate us from the deleterious effects of fanatic belief in monolithic ideologies.

Ultimately both *Amarcord* and *Prova d'orchestra* portray individuals mesmerized by collective myths—fascism in Italy's recent past and revolutionary Marxism in its confused present. It is Fellini's fervent belief that the role of the artist in society must be that of attacking precisely such dehumanizing collective ideologies: "*unmasking the lie, identifying the unauthentic, and taking apart the indefinite or false absolutes* continues to be, for now, the only corrective resource—a mocking, inexhaustible safeguard—against our bankrupt history while we are waiting to be prepared to propose and to live under a new hypothesis of the truth."[47] Such pernicious myths condition human conduct in negative ways by causing us to submerge our precious individuality in the meaningless abstractions of political ideology. *Amarcord* and *Prova d'orchestra* are the most obviously political of all of Fellini's works. But the overt political themes in these two films should not obscure the fact that all of Fellini's works attack the dead weight of outmoded mythologies and ideologies and their detrimental effects on the individual.

[47] Federico Fellini, "*Casanova*: An Interview with Aldo Tassone," in *Federico Fellini: Essays in Criticism*, ed. Bondanella, p. 35.

CHAPTER SEVEN

"The Great Fabricator and Dissolver of Clouds"

SEXUALITY AND THE IMAGE OF WOMEN IN *GIULIETTA DEGLI SPIRITI, CASANOVA, AND LA CITTÀ DELLE DONNE*

The intention of the film [Giulietta degli spiriti] . . . is to restore to the woman her true independence, her indisputable and inalienable dignity. A free man, I mean, cannot do without a free woman. The wife must not be the Madonna, or an instrument of pleasure; and least of all a servant. . . . The independence of women is the theme of the future. . . . No, woman mustn't emancipate herself for imitation—which would be a development within the projection of that famous masculine shadow—but to discover her own reality, a different one. Different, it seems to me, from that of the man, but profoundly complementary and integral to it. It would be a step toward a happier humanity.[1]

FEW ASPECTS of Fellini's cinema have aroused as much interest in the past or as much antipathy in the present as his treatment of women and sexuality. Much of the emotional appeal of his early films may be explained by the impact of Fellini's female protagonists on his audiences. Such characters as Gelso-

[1] Fellini, "The Long Interview: Tullio Kezich & Federico Fellini," p. 63.

mina, Cabiria, and Sylvia elicit far more of Fellini's sympathy than their male counterparts Zampanò, Oscar, or Marcello. The women in Fellini's early works, as well as those in films for which he provided scripts during his neorealist apprenticeship, are often victims (many are prostitutes), but there is little doubt that when compared to their always less admirable male partners, Fellini's women play a humanizing role in a cruel world dominated by insensitive masculine values, while his male protagonists are consistently depicted as emotionally limited, superficial, or even brutish and cruel. Certainly, the image of women in Fellini's early cinema also reflects both the dominant Hollywood representation in the commercial film of the 1950s and 1960s as well as its more specific Italian variant.[2] Fellini's fondness for the prostitute figure in these early films, and the frequent casting of his wife, Giulietta Masina, in a number of such roles he scripted or directed, may well reveal an aspect of his unconscious that a feminist critic might employ to attack Fellini's views on sexuality. But the frequent presence of such characters is certainly not surprising in his early films, since they often exploit the religious motif of conversion for symbolic purposes. The theme of the redeemed prostitute has a literary pedigree that stretches back at least as far as Mary Magdalene; moreover, the motif of the fallen woman with a heart of gold has a long history in melodrama as well as in European decadent literature. And it should not be forgotten that until 1958, Italian males were, in most instances, first introduced to sexuality through visits to the then-legal brothels.

Conventional wisdom about Italy defines Fellini's milieu as a male-dominated society. According to this stereotypical and somewhat racist view, perhaps best expressed in American film criticism by Molly Haskell, even the most enlightened Italian men tend to think of women as "the awesome and all-powerful mother" who controls Italian society through her control of the family, the "only cohesive force among an anarchic and decentralized race," while "the idea of a professional woman is either inconceivable or intrinsically comic" in Italy.[3] Italian males are said to divide women into two categories—virgins and whores. Italian men wish to marry women from the first category but carry on illicit affairs with mistresses chosen from the second group.

[2] For discussions of women in the Italian cinema, see Giuliana Bruno and Maria Nadotti, eds., *Off Screen: Women & Film in Italy* (New York: Routledge, 1988); Patrizia Carrano, *Malafemmina: la donna nel cinema italiano* (Florence: Guaraldi Editore, 1977); Giovanni Grazzini, *Eva dopo Eva: la donna nel cinema italiano dagli anni Sessanta a oggi* (Rome: Laterza, 1980); and Giuseppe Turroni, *Viaggio nel corpo: la commedia erotica nel cinema italiano* (Milan: Moizzi Editore, 1979).

[3] *From Reverence to Rape: The Treatment of Women in the Movies* (New York: Penguin, 1974), p. 308.

294   CHAPTER SEVEN

Given Fellini's age, background, and nationality, it would be almost impossible for him not to have been exposed to such a sexist view of women, even if Haskell's indictment of all of Italian society for such a sexist foundation, like most such superficial generalizations about national traits, reveals little understanding of the many revolutionary changes in Italy's sexual mores that have taken place in the postwar period. As Fellini's cinema following *La dolce vita* turned introspective after the director's encounter with Jung and dream analysis, there is, in fact, a marked increase in Fellini's works in the number of what have become popularly identified as "Italian-type roles," "busty, maternal-type actresses," as Haskell labels them,[4] such as Carla of *8 1/2*, Susy of *Giulietta degli spiriti*, Enotea of *Fellini Satyricon*, and Gradisca of *Amarcord*, to mention only the most important. These and other similar female characters are sexually available, invariably generously endowed with enormous breasts and bottoms, and they characteristically lick their lips and stick out their tongues at the camera to indicate their rapacious sexual appetites. Their mere appearance on the screen seems designed to trigger the sexual fantasies of the Italian male.

The few sketches from Fellini's dream notebooks that have been published contain drawings of several such female figures, and they tend to fit the pattern of the sexual bombshell. These suggestive female images are so central to Fellini's private fantasy world that in one of them (previously discussed in relation to *La dolce vita*), a young Fellini in a hot-air balloon is told by the pope that an enormous woman represents the "great fabricator and dissolver of clouds." The sketch clearly implies that the inspiration for all of Fellini's cinema lies in such powerful female apparitions. Before them, the mature director's unconscious can only represent itself as a timid young boy, completely unequal to the power emanating from the goddesslike apparition he is viewing. A more suggestive and problematic sketch dated 1 April 1975 depicts a gigantic nude woman riding on a cloud driven by the force of Fellini's breath, while the director whispers: "Now it is time to fertilize what lies below." As the nude woman (identified only by her initial, "Ms. P.") drifts along in the sky, she seizes her enormous breasts, and a shining rain shower begins to fall on the earth below.[5]

The woman defined as the "great fabricator and dissolver of clouds" in the first sketch functions as an inspirational source of Fellini's imagination, but the fact that she is mediated (and limited) by the presence of the pope will no doubt convince suspicious feminists that the sketch

[4] Ibid., p. 309.
[5] For a color photograph of this dream sketch and Fellini's analysis of it, see Fellini, "Fellini oniricon," p. 39.

39. Fellini's dream notebooks: a nude woman on a cloud fertilizes the ground below at Fellini's command

merely demonstrates how the Church, the ultimate origin of Guido's sexist mentality in *8 1/2*, also dominates the fantasy world of Guido's creator. In the second sketch the female figure represents a kind of fertility goddess, but the fact that Fellini himself appears in the dream image and manipulates the woman's actions by his presence may well imply that she is merely a projection of Fellini's unconscious, therefore embodying the same type of limited male image of woman that feminists criticize in Fellini's cinema.

Feminist viewers of Fellini's films will no doubt interpret such material as proof that Fellini's artistic vision is tainted by the same kind of sexist stereotyping of women that observers of the Italian scene so often criticize. Given the current climate of critical opinion, it is unlikely that Fellini will be given much credit for providing what he believes to be an honest picture of his fantasy life in his dream sketches even at the risk of making public the defects and prejudices that the director himself recognizes in his personality. There are more than a few critics who would agree with one feminist's recent evaluation that "in Fellini's films, as in all patriarchal representations of gender in Western culture, sexuality is located in Woman, but, like desire and meaning, it is the property and the prerogative of man. All of sexuality, that is, refers to man."[6] From a feminist perspective, Fellini's images of women and his treatment of sexuality privilege male fantasies or stereotypes projected upon women by Fellini and other Italian males. When such projections become part of Italian popular culture by virtue of the cinema's enormous impact on the popular imagination, these fantasies are transformed into restrictive impositions that limit women's potential. As a result, few critics concerned with feminist issues have examined Fellini's works sympathetically except to cite them as negative examples to be deplored, and Fellini's cinema has played little part in the contemporary critical discussion over the issue of how women have been or should be represented in the cinema.[7]

And yet, in his public pronouncements on the subject, Fellini has paradoxically agreed completely with the general feminist premise that condemns traditional commercial cinema for sexual stereotyping:

> I think the cinema is a woman by virtue of its ritualistic nature. This uterus which is the theater, the fetal darkness, the apparitions—all create a projected relationship, we project ourselves onto it, we become involved in a series of vicarious transpositions, and we make the screen assume the character of what we expect of it, just as we do with women,

[6] Teresa de Lauretis, "Fellini's 9 1/2," in *Technologies of Gender: Essays on Theory, Film, and Fiction* (Bloomington: Indiana University Press, 1987), pp. 104–5.

[7] At least one important feminist theorist, Germaine Greer, has defended Fellini's "Latin" perspective on women as worthy of more serious consideration, even if such a view stands in direct contrast to the Anglo-Saxon image of the liberated female as a professional woman rather than a mother: "Fellini is truly cunt-struck—intrigued, amazed, and in awe of the female. . . . Where *Homo sapiens* subsp. *nordicus* (e.g., Roman Polanski) is able to relate only to *girls*, the Latin man is subject to women, and in particular to monumental, stern, and silent women. The unseen woman to whose house the Italian man returns every night to sleep is an external superego or a reality principle anchoring his fantasies. The people who sneer at this mother fixation have absorbed a notion of the female (and especially the liberated female) as a non-mother. Perpetual girlhood is the nightmare from which modern feminism hopes to wake up; the Latin schema is an existing alternative, which, though probably invalid, is worth examination and consideration, by no means to be rejected out of hand" ("Fellinissimo," *Interview*, December 1988, p. 103). For a view of female sexuality remarkably atuned to Fellini's thinking, see Camille Paglia, *Sexual Personae: Art and Decadence from Neferiti to Emily Dickinson* (New Haven: Yale University Press, 1990).

upon whom we impose ourselves. Woman being a series of projections invented by man. In history, she became our dream image.[8]

While feminist critics and theorists suspect his cinema of reflecting an age-old masculine bias, Fellini concurs with their attack on mainstream cinema's representation of women through projections of male fantasies.[9] The fact that Fellini's statements on the representation of women in the cinema coincide with the general lines of recent feminist film theory suggests that the depiction of women and sexuality in Fellini's cinema may actually be far more complex a critical problem than has been previously realized by suspicious feminist critics.

That ambiguity characterizes Fellini's treatments of sexuality may best be observed in the harem sequence of *8 1/2*, the most blatant visualization of an unrepentant sexist fantasy in Fellini's cinema.[10] In this sequence, which takes place in a farmhouse kitchen from Guido's childhood, all the women in Guido's life are present and subservient to his wishes. His wife cooks, cleans, and makes no emotional demands on him; his mistress looks on without jealousy as other women pander to Guido's every infantile need; best of all, from Guido's point of view, the women are convinced that this is how things *should* be. Suddenly, Jacqueline Bonbon, a dancer and Guido's former girlfriend, rebels against Guido's house rules that exile women over the age of twenty-six to the quarters upstairs. There, Jacqueline will be well treated but forced to "live basking in her memories" (shot 541) without Guido's love. Jacqueline's objections to this male regulation lead to a general revolt against Guido's domination of the harem, but after a brief struggle with a bullwhip, Guido triumphs to the applause of the assembled and adoring women.

Such a brief description of the harem sequence indeed makes it appear to be the ultimate sexist dream, in which women exist only to satisfy male needs. But the perspective that Fellini provides the viewer offers not only a representation of Guido's sexist fantasy but also a cri-

[8] Cited in Gideon Bachmann, "Federico Fellini: 'The Cinema Seen as a Woman . . . ,' " *Film Quarterly* 34, no. 2 (1980–1981): 8.

[9] Laura Mulvey's "Visual Pleasure and Narrative Cinema," which first appeared in 1975 in *Screen*, has perhaps defined the boundaries of this critical debate more than any other single work. It is reprinted in the "Feminist Criticism" section in Bill Nichols, ed., *Movies and Methods: Volume II* (Berkeley and Los Angeles: University of California Press, 1985); and in Constance Penley, ed., *Feminism and Film Theory* (New York: Routledge, 1988). It has influenced all subsequent feminist work in film theory, including Teresa de Lauretis, *Alice Doesn't: Feminism, Semiotics, Cinema* (Bloomington: Indiana University Press, 1984); and her previously cited *Technologies of Gender*, in which Fellini's *Giulietta degli spiriti* is analyzed.

[10] For a shot-by-shot breakdown of the continuity script of this famous sequence, see Fellini, *"8 1/2": Federico Fellini, Director*, pp. 140–56 (shots 509–74).

tique of its assumptions. The fact that the harem occurs in Guido's mind in a place associated with his childhood suggests that the dream reflects Guido's desire to regress to the safety of infancy and is not the expression of the dreamworld of a mature male. The most surprising thing about the harem sequence is that it represents the exact opposite of what a harem usually connotes. Rather than a hedonistic garden of earthly delights where Guido chooses one or more compliant maidens to warm his bed, Guido is actually more interested in security, warmth, and protection than sex, a fact underlined by the way in which he is bathed and wrapped in swaddling clothes just as his nannies had done years earlier after baths in the wine vats. Of all the women in his wish-fulfillment dream, Guido's nannies—and not his ex-mistresses—are most dear to him. Far from selecting a whorish partner for bedroom gymnastics, Guido is actually looking for a protective mother more than a mistress. Fellini clearly intends the harem sequence to stand as a devastatingly comic critique of Guido's character, not as a praiseworthy and unself-conscious representation of a male sexual fantasy. While Fellini's harem sequence allows us to see the scene from Guido's perspective, it also provides the careful viewer with a vantage point from which Guido's sexist, wish-fulfillment fantasies are gently but effectively ridiculed.

While all of Fellini's works have something of significance to offer the viewer on the topic of women and sexuality, *Giulietta degli spiriti*, *Casanova*, and *La città delle donne* focus in large measure on these issues, and each film reflects an important stage in the evolution of Fellini's thinking on the matter. *Giulietta* analyzes a crisis of identity (sexual and otherwise) in the life of a middle-aged Italian housewife. *Casanova*, a box office disaster but one of Fellini's most original works, offers a personal interpretation of the archetypal Italian "Latin" lover, the Venetian rake and adventurer whom generations of Italian males would claim as their role model. And finally, in *La città delle donne*, Fellini introduces an Italian male into a feminist convention, forcing a modern would-be Casanova (played by Marcello Mastroianni) to confront a group of angry women who are demanding that traditional Italian sexual attitudes be radically altered. *Giulietta* may rightly be called one of the first significant postwar Italian films devoted to a sensitive analysis of women's social status in Italian culture, and, as such, it anticipated the perspective of the woman's movement in Italy. In it, Fellini attempts to represent the breakup of a marriage from the woman's point of view. *Casanova* and *La città delle donne* continue Fellini's exploration of human sexuality but maintain a masculine perspective that is nevertheless criticized. Fellini's portrayal of how men fantasize or dream about women in both these films and his depiction of how male representations of women are mediated by the cinema itself add an important dimension to Fellini's treatment of women and provide visual evidence to substantiate the director's view that mainstream cinema has distorted feminine reality by reducing its variety and complexity to the projection of male fantasies upon the silver screen.

Giulietta degli spiriti represents Fellini's first artistically motivated decision to shoot a feature-length film in color. His earlier and briefer *Le tentazioni del dottor Antonio* employed color only because the producers had decided to use it in all the episodes of *Boccaccio '70*.[11] The shift from black and white to color was dictated by Fellini's interest in dreams, Jungian dream analysis, and the composition of his dream notebooks:

> I don't think I would have done it [*Giulietta*] in black and white. It is a type of fantasy that is developed through colored illuminations. As you know, color is a part not only of the language but also of the idea and the feeling of the dream. Colors in a dream are concepts, not approximations or memories. . . . In a dream color is the idea, the concept, the feeling, just as it is in truly great painting.[12]

As in the conception of *8 1/2*, Fellini's encounter with Jung influenced the narrative structure of *Giulietta*. Indeed, one persuasive analysis of the film argues that the female protagonist of *Giulietta* (played by Fellini's wife, Giulietta Masina) embodies the characteristics of the Jungian *anima* of Guido, the protagonist of *8 1/2*.[13] In his essay "Marriage as a Psychological Relationship" (1925) Jung argued that "every man carries within him the eternal image of woman," an image that is "fundamentally unconscious, an hereditary factor of primordial origin engraved in the living organic system of the man, an imprint or 'archetype' of all the ancestral experiences of the female, a deposit, as it were,

---

[11] Fellini underlines this point in "The Long Interview: Tullio Kezich & Federico Fellini," p. 32.

[12] Ibid. Fellini goes on to add that black-and-white film offers "more room for the imagination" and that when film employs color to "mimic" reality, it actually impoverishes its imaginative qualities; he also characterizes as a romantic and reactionary remark his own comment, uttered during the shooting of *Le tentazioni del dottor Antonio*, that "there are only two colors you can use in the cinema—black and white" (ibid., p. 35).

[13] See Carolyn Geduld, "*Juliet of the Spirits*: Guido's Anima," in *Federico Fellini: Essays in Criticism*, ed. Bondanella, pp. 137–51. The story of Fellini's encounter with Jung's works through his friendship with the distinguished Jungian analyst Ernest Bernhard is recounted by Aldo Carotenuto in *Jung e la cultura italiana*, pp. 137–49. During the production of *Giulietta degli spiriti*, Fellini wanted to show the film to Bernhard, but the analyst suddenly died before he could do so, an event that had been foretold in one of Fellini's dreams.

of all the impressions ever made by woman. . . . The same is true of the woman: she too has her inborn image of man."[14] Jung calls this feminine aspect of men the *anima* and defines the masculine aspect of women as the *animus*; he believed that while the *anima* has an erotic and emotional character, the *animus* possesses a rationalizing one. Jung's most interesting idea in his explanation of these important psychological types is that both sexes project the aspect of their psyche of the opposite sex onto the objects of their desire. Thus, a man seeks out a woman onto whom he may project his particular *anima*, while a woman does much the same thing with her *animus*. The result, according to Jung, goes a long way toward explaining the age-old cliché that members of opposite sexes never fully understand each other.

With its discussion of unconscious male and female tendencies in members of the opposite sex, Jungian psychology implies that the unified human psyche would somehow be androgynous and incorporate something from both human genders. This is a notion that has fascinated Fellini since his reading of Jung's works first suggested it to him. One of his unrealized projects, *Una donna sconosciuta*, based on a story by Bernardino Zapponi, would have examined the various stages of a slow transformation or metamorphosis of a man into a woman.[15] It is Fellini's belief that male and female sexuality are not polar opposites but are complementary forces—a fundamental assumption of Jungian thought. It is the director's acceptance of the androgynous nature of human sexuality, and not because his sexist prejudices force him into representing Giulietta's problems from a purely male perspective, that prompts Fellini to structure the narrative of *Giulietta* after the story line of *8 1/2*.[16] Guido's childhood memories in the farmhouse kitchen to which he happily returns in his fantasies to construct his dream harem find a parallel in the school play in which young Giulietta plays a Christian martyr roasted on a grill by the Romans because she refuses to reject her faith. Giulietta's husband Giorgio (Mario Pisu) resembles Guido in many respects. He is a superficial philanderer who plans to run away with a model he has met in his public relations work. Giulietta's religious upbringing, like that of the young Guido, who suppos-

---

[14] *The Portable Jung*, p. 173.

[15] A discussion of this abandoned project, including two sketches by Fellini, may be found in Ciment, ed., *Federico Fellini*, pp. 22–27; it is also discussed by Zanelli, *Nel mondo di Federico*, pp. 54–58.

[16] For an extremely detailed outline of the structural similarities between the two films, see Geduld, "*Juliet of the Spirits*: Guido's Anima." Geduld's heuristic suggestion that Juliet represents Guido's anima is accepted by Teresa de Lauretis, whose negative feminist viewing of *Giulietta* departs from Geduld's insight but employs it as proof that Fellini's representation of Giulietta is fundamentally male-centered ("Fellini's 9 1/2," p. 103).

edly met the devil when he danced with the prostitute named La Saraghina on the beach near the church school he attended, has even more disastrous effects on the mature woman and wife Giulietta has become. And Giulietta's mother and sisters are little help in Giulietta's attempts to establish her independence from her husband and to achieve a measure of psychological freedom by following her own individuality.

That Giulietta lives in her husband's shadow is established in the film's first few scenes. An opening shot of the family's residence at the Roman beach resort of Fregene reminds the viewer both of a dollhouse and of Magritte's famous painting *The Empire of Light*. It is both an explicit comment on the status of Giulietta's marriage—a doll house contains a doll, not a mature woman in full control of her destiny—and an implicit cue that the unconscious, the surrealist painter's subject matter, will constitute the theme of the remainder of the film.[17] As the camera travels through the trees outside the house and inside the home, it constantly frames Giulietta in a variety of puzzling perspectives. She is photographed from behind as she sits at her makeup table, or gazing into the mirror and trying to decide whether to wear a wig or her natural hair for the special supper she has lovingly prepared on her wedding anniversary. As Giulietta moves about the house, we catch glimpses of everything but her face. This is revealed to us only as Giorgio's arrival home is announced. Only then are we shown her smiling face framed by a medium shot and illuminated by the kind of romantic backlighting typically employed to highlight female characters during the 1940s. This striking visual effect suggests that Giulietta's existence, like her illuminated face on the screen, depends entirely on the "light" of her husband's presence. Without it, she is totally eclipsed as an individual.

In a film analyzing a failed marriage from the wife's perspective, it comes as no surprise that Fellini sees Giulietta's insensitive husband Giorgio as a major cause of her crisis. But Giorgio is only part of Giulietta's problem. And it is a measure of Fellini's intellectual honesty (a

---

[17] The Italian script of *Giulietta degli spiriti* may be examined in Fellini, *Quattro film* (Turin: Einaudi, 1974); an English translation appears in Fellini, *Federico Fellini's "Juliet of the Spirits,"* the original manuscript of which is held in the Lilly Library's Fellini archive, catalogued as Fellini MS. 9 (Box 2). Criticism on this film is relatively sparse. In addition to the previously cited essays by de Lauretis and Geduld, see Costello, *Fellini's Road,* pp. 149–203, the longest and most important analysis of the film in English, or his "Fellini, Juliet, and the Feminists, or: What Does Fellini Think about Women?" *Michigan Academician* 15, no. 2 (1983): 293–300; Jon Solomon, "Fellini and Ovid," *Classical and Modern Literature* 3, 1 (1982): 39–44; and Marguerite Waller, "Neither an 'I' nor an 'Eye': The Gaze in Fellini's *Giulietta degli spiriti,"* in *Romance Languages Annual,* ed. Ben Lawton and Anthony Tamburri (West Lafayette, Ind.: Purdue Research Foundation, 1990), pp. 75–80.

trait rarely acknowledged by his critics) that *Giulietta degli spiriti* shows us more than merely the predicament of a middle-aged housewife who must deal with the infidelities of her husband. Giulietta's weak self-image must also be explained, in large measure, as a result of the *women* who surround her.[18] They offer contradictory advice, present radically different patterns of behavior that they expect Giulietta to follow, and constantly pound her with critical suggestions not unlike the frenetic nagging Guido suffers in *8 1/2*. Giulietta's elegant mother (Caterina Boratto) reprimands her for not using enough lipstick or dressing fashionably. She clearly implies that it is Giulietta's fault if Giorgio is no longer attracted to her. Her two sisters, Adele (Luisa Della Noce) and Silva (Silva Koscina), stand in dramatic contrast to Giulietta in physical appearance and attitude. One is happily pregnant, while the other is a sexy television announcer. Neither lacks a strong self-image or her mother's respect.

For Fellini, an individual's past represents a potential source both of psychic blockage and of growth and development. In every individual's past there are traumatic events that must be uncovered, confronted, and finally overcome in order to achieve a state of equilibrium. In *Giulietta degli spiriti*, as in *8 1/2*, Fellini employs a series of stunningly beautiful sequences that represent fantasies, daydreams, visions, and flashbacks to show the viewer how Giulietta's past impinges upon her present. The role "spirits" play in Giulietta's drama becomes clear in a seance that follows Giorgio's arrival home on their anniversary. An effeminate clairvoyant calls up two spirits—Iris and Olaf. The first female spirit, probably the personification of Iris, the deliverer of messages for the Greek gods, announces her message: "Love for everyone." But the second spirit, Olaf, calls one of Giulietta's friends a whore and then tells Giulietta that she is nothing to anyone, causing her to break the circle in a faint.

Soon afterward, while Giulietta is sunning herself on a nearby beach with some friends, she tells a doctor that as a child she was able to conjure up spirits merely by closing her eyes. As she does this, the figure of a beautiful woman appears on a trapeze. Opening her eyes, Giulietta sees the arrival of a strange boat and a group of equally strange people, including a sensual woman in a bikini who looks exactly like the ballerina of the trapeze act. During the course of the film, we shall discover that the ballerina is Fanny, a circus performer for whom Giu-

---

[18] The Italian women in Giulietta's life may well be dominated by values and role models American feminists find objectionable. But to argue that such women are totally motivated by the *male* values of the director and have no counterparts in Italian society during the mid-1960s denies the well-documented power of peer group pressure upon individuals, male or female, in any society.

lietta's grandfather (Lou Gilbert) abandoned his job as a schoolteacher. The woman on the beach who is Fanny's double is Susy (both roles are played by Sandra Milo). Susy seems to be the radical personification of both Iris and Fanny. She puts Iris's dictum of "Love for everyone" into practice with great vigor and determination, but she also lives in an exotic home next to Giulietta's by the beach that suggests, in many respects, the exotic circus where Fanny performs.

Before Giulietta can achieve psychic freedom, she must come to terms with these ghosts from her past and their manifestations in women from her present. Giulietta closes her eyes again on the beach and falls asleep. Now Fellini reconstructs a dream with obvious psychoanalytical implications. The color and tone of the images recall surrealistic painting. A man is pulling a rope ashore and hands it to Giulietta, who continues to pull on it, bringing ashore a boatload of savages armed with swords, several horses (one of which is dead), and a strange assortment of grotesque and frightening individuals. A passing jet plane brings Giulietta out of this nightmare suddenly, but we shall later learn that the man with the rope is the detective Giulietta has hired to track down Gabriella, her husband's mistress, while the frightening savages originate from the circus where Fanny met her grandfather.

Giulietta's disturbing visions continue to appear, and while they have initially been inspired by the crisis of confidence following Giulietta's suspicions of Giorgio's infidelity, her malaise goes much deeper than a marital crisis. In fact, the women in Giulietta's dreams seem to cause her the greatest psychological pain. At the request of several of her women friends, Giulietta visits an Indian mystic named Bhisma (Valeska Gert), an androgynous creature who criticizes Giulietta's sexual habits in a manner that deepens the rebukes of her mother and gives a completely sexual twist to Iris's message of "Love for everyone." Giulietta is informed that her body should be the battleground of love: love is a religion; she is its priestess, with her husband as her god and her body as its altar. Bhisma asks Giulietta if she has bought a pair of black net stockings and defines love as a "trade" before correcting him/herself to call it an "art." This last remark provokes Giulietta to exclaim indignantly that Bhisma's view of love equates it with prostitution. During this conversation, Iris suddenly appears to Giulietta as Fanny on her circus horse.

Returning from her visit to Bhisma in a car, Giulietta recalls how her grandfather ran off with Fanny, and her recollection triggers a flashback to the circus attended by a young Giulietta and her grandfather in the company of her elegantly dressed mother, who is described as an imperious queen. Giulietta imagines her grandfather escaping with Fanny in an old airplane. We see the circus savages and understand their ear-

lier presence in Giulietta's nightmare on the beach. And the grandfather delivers a line that most certainly reflects Fellini's personal senti-
ments: "A beautiful woman makes me feel more religious."

Some time later, after returning from a visit to the private detective's
office, in which she has examined proof of Giorgio's infidelity, Giulietta goes to see her sculptress friend Delores (Silvana Joachino), who
specializes in sensual male models and defines God as a "beautiful
body." Giulietta replies that as a child, she believed God to be concealed behind a window. Her remark triggers the most important flashback of the film, that of the play performed by the young Giulietta's
church school. Many of the characters from the circus flashback are
also present: Giulietta, her mother, her grandfather, the headmaster of
the school. The play tells the story of a Roman martyr who chose to die
rather than renounce her faith before the Roman emperor. Not surprisingly, it is little Giulietta who plays the martyr, a role she will continue
to act out during her marriage to Giorgio. Placed upon a grate over simulated coals, the virtuous martyr is hoisted up toward heaven and toward the window behind which Giulietta and her friend Laura believe
God is concealed. Just before the grate reaches the window (and the
vision of God), Giulietta's anticlerical grandfather intervenes and stops
the performance, to the embarrassment of Giulietta's mother and the
rage of the headmaster. We later learn that Laura commits suicide (one
of the alternatives presented to Giulietta during the course of the film),
and the fact that the two young girls never saw what was concealed
behind the window explains, in part, the traumatic impact of this childhood event.

Giulietta's recollection of the school play represents an enormous
step forward in her self-awareness, a development underlined by the
fact that both the adult Giulietta and the young child are present in the
school play sequence—the adult figure as spectator of the dream and
the child as its protagonist. Yet, Giulietta's reaction to this experience
does not lead her toward individual self-fulfillment. Instead, she decides to experiment with the radical libertinism Bhisma advocated by
attending a party at Susy's nearby home without Giorgio. Susy's home
is decorated in a lavishly extravagant manner, with a variety of bright
colors, especially the passionate hue of bright red. Giulietta now
dresses in a seductive fashion in a bright red dress, a costume and an
attitude in sharp contrast to her usual manner and clothing style,
which suggests the docility and subjugation of a downtrodden Chinese
coolie. As she enters the party, Giulietta has determined to follow Susy's example. The party atmosphere is established by a game re-creating
the ambience of a bordello: various guests walk down the stairs, simulating the common practice in a brothel, and the other guests make

lascivious comments. When Giulietta walks down the stairs and everyone watches, her face is once more concealed by shadows, recalling the
way her face was photographed while she was waiting for her husband
to return home to celebrate the wedding anniversary that he had forgotten. Fellini obviously believes that Giulietta's individuality suffers
not only from her subordination to her husband but also from her decision to adopt modes of behavior (in this case, the sexual libertinism
of Susy) dictated by her female peers and relatives.

Giulietta is accompanied to Susy's bedroom (complete with a mirror
on the ceiling and a seashell-shaped slide leading to a swimming pool),
where Susy introduces her to a young sheik, the godson of her Arabic
lover and the perfect touch for this garden of Oriental delights. Now,
however, a number of Giulietta's "spirits" begin to collide: when Susy
calls to Giulietta, we hear Bhisma's voice, not hers; the voice of Iris
tells Giulietta to accept Susy's advice and take her as a teacher; and
finally, just as Giulietta is about to be seduced, her past interrupts the
seduction as a vision of the martyr on her burning grate in the school
play appears overhead in the ceiling mirror, causing Giulietta to run
from the bedroom and from Susy's teachings.

At this point in the narrative, Giulietta begins to become unraveled,
just as Guido collapsed toward the end of 8 1/2 and imagined commit-
ting suicide. While a group of Giorgio's friends come home for a garden
party (and Giorgio busily arranges to leave his wife for his mistress Gabriella), the planes of everyday reality and fantasy collide. Giulietta begins to see strange spirits and apparitions all around her from both her
past and her current nightmares. The voice of her childhood friend
Laura calls from beneath the water of the lily pond and tells her to kill
herself to find tranquility, as she did. The nuns from the school play
intermingle with Nazi soldiers, the young sheik from Susy's party, the
headmaster, the grandfather, the private detective, the circus barbarians, and her grandfather's plane. However, it is Giulietta's mother who
seems to be the key to the difficulties Giulietta experiences as an adult.
With the imperious manner of the queen Giulietta remembers from the
circus scene, the mother orders Giulietta not to open a nearby door. But
Giulietta disobeys her, telling her that she is no longer frightened of
her, and with these words, as if by magic, the door opens, revealing the
young Giulietta inside tied down to the martyr's grate. As the adult
Giulietta frees the child Giulietta and they embrace, all the evil spirits
and apparitions haunting her suddenly begin to disappear by means of
rapid dissolves. Even the friendly figure of the grandfather leaves, telling Giulietta that she no longer needs him and that he, too, was a fig-
ment of her imagination, an invention of her fantasy. The film then
concludes with Giulietta outside her house, walking alone from screen

40. *Giulietta degli spiriti*: in her fantasy, the adult Giulietta releases the young Giulietta from captivity in the school play

left to screen right, "the conventional film sign for progress: moving on and ahead."[19] As Fellini has explained the film's ending,

> Juliet alone, at the end of the film, should mean the discovery of an individuality. The thing she feared the most, the departure of her husband, is revealed as a gift of providence. Juliet will no longer depend on the paternal figure of Giorgio, who has, nonetheless, enriched her life. To him, too, as to everyone and everything, Juliet feels grateful because they all—even those who seem the most fearful enemies—helped the process of her liberation.[20]

Fellini has declared over and over again that what interests him most is the freedom of the individual, the liberation of each man and woman from the outmoded mythologies or traditions of the past that obscure

[19] Geduld, "*Juliet of the Spirits*: Guido's Anima," p. 151.
[20] Fellini, "The Long Interview: Tulio Kezich & Federico Fellini," pp. 64–65.

their individuality and throw up obstacles to their growth into whole, integrated adults. Giulietta, like Guido before her, can come to grips with her problems only when she resolves the conflicts in her distant past. While Fellini sees each individual's past as a burden and an obstacle to be overcome, it also represents a source of potential freedom and liberation. For Fellini, the past may redeem the present through *acceptance*, not through rejection. Giulietta does not reject her past; in fact, she embraces it when she hugs the young child she once was. She feels no bitterness toward her husband, only disappointment and a sense of lost possibility. But she comes to realize that only she can free herself, that we are all liberated from our subservience to our past the moment we realize we have the capacity to be free. Even more importantly, with her grandfather's parting remark about his illusory character, Giulietta has embraced Fellini's view that our lives and our histories are fabricated from illusions and fantasies. If we react to them neurotically, we can destroy our lives. But if we accept such "spirits" as the building blocks of our present personality, just as Giulietta recognizes that even Giorgio has added something positive to her life, since his behavior has triggered her search for a stronger sense of self, then such spirits become benevolent—"friends," as Giulietta calls them at the close of the film. While Giulietta has liberated herself from the dead weight of her past and has transcended her husband's shadow to reach the clear sunlight of freedom, this development comes about as the result of self-acceptance, not because of any ideological consciousness-raising. Giulietta, like Guido, comes to realize that the most frightening monsters populating our nightmares are those we ourselves create. Giulietta is now free to choose the direction of her life by herself. The director offers no formulae for her future, nor any comforting vision through an edifying conclusion. Instead, Giulietta's journey has only begun.

With *Casanova*, Fellini presents a highly personal interpretation of Italy's archetypal Latin lover. The contrast between the optimistic and open-ended conclusion reflecting Giulietta's victory over the malevolent spirits within her, on the one hand, and the far darker, pessimistic, and even morbid analysis of male sexuality in the person of Giacomo Girolamo Casanova (1725–1798), on the other, could not be drawn more sharply.[21] Fellini's initial attitude toward his protagonist was

[21] For the Italian script of *Casanova*, see *Il "Casanova" di Federico Fellini*, ed. Gianfranco Angelucci and Liliana Betti (Bologna: Cappelli, 1977); in the absence of an English translation, a novelized "retelling" of the film, sometimes unfaithful to the final cut, may be examined in Bernardino Zapponi's *Fellini's "Casanova"* (New York: Dell, 1977). The dialect poetry composed by Andrea Zanzotto for the film may be found in his *Filò: per il "Casanova" di Fellini* (Milan: Mondadori, 1988). A fascinating collection of Italian commentary on the film, occasioned by a television spe-

completely negative. He described Casanova (Donald Sutherland) as a man who has traveled throughout the entire world but

> it is as if he never got out of bed. He is really an Italian, *The* Italian: the indefiniteness, the indifference, the commonplaces, the conventional ways, the facade, the attitude. And, therefore, it is clear why he has become a myth, because he is really nothingness, universality without meaning . . . a complete lack of individuality, the indeterminate. . . . The film is aimed at being precisely this kind of portrait of nothingness.[22]

Fellini further declared that his total lack of sympathy for the literary persona of the celebrated Venetian adventurer also suggested the "only possible point of view" for his film: "a film on nothingness . . . a mortuary-like film, rendered without emotion . . . nonlife with its empty forms which are composed and decomposed, the charm of an aquarium, an absentmindedness of sea-like profundity, where everything is completely hidden and unknown because there is no human penetration or intimacy."[23] The decision to dub the film in English, which was forced upon Fellini by his producer (Alberto Grimaldi) in exchange for a concession to shoot the work at Rome's Cinecittà rather than in London, provided an additional element of cultural alienation and linguistic estrangement to the project. This use of English imitated, quite unintentionally, the same linguistic operation undertaken by Casanova himself, who chose to compose his life's story in French rather than Italian to ensure a wider audience for his book.

Yet, Fellini's repeatedly expressed antipathy for the historical figure

---

cial in Italy on the topic, may be examined in Liliana Betti and Gianfranco Angelucci, eds., *Casanova rendez-vous con Federico Fellini* (Milan: Bompiani, 1975), and contains the single most important interview with Fellini on the film (pp. 138–45), translated as "*Casanova*: An Interview with Aldo Tassone." For critical commentary on *Casanova*, see Pier Marco De Santi and Raffaele Monti, eds., *Saggi e documenti sopra "Il Casanova" di Federico Fellini* (Pisa: Quaderni dell'Istituto di storia dell'arte dell'Università di Pisa, 1978); Antonio Chemasi, "Fellini's *Casanova*: The Final Nights," *American Film* 1, no. 10 (1976): 8–16; Elio Benevelli, *Analisi di una messa in scena: Freud e Lacan nel "Casanova" di Fellini* (Bari: Dedalo Libri, 1979); Millicent Marcus, "Fellini's *Casanova*: Portrait of the Artist," *Quarterly Review of Film Studies* 5 (1980): 19–34; and Markulin, "Plot and Character in Fellini's *Casanova*." Casanova's autobiography, upon which Fellini's shooting script is loosely based, was first published in 1821. Only in 1960 did a critical edition of the original manuscript in its entirety appear. For the only reliable English translation of it, see *History of My Life*, trans. Willard Trask, 12 vols. (New York: Harcourt, 1966). For Casanova's life and times, see John Masters, *Casanova* (New York: Bernard Geis, 1969); or Maurice Andrieux, *Daily Life in Venice in the Time of Casanova* (New York: Praeger, 1972).

[22] Fellini, "*Casanova*: An Interview with Aldo Tassone," pp. 29–30.

[23] Ibid., p. 28.

of Casanova, an extraordinary attitude for an artist engaged in spending millions of hard-to-raise dollars on a film dedicated to that figure, must surely constitute a textbook case of psychological resistance. Whenever Fellini has created extraordinary but despicable male protagonists in his works, such as Zampanò of *La strada*, his initial aversion to such characters seems to arise from the fact that the director reveals so much of himself in their negative qualities. As a major Italian Casanova scholar quite rightly remarked when asked about Fellini's selection of Casanova as the subject of a film, "I do not exclude the fact that Fellini may actually succeed in concealing himself in his character. Thus, this apparent hatred may hide, underneath, a true affection."[24]

Casanova must be interpreted from the perspective of the opening sequence, a fanciful creation of a Venetian carnival scene on the lot of Cinecittà. Fellini's set designer, Danilo Donati, created a Venice of the imagination in which the Rialto Bridge stands near the bell tower on Saint Mark's Square, an obvious falsification of the actual geography of the city on the sea.[25] On this fanciful city square surrounded by what will soon be revealed to be an equally artificial plastic body of water, Fellini creates a civic ritual celebrated by the Venetians accompanied by original poetry written by his friend Andrea Zanzotto, Italy's most important living poet. When Fellini asked Zanzotto to supply the lyrics chanted during this opening sequence, he explained the scene in this fashion:

> It is a ritual that unfolds at night on the Grand Canal, from whose depths must arise a gigantic black head of a woman. A kind of deity of the lagoon, the great Mediterranean mother, the mysterious female who lives in each of us, and I could continue on for a bit, adding with incautious nonchalance other suggestive psychoanalytical images. The ceremony is, in a sense, the ideological metaphor of the entire film; in fact, at a certain point this obscure and grandiose fetish object, not yet completely out of the water, returns to the water's depths because its pulleys snap and its ropes break; in short, the large head must submerge again, sinking deeply

[24] Piero Chiara, cited in Kezich, *Fellini*, p. 449. Millicent Marcus, in "Fellini's *Casanova*: Portrait of the Artist," argues that Fellini employs Casanova as the "perfect vehicle for the artist's anxieties about the loss of his own creative powers" (p. 29); Marie Jean Lederman, in "Art, Artifacts, and *Fellini's Casanova*," *Film Criticism* 2, no. 1 (1977), states that the film is about neither Casanova nor sex but, instead, "clearly a projection of feelings of guilt and fears of failure . . . his fears about his own place in time and eternity as a man and, more importantly, an artist" (p. 43).

[25] For Donati's discussion of how the sets were created in such a fanciful manner, the exact opposite of the kind of faithful reproduction typical of Luchino Visconti (with whom Donati worked in Milan), see "Danilo Donati: prime idee grafiche per *Il Casanova*," in De Santi and Monti, *Saggi e documenti*, pp. 93–97.

into the waters of the canal and remaining down there forever, unknown
and unreachable.[26]

As the crowd, dressed in traditional Venetian carnival costumes, looks
on, their doge, the titular ruler of the republic, grasps a scimitar and
cuts a long ribbon, declaring that he is cutting the placenta in order that
the figure represented by the large head may be reborn.[27] His action
releases a figure dressed as an angel and holding a sword, who descends
on a cable from the top of the nearby bell tower toward the water,
splashing into the lagoon. As the workmen pull on their ropes, the head
that Fellini describes in the letter above slowly emerges from the
murky waters. Its sexual connotations are underlined by the crowd as
they chant in dialect a refrain: "Aàh Venessia aàh Venissa aàh Venùsia."
This refrain establishes the link in Fellini's film between Casanova's
birthplace (Venice) and the ancient goddess of love (Venus). But the
chant then becomes a bawdy hymn in praise of the submerged sexual
powers of what Fellini calls the "Mediterranean mother," the alluring
yet terrifying potential for procreation all women possess that at the
same time both attracts men to women and makes them insecure in
their presence, since the female reveals to man his own incapacity to
give birth to new life: "Fornicating cunt, defecating ass, subterranean
old hag, stinking old woman, o great cunt, powerful cunt, coquette and
embroiler who is given to us by lot as bride and mother, mother-in-law
and step-mother, sister and grandmother, daughter and Madonna, we
order you with sweat and with work to flourish for him who knows
how to seize you."[28] The doge's reference to the cords of the placenta,
and the angel's sudden immersion into a body of water, make it clear
that Fellini's opening ritual celebrates a birth, Casanova's, just as the
conclusion of the film completes a life cycle and anticipates Casanova's
death. The image representing feminine procreative powers—the head
of Venice/Venus—appears but quickly returns to the depths of the
murky lagoon, a location suggesting the boundless possibilities of sexual creation, just as the mysterious labyrinth in *Fellini Satyricon* had
symbolized the myriad paths of the psyche. The angel whose immersion into the lagoon's dark waters triggered the momentary appearance
of the great Mediterranean mother Venice/Venus wears a strange corset

---

[26] Federico Fellini, private letter to Andrea Zanzotto (dated July 1976), in Zanzotto,
Filò, pp. 3–4.

[27] For the original Latin of the doge's declaration, see Fellini, *Il "Casanova" di
Federico Fellini*, p. 86.

[28] The original lines in Venetian dialect are reprinted in ibid., p. 87, showing a
slight change from Zanzotto's original verse, reprinted in Zanzotto, *Filò*, pp. 29–31.
I cite Millicent Marcus's translation from her essay "Fellini's *Casanova*: Portrait of
the Artist," p. 31.

41. *Casanova*: the head of Venus that sinks beneath the Venetian lagoon

or waistcoat, similar to the unusual undergarment Casanova wears in every one of his erotic encounters and never takes off even during his most intimate moments. Every viewer of the film has been puzzled by this bizarre costume. One plausible explanation for the garment is that it symbolizes his fear of castration.[29] Such a psychoanalytical explanation would also help to explain Casanova's sexual athleticism. Born in the shadow of Venice/Venus, and, like every other man, incapable of understanding or performing the ultimate mystery of procreation himself, Casanova can only combat his inadequacy with a frantic and ultimately insatiable compulsion to perform the sexual act over and over again.

The compulsive and mechanical nature of Casanova's lovemaking finds perfect expression in the strange, phallic-shaped bird that he carries everywhere with him, even into prison. The frenetic pumping motion of this mechanical toy, and the strange music that accompanies it on the sound track, suggest mechanical entertainments, such as merry-go-rounds. Moreover, in every instance that Casanova is framed by the camera as he is making love, he repeats the mechanical bobbing up and down of the bird, a movement closer to a gymnastic routine or even a stylized modern dance number than true passion or sexual arousal.[30] Casanova's amorous liaisons are spectacles or performances, not physical expressions of true emotion. When Casanova makes love with Maddalena (Margareth Clementi), the mistress of the French ambassador, just after the Venetian carnival scene opening the film, her lover observes the spectacle and comments on its fine points afterward. When Casanova makes love with the Marquise d'Urfé (Cicely Browne), as she believes she will be transformed into a man by Casanova's "great work" in her bed, Casanova is observed by his mistress Marcolina (Clara Algranti), who is forced to uncover her posterior to arouse Casanova's ardor with the older woman.

Sex is reduced to the level of an athletic event at the home of the English ambassador in Rome, Lord Talou (John Karlsen), who presides over a sexual contest between Casanova and his coachman Righetto (Mario Gagliardo) that is called a struggle between intelligence and brute force, the test of whether the "noble savage" exalted by "that great bore Rousseau" can match a "gentleman with style and culture."[31] At the Albergo dei Mori in Dresden, Casanova encounters a troupe of Italian opera singers and a former mistress named Astrodi (Marika Rivera), who introduces Casanova to a hunchbacked actress

[29] Benevelli, *Analisi di una messa in scena*, p. 16.
[30] See Markulin, "Plot and Character in Fellini's *Casanova*," p. 67, for a fine discussion of this question.
[31] Fellini, *Il "Casanova" di Federico Fellini*, p. 165.

with an enormous red tongue (Angelica Hansen). The encounter ends in an orgy in which Casanova copulates with a good part of the troupe while onlookers on the balcony masturbate, combining the notion of theatrical spectacle with that of mechanical sex. The usual mechanical music accompanying Casanova's bird speeds up and slows down exactly like that of a music box needing rewinding. This sense of lost energy is appropriate at that point in the film, since Casanova is rapidly approaching old age and death.

When Casanova finally reaches the end of his life in Bohemia, where he serves as the librarian to the castle of Dux, he has a dream of his native Venice which Fellini re-creates on the set where the head of Venus/Venice had sunk into the lagoon during the opening carnival sequence. Now we see the lagoon at night during the winter: the air is filled with fog and the water is frozen over, but underneath the ice Casanova can still discern the eerie eyes of the head gazing toward him and us. A number of the women in his life appear (including his mother), but they all run away and vanish on the ice. The pope, in a golden carriage, smiles at Casanova in a paternal way and motions to a figure nearby. It is Rosalba (Adele Angela Lojodice), a beautiful mechanical doll with whom Casanova had years earlier danced at the court of Württemberg and with whom he had made love in one of the few instances during his life when his passion was not accompanied by his mechanical bird. Casanova goes to Rosalba on the frozen lagoon, and after an extreme close-up of Casanova's old, bloodshot eyes, the camera frames the two dancing upon the ice. But now Casanova and the doll make no movements: Casanova's mechanical life and his frenzied sexual appetites have transformed him, like Rosalba, into a mechanical man who turns around and around with his partner on the frozen lagoon as if he were a cog in a machine.

I have already suggested that Casanova's sexual athleticism, manifested through the Venetian's mechanical perspective on sexuality, may well be the product of a sense of inferiority when confronted with the female and her potential for procreation. This idea finds substantial confirmation in one of the most unusual sequences of the film, that set in London. After Casanova is unceremoniously thrown out of a carriage with his mechanical bird by Madame Charpillon and her daughter (both his mistresses), he decides to commit suicide and walks into the Thames with rocks in his pockets, reciting the lyric poetry of Torquato Tasso (another man of letters that the Romantic period saw as destroyed by love). At the last moment, he spots a gigantic woman on the shore and decides to live, following her to a nearby circus. There, although Casanova does not realize that the woman (Sandy Allen) has disappeared into the body of an enormous female whale, Casanova sees

42. *Casanova*: Casanova dances with the only woman he ever really loved, a mechanical doll

a long line of men marching silently into the mouth of the whale, called by a circus barker "La grande Mouna." But the whale is clearly a euphemistic image for the female womb, a fact underlined by the name given to it by Tonino Guerra's verse which the barker shouts ("Mouna" suggests the Venetian word "mona" or "cunt," the key word in the chant opening the carnival scene). In addition, at least one of Fellini's preparatory drawings, published in Zanzotto's volume of verse written for *Casanova*, portrays the scene with a huge nude woman, not a whale, through whose outstretched legs the lines of men at the fair march.[32]

Inside the body of the whale/womb, Casanova encounters a magic lantern, the forerunner of the contemporary cinema, projecting frightening drawings by Roland Topor of the *vagina dentata*: they depict the female sexual member as a vortex into which men are dragged, as a spiderweb, and even in the likeness of the devil. This link of the projection of male sexual fantasies (or fears) to the Enlightenment equivalent of the cinema cannot help but recall Fellini's views on the feminine qualities of the cinema that were cited earlier in this chapter. In Fellini's early works, we have already observed how the director will frequently modify early versions of his scripts to tone down the overly obvious thematic ideas, preferring instead to rely on the evocative power of the image rather than the sometimes overly didactic dialogue. Bernardino Zapponi's prose "retelling" of the film in novel form probably reflects an earlier version of the script later modified during shooting or in editing when he describes Casanova's entrance into the whale in this fashion:

> "At last Casanova is back in the womb," says a voice. Who said that? Casanova wheels. No one is there (The voice was Fellini's).
>
> The spectacle that unfolds in the little whale-theater is amusing, if a bit shocking. A magic lantern projects images of female freaks on a screen. There are toothed vaginas, deformed bodies, and all the other features of a typical eighteenth-century '*summa monstruorum*.' . . .
>
> Giacomo looks on, fascinated by these horrendous deformities. Is this not perhaps, deep down, what women are really like? Is this the archetypal female to whom he, the eternal boy, is unconsciously drawn? Or is it a being to flee from—the terrible Vagina Dentata of legend?[33]

From Zapponi's retelling of the film's narrative, it is obvious that Fellini originally planned personal interventions into the screenplay similar to those we have already discussed in *Amarcord*. Later, realizing that such obvious emphasis on the film's narrative themes was unnec-

[32] Zanzotto, *Filò*, p. 36.
[33] Zapponi, *Fellini's "Casanova*,*"* pp. 113–14.

43. *Casanova*: the sketch of an early idea, a nude woman engulfing a line of men, that was later changed to the whale in the final film

essary and relying, as usual, on the expressive powers of the visual image, Fellini suppressed the temptation to interject his personal commentary into this sequence. But Zapponi's version does reveal the ambivalence toward the female that runs through this sequence. While the images projected by the magic lantern of the *vagina dentata* haunt the dark recesses of Casanova's psyche—and that of his creator—the giantess Casanova followed to the whale/womb and whom he meets there inside the animal's belly continues the theme of ambivalence toward women. She first defeats Casanova and a number of other men in tests of strength, thereby giving substance to male fears of the female's awesome powers. But later, as she bathes with her two dwarf attendants, she hums a childhood lullaby, "Cantilena londinese," composed by Zanzotto for the sound track.[34] She thus embodies a maternal aspect mysteriously combined with her awesome powers to overwhelm her male admirers.

Fellini has called Casanova's *Memoirs* only an aggravating "telephone book of artistically non-existent and sometimes most boring occurrences," and its author a proto-Fascist, an anticipation of the personality type depicted in *Amarcord* characterized by "protracted adolescence."[35] And yet, as always, Fellini's negative judgment of his embattled protagonist from the perspective of the prosecution is mitigated by extenuating circumstances brought forward by the major witness for the defense, the director himself. The final image of Casanova as an old man dreaming of his native Venice and dancing a last waltz upon the frozen lagoon with a mechanical doll, the only woman in his entire life he has really understood and whom he emulates in his last moments on the screen by becoming a mechanical creation himself, cannot be judged too harshly. As one critic has accurately described it, this closing vision is a celebration of the imaginative act of the artist, which, like the ice, can freeze an image and hold it before the mind's eye.[36] It is this implicit parallel between the aging Venetian rake and the no longer youthful director that ultimately moves Fellini to pardon Casanova's faults and to admit him to the pantheon alongside other flawed male protagonists in his cinema—Zampanò, Marcello, and Guido, to mention only the most important—who were just as incapable of comprehending the ultimate mystery of Woman as Fellini has shown Casanova to have been.

Casanova's confrontation with the Eternal Feminine constitutes a tragedy, in part precisely because he serves Fellini as an alter ego, representing the figure of the artist confronted with old age and mutabil-

---

[34] See Zanzotto, *Filò*, pp. 37–45; the poem reflects Zanzotto's interest in *petèl* (baby talk, infantile language).

[35] Fellini, "*Casanova*: An Interview with Aldo Tassone," pp. 27, 30–31.

[36] Marcus, "Fellini's *Casanova*: Portrait of the Artist," p. 33. Over a decade after the release of *Casanova*, in the 1988 BBC documentary "Real Dreams Into the Dark with Federico Fellini," Fellini admitted that his own views of women were similar to those of Casanova: "Casanova dances with an imaginary woman who is a shadow because . . . *that* is his destiny, or at least the destiny I gave the character Casanova, just as, in short, I identified him with . . . with me . . . not in the sense of a lover of women but in the sense of a man who *cannot* love women insofar as he loves a fantastic idea of women."

ity. In contrast, Fellini hoped his depiction of a modern-day, would-be
Casanova named Snàporaz (Marcello Mastroianni) and a group of
women at a feminist convention in *La città delle donne* would create a
comic portrait of the problematic relationships between men and
women in his cinema even if, by his own admission, the negative critical reaction to the film when it appeared suggests that his original intentions missed their mark.[37] While the link between Casanova and
Fellini was only implied, in *La città delle donne* the close relationship
between Fellini and his alter ego Mastroianni becomes an integral part
of the comic structure of the narrative and explains, in large measure,
the origin of the ideas behind the film's images of sexuality and desire.

The ironic tone of *La città delle donne* is revealed as the film credits
begin. A woman giggles off-screen and makes the remark, "With Marcello, again? Please, Maestro!"[38] Fellini thus reminds us even before a
single image is revealed that this is not the first time Mastroianni has
played a character identified with Fellini himself; the obvious reference
is to *8 1/2*, in which Mastroianni portrayed a movie director with
doubts and anxieties about his work as well as about the women in his
life that mirrored some of Fellini's own personal problems. The title
"City of Women" literally refers to a feminist convention the male protagonist attends. But it must also be understood figuratively as, first,
Snàporaz's unconscious, and, second, the cinema itself. With its attention to the dream state and metacinematic discourse, *La città delle
donne* continues an association that we have already examined in a
number of earlier and later works.[39]

[37] Fellini's remarks are to be found in the documentary "Real Dreams." While the
criticism on this film is not vast, given its negative performance at the box office
and the initially hostile reception it was given by some reviewers, two analyses of
the film are worth close attention: Marie Jean Lederman, "Dreams and Vision in
Fellini's *City of Women*," *Journal of Popular Film and Television* 9, no. 3 (1981):
114–22; and Gaetana Marrone-Puglia, "Memory in Fellini's *City of Women*," *Perspectives on Contemporary Literature* 9 (1983): 12–20. Sonia Schoonejans, in *Fellini*
(Rome: Lato Side Editor, 1980), offers a woman's perspective on the making of the
film, but Raffaele Monti, ed., in *Bottega Fellini—"La città delle donne": progetto,
lavorazione, film* (Rome: De Luca, 1981) provides the most detailed account of the
creation of *any* Fellini film; this work constitutes an invaluable source of information on Fellini's craftsmanship on the set. Of special interest, of course, is Fellini's
interview with Gideon Bachmann entitled "Federico Fellini: The Cinema Seen as a
Woman," which was given on the occasion of the release of *La città delle donne*.
Federico Fellini, *La città delle donne* (Milan: Garzanti, 1980) contains the third version of the film's script, but it differs significantly from the final version and should
be employed with caution, although the volume contains extremely interesting remarks by both Fellini and Andrea Zanzotto.

[38] I translate from the film itself; this line is not in the published script.

[39] Indeed, in at least one instance in the dialogue, Snàporaz asks the rhetorical

The story of *La città delle donne* consists of a long, uninterrupted dream experienced by Snàporaz (Fellini's nickname for Mastroianni in real life) that begins just as the credits end. The viewer does not realize this fact immediately, however, since the first scene of the film shows Snàporaz *waking up* in a train compartment, not going to sleep. Snàporaz's dream traces an imaginary visit to the "city of women" by the dreamer—a visit that takes place after he descends from the train. As Snàporaz awakens in his train compartment, he sees a beautiful, seductive woman in a fur hat and boots seated across from him (Bernice Stegers). Since her beguiling smile seems to promise a quick and uncomplicated sexual liaison, he follows her into the washroom, where his attempted couplings are hindered by the movements of the train, and then, more importantly, by the woman's imperious attitude as she challenges him to prove his virility. Suddenly this mysterious woman pulls the emergency lever to stop the train and walks off into a field. As Snàporaz follows her, she takes several photographs of him and then disappears into the Hotel Miramare, where she is attending a feminist convention.

The direct link between Fellini and Snàporaz becomes clear when this same mysterious woman from the train addresses an assembled crowd of militant feminists at the hotel, as Snàporaz looks on with increasing apprehension. In her speech she accuses Snàporaz of only pretending to want to know women better: "The eyes of that man who is circulating among us are the eyes of the eternal male that deform everything they see in the mirror of derision and ridicule. The rascal is always the same. We women are only pretexts to permit the narration on one more occasion of his bestiary, his circus, his neurotic avanspettacolo, and we are there just to serve as [his] clowns."[40] While her accusations are explicitly aimed at Fellini's alter ego, they obviously make much sense when applied to Fellini himself. That her charges are aimed both at the film's protagonist and at its director becomes crystal clear immediately after Snàporaz leaves the auditorium as quickly as possible under the woman's attacks and enters the hall of the hotel,

question "What kind of film is this?" rather than the question he might be expected to ask—"What is going on here?" (author's translation from the sound track). Even though the published script does not accurately reflect the dialogue of the final film and lacks this particular line, on at least two occasions, the published script contains similar metacinematic remarks by Snàporaz. Once he says to Katzone: "But don't I say anything in this film? Do you always talk?" (Fellini, *La città delle donne*, p. 95). At the end of the film in the published script, when Snàporaz asks his wife if he has been sleeping for as long as two hours, she replies: "Yes, during the entire film" (ibid., p. 120).

[40] Author's translation from the film (this scene is not included in the published script).

where a large crowd of angry feminists are waiting for him as he descends the staircase. On one side of the hall we see a poster of an enormous egg in a cup: the top half of the egg contains two large open eyes, while on the right side of the cup, a huge spoon is ready to open the egg and, presumably, to remove the eyes. The eyes on the egg belong to Fellini, and nowhere else in the entire film does the director better clarify the root cause of Snàporaz's anxieties, as well as his own, than in this scene underlining the fear of castration dominating the dreamer's experiences during the film's narrative.[41] While this particular scene links the protagonist's castration anxieties to those of the director, the entire film is filled with similar threats to Snàporaz as women kick the genitals of a male dummy in a gymnasium, fire pistols at airplanes, and eventually machine-gun balloons. Fellini not only exploits the well-known associations between flying and sex by showing the airplanes and balloons attacked by women, but he also employs the equally familiar linkages between blindness, eyesight, and castration as Snàporaz experiences increasing difficulties holding onto his glasses during the moments of his dream when he feels the most threatened.

Indeed, everything about Snàporaz's dream is menacing and fraught with double meanings. When a buxom girl named Donatella (Donatella Damiani) rescues him from the crowd of feminists and pushes him into a skating rink, his remark that he has not skated for many years, and the fact that numerous women are skating skillfully there without any other men present, reveals how skating and sex are linked in Snàporaz's unconscious. The relative ease with which the women skate represents, within the dream, Snàporaz's belief that female sexuality has unlimited potential. Male sexuality, on the other hand, is constantly threatened by a recalcitrant sexual organ often incapable of obeying its master's will and now the target of ideologically aroused women whose desire to change the traditional relationship between the sexes is seen as potential castration. Snàporaz's sexual anxieties arise from the gap between his fantasies of gargantuan sexual repasts and his less than sensational performance (a fact underlined by the coitus interruptus in the train). While the entire narrative of this film embodies the images

---

[41] Monti, in *Bottega Fellini*, pp. 84–85, notes that the eyes are those of Fellini, a detail that will escape viewers who have not met the director personally. Lederman, in "Dreams and Vision in Fellini's *City of Women*," seems unaware of the fact that the eyes in the egg belong to Fellini, but her discussion of Fellini's symbolic use of the scene is excellent, and she also calls our attention to an important dream Fellini experienced just before he began *Giulietta degli spiriti* in 1965 (reported by Kezich in "The Long Interview: Tullio Kezich & Federico Fellini," p. 23). In this dream, probably the ultimate origin of the scene with the egg in *La città delle donne*, Fellini imagines that he loses one of his eyes to a similar spoon. Lederman diagnoses this fear as symptomatic of castration anxiety.

from Snàporaz's dream, it is significant that none of the sexual activities Snàporaz recollects during his visit to this oneiric "city of women" constitutes a complete sexual experience to orgasm. Each time in the narrative/dream that the dreamer seems to approach the ultimate experience, he is thwarted or delayed in some comic and humiliating fashion. Besides this physical humiliation, Snàporaz's failures are doubly troubling to his unconscious since they occur in the presence of the threatening females whose implied sexual superiority over men is the root cause of his anxiety.

If Snàporaz represents the vulnerable, neurotic, and sympathetic aspect of male sexuality, the psyche of his counterpart Katzone (Ettore Manni) may be explained by the etymology of his name ("Big Cock") and the name of his villa (Dux, the Latin word for "leader" that Italian Fascists often employed to refer to Mussolini, Il Duce). Katzone admires d'Annunzio, inhabits an art deco mansion (the period style of both Mussolini and Fellini's childhood), and is about to celebrate his ten thousandth female conquest. In his home, there is a passageway with the photographs of all the women with whom he has made love, complete with recordings of their cries of passion. In Katzone's villa, Snàporaz mysteriously encounters his wife Elena (Anna Prucnal), as neurotic and estranged from him as Guido's wife was from him in *8 1/2*, but when Katzone's celebration is interrupted by a group of women dressed as police officers, Elena dances with one of them (perhaps underlining the dreamer's fear of being replaced by his wife with a lesbian lover) while Katzone goes off in tears after the police have killed one of his giant mastiffs, genuflecting before a marble statue of his mother and kissing her repeatedly. Fellini seems to suggest here, as he did earlier in *Casanova* and other works, that the Italian male's fixation on his mother may well represent the ultimate cause of the aggressively sexist behavior typical of individuals such as Katzone.

As Snàporaz realizes it is time to go to bed, Donatella appears once again with another girl on the stairway and dances down the steps. Snàporaz dons a top hat and dances with them both in imitation of Fred Astaire to American music before being given a nightshirt, as the adolescent he will always remain, and being tucked into bed. In psychoanalytical terms, Snàporaz has now begun to regress to his childhood, a happier and more secure time than the present, which is populated by castrating females. Elena now appears in hair curlers, and in a grotesque parody of their marital love life, she practically rapes him before turning away and immediately falling asleep, in imitation of Snàporaz's habitual practice when he makes love with Elena in real life.

Now Snàporaz's most important dream fantasy occurs, and, not surprisingly, it is directly linked to the cinema, the ultimate goal of this regression during the dream. Crawling under the bed, our hero leaves the bedroom and slides down a gigantic toboggan lit up by thousands of lights that recall those on a theater marquee. Fellini's camera moves through a series of eight scenes introduced by circles of these lights, each circle introducing a different sexual fantasy from Snàporaz's past. First we see the legs of a singing maid during Snàporaz's childhood from the young boy's perspective under the table; the buxom woman kisses the young boy and hugs him maternally.[42] The next woman is a sensual fishwife, who handles the eels she sells in a provocative fashion and licks her lips in anticipation. She is followed by a series of different women, all past objects of Snàporaz's desire: a masseuse at a spa; several female motorcyclists dressed in leather jackets from a circus sideshow; a woman dressing in a beach tent who sports a hairdo and bathing suit from the 1930s; a woman at the cemetery; and a prostitute in a brothel whose posterior is exaggerated by a wide-angle lens.

Not only is each of these scenes shown through the lights of a theater marquee, but each one is depicted in such a fashion that it clearly represents constructions from a film set, not merely figments from Snàporaz's past. Male sexual memories are thus inextricably connected to images from the cinema. Ultimately, Fellini seems to be telling us, the sexual desires of men are those learned from the cinema, and the cinema's image of women has been inherited by generations of males who project this image from the Hollywood dream factory upon flesh-and-blood women, with sometimes disastrous results. The sixth scene of this fascinating sequence linking male sexuality to the cinema is the most explicit, for it pictures a huge bed on which dozens of boys are masturbating under the sheets while they gaze at an enormous movie screen on the wall. At first they see the kind of historical potboiler Fellini re-created earlier in *Roma*; then they see provocative images of Marlene Dietrich and May West. The scene emphasizes the relationship between masculine sexual desire and the cinema, just as it depicts Fellini's belief (and that of contemporary feminist theorists) that the image of woman in the movies is not an authentic representation of women's reality but, instead, a projection of male sexual fantasies.

If Snàporaz's cinematic fantasies underline the comforting aspect of the female object of desire, as the dreamer reaches the bottom of the toboggan and is suddenly locked inside a cage by a group of angry women, we are reminded once again that in Fellini's universe, the comforting, maternal, sexually attractive side of women does not obscure the darker side of their nature, that which threatens to emasculate and

[42] According to the account Fellini gave Germaine Greer, one of Fellini's first sexual experiences was with a maid named Marcella (Greer, "Fellinissimo," p. 103).

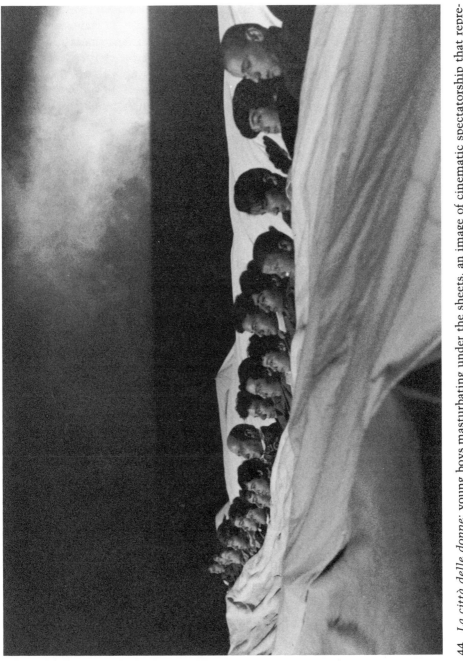

44. *La città delle donne*: young boys masturbating under the sheets, an image of cinematic spectatorship that represents for Fellini the essence of the cinema's male gaze

castrate. First Snàporaz is subjected to a kind of kangaroo court, what Fellini calls a "pre-ring," where he is asked to justify his having been born a male (to which he has no real response) and where other men are preparing to be sent into a huge boxing ring to compete with far superior women. When Snàporaz climbs up into the ring, he sees a huge balloon shaped like a woman with Donatella's features hovering above the ring with a long rope ladder dangling down from its basket. In a scene that the director himself has described as having been constructed from pure dream imagery,[43] Snàporaz climbs up into the basket. To the tune of an infantile lullaby (once again underlining his futile quest for security as well as sexual gratification), he attempts to fly away beneath this gigantic incarnation of the Eternal Feminine. But below on the ground, the real Donatella—now dressed as a terrorist with a ski mask covering her face and carrying a machine gun—shoots holes in the balloon. Snàporaz is brought down from the sky and abruptly awakens from his dream, as Fellini suddenly cuts to the film's opening setting, the train compartment.

Now wide awake, Snàporaz realizes he has been dreaming during the entire narrative of the film in the presence of his wife. Elena is seated opposite Snàporaz, wearing the fur hat and boots that the attractive woman of the first sequence in the compartment wore. That woman is there as well, along with the two dancers, Donatella and her partner (now students). All of the women smile at each other in a fashion that implies a sense of complicity between them and a superior understanding of Snàporaz's experience, while the dreamer, at first confused, decides to return to his dream and removes his glasses. As the train reenters the tunnel, Snàporaz reenters the womblike security of his dream. For Fellini, Snàporaz's experience has been a positive one: "This time he will dream because he is deciding to dream. It will be a vigilant dream, full of attention for the profound, a witnessing dream. He goes back consciously into the dream in order to have a more lucid contact with himself."[44]

Fellini believes that Snàporaz's misadventures in the "city of women," representing both the unconscious and memories from the cinema, are comic experiences, for they are produced by a total misunderstanding of the nature of the women populating this psychic city. In agreement with his feminist critics, Fellini admits that there are no real female protagonists in *La città delle donne*. Instead, there are only "thousands of faces, of mouths, of smiles, of looks, of voices."[45] No real

[43] Fellini makes this point in "Real Dreams."
[44] Bachmann, "Federico Fellini: The Cinema Seen as a Woman," p. 5.
[45] Ibid., p. 8.

CHAPTER EIGHT _____

La voce della luna
and the
Cinema of Poetry

How I like remembering, even more   _____
than living. And anyway, what dif-
ference is there?[1]

I have been invited to comment upon an event of this fantastic magnitude
[the capture of the moon]; forgive me, but I must confess to you my abso-
lute incapacity to do so. I can only repeat with the poet, "Nothing is
known, everything is imagined."[2]

I don't make films to debate theses or sustain theories. I make a film in
the same manner in which I live a dream, which is fascinating as long as
it remains mysterious and allusive but which risks becoming pointless
when it is explained. Just as we are doing now.[3]

VERY LOOSELY based on a first
novel by a young professor at the University of Bologna,[4] _La voce della_
luna returns Fellini to the provincial origins he treated with some nostalgia in _Amarcord_. Most of the shooting of the film was done not in
the studios of Cinecittà but in the newer studio complex on Rome's
Via Pontina known as "Dinocittà" because it was originally constructed by Fellini's former producer, Dino De Laurentiis. The setting
of the film is supposed to be the town of Reggiòlo, the home of Fellini's
adolescent idol, the caricaturist Nino Za, to whose residence Fellini
paid a visit to honor the artist's eighty-sixth birthday before he began
work on location for _La voce della luna_.

   The fact that the setting of _La voce della luna_ evokes a familiar pro-

---

[1] Federico Fellini, _La voce della luna_ (Turin: Einaudi, 1990), p. 27. This equation
of life and memory by Ivo Salvini also reflects Fellini's opinion.

[2] Professor Falzoni makes this comment (Fellini, _La voce della luna_, p. 127) when
asked to explain the significance of the capture of the moon by the inhabitants of
Reggiòlo. Falzoni's remark reflects an opinion held by Giacomo Leopardi, the nineteenth-century Italian poet whose verse is frequently quoted on the film's sound
track.

[3] Fellini, _E la nave va_, p. 169.

[4] Ermanno Cavazzoni, _Il poema dei lunatici_ (Turin: Bollati Boringhieri, 1987).

vincial atmosphere as well as one of the earliest artists to have an influence on Fellini points the attentive viewer of this film back in time toward Fellini's early cinema. The clear link between *La voce della luna* and Fellini's first films is most evident in the film's protagonists. Two of Italy's most popular comic actors portray characters with the same kind of diminished mental capacities that characterized Giudizio, the town fool of *I vitelloni*, or Gelsomina in *La strada*, a character type Fellini would employ successfully again with the mad Uncle Teo of *Amarcord*. One of these figures, Ivo Salvini (Roberto Benigni), has been released from a mental hospital. He has been proclaimed completely harmless, but he often hears voices coming from the depths of the many wells drilled in the farmlands of the area. In discussing the inspiration for Gelsomina in *La strada*, Fellini has described a curious figure from his grandmother's hometown:

> In Gambettola, there was a little boy, the son of farmers, who used to tell us that when the ox bellowed in the stable, he would see a huge piece of red lasagna come out of the wall, a sort of very long carpet floating in the air that would cross his head under his left eye and vanish, little by little, in the sun's reflection. This little boy used to say that once he even saw two large spheres of dark silver come off the bell tower while the clock struck two, and they passed through his head. He was a strange child, and Gelsomina had to be a bit like that.[5]

There seems to be a direct connection between Ivo and the boy who, years earlier, inspired in Fellini the figure of Gelsomina in Gambettola. Ivo describes equally paranormal experiences in the film in almost the same words Fellini uses in discussing his childhood memories of the strange little boy: "Do you see those little disks coming off the bell tower, don't you see them? There are the color of silver, antique silver. They enter through here and pass through my head in silence, yes they do!"[6]

Ivo's seemingly aimless wanderings about Reggiòlo provide what narrative structure *La voce della luna* contains, its picaresque quality constituting yet another link to Fellini's early cinema. Most of the characters Ivo encounters are slightly mad. Very few of the individuals populating this provincial setting are "normal," and most have some strange tic that sets them apart from average citizens. For example, a madcap oboist sleeps each night in the local cemetery in order to have a foretaste of death's silence. One of Ivo's friends, Nestore (Angelo Orlando), has married the town manicurist, a Gradisca-type bombshell named Marisa (Marisa Tomasi) who wants to make love constantly and

[5] Fellini, "The Genesis of *La Strada*," p. 183.
[6] Fellini, *La voce della luna*, p. 40.

is compared to a steam-powered locomotive in her single-minded pursuit of sexual passion. Nestore is slightly unbalanced, for after his wife leaves him for a virile motorcyclist, his favorite pastime is sitting on the rooftops amidst the ceramic tiles and television antennae. Nestore is also fascinated by the sound of the kitchen washing machine's centrifugal action, and in a burst of lyrical inspiration he compares it to the voice of a sea siren. The film's most absurd and poignant moments are produced by three somewhat demented brothers who manage to capture the moon with one of their huge farm machines and imprison it in their barn with ropes.

The most important of the characters Ivo meets is a former prefect named Adolfo Gonnella (Paolo Villaggio) who has lost his position because of his mental instability. While Ivo hears haunting voices, Gonnella interprets reality as merely a subterfuge, a fake canvas painted over the nothingness looming behind it. Gonnella is obsessed with what he sees as threatening plots all around him. Ivo, however, seems mesmerized by a young woman named Aldina Ferruzzi (Nadia Ottaviani). In one important scene, he gazes upon Aldina's moonlit face in her bedroom, linking the object of his sexual desire with the moon of the film's title in his confused mind. Aldina is elected "Miss Flour of 1989" in the local festival celebrating the famous flour dumplings (gnocche) consumed in the zone, a scene recalling I vitelloni and the many similar festivities in Fellini's early films.

Since Fellini's cinema is usually not directly indebted to literary models, the important role the poetry of Giacomo Leopardi plays in the dialogue of La voce della luna comes as somewhat of a surprise. But since Leopardi's Romantic verse employed the moon as a crucial poetic symbol in lyrics known to every Italian schoolchild, such uncharacteristic literary citations seem appropriate in this particular film. There is, in fact, a portrait of Leopardi in Ivo's childhood room where, as his grandmother remarks, his madness began. When Ivo gazes upon Aldina's face in the moonlight, forever linking the unattainable object of his sexual desire with earth's impassive satellite, his remarks combine lines from two of Leopardi's most famous poems treating the moon— "Canto notturno di un pastore errante dell'Asia" and "Alla luna."[7] Later, Ivo cites the second line of "La sera del dì di festa" in describing

[7] These lines are respectively "Che fai tu luna in ciel. Dimmi che fai, silenziosa luna" ("What are you doing in Heaven? O Moon, tell me, / What, O you silent Moon?"); and "travagliosa è la mia vita, ed è ne cambia stile o mia diletta luna" ("My life being full of travail; as it is still— / It does not change, O my sweet Moon"). For the context of these citations, see Fellini, La voce della luna, p. 32. I cite English translations of Leopardi's lyrics from Giacomo Leopardi: Selected Prose and Poetry, ed. and trans. Iris Origo and John Heath-Stubbs (New York: New American Library, 1967), pp. 258–59, 210–11.

the setting of the moon over the roofs and orchards of the town.[8] When a man named Onelio demands impatiently to know the meaning of the universe, eventually going berserk and shooting a pistol at the television screen set up in the town square for the press conference announcing the moon's capture, the entire scene provides a humorous parody of the unnamed narrator from Leopardi's "Canto notturno" whose desperate queries directed to an imperturbable moon about the meaning of life are never answered or even acknowledged by earth's indifferent satellite.

La voce della luna embodies a number of Leopardi's images or concepts connected with the moon, and includes, as well, a touch of Leopardi's depressing pessimism. While the setting of the film, the small town of Reggiòlo, may remind us in certain respects of the town made famous in *Amarcord*, Fellini's portrait of contemporary society is far less amusing and seems to have far less possibility of redemption than did the Amarcordians who lived under a Fascist dictator. The key to Fellini's critique of contemporary mass society, already introduced in *E la nave va*, *Ginger e Fred*, and *Intervista*, lies in his profound distrust of mass media, which, in his view, are more likely to convey irritating static than real information or communication. As a result, *La voce della luna* is characterized by an aggressive cacophony of competing sounds (blaring car radios, African street vendors screaming the merits of their wares, noisy beauty contests, the deafening roar of a hellish discothéque). This din is set in sharp contrast to the much quieter and reticent voices Ivo hears from the wells in the countryside, voices apparently inspired by the moon. Gonnella's visit to a discothéque reveals Fellini's impatience with the pandemonium of modern life: the ex-prefect stops disco dancers cold when he performs a stately waltz with an old girlfriend. When he seizes the disc jockey's microphone and asks the frenetic dancers if they have ever heard the sound of a violin, their complete lack of understanding shows that an entire generation of young people has apparently been rendered tone-deaf by the blaring amplifiers of contemporary popular music. Ivo and Gonnella are the only inhabitants of the town who seem to be listening to the real messages around them or are still open to any form of authentic human communication that has not been corrupted by the static of mass media. But both characters are considered by the townspeople to be insane. The notion that the mentally disturbed have a special capacity for human communication is not new to Fellini's work. But while *La voce della luna* consciously refers the attentive viewer back to the director's

---

[8] "E queta sovra i tetti e in mezzo agli orti / posa la luna" ("The quiet moon stands over roofs and orchards"): see *Giacomo Leopardi: Selected Prose and Poetry*, pp. 206–7. Ivo's citation (Fellini, *La voce della luna*, p. 75) differs slightly from Leopardi's original.

early "cinema of poetry"—and in particular to Gelsomina of *La strada*—as well as to the geographical setting of *Amarcord*, there is a sharply pessimistic tone in this film that was absent in both of the previous works.[9]

Viewers who interpret Fellini's impatience with rock music as yet another reactionary rejection of youth culture by a member of an older generation will miss the point. In fact, in numerous other films, Fellini has demonstrated a keen appreciation of the popular culture of the young. But, deeply concerned that the hectic pace of contemporary life has destroyed man's connections with the deepest reaches of his psyche—the source, for Fellini, of all useful knowledge as well as the poetic inspiration for the creation of any work of art—Fellini employs unmistakable symbols of our era, such as the discothéque or the television commercial, to dramatize his concerns.

The conclusion of *La voce della luna* depends upon our familiarity with the frequent interruptions of television broadcasts by advertising. As Ivo wanders near one of the wells from which emanate his secret voices, he gazes at a huge full moon upon which Aldina's shining face is illuminated. Throughout the film, Ivo has associated the moon with Aldina, the object of his sexual desire. Now the moon/Aldina informs Ivo that he is fortunate to have his voices, even if they disturb him and cause him headaches. Hearing them is a "great gift," and the moon/Aldina tells Ivo he should stop complaining about not understanding these voices: "You make me angry you're so lucky. You mustn't understand! It would be terrible if you understood! And what would you do then? You must only listen to them, only hear those voices and hope that they never tire of calling you."[10]

In the midst of this extremely important conversation focusing the viewer's attention on what is the central theme of *La voce della luna*, Fellini dramatizes the intrusive and aggressive quality of mass media by introducing a shocking interruption of the scene that parallels commercial messages on television. Aldina, the personification of the moon, clears her throat and shouts at the top of her lungs: "Commercial!" As if in response to her cry, even the sounds of nature obey her command. The sound track intensifies to a peak of disturbing static-filled noises that are nevertheless recognizable as the cries of locusts magnified many times over. With the full moon in the background, in the film's last shot, Ivo leans over a well in the field and remarks, "And

---

[9] See Gianfranco Angelucci, "Su *La voce della luna* e altre fellinità," *Cineteca* 6, no. 2/3 (1990): 10–11, for the most incisive critical analysis of this film which underlines Fellini's increasingly polemical distance from his contemporaries. For a photographic record of Fellini's work on the set of this film, see Federico Fellini, *La voce della luna*, ed. Lietta Tornabuoni (Florence: La Nuova Italia, 1990).

[10] Fellini, *La voce della luna*, p. 136.

45. *La voce della luna*: Ivo listens enraptured to the strange, suggestive voices emanating from the open wells under the moonlight

yet, I believe that if there were a bit more silence, if we all were a little bit quieter . . . perhaps then we could understand!"[11]

Ivo's closing remarks embody Fellini's personal belief that our instincts are a surer guide to the truth than our reason. This is why he has often created protagonists who may be judged as abnormal or slightly mad, from society's point of view, because only such characters are still capable of hearing the secret messages originating from our unconscious. The wells and their voices only Ivo can hear (even though

[11] Ibid., p. 137

with some difficulty) cannot help but remind us of the secret voices or sounds from nature that only Gelsomina was capable of comprehending in *La strada*.

Fellini's long career in the cinema has progressed through a number of very different films and a variety of stylistic innovations from his early *Luci del varietà* to the present. But there has been one crucial element in both his art and his life that has remained constant over more than four decades—his reliance upon the irrational, lyrical, and poetic insights that have their origins in his unconscious. In his early films, Fellini's special sensitivity to the irrational dimensions of human existence was mainly a result of instinct and was as yet uninformed by any disciplined study of the unconscious. In midcareer, Fellini encountered the works of Jung, and the Swiss psychoanalyst's insights inspired not only Fellini's personal dream notebooks but also an entirely different direction in his cinematic style after *8 1/2*. In Fellini's subsequent works, his interest in dreams and the unconscious merged with his fascination with metacinema. Fellini began to realize that, at least in his own life, recalling memories from a distant past, dreaming dreams, and making films were integrally linked together within his artistic temperament.

Federico Fellini's career began as a scriptwriter during the height of the neorealist era, when Italian directors were expected to take their cameras out into the streets of a war-ravaged nation and bring back a faithful portrait of the "reality" of everyday life. But Fellini believed then, and still believes now after over four decades of filmmaking, that the only reality the camera can describe is that which is within each one of us—the personal, subjective, and (in Fellini's case) poetic fantasy that each one of us possesses and can discover if only we will listen to its faint voice within us, as Ivo does in *La voce della luna*.

As Fellini has remarked, it is a mistake to define the cinema merely in terms of a camera full of film and a reality "out there," potentially ready to be captured by photography. Instead, in the director's words, when you make a film, "you only put yourself in front of the camera lens."[12] And yet Fellini would reject any accusation that he and his artistic creations merely embody an irrational impulse in contemporary culture. As Fellini is so fond of saying, the visionary, the creative artist who best succeeds in revealing himself through his art, is the only true realist.[13]

[12] Fellini, *Block-notes di un regista*, p. 62.

[13] Fellini, *Fellini on Fellini*, p. 120; Fellini, *Fare un film*, p. 113; or Fellini, *Fellini's Films: The Four Hundred Most Memorable Stills from Federico Fellini's Fifteen and a Half Films*, ed. Christian Strich (New York: Putnam's, 1977), title page.

FILMS SCRIPTED FOR OTHER DIRECTORS

(*Note*: This list includes *only* films that were actually completed, not scripts written for films never shot.)

1939: *Imputato alzatevi! (Defendant, On Your Feet!)*
DIRECTOR: Mario Mattoli
SCRIPT: Vittorio Metz, Mario Mattoli (Fellini not credited)

1939: *Lo vedi come sei? (Do You See How You Are?)*
DIRECTOR: Mario Mattoli
SCRIPT: Vittorio Metz, Steno, Mario Mattoli (Fellini not credited)

1940: *Non me lo dire! (Don't Tell Me!)*
DIRECTOR: Mario Mattoli
SCRIPT: Vittorio Metz, Marcello Marchesi, Steno, Mario Mattoli (Fellini not credited)

1940: *Il pirata sono io (The Pirate Is Me)*
DIRECTOR: Mario Mattoli
SCRIPT: Vittorio Metz, Steno, Marcello Marchesi, Mario Mattoli (Fellini not credited)

1942: *Avanti c'è posto (There's Room Up Ahead)*
DIRECTOR: Mario Bonnard
SCRIPT: Aldo Fabrizi, Cesare Zavattini, Piero Tellini, Federico Fellini (listed as scriptwriter in film's registration documents but not credited by film's titles)

1942: *Documento Z3 (Document Z3)*
DIRECTOR: Alfredo Guarini
SCRIPT: Sandro De Feo, Alfredo Guarini, Ercoli Patti (Fellini not credited)

1943: *Campo de' fiori (Campo de' fiori Square)*
DIRECTOR: Mario Bonnard
SCRIPT: Aldo Fabrizi, Federico Fellini, Piero Tellini, Mario Bonnard

1943: *L'ultima carrozzella (The Last Carriage)*
DIRECTOR: Mario Mattoli
SCRIPT: Aldo Fabrizi, Federico Fellini

1943: *Quarta pagina (The Fourth Page)*
DIRECTOR: Nicola Manzari
SCRIPT: Piero Tellini, Federico Fellini, Edoardo Anton, Ugo Betti, Nicola Manzari, Spiro Manzari, Giuseppe Marotta, Gianni Puccini, Steno, Cesare Zavattini (seven episodes, each scripted by different writers)

1943 (released in 1945): *Chi l'ha visto? (Who Has Seen Him?)*
DIRECTOR: Goffredo Alessandrini
SCRIPT: Federico Fellini, Piero Tellini

1943: *Gli ultimi Tuareg (The Last Tuaregs)*
DIRECTOR: Gino Talamo
SCRIPT: Federico Fellini and others (?)—film shot but never released

1944: *Apparizione (Apparition)*
DIRECTOR: Jean de Limur
SCRIPT: Piero Tellini, Lucio De Caro, Giuseppe Amato (Fellini not credited)

1945: *Tutta la città canta (The Whole City Is Singing)*
DIRECTOR: Riccardo Freda
SCRIPT: Vittorio Metz, Marcello Marchesi, Steno (Fellini not credited)

1945: *Roma città aperta (Rome, Open City)*
DIRECTOR: Roberto Rossellini
SCRIPT: Alberto Consiglio, Sergio Amidei, Roberto Rossellini, Federico Fellini

1946: *Paisà (Paisan)*
DIRECTOR: Roberto Rossellini
SCRIPT: Sergio Amidei, Klaus Mann, Alfred Hayes, Marcello Pagliero, Roberto Rossellini, Federico Fellini

1947: *Il delitto di Giovanni Episcopo (The Crime of Giovanni Episcopo)*
DIRECTOR: Alberto Lattuada
SCRIPT: Piero Tellini, Suso Cecchi D'Amico, Aldo Fabrizi, Alberto Lattuada, Federico Fellini

1947: *Il passatore (A Bullet for Stefano)*
DIRECTOR: Duilio Coletti
SCRIPT: Tullio Pinelli, Federico Fellini

1948: *Senza pietà (Without Pity)*
DIRECTOR: Alberto Lattuada
SCRIPT: Tullio Pinelli, Alberto Lattuada, Federico Fellini, Ettore Maria Margadonna

1948: *Il miracolo (The Miracle)*, part 2 of *L'amore (The Ways of Love)*
DIRECTOR: Roberto Rossellini
SCRIPT: Federico Fellini, Tullio Pinelli, Roberto Rossellini

1949: *Il mulino del Po (The Mill on the Po)*
DIRECTOR: Alberto Lattuada
SCRIPT: Riccardo Bacchelli, Mario Bonfantini, Luigi Comencini, Carlo Musso, Sergio Romano, Alberto Lattuada, Tullio Pinelli, Federico Fellini

1949: *In nome della legge (In the Name of the Law)*
DIRECTOR: Pietro Germi
SCRIPT: Aldo Bizzarri, Pietro Germi, Giuseppe Mangione, Mario Monicelli, Tullio Pinelli, Federico Fellini

1950: *Francesco, giullare di Dio (The Flowers of Saint Francis)*
DIRECTOR: Roberto Rossellini
SCRIPT: Roberto Rossellini, Federico Fellini, with the assistance of Father Félix Morlion and Father Antonio Lisandrini

1950: *Il cammino della speranza (The Path of Hope)*
DIRECTOR: Pietro Germi
SCRIPT: Pietro Germi, Tullio Pinelli, Federico Fellini

1951: *La città si difende (The City Defends Itself)*
DIRECTOR: Pietro Germi
SCRIPT: Pietro Germi, Tullio Pinelli, Giuseppe Mangione, Federico Fellini

1951: *Persiane chiuse (Drawn Shutters)*
DIRECTOR: Luigi Comencini
SCRIPT: Tullio Pinelli, Federico Fellini

1952: *Europa '51 (Europe '51)*
DIRECTOR: Roberto Rossellini
SCRIPT: Sandro De Feo, Roberto Rossellini, Mario Pannunzio, Ivo Perilli, Diego Fabbri, Antonio Pietrangeli, Brunello Rondi (Fellini not credited)

1952: *Il brigante di Tacca del Lupo (The Bandit of Tacca del Lupo)*
DIRECTOR: Pietro Germi
SCRIPT: Tullio Pinelli, Pietro Germi, Fausto Tozzi, Federico Fellini

1958: *Fortunella (Fortunella)*
DIRECTOR: Eduardo De Filippo
SCRIPT: Federico Fellini

1979: *Viaggio con Anita (A Journey with Anita)*
DIRECTOR: Mario Monicelli
SCRIPT: Tullio Pinelli (Fellini not credited)

FILMS DIRECTED BY FELLINI

1950: *Luci del varietà (Variety Lights)*
SCRIPT: Alberto Lattuada, Federico Fellini, Tullio Pinelli, Ennio Flaiano

PHOTOGRAPHY: Otello Martelli
MUSIC: Felice Lattuada
SET DESIGN: Aldo Buzzi
EDITING: Mario Bonotti
PRODUCER: Capitolium Film
CAST: Peppino De Filippo (Checco), Carlo Del Poggio (Liliana), Giulietta Masina (Melina), Johnny Kitzmiller (Johnny), Giulio Cali (Edison Will), Carlo Romano (Renzo), Folco Lulli (Conti)

1952: *Lo sceicco bianco* (*The White Sheik*)
SCRIPT: Federico Fellini, Tullio Pinelli, Ennio Flaiano
PHOTOGRAPHY: Arturo Gallea
MUSIC: Nino Rota
SET DESIGN: Federico Fellini
EDITING: Rolando Benedetti
PRODUCER: Luigi Rovere
CAST: Brunella Bovo (Wanda Cavalli), Leopoldo Trieste (Ivan Cavalli), Alberto Sordi (Fernando Rivoli), Giulietta Masina (Cabiria), Fanny Marchiò (Marilena Velardi), Ernesto Almirante (fotoromanzo director), Ettore Margadonna (Ivan's uncle)

1953: *I vitelloni* (*I Vitelloni, The Young and the Passionate*)
SCRIPT: Federico Fellini, Tullio Pinelli, Ennio Flaiano
PHOTOGRAPHY: Otello Martelli
MUSIC: Nino Rota
SET DESIGN: Mario Chiari
EDITING: Rolando Benedetti
PRODUCER: Peg Films–Cité Films
CAST: Franco Interlenghi (Moraldo), Franco Fabrizi (Fausto), Alberto Sordi (Alberto), Leopoldo Trieste (Leopoldo), Riccardo Fellini (Riccardo), Eleonora Ruffo (Sandra), Jean Brochard (Fausto's father), Claude Farrell (Alberto's sister), Carlo Romano (Signor Michele), Enrico Viarisio (Sandra's father), Lida Baarova (Giulia), Arlette Sauvage (woman in the cinema)

1953: *Un'agenzia matrimoniale* (*A Marriage Agency*), one episode in *Amore in città* (*Love in the City*)
SCRIPT: Federico Fellini and Tullio Pinelli
PHOTOGRAPHY: Gianni di Venanzo
MUSIC: Mario Nascimbene
SET DESIGN: Gianni Polidori
EDITING: Eraldo da Roma
PRODUCER: Faro Films
CAST: Antonio Cifariello (journalist), Livia Venturini (Rossana)

1954: *La strada* (*La Strada*)
SCRIPT: Federico Fellini, Tullio Pinelli, Ennio Flaiano
PHOTOGRAPHY: Otello Martelli
MUSIC: Nino Rota

SET DESIGN: Mario Ravasco
EDITING: Leo Catozzo
PRODUCER: Carlo Ponti and Dino De Laurentiis
CAST: Giulietta Masina (Gelsomina), Anthony Quinn (Zampanò), Richard Basehart (The Fool), Aldo Silvani (circus owner), Marcella Rovere (widow), Livia Venturini (nun)

1955: *Il bidone (Il Bidone, The Swindle)*
SCRIPT: Federico Fellini, Tullio Pinelli, Ennio Flaiano
PHOTOGRAPHY: Otello Martelli
MUSIC: Nino Rota
SET DESIGN: Dario Cecchi
EDITING: Mario Serandrei and Giuseppe Vari
PRODUCER: Titanus
CAST: Broderick Crawford (Augusto), Richard Basehart (Picasso), Franco Fabrizi (Roberto), Giulietta Masina (Iris), Lorella De Luca (Patrizia), Giacomo Gabrielli (Vargas), Sue Ellen Blake (Anna), Alberto De Amicis (Goffredo), Irena Cefaro (Marisa)

1957: *Le notti di Cabiria (The Nights of Cabiria)*
SCRIPT: Federico Fellini, Tullio Pinelli, Ennio Flaiano, with the collaboration of Pier Paolo Pasolini for dialogue
PHOTOGRAPHY: Aldo Tonti and Otello Martelli
MUSIC: Nino Rota
SET DESIGN: Piero Gherardi
EDITING: Leo Catozzo
PRODUCER: Dino De Laurentiis
CAST: Giulietta Masina (Cabiria), Amedeo Nazzari (actor), François Périer (Oscar D'Onofrio), Aldo Silvani (hypnotist), Franca Marzi (Wanda), Dorian Gray (Jessy), Franco Fabrizi (Giorgio), Mario Passange (cripple), Pina Gualandri (Matilda)

1959: *La dolce vita (La Dolce Vita)*
SCRIPT: Federico Fellini, Tullio Pinelli, Ennio Flaiano, Brunello Rondi
PHOTOGRAPHY: Otello Martelli
MUSIC: Nino Rota
SET DESIGN: Piero Gherardi
EDITING: Leo Catozzo
PRODUCER: Riama Film–Pathé Consortium Cinéma
CAST: Marcello Mastroianni (Marcello Rubini), Anouk Aimée (Maddalena), Anita Ekberg (Sylvia), Walter Santesso (Paparazzo), Lex Barker (Robert), Yvonne Fourneaux (Emma), Alain Cuny (Steiner), Annibale Ninchi (Marcello's father), Polidor (clown), Nadia Gray (Nadia), Valeria Ciangottini (Paola), Magali Noël (Fanny), Alan Dijon (Frankie Stout), and numerous minor characters

1962: *Le tentazioni del dottor Antonio* (*The Temptations of Doctor Antonio*), an episode in *Boccaccio '70* (*Boccaccio '70*)
SCRIPT: Federico Fellini, Tullio Pinelli, Ennio Flaiano
PHOTOGRAPHY: Otello Martelli
MUSIC: Nino Rota
SET DESIGN: Piero Zuffi
EDITING: Leo Catozzo
PRODUCER: Carlo Ponti and Antonio Cervi
CAST: Peppino De Filippo (Doctor Antonio Mazzuolo), Anita Ekberg (Anita), Donatella Della Nora (Mazzuolo's sister), Antonio Acqua (Commendatore La Pappa), Elenora Maggi (Cupid)

1963: *8 1/2* (*8 1/2*)
SCRIPT: Federico Fellini, Tullio Pinelli, Ennio Flaiano, Brunello Rondi
PHOTOGRAPHY: Gianni di Venanzo
MUSIC: Nino Rota
SET DESIGN: Piero Gherardi
EDITING: Leo Catozzo
PRODUCER: Angelo Rizzoli
CAST: Marcello Mastroianni (Guido Anselmi), Anouk Aimée (Luisa), Sandra Milo (Carla), Claudia Cardinale (Claudia), Rossella Falk (Rossella), Edra Gale (La Saraghina), Caterina Boratto (Beautiful Unknown Woman), Madeleine Lebeau (French actress), Barbara Steel (Gloria Morin), Mario Pisu (Mario Mezzabotta), Guido Alberti (Pace the producer), Jean Rougeul (Daumier the critic), Ian Dallas (Maurice the magician), Tito Masini (cardinal), Annibale Ninchi (Guido's father), Giuditta Rissone (Guido's mother), Yvonne Casadei (Jacqueline Bonbon), Marco Gemini (Guido as a schoolboy), Riccardo Guglielmi (Guido at farmhouse), and numerous other minor characters

1965: *Giulietta degli spiriti* (*Juliet of the Spirits*)
SCRIPT: Federico Fellini, Tullio Pinelli, Ennio Flaiano, Brunello Rondi
PHOTOGRAPHY: Gianni di Venanzo
MUSIC: Nino Rota
SET DESIGN: Piero Gherardi
EDITING: Ruggero Mastroianni
PRODUCER: Angelo Rizzoli
CAST: Giulietta Masina (Giulietta), Mario Pisu (Giorgio, Giulietta's husband), Sandra Milo (Susy/Iris/Fanny), Lou Gilbert (grandfather), Caterina Boratto (Giulietta's mother), Luisa Della Noce (Adele), Sylva Koscina (Sylva), Valentina Cortese (Val), Valeska Gert (Bhisma), Alberto Plebani (Lynx-Eyes, the private detective), José de Villalonga (José), Silvana Jachino (Dolores), Elena Fondra (Elena), and numerous minor characters

1968: *Toby Dammit* (*Toby Dammit*), an episode in *Tre passi nel delirio* (*Spirits of the Dead*)
SCRIPT: Federico Fellini, Bernardino Zapponi
PHOTOGRAPHY: Giuseppe Rotunno
MUSIC: Nino Rota
SET DESIGN: Piero Tosi
EDITING: Ruggero Mastroianni
PRODUCER: Les Films Marceau/Cocinor–P.E.A. Cinematografica
CAST: Terence Stamp (Toby Dammit), Salvo Randone (priest), Antonia Pietrosi (actress), Polidor (old actor), Marina Yaru (the devil as a young girl)

1969: *Block-notes di un regista* (*Fellini: A Director's Notebook*)
SCRIPT: Federico Fellini
PHOTOGRAPHY: Pasquale De Santis
MUSIC: Nino Rota
SET DESIGN: Federico Fellini
EDITING: Ruggero Mastroianni
PRODUCER: NBC and Peter Goldfarb
CAST: Federico Fellini, Giulietta Masina, Marcello Mastroianni, Marina Boratto, Caterina Boratto, Pasquale De Santis, Genius the Medium, and numerous nonprofessionals

1969: *Fellini Satyricon* (*Fellini's Satyricon*)
SCRIPT: Federico Fellini, Bernardino Zapponi
PHOTOGRAPHY: Giuseppe Rotunno
MUSIC: Nino Rota
SET DESIGN: Danilo Donati
EDITING: Ruggero Mastroianni
PRODUCER: Alberto Grimaldi
CAST: Martin Potter (Encolpio), Hiram Keller (Ascilto), Max Born (Gitone), Mario Romagnoli (Trimalchione), Fanfulla (Vernacchio), Gordon Mitchell (robber), Alain Cuny (Lica), Joseph Wheeler (husband suicide), Lucia Bosè (wife suicide), Donyale Luna (Enotea), Salvo Randone (Eumolpo), Magali Noël (Fortunata), Hylette Adolphe (slave girl), Pasquale Baldassare (hermaphrodite), Luigi Montefiori (Minotaur), Gennaro Sabatino (ferryman), Marcello di Falco (Proconsul), Tanya Lopert (emperor)

1970: *I clowns* (*The Clowns*)
SCRIPT: Federico Fellini, Bernardino Zapponi
PHOTOGRAPHY: Dario di Palma
MUSIC: Nino Rota
SET DESIGN: Danilo Donati
EDITING: Ruggero Mastroianni
PRODUCER: Federico Fellini, Ugo Guerra, Elio Scardamaglia
CAST: Film crew—Maya Morin, Lina Alberti, Gasperino, Alvaro Vitali; French clowns—Alex, Bario, Père Loriot, Ludo, Nino, Charlie

Rivel; Italian clowns—Riccardo Billi, Fanfulla, Tino Scotti, Carlo Rizzo, Freddo Pistoni, the Colombaioni, Merli, Maggio, Valdemaro Bevilacqua, Janigro, Terzo, Vingelli, Fumagalli; others (as themselves)—Federico Fellini, Liana Orfei, Tristan Rémy, Anita Ekberg, Victoria Chaplin, Franco Migliorini, Baptiste, Pierre Etaix

1972: *Roma (Fellini's Roma)*
SCRIPT: Federico Fellini, Bernardino Zapponi
PHOTOGRAPHY: Giuseppe Rotunno
MUSIC: Nino Rota
SET DESIGN: Danilo Donati
EDITING: Ruggero Mastroianni
PRODUCER: Turi Vasile
CAST: Peter Gonzales (young Fellini), Fiona Florence (beautiful prostitute), Pia De Doses (aristocratic princess), Alvaro Vitali (tap-dancer), Libero Frissi, Mario Del Vago, Galliano Sbarra, Alfredo Adami (performers in music hall), Federico Fellini, Marcello Mastroianni, Gore Vidal, Anna Magnani, Alberto Sordi (as themselves)

1973: *Amarcord (Amarcord)*
SCRIPT: Federico Fellini, Tonino Guerra
PHOTOGRAPHY: Giuseppe Rotunno
MUSIC: Nino Rota
SET DESIGN: Danilo Donati
EDITING: Ruggero Mastroianni
PRODUCER: Franco Cristaldi
CAST: Bruno Zanin (Titta), Pupella Maggio (Titta's mother), Armando Brancia (Aurelio), Nando Orfei (Pataca), Peppino Ianigro (grandfather), Ciccio Ingrassia (Uncle Teo), Magali Noël (Gradisca), Josiane Tanzilli (Volpina), Maria Antonietta Beluzzi (tobacconist), Gennaro Ombra (Biscein the liar), Aristide Caporale (Giudizio), Alvaro Vitali (Naso), Bruno Scagnetti (Ovo), Bruno Lenzi (Gigliozzi), Fernando de Felice (Ciccio), Donatella Gambini (Aldina), Franco Magno (Zeus the headmaster), Mauro Misul (philosophy teacher), Dina Adorni (math teacher), Francesco Maselli (physics teacher), Mario Silvestri (Italian teacher), Fides Stagni (art history teacher), Mario Liberati (owner of movie theater), Domenica Pertica (blind accordion player)

1976: *Casanova (Fellini's Casanova)*
SCRIPT: Federico Fellini, Bernardino Zapponi, with lyrics by Andrea Zanzotto and Tonino Guerra
PHOTOGRAPHY: Giuseppe Rotunno
MUSIC: Nino Rota
SET DESIGN: Danilo Donati
EDITING: Ruggero Mastroianni
PRODUCER: Alberto Grimaldi and Universal-Fox-Gaumont-Titanus
CAST: Donald Sutherland (Casanova), Cicely Browne (Madame

d'Urfé), Tina Aumont (Henriette), Margareth Clementi (Maddalena), Olimpia Carlisi (Isabella), Daniel Emilfork (Dubois), Sandy Allen (giantess), Claretta Algrandi (Marcolina), Clarissa Roll (Annamaria), Marika Rivera (Astrodi), Adele Angela Lojodice (mechanical doll), John Karlsen (Lord Talou), Mario Gagliardo (Righetto), Angelica Hansen (hunchbacked actress)

1979: *Prova d'orchestra (Orchestra Rehearsal)*
SCRIPT: Federico Fellini, Brunello Rondi
PHOTOGRAPHY: Giuseppe Rotunno
MUSIC: Nino Rota
SET DESIGN: Dante Ferretti
EDITING: Ruggero Mastroianni
PRODUCER: Daime Cinematografica and RAI, Albatros Produktion
CAST: Balduin Baas (orchestra conductor), David Mauhsell (first violinist), Francesco Aluigi (second violinist), Angelica Hansen, Heinz Kreuger (violinists), Elisabeth Labi (pianist), Ronaldo Bonacchi (contrabassoon player), Giovanni Javarone (tuba player), Andy Miller (oboist), Umberto Zuanelli (copyist), Claudio Ciocca (union leader), Sibyl Mostert (flutist), Franco Mazzieri (trumpet player), Daniele Pagani (trombone player)

1980: *La città delle donne (City of Women)*
SCRIPT: Federico Fellini, Bernardino Zapponi, Brunello Rondi
PHOTOGRAPHY: Giuseppe Rotunno
MUSIC: Luis Bacalov
SET DESIGN: Dante Ferretti
EDITING: Ruggero Mastroianni
PRODUCER: Opera Film Production and Gaumont
CAST: Marcello Mastroianni (Snàporaz), Anna Prucnal (Snàporaz's wife), Bernice Stegers (mysterious woman on the train), Ettore Manni (Katzone), Donatella Damiani, Rosaria Tafuri (the two *soubrettes*)

1983: *E la nave va (And the Ship Sails On)*
SCRIPT: Federico Fellini, Tonino Guerra, with opera lyrics by Andrea Zanzotto
PHOTOGRAPHY: Giuseppe Rotunno
MUSIC: Gianfranco Plenizio
SET DESIGN: Dante Ferretti
EDITING: Ruggero Mastroianni
PRODUCER: Franco Cristaldi, RAI, Vides Produzione, Gaumont
CAST: Freddie Jones (Orlando), Barbara Jefford (Ildebranda Cuffari), Janet Suzman (Edmea Tetua), Victor Poletti (Aureliano Fuciletto), Peter Cellier (Sir Reginald Dongby), Norma West (Lady Violet Dongby), Pina Bausch (princess), Pasquale Zito (Count of Bassano), Fiorenzo Serra (Grand Duke), Philip Locke (prime minister)

1985: *Ginger e Fred (Ginger and Fred)*
SCRIPT: Federico Fellini, Tullio Pinelli, Tonino Guerra
PHOTOGRAPHY: Tonino Delli Colli
MUSIC: Nicola Piovani
SET DESIGN: Dante Ferretti
EDITING: Nino Baragli, Ugo De Rossi, Ruggero Mastroianni
PRODUCER: Alberto Grimaldi
CAST: Giulietta Masina (Amelia or "Ginger"), Marcello Mastroianni (Pippo or "Fred"), Franco Fabrizi (master of ceremonies of variety show), Frederick Ledenburg (admiral), Augusto Poderosi (transvestite), Jacque Henri Lartigue (priest), Totò Mignone (Totò), Luciano Lombardo (defrocked priest), and numerous minor characters

1988: *Intervista (Interview)*
SCRIPT: Federico Fellini, Gianfranco Angelucci
PHOTOGRAPHY: Tonino Delli Colli
MUSIC: Nicola Piovani
SET DESIGN: Danilo Donati
EDITING: Nino Baragli
PRODUCER: Ibrahim Moussa, Aljosha Productions, RAI-Uno
CAST: Sergio Rubini (journalist), Paola Liguori (movie star), Maurizio Mein (assistant director), Nadia Ottaviani (custodian of Cinecittà's archives), Anita Ekberg, Federico Fellini, Marcello Mastroianni, and numerous other members of the troupe (as themselves)

1990: *La voce della luna (The Voice of the Moon)*
SCRIPT: Federico Fellini, Tullio Pinelli, Ermanno Cavazzoni
PHOTOGRAPHY: Tonino Delli Colli
MUSIC: Nicola Piovani
SET DESIGN: Dante Ferretti
EDITING: Nino Baragli
PRODUCER: Mario Cecchi Gori and Vittorio Cecchi Gori, RAI-Uno
CAST: Roberto Benigni (Ivo Salvini), Paolo Villaggio (Prefect Gonnella), Marisa Tomasi (Marisa), Nadia Ottaviani (Aldina Ferruzzi), Algelo Orlando (Nestore), Uta Schmidt (Ivo's grandmother), George Taylor (Marisa's lover), Susy Blady (Susy)

SELECTED
BIBLIOGRAPHY

ORIGINAL MANUSCRIPTS OF STORIES, TREATMENTS, SCRIPTS, AND
SCREENPLAYS

Fellini, Federico. "Fare un film." Fellini MS. 1 (Box 1). Lilly Library of Rare
Books, Bloomington, Ind. (Original typescript of *Fare un film*, published
by Einaudi in 1980).
———. "Filmetto pubblicitario per la soc. Campari: 'Oh, che bel paesag-
gio!'—sceneggiatura (Roma, 19 febbraio 1984)." Fellini MS. 7 (Box 2).
Lilly Library of Rare Books, Bloomington, Ind. (Unpublished script for
Campari soda commercial).
———. "Prova d'orchestra." Fellini MS. 6 (Box 1). Lilly Library of Rare
Books, Bloomington, Ind. (Copy of one version of script and additional
dialogue, with variations from that published by Garzanti in 1979).
———. "Prova d'orchestra: chiaccherata sul filmetto che avrei in animo di
fare." Fellini MS. 5 (Box 1). Lilly Library of Rare Books, Bloomington, Ind.
(Version of the film's soggetto, with variations from that published by
Garzanti in 1979; also contains a loose-leaf drawing from Fellini's dream
notebook).
Fellini, Federico, with the collaboration of Gianfranco Angelucci. "Block
notes di un regista: appunti di Federico Fellini (prima versione provviso-
ria)." Fellini MS. 2 (Box 1). Lilly Library of Rare Books, Bloomington, Ind.
(Provisional and incomplete version of script for *Intervista*).
Fellini, Federico, and Tonino Guerra. "E la nave va: soggetto di Federico
Fellini e Tonino Guerra." Fellini MS. 8 (Box 2). Lilly Library of Rare
Books, Bloomington, Ind. (Original copy of story for film, subsequently
published by Longanesi in 1983).
Fellini, Federico, and Tonino Guerra, with the collaboration of Tullio Pi-
nelli. "Ginger e Fred." Ed. Mino Guerrini. Fellini MS. 3 (Box 1). Lilly Li-
brary of Rare Books, Bloomington, Ind. (Original manuscript of book on
the film published by Longanesi in 1985).
———. "Ginger e Fred di Federico Fellini." Fellini MS. 4 (Box 1). Lilly Library of Rare Books, Bloomington, Ind. (Unpublished English translation
of film's dialogue).
———. "Ginger e Fred: soggetto e sceneggiatura di Federico Fellini e Tonino
Guerra con la collaborazione di Tullio Pinelli." Pinelli MS. 13 (Box 4, IIE).
Lilly Library of Rare Books, Bloomington, Ind. (Original copy of script

without story as mentioned in the title; story published by Longanesi
with script in 1985).

Fellini, Federico, and Tullio Pinelli. "La famiglia." Pinelli MS. 12 (Box 5,
IIIA). Lilly Library of Rare Books, Bloomington, Ind. (Unpublished original copy of story).

———. "G. degli spiriti (titolo provvisorio): sceneggiatura provvisoria." Pinelli MS. 12 (Box 4, IID). Lilly Library of Rare Books, Bloomington, Ind.
(Unpublished early version of the script).

———. "Giulietta of the Spirits (Provisional Title)." Fellini MS. 9 (Box 2).
Lilly Library of Rare Books, Bloomington, Ind. (Original copy of an En-
glish translation of Italian script, a version of which was published by
Orion in 1965).

———. "Happy Country (Paese felice)." Pinelli MS. 13 (Box 5, IIIB). Lilly
Library of Rare Books, Bloomington, Ind. (Unpublished original copy of
script based on an idea by Luigi Barzini, Jr.).

———. "La strada." Pinelli MS. 7 (Box 3, IIA). Lilly Library of Rare Books,
Bloomington, Ind. (Unpublished original copy of story with carbon copy;
apparently final draft).

———. "La strada." Pinelli MS. 7 (Box 3, IIA). Lilly Library of Rare Books,
Bloomington, Ind. (Unpublished original copy of script; apparently next-
to-last version).

———. "La strada: soggetto e sceneggiatura—Tullio Pinelli/Federico Fellini." Pinelli MS. 5 (Box 2, IE). Lilly Library of Rare Books, Bloomington,
Ind. (Unpublished original copy of next-to-last version of the story plus
original copy of final version of the script, bound together).

Fellini, Federico, Tullio Pinelli, and Ennio Flaiano. "Il bidone: soggetto e
sceneggiatura di Federico Fellini, Ennio Flaiano, Tullio Pinelli." Pinelli
MS. 6 (Box 3, IF). Lilly Library of Rare Books, Bloomington, Ind. (Original
copy of final version of script without the story as listed in the title).

———. "Le notti di Cabiria: sceneggiatura di Federico Fellini, Ennio
Flaiano, Tullio Pinelli." Pinelli MS. 8 (Box 3, IIB). Lilly Library of Rare
Books, Bloomington, Ind. (Original copy of script).

———. "Le notti di Cabiria: soggetto di Fellini, Flaiano, Pinelli." Pinelli
MS. 9 (Box 4, IIB-1). Lilly Library of Rare Books, Bloomington, Ind. (Original unpublished copy of story).

———. "Lo sceicco bianco." Pinelli MS. 3 (Box 1, IC). Lilly Library of Rare
Books, Bloomington, Ind. (Original copy of script).

———. " 'I vitelloni' (titolo provvisorio): soggetto e trattamento di Federico
Fellini, Tullio Pinelli, Ennio Flaiano." Pinelli MS. 4 (Box 2, ID). Lilly Library of Rare Books, Bloomington, Ind. (Original unpublished copy of
story [88 pp.] and script [390 pp.]).

Fellini, Federico, Tullio Pinelli, and Ennio Flaiano, with the collaboration
of Brunello Rondi. "La dolce vita: soggetto e sceneggiatura di: Federico
Fellini, Ennio Flaiano, Tullio Pinelli: collaboratore alla sceneggiatura:
Brunello Rondi." Pinelli MS. 10 (Box 4, IIC-1). Lilly Library of Rare Books,
Bloomington, Ind. (Original copy of script for primo tempo of film with-
out story as title indicates).

———. "La dolce vita (secondo tempo)." Pinelli MS. 11 (Box 4, IIC-2). Lilly

Library of Rare Books, Bloomington, Ind. (Original copy of script for secondo tempo of film).

Fellini, Federico, Tullio Pinelli, and Pietro Germi. "Il brigante di Tacco del Lupo." Pinelli MS. 14 (Box 5, IIIC). Lilly Library of Rare Books, Bloomington, Ind. (Original unpublished copy of script).

Fellini, Federico, Tullio Pinelli, and Alberto Lattuada. "Senza pietà." Pinelli MS. 1 (Box 1, IA). Lilly Library of Rare Books, Bloomington, Ind. (Original unpublished copy of script).

Fellini, Federico, Tullio Pinelli, and Giorgio Pastina. "Il diavolo in convento." Pinelli MS. 16 (Box 5, IIIE). Lilly Library of Rare Books, Bloomington, Ind. (Original unpublished copy of primo tempo of script).

Fellini, Federico, Tullio Pinelli, Alberto Lattuada, and Ennio Flaiano. "Luci del varietà." Pinelli MS. 2 (Box 1, IB). Lilly Library of Rare Books, Bloomington, Ind. (Original copy of script).

Fellini, Federico, Tullio Pinelli, and Gianni Puccini. "Persiane chiuse." Pinelli MS. 15 (Box 5, IIID). Lilly Library of Rare Books, Bloomington, Ind. (Original unpublished copy of script).

Fellini, Federico, and Bernardino Zapponi. "Inizio Roma—episodio." Fellini MS. 10-1 (Box 2). Lilly Library of Rare Books, Bloomington, Ind. (First notebook containing a version of opening scenes in Roma).

———. "Roma: l'arrivo a Roma." Fellini MS. 10-2 (Box 2). Lilly Library of Rare Books, Bloomington, Ind. (Second notebook containing a version of the arrival sequence in Roma).

———. "Roma: raccordo anulare." Fellini MS. 10-3 (Box 2). Lilly Library of Rare Books, Bloomington, Ind. (Third notebook containing a version of the autostrada episode in Roma).

———. "Film 'Roma' di F. Fellini: Il defilé." Fellini MS. 10-4 (Box 2). Lilly Library of Rare Books, Bloomington, Ind. (Fourth notebook containing a more complete and revised version of the ecclesiastical fashion parade episode in Roma).

———. "Roma: ricordo dei casini." Fellini MS. 10-7 (Box 2). Lilly Library of Rare Books, Bloomington, Ind. (Fifth notebook containing a version of the brothel episode in Roma).

———. "Roma: gli aristocratici e il defilé." Fellini MS. 10-8 (Box 2). Lilly Library of Rare Books, Bloomington, Ind. (Sixth notebook containing a shorter and earlier version of the ecclesiastical fashion parade episode in Roma).

———. " 'Toby Dammit' dal racconto di Poe 'Non scommettere la testa col diavolo': riduzione di Fellini & Zapponi." Fellini MS. 11 (Box 2). Lilly Library of Rare Books, Bloomington, Ind. (Original copy of director's shooting script, subsequently revised and published by Cappelli in 1968).

PUBLISHED BOOKS AND ARTICLES

Affron, Charles. "8 1/2 What?" In Federico Fellini, "8 1/2": Federico Fellini, Director, ed. Charles Affron, 3–19. New Brunswick, N.J.: Rutgers University Press, 1987.

Agel, Geneviève. "*Il Bidone.*" In *Federico Fellini: Essays in Criticism*, ed. Peter Bondanella, 66–79. New York: Oxford University Press, 1977.

———. *Les Chemins de Fellini.* Paris: Éditions du Cerf, 1956.

Alpert, Hollis. *Fellini: A Life.* New York: Atheneum, 1986.

Amengual, Barthélemy. "Fin d'itinéraire: du 'côté de chez Lumière' au 'côté de Méliès.' " *Études cinématographiques* 127–30 (1981): 81–111.

———. "Une mythologie fertile: '*Mamma Puttana.*' " In *Federico Fellini*, ed. Gilles Ciment, 32–39. Paris: Éditions Rivages, 1988.

Amiel, Vincent. "Critique." In *Federico Fellini*, ed. Gilles Ciment, 174–75. Paris: Éditions Rivages, 1988.

Angelini, Pietro. *Controfellini.* Milan: Ottaviano, 1974.

Angelucci, Gianfranco. Interview with author. Rome, 15 November 1987.

———. "Su *La voce della luna* e altre fellinità." *Cineteca* 6, no. 2/3 (1990): 10–11.

———. "Un'intervista tutta da vedere." *Intermedia Journal* 1, no. 5 (1987): 36–39, 41.

———, ed. "*La dolce vita*": un film di Federico Fellini. Rome: Editalia, 1989.

Aristarco, Guido. *Antologia di "Cinema nuovo" 1952–1958.* Florence: Guaraldi Editore, 1975.

Armes, Roy. *Patterns of Realism: A Study of Italian Neo-Realism.* Cranbury, N.J.: A. S. Barnes, 1971.

Attolini, Vito. *Il cinema di Pietro Germi.* Lecce: Elle Edizioni, 1986.

Bachman, Gideon. *Ciao, Federico!* Documentary film on *Fellini Satyricon*, 1969.

———. "Federico Fellini: 'The Cinema Seen as a Woman. . . .' " *Film Quarterly* 34, no. 2 (1980–1981): 2–9.

Baranski, Zygmunt G. "Antithesis in Fellini's *I vitelloni*." *The Italianist* 1 (1981): 24–42.

Bazin, André. "*Cabiria*: The Voyage to the End of Neorealism." In *Federico Fellini: Essays in Criticism*, ed. Peter Bondanella, 94–102. New York: Oxford University Press, 1977.

———. *Qu'est-ce que le cinéma?—IV. Une esthétique de la Réalité: le néoréalisme.* Paris: Éditions du Cerf, 1962. Partially reprinted in *What Is Cinema? Vol. II*, trans. Hugh Gray. Berkeley and Los Angeles: University of California Press, 1971.

Begnal, Michael. "Fellini & Poe: A Story with a Moral?" *Literature/Film Quarterly* 10, no. 2 (1982): 130–33.

Benayoun, Robert. "Les Conquérants de la planète mère." In *Federico Fellini*, ed. Gilles Ciment, 65–68. Paris: Éditions Rivages, 1988.

———. "Fellini-Fellini: une pub pour le cinema?" In *Federico Fellini*, ed. Gilles Ciment, 164–66. Paris: Éditions Rivages, 1988.

Benderson, Albert E. *Critical Approaches to Federico Fellini's "8 1/2."* New York: Arno Press, 1974.

Benevelli, Elio. *Analisi di una messa in scena: Freud e Lacan nel "Casanova" di Fellini.* Bari: Dedalo Libri, 1979.

Bertelli, Gian Carlo, and Pier Marco De Santi, eds. *Omaggio a Flaiano*. Pisa: Giardini, 1987.

Bertetto, Paolo. *Il più brutto del mondo: il cinema italiano oggi*. Milan: Bompiani, 1982.

Bertieri, Claudio. *Fumetti all'italiana: le fiabe a quadretti 1908–1945*. Rome: Comic Art, 1989.

Betti, Liliana. "Alla ricerca di Toby Dammit." In *Tre passi nel delirio di F. Fellini, L. Malle, R. Vadim*, ed. Liliana Betti et al., 31–59. Bologna: Cappelli, 1968.

———. *Fellini: An Intimate Portrait*. Trans. Joachim Neugroschel. Boston: Little, Brown, 1979.

———, ed. *Federico A. C.: disegni per il "Satyricon" di Federico Fellini*. Milan: Libri Edizioni, 1970.

Betti, Liliana, and Gianfranco Angelucci, eds. *Casanova rendez-vous con Federico Fellini*. Milan: Bompiani, 1975.

Betti, Liliana, and Oreste Del Buono, eds. *Federcord: disegni per "Amarcord" di Federico Fellini*. Milan: Libri Edizioni, 1974.

Bìspurri, Ennio. *Federico Fellini: il sentimento latino della vita*. Rome: Editrice Il Ventaglio, 1981.

Bohne, Frederick. "Fellini's *Toby Dammit*: An Original Adaptation." *Film Criticism* 1, no. 1 (1976): 26–29.

Bondanella, Peter. "Early Fellini: *Variety Lights, The White Sheik, The Vitelloni*." In *Federico Fellini: Essays in Criticism*, ed. Peter Bondanella, 220–39. New York: Oxford University Press, 1978.

———. *The Eternal City: Roman Images in the Modern World*. Chapel Hill: University of North Carolina Press, 1987.

———. *Italian Cinema: From Neorealism to the Present*. 2d ed. New York: Continuum, 1990.

———. "Literature as Therapy: Fellini and Petronius." *Annali d'Italianistica* 6 (1988): 179–98.

———, ed. *Federico Fellini: Essays in Criticism*. New York: Oxford University Press, 1978.

Boyer, Deena. *The Two Hundred Days of "8 1/2."* New York: Garland, 1978.

Branigan, Edward. *Point of View in the Cinema: A Theory of Narration and Subjectivity in Classical Film*. Berlin: Mouton Publishers, 1984.

Brunetta, Gian Piero. *Storia del cinema italiano dal 1945 agli anni ottanta*. Rome: Editori Riuniti, 1982.

Brunette, Peter. *Roberto Rossellini*. New York: Oxford University Press, 1987.

Budgen, Suzanne. *Fellini*. London: British Film Institute, 1966.

Burke, Frank. *Federico Fellini: "Variety Lights" to "La Dolce Vita."* Boston: Twayne, 1984.

———. "Fellini: Changing the Subject." *Film Quarterly* 43, no. 1 (1989): 36–48.

Burke, Frank. "Fellini's *Luci del varietà*: The Limitations of the Stage and the 'Morality of Movies.' " *Italica* 55, no. 2 (1978): 225–35.

———. "Reason and Unreason in Federico Fellini's *I Vitelloni*." *Literature/Film Quarterly* 8 (1980): 116–24.

———. "*Variety Lights, The White Sheik*, and Italian Neorealism." *Film Criticism* 3 (1979): 53–66.

Cabutti, Lucio. "La dolce matita di Federico." *Arte* 19, no. 190 (1988): 98–101, 162–63.

Calvino, Italo. "Autobiografia di uno spettatore." In Federico Fellini, *Quattro film*, ix–xxiv. Turin: Einaudi, 1974.

———. "Major Currents in Italian Fiction Today." *Italian Quarterly* 4 (1960): 3–15.

———. *The Path to the Nest of Spiders*. Trans. Archibald Colquhoun. New York: Ecco Press, 1976.

Carotenuto, Alberto. *Jung e la cultura italiana*. Rome: Astrolabio, 1977.

Cavazzoni, Ermanno. *Il poema dei lunatici*. Turin: Bollati Boringhieri, 1987.

Chemasi, Antonio. "Fellini's *Casanova*: The Final Nights." *American Film* 1 (1976): 8–16.

Cederna, Camilla. "La bella confusione." In Federico Fellini, "*8 1/2*" *di Federico Fellini*, ed. Camilla Cederna, 15–85. Bologna: Cappelli, 1965.

Chiesa, Adolfo, ed. *Antologia del "Marc'Aurelio" 1931–1954*. Rome: Casa Editrice Roberto Napoleone, 1974. Reprinted in 1988 as *Il meglio del "Marc'Aurelio": periodico umoristico 1931/1954*.

Cianfarani, Carmine, ed. *Federico Fellini: Leone d'Oro, Venezia 1985*. Rome: ANICA, 1985. (Catalogue of Fellini retrospective at 1985 Venice Film Festival).

Ciment, Gilles, ed. *Federico Fellini*. Paris: Éditions Rivages, 1988. (Anthology of articles on Fellini published by *Positif*).

Ciment, Michel. "Entretién avec Federico Fellini." In *Federico Fellini*, ed. Gilles Ciment, 112–16. Paris: Éditions Rivages, 1988.

Codelli, Lorenzo. "Entretien avec Bernardino Zapponi." *Positif*, no. 230 (May 1980): 34–45. (Includes filmography of Zapponi's scripts).

Collet, Jean. *La Création selon Fellini*. Paris: José Corti, 1990.

Costello, Donald. *Fellini's Road*. Notre Dame, Ind.: University of Notre Dame Press, 1983.

———. "Layers of Reality: *8 1/2* as Spiritual Autobiography." *Notre Dame English Journal* 13, no. 2 (1981): 1–12.

Cosulich, Callisto. *I film di Alberto Lattuada*. Rome: Gremese Editore, 1985.

Curchod, Olivier. " 'J'écris *Paludes*.' " In *Federico Fellini*, ed. Gilles Ciment, 168–72. Paris: Éditions Rivages, 1988.

d'Amico, Masolino. *La commedia all'italiana: il cinema comico in Italia dal 1945 al 1975*. Milan: Mondadori, 1985.

del Buono, Oreste. "Da Fortunello a Giudizio, passando per Little Nemo."

In Federico Fellini, *I Clown*, 2d ed., ed. Renzo Renzi, 73–76. Bologna: Cappelli, 1988.

———. "Un esordio difficile." In Federico Fellini, *Lo sceicco bianco*, 5–15. Milan: Garzanti, 1980.

Delouche, Dominique. "Journal d'un bidoniste." In Geneviève Agel, *Les chemins de Fellini*, 98–157. Paris: Éditions du Cerf, 1956.

de Miro, Ester, and Mario Guaraldi, eds. *Fellini della memoria*. Florence: La Casa Usher, 1983. (Catalogue for the 1983 Fellini retrospective at Rimini).

De Santi, Pier Marco. *I disegni di Fellini*. Rome: Laterza, 1982.

———. *La musica di Nino Rota*. Rome: Laterza, 1983.

De Santi, Pier Marco, and Raffaele Monti, eds. *Saggi e documenti sopra "Il Casanova" di Federico Fellini*. Pisa: Quaderni dell'Istituto di storia dell'arte dell'Università di Pisa, 1978.

Dick, Bernard F. "Adaptation as Archaeology: *Fellini Satyricon* (1969)." In *Modern European Filmmakers and the Art of Adaptation*, ed. Andrew Horton and Joan Magretta, 145–57. New York: Frederick Ungar, 1981.

Fahe, Marilyn. "*8 1/2*": *The Saraghina Sequence*. New York: Macmillan Films, 1975.

Faldini, Franca, and Goffredo Fofi, eds. *L'avventurosa storia del cinema italiano raccontata dai suoi protagonisti 1935–1959*. Milan: Feltrinelli, 1979.

———, eds. *L'avventurosa storia del cinema italiano raccontata dai suoi protagonisti 1960–1969*. Milan: Feltrinelli, 1981.

———, eds. *Il cinema italiano d'oggi 1970–1984 raccontato dai suoi protagonisti*. Milan: Feltrinelli, 1984.

Farassino, Alberto, and Tatti Sanguineti. *Lux Film: Esthétique et système d'un studio italien*. Locarno: Éditions du Festival international du film de Locarno, 1984.

Fava, Claudio G., and Aldo Viganò. *I film di Federico Fellini*. 2d ed. Rome: Gremese Editore, 1987. Translated as *The Films of Federico Fellini*. Trans. Shula Curto. Secaucus, N.J.: Citadel Press, 1985.

Federico Fellini: Working Drawings 1952–1982 for the Films "La Dolce Vita," "Satyricon," "Amarcord," "Il Casanova," and Others. New York: Pierre Matisse Gallery, 1986. (Catalogue for New York showing of Fellini's drawings).

Fellini, Federico. "A Brief Introduction." In Claudio G. Fava and Aldo Viganò, *The Films of Federico Fellini*, trans. Shula Curto, 11–12. Secaucus, N.J.: Citadel Press, 1985.

———. "Amarcord Maciste." In *Gli uomini forti*, ed. Alberto Farassino and Tatti Sanguineti, 182. Milan: Mazzotta, 1983. (Fellini's memories of his first cinematic experience).

———. "*Amarcord*: The Fascism Within Us—An Interview with Valerio Riva." In *Federico Fellini: Essays in Criticism*, ed. Peter Bondanella, 20–26. New York: Oxford University Press, 1978.

Fellini, Federico. "America and I." *Amica—International Italian Fashion.* Autumn 1987–Winter 1988, p. 39.

———. *Block–notes di un regista.* Milan: Longanesi, 1988.

———. *Casanova.* Ed. Federico Fellini and Bernardino Zapponi. Turin: Einaudi, 1977.

———. "*Casanova*: An Interview with Aldo Tassone." In *Federico Fellini: Essays in Criticism,* ed. Peter Bondanella, 27–35. New York: Oxford University Press, 1978.

———. *Il "Casanova" di Federico Fellini.* Ed. Gianfranco Angelucci and Liliana Betti. Bologna: Cappelli, 1977.

———. *La città delle donne.* Milan: Garzanti, 1980.

———. *I clown.* 2d ed., ed. Renzo Renzi. Bologna: Cappelli, 1988.

———. *Comments on Film.* Ed. Giovanni Grazzini. Trans. Joseph Henry. Fresno: The Press of California State University at Fresno, 1988.

———. *La Dolce Vita.* New York: Ballantine, 1961.

———. *La dolce vita.* Milan: Garzanti, 1981.

———. *Early Screenplays: "Variety Lights" and "The White Sheik."* New York: Grossman, 1971.

———. "*8 1/2" di Federico Fellini.* Ed. Camilla Cederna. Bologna: Cappelli, 1965.

———. "*8 1/2": Federico Fellini, Director.* Ed. Charles Affron. New Brunswick, N.J.: Rutgers University Press, 1987.

———. *E il segno va: disegni di Federico Fellini.* Turin: Edizioni Omega, 1988.

———. *E la nave va.* Ed. Federico Fellini and Tonino Guerra. Milan: Longanesi, 1983.

———. *Fare un film.* Turin: Einaudi, 1980.

———. "Federico Fellini" (interview with Pierre Kast). In *Interviews with Film Directors,* ed. Andrew Sarris, 175–92. New York: Avon, 1969.

———. *Fellini on Fellini.* Ed. Anna Keel and Christian Strich. Trans. Isabel Quigly. London: Eyre Methuen, 1976.

———. "Fellini oniricon." Ed. Lietta Tornabuoni. *Dolce vita* 1, no. 3 (1987): 29–44.

———. "Fellini on Television: *A Director's Notebook* and *The Clowns.*" In *Federico Fellini: Essays in Criticism,* ed. Peter Bondanella, 11–16. New York: Oxford University Press, 1978.

———. "*Fellini Satyricon" di Federico Fellini.* Ed. Dario Zanelli. Bologna: Cappelli, 1969.

———. *Fellini's Casanova.* Ed. Bernardino Zapponi. New York: Dell, 1977.

———. *Fellini's "Satyricon."* Ed. Dario Zanelli. New York: Ballantine, 1970.

———. *Fellini TV: "Blocknotes di un regista"/"I clowns."* Ed. Renzo Renzi. Bologna: Cappelli, 1972.

———. *Fellini: Zeichnungen.* Zurich: Diogenes Verlag, 1976.

———. *Fellini: Zeichnungen.* Ed. Gabriele Schulteiss. Frankfurt: Deutsches Filmmuseum, 1984.

————. *Il film "Amarcord" di Federico Fellini*. Ed. Gianfranco Angelucci and Liliana Betti. Bologna: Cappelli, 1974.

————. *Ginger e Fred*. Ed. Mino Guerrini. Milan: Longanesi, 1986.

————. "Ho inventato tutto, anche me." *Panorama* 18 (14 January 1980): 84–95.

————. "How I Create." *Atlas* 9 (1965): 182–85.

————. "In chiave di Fellini." *Panorama* 16 (17 October 1978): 168–85.

————. Interview with Aldo Tassone. Typescript, 1976.

————. *Intervista sul cinema*. Ed. Giovanni Grazzini. Rome: Laterza, 1983.

————. Introduction to James Steranko, *The Steranko History of Comics*, 3. Reading, Pa.: Supergraphics, 1970.

————. "Io e la bio-energia." In *Pulsazione*, ed. Luigi De Marchi, 11–25. Milan: Sugar, n.d. (probably 1976).

————. "I Was Born for the Cinema." *Film Comment* 4 (1966): 77–84.

————. *Federico Fellini's "Juliet of the Spirits."* Ed. Tullio Kezich. New York: Orion Press, 1965.

————. "Lettre à Alberto Grimaldi sur un projet de film." In *Federico Fellini*, ed. Gilles Ciment, 22–24. Paris: Éditions Rivages, 1988.

————. "The Long Interview: Tullio Kezich & Federico Fellini." In *Federico Fellini's "Juliet of the Spirits,"* ed. Tullio Kezich, 11–65. New York: Orion Press, 1965.

————. *La mia Rimini*. Ed. Renzo Renzi. Bologna: Cappelli, 1987.

————. "La mia Roma." Ed. Costanzo Costantini. *Roma ieri, oggi, domani* 1 (1988): 19–21.

————. *"Moraldo in the City" and "A Journey with Anita."* Ed. and trans. John C. Stubbs. Urbana: University of Illinois Press, 1983. (Unrealized screenplays).

————. "My Experiences as a Director." In *Federico Fellini: Essays in Criticism*, ed. Peter Bondanella, 3–11. New York: Oxford University Press, 1978.

————. "1970: notes sur *Une femme inconnue* (ou *La Femme inconnue*)." In *Federico Fellini*, ed. Gilles Ciment, 24–27. Paris: Éditions Rivages, 1988.

————. *Le notti di Cabiria*. Milan: Garzanti, 1981.

————. "Preface to *Satyricon*." In *Federico Fellini: Essays in Criticism*, ed. Peter Bondanella, 16–19. New York: Oxford University Press, 1978.

————. *Il primo Fellini: "Lo sceicco bianco," "I vitelloni," "La strada," "Il bidone."* Ed. Renzo Renzi. Bologna: Cappelli, 1969.

————. *Prova d'orchestra*. Milan: Garzanti, 1980.

————. *Quattro film*. Introduction by Italo Calvino. Turin: Einaudi, 1974.

————. *Un regista a Cinecittà*. Milan: Mondadori, 1988.

————. *"Roma" di Federico Fellini*. Ed. Bernardino Zapponi. Bologna: Cappelli, 1972.

————. *Lo sceicco bianco*. Milan: Garzanti, 1980.

————. *La Strada*. Ed. François-Regis Bastide, Juliette Caputo, and Chris Marker. Paris: Éditions du Seuil, 1955.

Fellini, Federico. *"La Strada." L'Avant-Scène du Cinéma* 102 (April 1970): 7–51.

——. *"La Strada": Federico Fellini, Director.* Ed. Peter Bondanella and Manuela Gieri. New Brunswick, N.J.: Rutgers University Press, 1987.

——. *"La strada": sceneggiatura originale di Federico Fellini e Tullio Pinelli.* Rome: Edizioni di Bianco e Nero, 1955.

——. *Three Screenplays: "I Vitelloni," "Il Bidone," "The Temptations of Dr. Antonio."* New York: Grossman, 1970.

——. "Totò: per pochi minuti fui il suo regista." *La Repubblica: Il venerdì* 2, no. 29 (4 June 1988): 96–105.

——. *"Tre passi nel delirio" di F. Fellini, L. Malle, R. Vadim.* Ed. Liliana Betti, Ornella Volta, and Bernardino Zapponi. Bologna: Cappelli, 1968.

——. *"I vitelloni" e "La strada."* Milan: Longanesi, 1989.

——. *La voce della luna.* Turin: Einaudi, 1990.

——. *La voce della luna.* Ed. Lietta Tornabuoni. Florence: La Nuova Italia, 1990.

Foreman, Walter C. "Fellini's Cinematic City: *Roma* and Myths of Foundation." *Forum Italicum* 14 (1980): 78–98.

——. "The Poor Player Struts Again: Fellini's *Toby Dammit* and the End of the Actor." In *1977 Film Studies Annual: Part One,* ed. Ben Lawton and Janet Staiger, 111–23. Pleasantville, N.Y.: Redgrave, 1977.

Free, William J. "Fellini's *I clowns* and the Grotesque." In *Federico Fellini: Essays in Criticism,* ed. Peter Bondanella, 188–201. New York: Oxford University Press, 1978.

Fumento, Rocco. "Maestro Fellini, Studente Angelucci." *Literature/Film Quarterly* 10, no. 4 (1982): 226–33.

Geduld, Carolyn. *"Juliet of the Spirits:* Guido's Anima." In *Federico Fellini: Essays in Criticism,* ed. Peter Bondanella, 137–51. New York: Oxford University Press, 1978.

Giacchero, Norma. Interview with author. Rome, 5 April 1988.

Gili, Jean A. " 'Ce mot magique, Cinecittà': Entretien avec Federico Fellini." In *Federico Fellini,* ed. Gilles Ciment, 178–82. Paris: Éditions Rivages, 1988.

——. "Du journalisme au cinéma: l'itinéraire de Fellini, de 1939 à 1946," *Études cinématographiques* 127–30 (1981): 5–18.

Gorbman, Claudia. "Music as Salvation: Notes on Fellini and Rota." In *Federico Fellini: Essays in Criticism,* ed. Peter Bondanella, 80–94. New York: Oxford University Press, 1978.

Gori, Gianfranco Miro, ed. *Rimini et le cinéma: images, cinéastes, histoires.* Paris: Éditions du Centre Pompidou, 1989.

Grau, Jordi. *Fellini desde Barcelona.* Barcelona: Ambit Servicios Editoriales, 1985.

Greer, Germaine. "Fellinissimo." *Interview,* December 1988, pp. 100–106.

Hay, James. *Popular Film Culture in Fascist Italy: The Passing of the Rex.* Bloomington: Indiana University Press, 1987.

Horton, Andrew S., and Joan Magretta, eds. *Modern European Filmmakers and the Art of Adaptation.* New York: Frederick Ungar, 1981.

Hume, Kathryn. *Fantasy and Mimesis: Responses to Reality in Western Literature.* New York: Methuen, 1984.

Hyman, Timothy. "*8 1/2* as an Anatomy of Melancholy." In *Federico Fellini: Essays in Criticism,* ed. Peter Bondanella, 121–29. New York: Oxford University Press, 1978.

Kaufman, Hank, and Gene Lerner. *Hollywood sul Tevere.* Milan: Sperling & Kupfer. 1982.

Ketcham, Charles B. *Federico Fellini: The Search for a New Mythology.* New York: Paulist Press, 1976.

———. "Samsonite Agonistes: A Fellinisque Journey to Fellini." *Film Criticism* 1 (1976): 30–35.

Keyser, Lester J. "Three Faces of Evil: Fascism in Recent Movies." *Journal of Popular Film* 4 (1975): 21–31.

Kezich, Tullio. *Il dolce cinema.* Milan: Bompiani, 1978.

———. *Fellini.* Milan: Camunia, 1987.

———, ed. *Giulietta Masina (La Chaplin Mujer): Entrevista realizada por Tullio Kezich.* Valencia: Fernando Torres, 1985.

Kolker, Robert P. *The Altering Eye: Contemporary International Cinema.* New York: Oxford University Press, 1983.

Kovács, Steven. "Fellini's *Toby Dammit*: A Study of Characteristic Themes and Techniques." *Journal of Aesthetics and Art Criticism* 31 (1972): 255–61.

Lambertini, Luigi. *Nino Za: il caricaturista degli anni '30.* Bologna: Edizioni Bora, 1982.

Latil-Le Dantec, Mireille. "Le Monde du cirque et le monde comme cirque: *Les Clowns.*" *Études cinématographiques* 127–30 (1981): 49–64.

Lavery, David. " 'Major Man': Fellini as an Autobiographer." *Literature/Film Quarterly* 16, no. 1 (1988): 14–29.

Lawton, Ben. "Fellini and the Literary Tradition." *Italian Journal* 4, no. 3–4 (1990): 32–40.

Lederman, Marie Jean. "Art, Artifacts, and *Fellini's Casanova.*" *Film Criticism* 2, no. 1 (1977): 43–45.

———. "Dreams and Vision in Fellini's *City of Women.*" *Journal of Popular Film and Television* 9, no. 3 (1981): 114–22.

Legrand, Gérard. "La Soprano et le rhinocéros." In *Federico Fellini,* ed. Gilles Ciment, 146–49. Paris: Éditions Rivages, 1988.

Lewalski, Barbara K. "Federico Fellini's *Purgatorio.*" In *Federico Fellini: Essays in Criticism,* ed. Peter Bondanella, 113–20. New York: Oxford University Press, 1978.

Librach, Ronald S. "Reconciliation in the Realm of Fantasy: The Fellini World and the Fellini Text." *Literature/Film Quarterly* 15, no. 2 (1987): 85–98.

Liehm, Mira. *Passion and Defiance: Film in Italy from 1942 to the Present.* Berkeley and Los Angeles: University of California Press, 1984.

Lizzani, Carlo. *Il cinema italiano dalle origini agli anni ottanta.* 2d ed. Rome: Editori Riuniti, 1982.

Lucente, Gregory L. *Beautiful Fables: Self-consciousness in Italian Narrative from Manzoni to Calvino.* Baltimore: Johns Hopkins University Press, 1986.

McBride, Joseph. "The Director as Superstar." In *Federico Fellini: Essays in Criticism,* ed. Peter Bondanella, 152–60. New York: Oxford University Press, 1978.

McDougal, Stuart Y., ed. *Made into Movies: From Literature to Film.* New York: Holt, Rinehart and Winston, 1985.

Madrignani, Carlo. "Il fallo Ginger-Frediano." *Belfagor* 41 (1986): 341–44.

Manara, Milo. "Senza titolo quasi un preludio." *Corto Maltese* 7, no. 7 (July 1989): 4–7.

———. "Viaggio a Tulum da un soggetto di Federico Fellini per un film da fare." *Corto Maltese* 7, no. 7 (July 1989): 10–19; 7, no. 8 (August 1989): 4–14.

Marcus, Millicent. "Fellini's *Amarcord*: Film as Memory." *Quarterly Review of Film Studies* 2 (1977): 418–25.

———. "Fellini's *Casanova*: Portrait of the Artist." *Quarterly Review of Film Studies* 5 (1980): 19–34.

———. *Italian Film in the Light of Neorealism.* Princeton: Princeton University Press, 1986.

Markulin, Joseph. "Plot and Character in Fellini's *Casanova*: Beyond *Satyricon*." *Italian Quarterly* 23 (1982): 65–74.

Masi, Stefano. *Nel buio della moviola: introduzione alla storia del montaggio.* L'Aquila: La Lanterna Magica, 1985.

———. *Storie della luce.* L'Aquila: La Lanterna Magica, 1985.

Masi, Stefano, and Enrico Lancia. *I film di Roberto Rossellini.* Rome: Gremese Editore, 1987.

Mesnil, Michel. "*Casanova*: le vieil homme et la mort." *Études cinématographiques* 127–30 (1981): 71–80.

———. "*La Cité des femmes*: ombilic des limbes." *Études cinématographiques* 127–30 (1981): 113–26.

Metz, Christian. "Mirror Construction in Fellini's *8 1/2*." In *Federico Fellini: Essays in Criticism,* ed. Peter Bondanella, 130–36. New York: Oxford University Press, 1978.

Mezzavilla, Silvano, ed. *Cinema in fumetto.* Montepulciano: Editori del Grifo, 1988.

Miccichè, Lino, ed. *Il cinema italiano degli anni '60.* Venice: Marsilio Editori, 1975.

———, ed. *Cinema italiano degli anni '70: cronache 1969–78.* Venice: Marsilio Editori, 1980.

———, ed. *Il neorealismo cinematografico italiano.* Venice: Marsilio Editori, 1975.

Milo, Sandro. *Caro Federico.* Milan: Rizzoli, 1982.

Mollica, Vincenzo. "Viaggio a Tulum da un soggetto di Federico Fellini per un film da fare." *Corto Maltese* 7, no. 7 (July 1989): 8–9.

———, ed. *Il fumetto e il cinema di Fellini*. Montepulciano: Editori del Grifo, 1984.

Monti, Raffaele, ed. *Bottega Fellini—"La città delle donne": progetto, lavorazione, film*. Rome: De Luca, 1981.

Monti, Raffaele, and Pier Marco De Santi, eds. *L'invenzione consapevole: disegni e materiali di Federico Fellini per il film "E la nave va."* Florence: Artificio, 1984.

Montini, Franco. "Fellini? É come Garibaldi." *La Repubblica: Il Venerdì*, insert 2, no. 46 (6 November 1988): 124–27.

Moravia, Alberto. "Dreaming Up Petronius." In *Federico Fellini: Essays in Criticism*, ed. Peter Bondanella, 161–68. New York: Oxford University Press, 1978.

Morlion, Felix A. "The Philosophical Basis of Neo-Realism." In *Springtime in Italy: A Reader on Neo-realism*, ed. David Overbey, 115–24. Hamden, Conn.: Archon Books, 1979.

Murray, Edward. *Fellini the Artist*. 2d ed. New York: Frederick Ungar, 1985.

Nemiz, Andrea. *Vita, dolce vita*. Rome: Network Edizioni, 1983.

Olivieri, Angelo. *L'imperatore in platea: i grandi del cinema italiano dal "Marc'Aurelio" allo schermo*. Bari: Edizioni Dedalo, 1986.

Overbey, David, ed. *Springtime in Italy: A Reader on Neo-realism*. Hamden, Conn.: Archon Books, 1979.

Parshall, Peter F. "Fellini's Thematic Structuring: Patterns of Fascism in *Amarcord*." *Film Criticism* 7, no. 2 (1983): 19–30.

Pasco, Allan H. "The Thematic Structure of Fellini's *Amarcord*." In *1976 Film Studies Annual*, ed. Ben Lawton et al., 259–71. West Lafayette, Ind.: Purdue University, 1976.

Pasolini, Pier Paolo. "The Catholic Irrationalism of Fellini." *Film Criticism* 9, no. 1 (1984): 63–73.

Pecori, Franco. *Federico Fellini*. Florence: La Nuova Italia, 1974.

Peri, Enzo. "Federico Fellini: An Interview." *Film Quarterly* 15 (1961): 30–33.

Perry, Ted. *Filmguide to "8 1/2."* Bloomington: Indiana University Press, 1975.

———. "Signifiers in Fellini's *8 1/2*." *Forum Italicum* 6 (1972): 79–86.

Pieri, Françoise. "Aux sources d'*Amarcord*: les récits felliniens du *Marc'Aurelio*." *Études cinématographiques* 127–30 (1981): 19–36.

———. "Federico Fellini écrivain du *Marc'Aurelio*." *Positif* 244–45 (1981): 20–32.

Pilliteri, Paolo. *Appunti su Fellini*. Milan: Franco Angeli, 1990.

Pinelli, Tullio. Interview with author. Rome, 8 October 1987.

Prats, A. J. *The Autonomous Image: Cinematic Narration and Humanism*. Lexington: University Press of Kentucky, 1981.

———. "The Individual, the World, and the Life of Myth in *Fellini Satyricon*." *South Atlantic Bulletin* 44 (1979): 45–58.

Prédal, René. *La Photo de cinéma suivi d'un dictionnaire de cent chefs opérateurs.* Paris: Éditions du Cerf, 1985.

Price, Barbara Anne, and Theodore Price. *Federico Fellini: An Annotated International Bibliography.* Metuchen, N.J.: Scarecrow Press, 1978.

Questerbert, Marie-Christine. *Les Scénaristes italiens: 50 ans d'écriture cinématographique.* Renans: 5 Continents/Hatier, 1988.

"Real Dreams: Into the Dark with Federico Fellini." BBC television program, 1987. (Videotape of broadcast and transcript of dialogue).

Renzi, Renzo. *Il fascismo involontario e altri scritti.* Bologna: Cappelli, 1975.

Richardson, Robert. "Waste Lands: The Breakdown of Order." In *Federico Fellini: Essays in Criticism*, ed. Peter Bondanella, 103–12. New York: Oxford University Press, 1978.

Risset, Jacqueline. *Fellini: "Le Cheik Blanc"—l'annonce faite à Federico.* Paris: Adam Birro, 1990.

Rocher, Daniel. "Note sur *Amarcord* ou l'antichambre de la mort." *Études cinématographiques* 127–30 (1981): 65–69.

Rondi, Brunello. *Il cinema di Fellini.* Rome: Edizioni di Bianco e Nero, 1965.

———. Interview with author. Rome, 20 October 1987.

Rosenthal, Stuart. *The Cinema of Federico Fellini.* South Brunswick, N.J.: A. S. Barnes, 1976.

Rossellini, Robert. "Ten Years of Cinema." In *Springtime in Italy: A Reader on Neo-realism*, ed. David Overbey, 93–113. Hamden, Conn.: Archon Books, 1979.

Rossi, Patrizio, and Ben Lawton. "Reality, Fantasy, and Fellini." In *Federico Fellini: Essays in Criticism*, ed. Peter Bondanella, 254–61. New York: Oxford University Press, 1978.

Salachas, Gilbert. *Federico Fellini: An Investigation into His Films and Philosophy.* Trans. Rosalie Siegel. New York: Crown, 1969. (Translation of original 1963 French edition).

———. "Fellini's Imagery from *Variety Lights* to *Juliet of the Spirits*." In *Federico Fellini: Essays in Criticism*, ed. Peter Bondanella, 205–19. New York: Oxford University Press, 1978.

Samuels, Charles Thomas, ed. *Encountering Directors.* New York: Putnam's, 1972.

Schoonejans, Sonia. *Fellini.* Rome: Lato Side Editori, 1980.

Segal, Erich. "Arbitrary *Satyricon*: Petronius & Fellini." *Diacritics* 1 (1971): 54–57.

Shale, Richard, ed. *Academy Awards.* 2d ed. New York: Frederick Ungar, 1982.

Silke, James R., ed. *Federico Fellini: Discussion.* Los Angeles: American Film Institute, 1970.

Skska, William. "Metacinema: A Modern Necessity." *Literature/Film Quarterly* 7, no. 4 (1979): 285–89.

Snyder, Stephen. "Color, Growth, and Evolution in *Fellini Satyricon*." In

Federico Fellini: Essays in Criticism, ed. Peter Bondanella, 168–87. New York: Oxford University Press, 1978.

———. "Fellini's *The White Sheik*: Discovering the Story in the Medium." In *1977 Film Studies Annual: Part One*, ed. Ben Lawton and Janet Staiger, 100–110. Pleasantville, N.Y.: Redgrave, 1977.

Solmi, Angelo. *Fellini*. London: Merlin Press, 1967.

Solomon, Jon. "Fellini and Ovid." *Classical and Modern Literature* 3, no. 1 (1982): 39–44.

Stam, Robert. *Reflexivity in Film and Literature: From Don Quixote to Jean-Luc Godard*. Ann Arbor, Mich.: UMI Research Press, 1985.

Strazzulla, Gaetano. *I fumetti*. 2 vols. Florence: Sansoni Editore, 1980.

Strich, Christian, ed. *Fellini's Faces*. New York: Holt, Rinehart and Winston, 1982.

———, ed. *Fellini's Films: The Four Hundred Most Memorable Stills from Federico Fellini's Fifteen and a Half Films*. New York: Putnam's, 1977.

Stubbs, John C. *Federico Fellini: A Guide to References and Resources*. Boston: G. K. Hall, 1978.

Tassone, Aldo. "From Romagna to Rome: The Voyage of a Visionary Chronicler (*Roma* and *Amarcord*)." In *Federico Fellini: Essays in Criticism*, ed. Peter Bondanella, 261–88. New York: Oxford University Press, 1978.

Taylor, John Russell. *Cinema Eye, Cinema Ear*. New York: Hill and Wang, 1964.

Thiraud, Paul-Louis. "Les Nuits blanches de Fellini." In *Federico Fellini*, ed. Gilles Ciment, 45–49. Paris: Éditions Rivages, 1988.

Tinazzi, Giorgio, ed. *Il cinema italiano degli anni '50*. Venice: Marsilio Editori, 1979.

Tonino Guerra. Rimini: Maggioli Editore, 1985. (Exhibit catalogue with no editor's name listed).

Viviani, Christian. "Les Sunlights de Fellini et les feux du music-hall." *Études cinématographiques* 127–30 (1981): 37–48.

Volta, Ornella. "Une analyse." In *Federico Fellini*, ed. Gilles Ciment, 138–41. Paris: Éditions Rivages, 1988.

———. "Autour de *La Cité des femmes*." In *Federico Fellini*, ed. Gilles Ciment, 117–23. Paris: Éditions Rivages, 1988.

———. "Avant-première." In *Federico Fellini*, ed. Gilles Ciment, 156–63. Paris: Éditions Rivages, 1988.

———. "Come é nato *Tre passi nel delirio*." In *Tre passi nel delirio di F. Fellini, L. Malle, R. Vadim*, ed. Liliana Betti, Ornella Volta, and Bernardino Zappani, 25–28. Bologna: Cappelli, 1968.

———. "Entretien avec Federico Fellini." In *Federico Fellini*, ed. Gilles Ciment, 130–37. Paris: Éditions Rivages, 1988. (On *La città delle donne*).

———. "Entretien avec Federico Fellini." In *Federico Fellini*, ed. Gilles Ciment, 150–55. Paris: Éditions Rivages, 1988. (On *E la nave va*).

———. "Federico Fellini: l'interview d'*Intervista*." In *Federico Fellini*, ed. Gilles Ciment, 176–77. Paris: Éditions Rivages, 1988.

Volta, Ornella. "Le Film que Fellini ne tourne pas." In *Federico Fellini*, ed. Gilles Ciment, 75–78. Paris: Éditions Rivages, 1988.

———. "Le Journal des rêves de Federico Fellini (dessins et propros recueillis par Ornella Volta)." In *Federico Fellini*, ed. Gilles Ciment, 14–21. Paris: Éditions Rivages, 1988.

———. "Quelques notes en plus, prises au cours du tournage." In *Federico Fellini*, ed. Gilles Ciment, 142–45. Paris: Éditions Rivages, 1988.

Waller, Marguerite. "Neither an 'I' nor an 'Eye': The Gaze in Fellini's *Giulietta degli spiriti*." In *Romance Languages Annual*, ed. Ben Lawton and Anthony Tamburri, 75–80. West Lafayette, Ind.: Purdue Research Foundation, 1990.

Welle, John. "Fellini's Use of Dante in *La Dolce Vita*." *Studies in Medievalism* 2, no. 3 (1983): 53–66.

Zand, Nicole. "The Guilty Conscience of a Christian Consciousness." In *Federico Fellini, "8 1/2": Federico Fellini, Director*, ed. Charles Affron, 274–81. New Brunswick, N.J.: Rutgers University Press, 1987.

Zanelli, Dario. *Nel mondo di Federico*. Preface by Federico Fellini. Turin: Nuova ERI Edizioni Rai, 1987.

Zanzotto, Andrea. *Filò: per il "Casanova" di Fellini*. Milan: Mondadori, 1988. (Poems written for the film, including a letter from Fellini and five of his drawings).

Zapponi, Bernardino. "Edgar Poe e il cinema." In *Tre passi nel delirio di F. Fellini, L. Malle, R. Vadim*, ed. Liliana Betti, Ornella Volta, and Bernardino Zapponi, 15–22. Bologna: Cappelli, 1968.

———. *Gobal*. Milan: Longanesi, 1967.

———. Interview with author. Rome, 21 October 1987.

Zavattini, Cesare. "A Thesis on Neo-Realism." In *Springtime in Italy: A Reader on Neo-realism*, ed. David Overbey, 67–78. Hamden, Conn.: Archon Books, 1979.

INDEX